Frommer's®

W9-AZA-664

Fiji

1st Edition

by Bill Goodwin

WITHDRAWN

lere's what the critics say about Frommer's:

Amazingly easy to use. Very portable, very complete."

—*Booklist*

Detailed, accurate, and easy-to-read information for all price ranges."
—*Glamour Magazine*

Hotel information is close to encyclopedic."

—*Des Moines Sunday Register*

Frommer's Guides have a way of giving you a real feel for a place."
—*Knight Ridder Newspapers*

WILEY

Wiley Publishing, Inc.

Published by:

Wiley Publishing, Inc.

111 River St.
Hoboken, NJ 07030-5774

ISBN 978-0-470-25707-4

Editor: Alexia Travaglini
Production Editor: Eric T. Schroeder
Cartographer: Guy Ruggiero
Photo Editor: Richard Fox
Production by Wiley Indianapolis Composition Services

Front cover photo: Raranitingga: uninhabitied island beach
Back cover photo: Typical underwater scene: tropical fish

For information on our other products and services or to obtain technical support, please contact our Customer Care Department within the U.S. at 800/762-2974, outside the U.S. at 317/572-3993 or fax 317/572-4002.

Wiley also publishes its books in a variety of electronic formats. Some content that appears in print may not be available in electronic formats.

Manufactured in the United States of America

5   4   3   2   1

Contents

List of Maps

To my father,

*with love and with grateful thanks for supporting my being a writer
rather than a lawyer*

Acknowledgments

I owe a debt of gratitude to many individuals and organizations without whose help this book would have been impossible to research and write. You will become acquainted with many of them in these pages, and it will be your good fortune if you meet them in the islands.

My good fortune was to be assisted by Valerie Haeder, who had the enviable task of reporting on Fiji's beautiful Yasawa Islands. You will read her well-chosen words in chapter 6.

I am particularly grateful to Cherill Watson, Ili Matatolu, Thomas Valentine, Susan Bejeckian, and especially to Keti Wagavonovono of the Fiji Visitors Bureau, who went out of their way to help me research this book.

My deep personal thanks go to Connie Haeder, Curtis and Judy Moore, Anne Simon, Suzanne McIntosh, Nancy Monseaux, and Max Parrish, who have tended the home fires while I have been away in paradise over the years; to my sister, Jean Goodwin Santa-Maria, who has consistently given much-needed moral support; and to Dick Beaulieu, always a font of information, advice, and ice-cold Fiji Bitters.

I am truly blessed to have all of them in my life.

—Bill Goodwin

An Invitation to the Reader

In researching this book, we discovered many wonderful places—hotels, restaurants, shops, and more. We're sure you'll find others. Please tell us about them, so we can share the information with your fellow travelers in upcoming editions. If you were disappointed with a recommendation, we'd love to know that, too. Please write to:

Frommer's Fiji, 1st Edition
Wiley Publishing, Inc. • 111 River St. • Hoboken, NJ 07030-5774

An Additional Note

Please be advised that travel information is subject to change at any time—and this is especially true of prices. We therefore suggest that you write or call ahead for confirmation when making your travel plans. The authors, editors, and publisher cannot be held responsible for the experiences of readers while traveling. Your safety is important to us, however, so we encourage you to stay alert and be aware of your surroundings. Keep a close eye on cameras, purses, and wallets, all favorite targets of thieves and pickpockets.

About the Author

Bill Goodwin is one of the world's experts on travel to Fiji and the South Pacific islands. Before falling in love with the islands, he traveled widely as a decorated officer in the U.S. Navy and was an award-winning newspaper reporter for the *Atlanta Journal,* which sent him to Washington, D.C., as a political correspondent. He then served as legal counsel and speechwriter for two influential U.S. senators—Sam Nunn of Georgia and the late Sam Ervin of North Carolina. In 1977 he and a friend sailed a 41-foot yacht from Annapolis, Maryland, to Tahiti. He left the boat in Papeete and, with girlfriend and backpack, spent more than a year exploring French Polynesia, American Samoa, Samoa, Tonga, Fiji, New Zealand, and Australia. After another stint with Senator Nunn and a year in Hawaii, he researched and wrote the first edition of *Frommer's South Pacific* in 1986–87. He also is the author of *Frommer's Tahiti & French Polynesia* and, at home, *Frommer's Virginia.* Visit him at www.billgoodwin.com.

Other Great Guides for Your Trip:

Frommer's Tahiti & French Polynesia
Frommer's South Pacific
Frommer's Australia
Frommer's New Zealand
Frommer's Southeast Asia

Frommer's Star Ratings, Icons & Abbreviations

Every hotel, restaurant, and attraction listing in this guide has been ranked for quality, value, service, amenities, and special features using a **star-rating system.** In country, state, and regional guides, we also rate towns and regions to help you narrow down your choices and budget your time accordingly. Hotels and restaurants are rated on a scale of zero (recommended) to three stars (exceptional). Attractions, shopping, nightlife, towns, and regions are rated according to the following scale: zero stars (recommended), one star (highly recommended), two stars (very highly recommended), and three stars (must-see).

In addition to the star-rating system, we also use **seven feature icons** that point you to the great deals, in-the-know advice, and unique experiences that separate travelers from tourists. Throughout the book, look for:

Finds	Special finds—those places only insiders know about
Fun Fact	Fun facts—details that make travelers more informed and their trips more fun
Kids	Best bets for kids and advice for the whole family
Moments	Special moments—those experiences that memories are made of
Overrated	Places or experiences not worth your time or money
Tips	Insider tips—great ways to save time and money
Value	Great values—where to get the best deals

The following **abbreviations** are used for credit cards:

AE	American Express	DISC	Discover	V	Visa
DC	Diners Club	MC	MasterCard		

Frommers.com

Now that you have the guidebook to a great trip, visit our website at **www.frommers.com** for travel information on more than 4,000 destinations. We update features regularly to give you instant access to the most current trip-planning information available. At Frommers.com, you'll find scoops on the best airfares, lodging rates, and car rental bargains. You can even book your travel online through our reliable travel booking partners. Other popular features include:

- Online updates of our most popular guidebooks
- Vacation sweepstakes and contest giveaways
- Newsletters highlighting the hottest travel trends
- Podcasts, interactive maps, and up-to-the-minute events listings
- Opinionated blog entries by Arthur Frommer himself
- Online travel message boards with featured travel discussions

The Best of Fiji

The best thing about Fiji isn't its palm-draped beaches, blue lagoons, or rugged mountains. I think it's the enormous friendliness of the Fijian people.

Picking the best of everything else in Fiji is no easy task, for this is a diverse tropical country with many choices. In this chapter, I point out the best of the best—not necessarily to pass qualitative judgment, but to help you choose among many options. I list them here in the order in which they appear in the book.

Your choice of where you go and what you do will depend on why you are coming to Fiji, and how much money you have to spend while you're here. You can scuba dive to exhaustion over some of the world's most beautiful reefs or just laze on the beach with a trashy novel. You can share a 300-room hotel with package tourists, or get away from it all on a tiny islet. Even out there, you can be left alone with your lover or join your fellow guests at lively dinner parties. You can totally ignore the islanders around you or enrich your own life by learning about theirs. You can listen to the day's events on CNN International or get out and see what Fiji was like a century ago. Those decisions are all yours.

Regardless of where you stay and what you do, you are in for a memorable time. The friendly Fijians will see to that.

1 The Most Beautiful Islands

"In the South Seas," Rupert Brooke wrote in 1914, "the Creator seems to have laid himself out to show what He can do." How right the poet was, for all across the South Pacific lie some of the world's most dramatically beautiful islands. In my opinion, the best of the lot have jagged mountain peaks plunging into aquamarine lagoons. All these islands are beautiful, but I think the following stand out from the pack.

- **Monuriki:** Tom Hanks spent a lot time filming *Castaway* on lovely Monuriki, one of the westernmost of the Mamanuca Islands. A rocky central mountain drops down to the beach where Hanks figured out how to pry open a coconut. See chapter 6.

- **Yasawa:** This long, narrow island off the northwest coast of Viti Levu has several of Fiji's best beaches scattered among its rolling hills. It's also home to Yasawa Island Resort and Spa, one of Fiji's best offshore hotels. See chapter 6.

- **Waya:** Near the southern end of the Yasawa chain, Waya Island is one of the few in Fiji with the combination of cliffs and sheer basaltic peaks I find so appealing in the Pacific islands. See chapter 6.

- **Beqa:** Off Viti Levu's southern coast, Beqa has no roads cutting through its hills. Lovely Malumu Bay, one of Fiji's more scenic spots, nearly bisects Beqa, and it's all surrounded by the magnificent Beqa Lagoon. See chapter 8.

- **Kadavu:** About 60km (37 miles) long and just 14km (8½ miles) across at its widest point, Kadavu is Fiji's unspoiled nature preserve. Native birds and other wildlife live in abundance on Kadavu, given the absence of mongooses, iguanas, myna birds, and other introduced predators. The Great Astrolabe Reef provides great diving off the eastern and southern shores. See chapter 9.

- **Ovalau:** The sheer cliffs of Ovalau kept the town of Levuka from becoming Fiji's modern capital, but they create a dramatic backdrop to an old South Seas town little changed in the past century. Ovalau has no good beaches, which means no resorts alter its landscape. See chapter 12.

- **Savusavu:** Savusavu isn't an island but almost seems like it, since it sits on a peninsula separated from the main part of Vanua Levu by spectacular, mountain-surrounded Savusavu Bay, which is so large the U.S. Navy considered hiding the Pacific fleet there during World War II. See chapter 13.

- **Qamea and Matagi:** These little jewels off the northern coast of Taveuni are lushly beautiful, with their shorelines either dropping precipitously into the calm surrounding waters or forming little bays with idyllic beaches. See chapter 14.

2 The Best Beaches

Because all but a few islands in Fiji are surrounded by coral reefs, it has no real surf beaches like those so common in, say, Hawaii and Florida. Most islands (and all but a few resorts) have bathtublike lagoons lapping on coral sands draped by coconut palms. Unfortunately, most lagoons in Fiji are shallow at low tide, thus limiting watersports for half the day. This is especially true on the Coral Coast. Fortunately for the environmentalists among us, some of the most spectacular beaches are on remote islands and are protected from development by the islanders' devotion to their cultures and villages' land rights. Needless to say, resort developers have placed their establishments on most of the best. These stand out from the many.

- **Qalito (Castaway) Island** (the Mamanucas): Better known as the home of **Castaway Island Resort** (p. 138), hilly Qalito Island ends at a point flanked on both sides by beaches of deep white sand, which helps make Castaway one of Fiji's most popular resorts.

- **Malolo Island** (the Mamanucas): The beach fronting **Malolo Island Fiji** resort (p. 137) has deep sand, and the lagoon here is deep enough for swimming and snorkeling at most tides. The resort has one of Fiji's best beach bars.

- **Mana Island** (the Mamanucas): Mana Island has beaches on both its sides, but the one on the south coast is worth writing home about. It's so long that it's shared by both **Mana Island Resort** (p. 137) and bottom-end backpacker hostels.

- **Matamanoa Island** (the Mamanucas): Just enough room exists between Matamanoa's rocky central hill and its beach to shoe-horn in **Matamanoa Island Resort** (p. 138). Both the sands and the lagoon here are deep enough to enjoy all the time.

- **Malololailai Island** (the Mamanucas): Connected to the larger Malolo Island by a marshy isthmus, Malololailai is home to three resorts: **Musket Cove Island Resort** (p. 134), **Lomani Island Resort** (p. 134), and **Plantation Island Resort** (p. 135). Although the lagoon is shallow, the beach in front of Lomani and Plantation Island resorts is one of Fiji's most

Fiji's Best Beaches

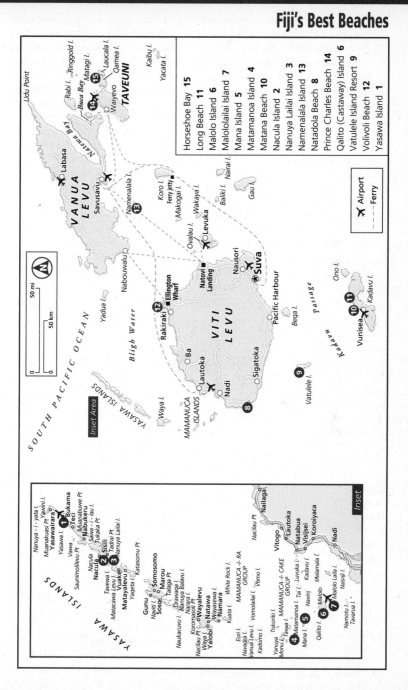

Horseshoe Bay **15**
Long Beach **11**
Malolo Island **6**
Malololailai Island **7**
Mana Island **5**
Matamanoa Island **4**
Matana Beach **10**
Nacula Island **2**
Nanuya Lailai Island **3**
Namenalala Island **13**
Natadola Beach **8**
Prince Charles Beach **14**
Qalito (Castaway) Island **6**
Vatulele Island Resort **9**
Volivoli Beach **12**
Yasawa Island **1**

✈ Airport
----- Ferry

picturesque, with coconut palms hanging over it in places.

- **Yasawa Island** (the Yasawas): Several of Fiji's best beaches are on Yasawa, the northernmost island in the Yasawa chain. One long stretch of sand near the north end is divided by big black rocks flanked by two Fijian villages. Another in front of **Yasawa Island Resort and Spa** (p. 148) also has rocks plus waves, a rarity among Fijian beaches.

- **Nanuyalailai Island** (the Yasawas): About midway along the Yasawa chain, Nanuya is skirted on its south side by a long beach that wraps around a coconut palm–studded peninsula and keeps on going. **Nanuya Island Resort** (p. 146) sits on the western end, while **Blue Lagoon Cruises** (p. 131) uses the sands on the other side of the peninsula.

- **Nacula Island** (the Yasawas): The inexpensive **Oarsmans Bay Lodge** (p. 147), on Nacula Island, sits beside one of the top beaches in Fiji, a glorious strip of sand emptying into a lagoon that is deep at all tides.

- **Natadola Beach** (the Coral Coast): Fiji's main island of Viti Levu doesn't have the high-quality beaches found on the country's small islands, but Natadola is the exception (p. 152). Until recently this long stretch was spared development, but a big resort is coming.

- **Vatulele Island Resort** (Vatulele): The luxury resort on Vatulele Island has new owners and has been undergoing significant changes, but the 1km (½ mile) of sand in front of it remains one of the most brilliantly white beaches in Fiji. See p. 163.

- **Long Beach** (Kadavu): Fiji's longest beach runs for several kilometers along the north shore of Kadavu Island, where one resort is under development. In the meantime, visitors have it all to themselves but will have to stay at nearby **Papageno Resort** (p. 176) or **Dive Kadavu/Matana Beach Resort** (p. 175).

- **Matana Beach** (Kadavu): Also on Kadavu's north shore, Matana Beach combines deep white sand with a deep lagoon. Bordered by a Fijian village and **Dive Kadavu/Matana Beach Resort** (p. 175), Matana has a fine view westward along Kadavu's shore.

- **Volivoli Beach** (Rakiraki): At the very northern tip of Viti Levu a few kilometers from Rakiraki, lovely Volivoli also has soft white sand, a deep lagoon, and a spectacular view southwestward toward Viti Levu's mountains. You don't have to pay a fortune either, with inexpensive **Volivoli Beach Resort** (p. 201) just around the corner.

- **Namenalala Island** (off Savusavu): The main beach at the remote little resort known as **Moody's Namena** is one of the finest I've seen in Fiji, but owners Tom and Joan Moody have marked four other private beaches with OCCUPIED/UNOCCUPIED signs. See p. 226.

- **Prince Charles Beach** (Taveuni): The northern coast of Taveuni has three great beaches within walking distance of each other, the best being Prince Charles Beach, so named because said prince once took a dip in its warm lagoon. See p. 236.

- **Horseshoe Bay** (Matagi Island): Matagi is an extinct volcano whose crater fell away on one side and formed picturesque Horseshoe Bay. The half-moon-shape beach at its head is one of the finest in the islands, but you have to be on a yacht or a guest at **Matangi Island Resort** to enjoy it (p. 242).

3 The Most Romantic Resorts

Fiji is a marvelous place for honeymoons and other romantic escapes. I've never stayed anywhere as love-enhancing as a thatched-roof bungalow on the beach. You'll find lots of these in Fiji. A few are built on stilts out over the lagoon, while others have their own swimming pools and hot tubs.

Fiji's numerous small, relatively remote offshore resorts offer as much privacy as you are likely to desire. Many of these establishments have less than 20 bungalows each, instead of the 40 or more found in French Polynesia and elsewhere, which means they are usually widely spaced. Many are even on islands all by themselves.

They are so romantic that a friend of mine says her ideal wedding would be to rent an entire small resort, take her wedding party with her, get married in Fijian costume beside the beach, and make the rest of her honeymoon a diving vacation.

Every offshore resort in Fiji qualifies as a very good romantic retreat, but I'm headed to one of the following when Cupid strikes. Most have full-service spas for your pampering pleasure.

- **Likuliku Lagoon Resort** (Malolo Island, the Mamanucas; ✆ **672 4275** or 666 3344; www.likulikulagoon. com). This exquisitely designed resort is tops in the Mamanuca Islands, primarily because it's the first in Fiji with overwater bungalows. See p. 136.
- **Tokoriki Island Resort** (Tokoriki Island, the Mamanucas; ✆ **666 1999;** www.tokoriki.com): The beach at Tokoriki has erosion problems, but it has five bungalows with their own plunge pools (p. 140).
- **Matamanoa Island Resort** (Matamanoa Island, the Mamanucas; ✆ **666 0511;** www.matamanoa.com): It's less luxurious than Tokoriki, but Matamanoa is a good choice for cost-conscious honeymooners, and it has one of Fiji's best beaches. See p. 138.
- **Turtle Island** (Nanuya Levu Island, the Yasawas; ✆ **877/288-7853** or 672 2921; www.turtlefiji.com): Fiji's first top-end resort continues to offer romance beside its seemingly landlocked "Blue Lagoon." Its most private bungalow lacks a whirlpool but has a 360-degree view of the lagoon and surrounding islands. See p. 146.
- **Yasawa Island Resort and Spa** (Yasawa Island, the Yasawas; ✆ **672 2266;** www.yasawa.com): Sitting on one of the prettiest beaches in Fiji, Yasawa Island Resort and Spa has a very low-key, friendly ambience to go with its very large bungalows, the choicest being the secluded honeymoon unit with its own beach (it even has a private pool). See p. 148.
- **Navutu Stars Resort** (Yaqueta Island, the Yasawas; ✆ **664 0553;** www. navutustarsfiji.com): Also in the Yasawa Islands, Navutu Stars Resort has a spa and yoga sessions in addition to fine food brought to you by its Italian owners. See p. 142.
- **The Wakaya Club** (Wakaya Island; ✆ **344 0128;** www.wakaya.com): In central Fiji near Ovalau Island, the Wakaya Club is generally considered Fiji's top resort. It has some of the country's largest bungalows, plus a palatial mansion with its own pool, perched high atop a ridge. The staff leaves the guests to their own devices, and you might see a movie star or two relaxing here. See p. 213.
- **Jean-Michel Cousteau Fiji Islands Resort** (Savusavu; ✆ **800/246-3454** or 885 0188; www.fijiresort.com): "Cousteau" is Fiji's best family hotel. It expertly herds the kids away in the award-winning Bula Club, and young

---

Fun Fact **Getting Hitched in Fiji**

These romantic islands are marvelous places to get married, and becoming officially hitched is relatively easy in Fiji. You do not have to be a resident, and obtaining the necessary licenses and permits requires only a few days. Most resorts will take care of the formalities and organize traditional ceremonies (which can take place on the beach if you like). Their wedding coordinators will tell you what documents you will need to bring (or send in advance) and what local formalities you will need to execute. Do not even think of making the arrangements yourself.

---

ones are seldom if ever seen in a beautiful honeymoon villa with its own swimming pool. See p. 222.

- **Namale – The Fiji Islands Resort & Spa** (Savusavu; ℂ **800/727-3454** or 885 0435; www.namalefiji.com): Motivational speaker Anthony Robbins's luxurious resort also has private, pool-equipped villas plus a bowling alley, golf simulator, and a ton of other toys. See p. 223.
- **Coconut Grove Beachfront Cottages** (Taveuni; ℂ/fax **888 0328;** www.coconutgrovefiji.com): Ronna Goldstein's charming three-unit, bed-and-breakfast-like hotel is one of Fiji's best bargains for anyone, including honeymooners on a budget. See p. 237.
- **Maravu Plantation Beach Resort & Spa** (Taveuni; ℂ **866/528-3864** or 888 0555; www.maravu.net): Maravu is not directly on the beach (a picturesque one is just across the road); but bungalows come equipped

with hot tubs, and the honeymoon unit is built up in a tree. See p. 238.
- **Matangi Island Resort** (Matagi Island, off Taveuni; ℂ **888/628-2644** or 888 0260; www.matangi island.com): One of the widely spaced bungalows at Matangi Island Resort is built up in a Pacific almond tree, while two others are carved in the side of a cliff. They all have outdoor bathrooms. See p. 242.
- **Qamea Resort and Spa** (Qamea Island, off Taveuni; ℂ **866/867-2632** or 888 0220; www.qamea. com): Among my favorite places to stay are the charming, old South Seas–style bungalows at Qamea Island Resort and Spa. More luxurious still are the two units specifically designed for honeymooners and two more with their own plunge pools. Kerosene lanterns romantically light the 16m-high (52-ft.) thatched roof of Qamea's main building at night. See p. 243.

4 The Best Places to Get Away from It All

Some of Fiji's offshore resorts are better at getting away from it all than others. The ones I list below are small enough that you won't have a lot of company, and—since they are on islands all by themselves—you won't have people from

another property walking along your stretch of private beach.

- **Wadigi Island Resort** (Wadigi Island, the Mamanucas; ℂ **672 0901;** www.wadigi.com): On a tiny islet, Wadigi Island Resort has just three units, all on top of a peak with a glorious view of nearby Malolo Island and the surrounding Mamanucas. It's expensive and very private, so no one will care if you run around naked. See p. 141.

- **Matamanoa Island Resort** (Matamanoa Island, the Mamanucas; ✆ **666 0511;** www.matamanoa.com): In the westernmost of the Mamanucas, this remote little resort is one of Fiji's most reasonably priced romantic resorts, and its beach is superb. See p. 138.

- **Yasawa Island Resort and Spa** (Yasawa Island, the Yasawas; ✆ **672 2266;** www.yasawa.com): Another great honeymoon choice, Yasawa Island Resort and Spa has no neighbors and is therefore very private. Its secluded honeymoon *bure* (bungalow) has its own private beach and pool. See p. 148.

- **Lalati Resort & Spa** (Beqa Island; ✆ **347 2033;** www.lalati-fiji.com): Beside picturesque Malumu Bay and enjoying a fine view of the Beqa Lagoon and Viti Levu's southern shore, Lalati appeals to couples looking to dive, or to just get away. The full-service spa is augmented by an air-conditioned lounge with TV and DVD player, and the outdoor pool helps compensate for a poor beach. See p. 170.

- **Royal Davui Island Fiji** (in Beqa Lagoon; ✆ **330 7090;** www.royal davui.com): On a tiny, rocky islet in Beqa Lagoon, this luxury resort is set above a small beach. Bungalows are built in an old-growth hillside, but guests are compensated by marvelous views from each unit's plunge pool–equipped veranda. See p. 170.

- **Dive Kadavu/Matana Beach Resort** (Kadavu Island; ✆ **368 3502;** www.divekadavu.com): Only a 10-minute boat ride from Kadavu's airstrip, this little resort has been a top dive base since 1983, but it has begun using the name Matana Beach Resort to take advantage of its location on one of Fiji's most beautiful beaches. See p. 175.

- **Matava—The Astrolabe Hideaway** (Kadavu Island; ✆ **333 6222;** www.matava.com): Much farther than Dive Kadavu from the airstrip—at least 45 minutes by small boat—Matava is so eco-friendly it has no air-conditioners and turns on the solar-powered lights only at night. Made primarily of thatch and other natural materials, its bungalows are both basic and charming. It's close to many Great Astrolabe Reef dive sights, but it also specializes in kayaking trips and bird-watching. See p. 176.

- **The Wakaya Club** (Wakaya Island; ✆ **344 0128;** www.wakaya.com): Except for a few private villas owned by Hollywooders and other well-heeled types, Fiji's top resort has all of Wakaya Island to itself. Nicole Kidman, Russell Crowe, and other Aussie celebs have been known to take a break at Wakaya on their way home. See p. 213.

- **Moody's Namena** (Namenalala Island, off Savusavu; ✆ **881 3764;** www.moodysnamenafiji.com): You either take a seaplane or ride a boat for more than an hour to reach Joan and Tom Moody's little resort. Not only is Namenalala surrounded by the fabulous Namea Reef, but the island also has five beaches, four of them so private the pathways leading to them have OCCUPIED/UNOCCUPIED signs to prevent your fellow guests from disturbing you. See p. 227.

- **Matangi Island Resort** (Matagi Island, off Taveuni; ✆ **888/628-2644** or 888 0260; www.matangi island.com): This couples-only resort's honeymoon bungalow up in a Pacific almond tree is both charming and private, and you can walk over the hill and have the gorgeous beach in Horseshoe Bay all to yourselves. See p. 242.

- **Qamea Resort and Spa** (Qamea Island, off Taveuni; ⓒ **866/867-2632** or 888 0220; www.qamea.com): Qamea's two luxurious honeymoon bungalows are situated on one end of the resort, although I prefer the two other villas with their own plunge pools. See p. 243.

5 The Best Family Resorts

There are no Disney Worlds or other such attractions in Fiji. That's not to say that children won't have a fine time here, for Fiji draws many Australians and New Zealanders on family holidays. It has one of the South Pacific's finest family resorts, and others make provisions for families as well as honeymooners. Kids who like being around and in the water will enjoy themselves most.

With their innate love of children, Fijians are very good at babysitting and staffing the kids' programs at the major resorts.

On the other hand, many of Fiji's small resorts do not accept young children. I point these out in my hotel reviews.

Obvious family choices are the large hotels on Denarau Island. The **Fiji Beach Resort & Spa Managed by Hilton,** the **Sheraton Fiji Resort,** the **Sheraton Denarau Villas,** the **Sofitel Fiji Resort & Spa,** the **Radisson Resort Fiji Denarau Island,** and the **Westin Denarau Island Resort & Spa** are all equipped for families with children. Of them, the Radisson, has Fiji's best swimming-pool complex. See chapter 5.

Likewise, the **Outrigger on the Lagoon Fiji,** the **Warwick Fiji Resort & Spa,** and the **Naviti Resort** on the Coral Coast all have plenty to keep the kids occupied. See chapter 7.

Here are my recommendations among the smaller resorts.

- **Treasure Island Resort** (Luvuka Island, the Mamanucas; ⓒ **666 6999;** www.fiji-treasure.com): Modest but comfortable Treasure Island occupies a tiny, beach-fringed islet, the middle of which has a children's program, a miniature golf course, and baby sea turtles swimming in a breeding pool. See p. 132.

- **Castaway Island Resort** (Qalito Island, the Mamanucas; ⓒ **800/888-0120** or 666 1233; www.castaway fiji.com): One of Fiji's oldest resorts but thoroughly refurbished, Castaway has plenty to keep both adults and children occupied, from a wide array of watersports to a kids' playroom and a nursery. See p. 138.

- **Malolo Island Fiji** (Malolo Island, the Mamanucas; ⓒ **666 9192;** www.maloloisland.com): This sister of the adults-only Likuliku Lagoon Resort has a fine beach, as well as a shaded swimming pool designed with children in mind. See p. 137.

- **Mana Island Resort** (Mana Island, the Mamanucas; ⓒ **665 0423;** www.manafiji.com): Relatively large Mana Island Resort caters to everyone and gets many day-trippers from Nadi; but the beach is safe, and it has one of the better children's programs in the Mamanuca Islands. See p. 137.

- **Plantation Island Resort** (Malololailai Island, the Mamanucas; ⓒ **666 9333;** www.plantationisland.com): The largest resort in the Mamanucas has long appealed to Australian families, offering a wide range of accommodations and activities, including a children's program with a full-time babysitter. See p. 135.

- **Outrigger on the Lagoon Fiji** (Coral Coast; ℂ 800/688-7444 or 650 0044; www.outrigger.com): The beach and shallow lagoon at the Outrigger leave much to be desired, but it has an exceptional swimming pool. See p. 156.

- **Shangri-La's Fijian Resort & Spa** (Yanuca Island, the Coral Coast; ℂ 866/565-5050 or 652 0155; www.shangri-la.com): The country's largest resort with 442 units, "The Fijian" has a better beach and lagoon than its big rivals on Denarau Island and the Coral Coast. You may exhaust yourself chasing the youngsters around its sprawling grounds, but the hotel has plenty of activities for all ages. See p. 155.

- **Jean-Michel Cousteau Fiji Islands Resort** (Savusavu; ℂ 800/246-3454 or 885 0188; www.fijiresort.com): Although it appeals equally to couples, Fiji's finest family resort encourages parents to enroll their kids in its exceptional Bula Club, thus keeping the youngsters educated, entertained, and out of sight from breakfast to bedtime. See p. 222.

6 The Best Cultural & Environmental Experiences

The Fijians are justly proud of their ancient culture, and they eagerly inform anyone who asks about both their ancient and modern ways. Here are some of the best ways to learn about their lifestyle and explore the environment of their islands.

- **Fijian Village Visits** (nationwide): Many tours from Nadi, the Coral Coast, and most offshore resorts include visits to traditional Fijian villages, whose residents stage welcoming ceremonies (featuring the slightly narcotic drink kava, or *yaqona* as it's known in Fiji). The hosts then show visitors around and explain how the old and the new combine in today's villages. See "Exploring the Nadi Area," p. 100.

- **Kalevu South Pacific Cultural Centre** (the Coral Coast; ℂ 652 0200; www.fijiculturalcentre.com): Opposite Shangri-La's Fijian Resort & Spa, this cultural center exhibits handicraft making, cooking, and skills of Fiji, Samoa, and other Pacific islands. See p. 153.

- **Sigatoka Sand Dunes National Park** (near Sigatoka, the Coral Coast; ℂ 652 0243): Ancient Fijian burial grounds and pieces of pottery dating from 5 B.C. to A.D. 240 have been found among these dunes, which stretch for several miles along Viti Levu's southern coast. See p. 153.

- **Tavuni Hill Fort** (near Sigatoka, the Coral Coast; ℂ 650 0818): This best example of a traditional Fijian fort stands atop a hill east of Sigatoka. It renders both a glimpse of what war was like in the old days and a splendid view over the Sigatoka River Valley. See p. 154.

- **Kula Eco Park** (Korotogo, the Coral Coast; ℂ 650 0505; www.fijiwild.com): Opposite the Outrigger on the Lagoon Fiji, this nature park exhibits most of Fiji's endemic species of birds, reptiles, and mammals. Children are given a chance to handle some of the creatures in a petting zoo. See p. 154.

- **Waterfall and Cave Tours** (the Coral Coast): On walking tours offered by **Adventures in Paradise Fiji** (ℂ 652 0833; www.adventuresinparadisefiji.com), you will be welcomed into a Fijian village plus see a cave and one of the country's many waterfalls. See p. 154.

- **Arts Village Cultural Centre** (Pacific Harbour; © **345 0065;** www.arts village.com): A reconstructed traditional Fijian village built of thatch and other local materials is the centerpiece of this cultural center, which has fire-walking shows in addition to demonstrations of old-time Fijian skills. See p. 165.

- **Rafting on the Navua River** (Pacific Harbour): The Navua River begins in the highlands and ends on the southern coast of Viti Levu, on the way cutting two gorges, one of them dubbed the "Grand Canyon of Fiji." Rafting on the river—either by inflatable raft through the white-water gorge with **Rivers Fiji** (© **800/446-2411** in the U.S., or 345 0147; www. riversfiji.com) or while riding lashed-together bamboo poles (a bilibili raft) through the lazy lowlands with **Discover Fiji Tours** (© **345 0180;** www.discoverfijitours.com)—is one of Fiji's top outdoor experiences. See p. 166.

- **Fiji Museum** (Thurston Park, Suva; © **331 5944;** www.fijimuseum. org.fj): The small but very good Fiji Museum has a terrific collection of war clubs, cannibal forks, and other ancient artifacts, plus the rudder of HMS *Bounty.* See p. 182.

- **Suva Municipal Market** (Usher St. at Rodwell Rd., Suva; no phone):

You'll see an enormous amount of tropical produce for sale at Suva's main supplier of food. The market is especially active on Saturday morning. See p. 182.

- **Rainforest Walks** (Savusavu): No wires are in place to allow exploration of the canopy, but earthly gravel pathways lead to a waterfall in **Waisali Rainforest Reserve** (no phone), a 116-hectare (290-acre) national forest up in the central mountains of Vanua Levu. See p. 219.

- **Adventure Cruises on the *Tui Tai*** (Savusavu; © **885 3032;** www.tuitai. com): Passengers on the small but luxurious sailing ship *Tui Tai* spend much of their time snorkeling, diving, and mountain biking, but they also get to visit Fijian villages on remote islands such as Kioa. See p. 220.

- **Bouma Falls and Lavena Coastal Walk** (Taveuni): Although Taveuni is best known for world-class scuba diving, it's also one of the best places in Fiji to explore the mountainous interior. **Bouma Falls National Heritage Park** (© **888 0390**) has three waterfalls, and the **Lavena Coastal Walk** (© **923 9080**) leads along the island's nearly deserted east coast to yet another falls—though you'll need to swim to reach it. See p. 233.

7 The Best of the Old South Seas

Fiji is developing rapidly, with modern, fast-paced towns replacing what were once small villages and sleepy backwater ports. However, a few places still harken back to the old South Sea days of coconut planters, beach bums, and missionaries.

- **Lautoka:** Fiji's second-largest city is still small enough to walk around, and it's genteel citizens normally won't hassle you to "come in, take a

look" at their shops. The town was laid out by the British, with broad streets, shady sidewalks, and pleasant parks. See "Lautoka," in chapter 5.

- **Sigatoka:** The riverfront town of Sigatoka, on the Coral Coast, isn't as pleasing to the eye as Lautoka, but it still makes its living not from tourists but from trading with the farmers in the picturesque Sigatoka River Valley.

It's the only place in Fiji where I've seen Muslim women wearing head-to-toe *burkas*. See chapter 7.

- **Kadavu:** The long, skinny island of Kadavu, some 100km (60 miles) south of Viti Levu, has a road on one end, but you must take a boat to reach all its best spots. That's one bit of evidence of how little Kadavu has changed. Unlike Fiji's other large islands, it has no sugar-cane farms, no mongooses, no iguanas, no myna birds, and few if any Fiji Indians. The result: It's like the rest of Fiji used to be. See chapter 9.

- **Suva:** The British are long gone, and Suva today is the largest, most vibrant city in the South Pacific islands. But among its new high-rise office towers are grand colonial buildings, orderly parks, and a mixed population that dates back to the days of the Raj. See chapter 10.

- **Rakiraki:** On the northern tip of Viti Levu, the Fijian village of Rakiraki and its surrounding countryside seem caught in a time warp, provided you don't notice the few small real-estate developments creeping into the hills (will we Westerners ever stop wanting to buy our own piece of paradise?). See chapter 11.

- **Levuka** (Ovalau Island): No other town has remained the same after a century as much as has Levuka, Fiji's first European-style town and its original colonial capital in the 1870s. The dramatic cliffs of Ovalau Island hemmed in the town and prevented growth, so the government moved to Suva in 1882. Levuka looks very much as it did then, with a row of clapboard general stores along picturesque Beach Street. See chapter 12.

- **Savusavu:** You're apt to see more Americans strolling the streets of picturesque Savusavu than anywhere else in Fiji, since so many of them have purchased land near there, but the town still has the feel of the days when schooners would pick up cargo at places like the Copra Shed. See chapter 13.

- **Taveuni:** Fiji's lush "Garden Island" has changed little since Europeans bought land holdings and started coconut plantations in the 19th century. You can stay with descendants of one of those early planters at **Vatuwiri Farm Resort** (© **888 0316;** www.vatuwirifiji.com; p. 240). With a large population of indigenous plants and animals, Taveuni is a nature lover's delight and the best place to go hiking in Fiji. See chapter 14.

8 The Best Dining Experiences

You won't be stuck eating only island-style food cooked in an earth oven (see "Eating & Drinking in Fiji," in chapter 2), nor will you be limited by New Zealanders' and Australians' traditionally bland tastes, which until recently predominated at many restaurants in Fiji. The Indians brought curries to Fiji, and exciting new restaurants are offering cuisine from around the world.

Here are some of my favorites.

- **Indigo** (Denarau Island; © **675 0026**): In the Port Denarau shopping and dining complex, Indigo is the second-best Indian restaurant in Fiji, behind Saffron (see below), but it also pulls from Southeast Asian culinary tradition with Thai-style crab and Rendang curry. Most dining is alfresco. See p. 122.

- **Bullacino** (Nadi Town; © **672 8638**): I've had terrific breakfasts and lunches at this sophisticated coffee shop beside the Nadi River. Unfortunately, it is not open for dinner. See p. 122.

- **Chefs The Restaurant** (Nadi Town; ✆ **670 3131**): Along with Indigo, this formal restaurant is the creation of Chef Eugene Gomes, who came here from Goa, India. The service is attentive, and the international fare is very good. See p. 123.
- **Saffron** (Nadi Town; ✆ **670 1233**): Another Eugene Gomes creation, Saffron consistently serves Fiji's best northern Indian cuisine, and it's tops for vegetarians, too. See p. 123.
- **Nadina Authentic Fijian Restaurant** (Queen's Rd., Martintar, Nadi; ✆ **672 7313**): While most resorts serve native food only on the buffets at their nighttime island feasts, this little restaurant serves great Fijian fare—such as the luscious *ota miti*, the tender young shoots of the wood fern served with coconut milk—round-the-clock. See p. 124.
- **The Outer Reef Seafood Café/Sandbar Restaurant** (Queen's Rd., Martintar, Nadi; ✆ **672 7201**): No other restaurant has as wide an array of seafood as this stylish outdoor cafe. Much of it is flown in fresh from Australia. See p. 124.
- **Vilisite's Seafood Restaurant** (The Coral Coast; ✆ **653 0054**): This seaside restaurant, owned and operated by a friendly Fijian woman named Vilisite, doesn't look like much from the outside, but it offers a handful of excellent seafood meals to augment a terrific view along the Coral Coast. See p. 162.
- **Hare Krishna Restaurant** (16 Pratt St., Suva; ✆ **331 4154**): I always have at least one lunch at this clean, casual vegetarian restaurant. Choosing is easy, since everything is presented cafeteria-style. See p. 193.
- **Maya Dhaba** (281 Victoria Parade, Suva; ✆ **331 0045**): Although

inexpensive, Maya Dhaba is Suva's most sophisticated restaurant, offering authentic Indian cuisine at extraordinarily reasonable prices in a hip, urbane environment. Both meat and vegetarian dishes appear here. See p. 194.
- **Old Mill Cottage** (47–49 Carnavon St., Suva; ✆ **331 2134**): Diplomats and government workers pack this old colonial cottage at breakfast and lunch for some of the region's best and least expensive local fare. Offerings range from English-style roast chicken with mashed potatoes and peas to Fijian-style *palusami* (fresh fish wrapped in taro leaves and steamed in coconut milk). See p. 194.
- **Surf 'n' Turf** (Copra Shed, Savusavu; ✆ **881 0966**): A veteran of Jean-Michel Cousteau Fiji Islands Resort, Chef Vijendra Kumar is very good with tropical lobsters, and he often accompanies them with ota miti, my favorite Fijian vegetable. See p. 227.
- **Coconut Grove Restaurant** (Matei, Taveuni; ✆ **888 0328**): I love the fresh banana bread and the Thai fish at Ronna Goldstein's little hotel on Taveuni. Adding to the enjoyment is the view from her veranda of the rocky islets off Taveuni. See p. 241.
- **Tramontu Bar & Grill** (Matei, Taveuni; ✆ **888 2224**): The pizzas and other fare at this local restaurant aren't that great, but it has a million-dollar view of the Somosomo Strait from its clifftop perch. See p. 242.
- **Vunibokoi Restaurant** (Matei, Taveuni; ✆ **888 0560**): This plain restaurant on the front porch of the inexpensive Tovu Tovu Resort has one of the best Friday night buffets of Fijian *lovo* food (cooked in an underground oven). See p. 242.

Take some extra money along to spend on handicrafts, black pearls, and tropical clothing. For the locations of the best shops, see the shopping sections in chapters 5, 10, and 13.

- **Black Pearls:** Long the specialty of French Polynesia and the Cook Islands, black pearls are now being produced in Fiji, and they are reasonably high-quality. The top farm is **J. Hunter Pearls** (© 885 0821; www.pearlsfiji.com; p. 221) in Savusavu. The peculiarities of the seawater in Savusavu Bay result in unique yellow pearls known as Fiji Gold. The farm shop is the best place to buy them, but they are available in some hotel boutiques and in the Tappoo department stores in Nadi Town and elsewhere.

- **Handicrafts:** Although many of the items you will see in souvenir shops are actually made in Asia, locally produced handicrafts are some of Fiji's best souvenir buys. The most widespread are hats, mats, and baskets woven of *pandanus* or other fibers, usually by women who have maintained this ancient art. Before the European traders brought printed cotton, Fijians used *tapa*, the beaten bark of the paper mulberry tree, known here as *masi*. The resulting cloth is painted with dyes made from natural substances, usually in geometric designs that have ancestries dating back thousands of years. Tapa is an excellent souvenir because it can be folded and brought back in a suitcase. Woodcarvings are also popular. Spears, war clubs, knives made from sharks' teeth, canoe prows, and cannibal forks are some examples. Many carvings, however, tend to be produced for the tourist trade and often lack the imagery of bygone days, and some are now machine-produced.

- **Tropical Clothing:** Colorful hand-screened, hand-blocked, and hand-dyed fabrics are very popular in the islands for making dresses or the wraparound skirt known as a *sulu* in Fiji. Heat-sensitive dyes are applied by hand to cotton, which is then laid in the sun for several hours. Flowers, leaves, and other designs are placed on the fabric, and, as the heat of the sun darkens and sets the dyes, the shadows from these objects leave their images behind on the finished product.

10 The Best Diving & Snorkeling

With nutrient-rich waters welling up from the Tonga Trench offshore and being carried by strong currents funneling through narrow passages, Fiji is famous for some of the world's most colorful soft corals.

All the islands have excellent scuba diving and snorkeling, and all but a few of the resorts either have their own dive operations or can easily make arrangements with a local company. Many dive operators will take snorkelers along; that's my favorite way to go snorkeling in Fiji.

The best areas to dive are listed here. See "Diving & Snorkeling" under "The Active Traveler," in chapter 3, for additional advice and information.

- **Shark Diving** (Pacific Harbour): The dive masters lure tiger, bull, and other sharks by feeding them in these exciting dives off southern Viti Levu. It's not for novices. See chapter 8.

- **Beqa Lagoon** (off Beqa Island): Beqa Lagoon has soft corals, especially at Frigate Passage, where they seem to fall over one another. See chapter 8.

- **Great Astrolabe Reef** (off Kadavu): Skirting the eastern and southern sides of Kadavu, the Great Astrolabe Reef has lost much of its reef-top soft corals but still has plenty over the sides. It also attracts Fiji's largest concentration of manta rays. See chapter 9.
- **Namena Marine Protected Reserve** (off Savusavu): This magnificent barrier reef that nearly surrounds Moody's Namena resort (p. 227) is now a protected marine reserve populated by both soft and hard corals. See chapter 13.
- **Somosomo Strait** (off Taveuni): The narrow passage between Vanua Levu and Taveuni is Fiji's most famous site for soft corals, especially its Great White Wall and Rainbow Reef. The snorkeling is very good here, too, but watch out for strong currents and sharks. See chapter 14.

11 The Best Offbeat Travel Experiences

Some cynics might say that a visit to Fiji itself is an offbeat experience, but these five really are.

- **Getting Asked to Dance** (nationwide): I've seen so many traditional Fijian *meke* dance shows that I now stand by the rear door, ready to beat a quick escape before those lovely young women can grab my hand and force me to make a fool of myself by joining them on stage. It's part of the tourist experience at all resorts, and it's all in good fun.
- **Rise of the *Balolo*** (nationwide): Dawn after the full moon in October sees thousands of Fijians out on the reefs with buckets to snare the wiggling *balolo,* a coral worm that comes out to mate only then. Actually, the rear ends of the worms break off and swim to the surface, spewing eggs and sperm in a reproductive frenzy lasting only a few hours. Fijians consider the slimy balolo to be their caviar.
- **Sliding Through a Jungle Canopy** (Pacific Harbour): Those of you who have been to Costa Rica or the Amazon may think it's an ordinary thing to do, but sliding along cables strung across a rainforest canopy in Fiji strikes me as offbeat. You can do just that with **ZIP Fiji** (© **930 0545;** www.zip-fiji.com) in Pacific Harbour. See p. 166.
- **Jet-Skiing to Your Hotel** (Taveuni): You can get to your Fiji hotel by taxi, ferry, boat, plane, seaplane, helicopter, even on foot, but only at **Paradise Taveuni** (©/fax **888 0125;** www.paradiseinfiji.com) will you have the option of riding a jet ski. See p. 235.
- **Living on a Copra Plantation** (Taveuni): The first successful industry in Fiji was extracting the meat from coconuts and drying it into *copra,* from which the oil is extracted for cooking, cosmetics, and other products. In the 19th century, Europeans created large copra plantations, many of which are still operational. You can actually share one of them with the descendants of the original English planter at **Vatuwiri Farm Resort** (© **888 0316;** www.vatuwiri fiji.com). See p. 240.

Fiji in Depth

You'll see why I like Fiji so much as soon as you get off the plane, clear Customs and Immigration, and are greeted by a procession of smiling faces, all of them exclaiming an enthusiastic *"Bula!"* That one word—"health" in Fijian—expresses the warmest and most heartfelt welcome I have ever received anywhere.

Fiji's great diversity will also be immediately evident, for the taxi drivers who whisk you to your hotel will not be Fijians of Melanesian heritage, but Indians whose ancestors migrated to Fiji from places like Calcutta and Madras. Now about 38% of the population, these Fiji Indians have played major roles in making their country the most prosperous of the independent South Pacific island nations.

Fiji has a lot to offer in terms of raw material for building the region's largest tourism industry. In the most-visited areas—and especially on Fiji's marvelous offshore islets— you'll find gorgeous white-sand beaches bordered by curving coconut palms, azure lagoons, and colorful reefs offering world-class scuba diving and snorkeling, green mountains sweeping to the sea, and a tropical climate in which to enjoy it all.

Fiji has something for every budget. Its wide variety of accommodations ranges from deluxe resorts nestled in tropical gardens beside the beach to down-to-basics hostels that cater to the young and young-at-heart. Out on its 300-plus islands is one of the largest and finest collections of small, Robinson Crusoe–like offshore resorts I have ever seen.

Although it has been in the news because of its military coups (four of them, most recently in Dec 2006), visitors have not directly been affected by the political tensions. The 2006 coup was completely peaceful and not completely unwelcomed by many in Fiji. I recently spent the better part of 2 months traveling throughout the country, and I saw no evidence that there had even been a coup. From a traveler's point of view, everything was working normally. Travel advisories by the New Zealand government notwithstanding, politics in Fiji, to my mind, should not determine whether you visit these marvelous islands and their extraordinarily friendly inhabitants.

Before you start making your plans, let's see what Fiji is like today, review the fascinating story of how it got to this point, take a look at its mix of cultures and languages, and get a glimpse of its natural environment.

1 Fiji Today

You are unlikely to see any signs that it even occurred, but Fiji's 2006 coup still headlines the local news, as it will until the interim government steps aside and the country holds democratic elections, perhaps in 2009.

About half the people in Fiji reside in urban areas and deal with typical matters like traffic jams, while the others live out in the countryside trying to squeeze a living from sugar-cane farms, or to provide provisions for their traditional Fijian

*There is no part of Fiji which is not civilized, although bush natives prefer a
more naked kind of life.*
—James A. Michener, *Return to Paradise*, 1951

villages. Wherever they are, politics is not first and foremost on their agendas.

Thanks to its industrious Indian residents, Fiji is a relatively developed Third World country. With a multitude of buses and taxis, the transportation system is efficient and relatively inexpensive, though service from the two domestic airlines is a little more unpredictable. The electrical system is reliable, as are communications. Only one TV station serves the country's viewers, but more are on the way. Despite periodic disruptions in some areas, the water pipes provide clean water to the taps.

All of which means that travel in Fiji is overall both efficient and comfortable.

GOVERNMENT

Fiji had a Westminster-style government prior to the 2006 coup. A 71-member parliament consisted of 23 seats reserved for Fijians, 19 for Indians, 1 for Rotuma (a Polynesian island north of Viti Levu), 3 for general electors (anyone who's a Fijian, Indian, or Rotuman), and 25 for any citizen regardless of race. The Great Council of Chiefs picked the country's largely figurehead president, who presided over an appointed senate with relatively little power.

Since the coup the country has had an interim government headed by the military commander, navy Commodore Frank Bainimarama, who had threatened for most of 2006 to "clean up" elected Prime Minister Laisenia Qarase's Fiji nationalist government, which he accused of being both corrupt and racist. His interim government consists of a broad range of local leaders, including Mahendra Chaudhry as finance minister.

Chaudhry was deposed as prime minister during the country's racially motivated insurrection in 2000 and was a key player in the coalition government removed by Fiji's first coup in 1987.

Bainimarama has agreed in principle to hold elections in 2009 after changes to the country's constitution, specifically removal of the race-based electoral system by which nationalist Fijians maintained a majority in parliament.

While the Fijian-Indian racial divide gets most of the blame for the coups, the situation is more complicated. Many indigenous Fijians are educated, live in urban areas, hold responsible positions in tourism and other industries, and deal with Indians on a daily basis. They are at opposites with other Fijians, especially some fundamentalist Christians, who see Indians as heathens who should be deported. In addition, the country has a hereditary system of Fijian chiefs, some of whom have always been rivals. Some descendants of Cakobau, the chief of tiny Bau Island who rose to national power with the help of European settlers in the 1840s (see "Looking Back at Fiji," below), were prime backers of the Fiji nationalist government ousted in 2006. Their rivals are members of the high-ranking Ganilau clan, two of whom are serving as ministers in today's interim government.

ECONOMY

Tourism is far and away Fiji's largest industry. Although the number of visitors dropped off following the December 2006 coup, earlier record demand spurred a hotel construction boom. Sugar and garment manufacturing—Fiji's other economic mainstays—have also fallen off. Grown primarily by Indian farmers on land leased from Fijians, the sugar cane is harvested between June and November and crushed in five aging sugar mills—all of which need repair and upgrading—operated by the government-owned Fiji Sugar Corporation. The number of farmers has decreased since Fijian landowners have not renewed many of their land leases (some displaced farmers have moved into shanties around Suva). In addition, the country lost European Union sugar price supports and favorable trade preferences for garments sold to the United States and Australia.

Behind sugar, the country's leading exports are the famous "Fiji" mineral water, fresh and frozen fish, tuna canned at Levuka, timber and wood products, taro and cassava, and gold mined in northern Viti Levu. For domestic consumption, Fiji produces furniture, coffee (you'll get a rich, strong brew throughout the country), and other consumer goods (the Colgate toothpaste you buy in Fiji most likely will have been made here). Suva is also a major transshipment point for goods destined for other South Pacific islands. Remittances from locals overseas also contribute significantly to the economy.

Nevertheless, unemployment is a persistent problem in Fiji. More than half the population is under 25, and there just aren't enough jobs being created for young people joining the workforce. About 50% of all households live below the official poverty line or just above it. As a consequence, the country has seen a marked increase in burglaries, robberies, home invasions, and other crimes.

2 Looking Back at Fiji

Fiji's oral history goes back some 2,500 years, when the current indigenous residents' ancestors landed on Viti Levu, but the first European eyes in these parts belonged to Dutch navigator Abel Tasman, who sighted Vanua Levu Island and some others in 1643. British Capt. James Cook, the famous South Pacific explorer, visited one of the southernmost islands in 1774. Capt. William Bligh was the first European to sail through and plot the group, after the mutiny on HMS *Bounty* in April 1789. Bligh and his loyal crew sailed their longboat through Fiji on their way to safety in Indonesia. They passed Ovalau and sailed between Viti Levu and Vanua Levu. Large Fijian *druas* (war canoes) gave chase near the Yasawas, but with some furious paddling and the help of a fortuitous squall, Bligh and his men

Dateline

- **1500 B.C.** Polynesians arrive from the west.
- **500 B.C.** Melanesians settle in Fiji, push Polynesians eastward.
- **A.D. 1300–1600** Polynesians, especially Tongans, invade from the east.
- **1643** Abel Tasman sights Vanua Levu, other islands in Fiji.

- **1774** Capt. James Cook visits Vatoa.
- **1789** After the mutiny on the *Bounty*, Capt. William Bligh navigates his longboat through Fiji and is nearly captured by a war canoe.
- **1808** Swedish mercenary Charlie Savage arrives at Bau and supplies guns to Chief Tanoa in successful wars to conquer western Fiji.
- **1822** European settlement begins at Levuka.

- **1830** First Christian missionaries arrive at Lakeba in the Lau Group.
- **1840** A U.S. exploring expedition under Capt. John Wilkes visits the islands.
- **1848** Prince Enele Ma'afu exerts Tongan control over eastern Fiji from outpost in Lau Group.
- **1849** U.S. Consul John Brown Williams's home is burned and looted during

continues

History of Fiji

❶ First Fijians arrive at Vuda Point about 5000 B.C.E.

❷ Dutch explorer Abel Tasman sights Vanua Levu in 1643.

❸ Capt. William Bligh narrowly escapes Fijian warriors after mutiny on the Bounty in 1789.

❹ First Christian missionaries arrive at Lekeba in 1830.

❺ Europeans establish coconut plantations at Savusavu in 1860s.

❻ Highland cannibals devour the Rev. Shirley Baker in 1867.

❼ Fijian chiefs cede their island to the British at Levuka in 1874.

❽ Col. Sitiveni Rabuka stages first coup at Suva in 1987; three more follow in 1987, 2000, 2006.

❾ German raider Count Felix von Luckner unwittingly captured on Wakaya in 1917.

❿ Fiji Water first shipped from northern Viti Levu in 1997.

⓫ Actor Mel Gibson buys Mago Island in 2005.

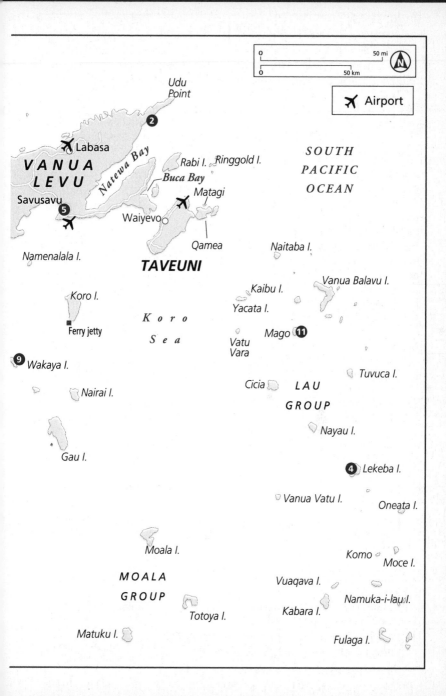

50 mi
50 km

✈ Airport

Udu
Point

2

✈ Labasa

**VANUA
LEVU**

Natewa Bay

Rabi I. Ringgold I.

Buca Bay

Matagi

Savusavu

5

✈

Waiyevo○

Qamea

Namenalala I.

TAVEUNI

*SOUTH
PACIFIC
OCEAN*

Naitaba I.

Vanua Balavu I.

Kaibu I.

Koro I.

K o r o

Yacata I.

S e a

■
Ferry jetty

Mago **11**

Vatu
Vara

9 Wakaya I.

Cicia

LAU

Tuvuca I.

Nairai I.

GROUP

Nayau I.

Gau I.

4 Lekeba I.

Vanua Vatu I.

Oneata I.

Moala I.

Komo

Moce I.

MOALA

Vuaqava I.

GROUP

Namuka-i-lau I.

Kabara I.

Totoya I.

Matuku I.

Fulaga I.

escaped to the open ocean. For a while, Fiji was known as the Bligh Islands, and the passage between Viti Levu and Vanua Levu still is named Bligh Water.

The Tongans warned the Europeans who made their way west across the South Pacific that Fiji was inhabited by ferocious cannibals, and the reports by Bligh and others of reef-strewn waters added to the dangerous reputation of the islands. Consequently, European penetration into Fiji was limited for many years to beach bums and convicts who escaped from the British penal colonies in Australia. There was a sandalwood rush between 1804 and 1813. Other traders arrived in the 1820s in search of *bêche-de-mer* (sea cucumber). This trade continued until the 1850s and had a lasting impact on Fiji because along with the traders came guns and whiskey.

CAKOBAU RISES & FALLS

The traders and settlers established the first European-style town in Fiji at Levuka on Ovalau in the early 1820s, but for many years the real power lay on Bau, a tiny island just off the east coast of Viti Levu. With the help of a Swedish mercenary named Charlie Savage, who supplied the guns, High Chief Tanoa of Bau defeated several much larger confederations and extended his control over most of western Fiji. Bau's influence grew even more under his son and successor, Cakobau, who rose to the height of power in the 1840s. Cakobau never ruled over all the islands, however, for Enele Ma'afu, a member of Tonga's royal family, moved to the Lau Group in 1848 and exerted control over eastern Fiji. Ma'afu brought along Wesleyan missionaries from Tonga and gave the Methodist church a foothold in Fiji (it still is the predominate denomination here).

Although Cakobau governed much of western Fiji, local chiefs continued to be powerful enough to make his control tenuous. The lesser chiefs, especially those in the mountains, also saw the Wesleyan missionaries as a threat to their power,

July 4 celebrations; he blames Cakobau, high chief of eastern Viti Levu.
- **1851** U.S. warship arrives, demands that Cakobau pay $5,000 for Williams's losses.
- **1853** Cakobau is installed as high chief of Bau, highest post in Fiji.
- **1855** United States claims against Cakobau grow to $40,000; U.S. warship arrives, claims some islands as mortgage.
- **1858** Cakobau offers to cede Fiji to Britain for $40,000.
- **1862** Britain rejects Cakobau's offer.
- **1867** Unrest grows; Europeans crown Cakobau King of Bau; Rev. Thomas Baker is eaten.
- **1868** Polynesia Company buys Suva in exchange for paying Cakobau's debts.
- **1871** Europeans form central government at Levuka, make Cakobau king of Fiji.
- **1874** Cakobau's government collapses; he and other chiefs cede Fiji to Britain without price tag.
- **1875** Sir Arthur Gordon becomes first governor.
- **1879** First Indians arrive as indentured laborers.
- **1882** Capital moved from Levuka to Suva.
- **1916** Recruitment of indentured Indians ends.

Impressions

Many of the missionaries were eaten, leading an irreverent planter to suggest that they triumphed by infiltration.

—James A. Michener, *Return to Paradise*, 1951

---

and most of them refused to convert or even to allow the missionaries to establish outposts in their villages. Some mountaineers made a meal of the Rev. Thomas Baker when he tried to convert them in 1867 (see "A Holy Meal" box, later in this chapter).

Cakobau's slide from power began in earnest July 4, 1849, when John Brown Williams, the American consul, celebrated the birth of his own nation. A cannon went off and started a fire that burned Williams's house. The Fijians promptly looted the burning building. Williams blamed Cakobau and demanded US$5,000 in damages. Within a few years the U.S. claims against the chief totaled more than US$40,000, an enormous sum in those days. In the late 1850s, with Ma'afu and his confederation of chiefs gaining power—and disorder growing in western Fiji—Cakobau offered to cede the islands to Great Britain if Queen Victoria would pay the Americans. The British pondered his offer for 4 years and turned him down.

Cakobau worked a better deal when the Polynesia Company, an Australian planting and commercial enterprise, came to Fiji looking for suitable land after the price of cotton skyrocketed during the U.S. Civil War. Instead of offering his entire kingdom, Cakobau this time tendered only 80,000 hectares (200,000 acres) of it. The Polynesia Company accepted, paid off the U.S. claims, and in 1870 landed Australian settlers on 9,200 hectares (23,000 acres) of its land on Viti Levu, near a Fijian village known as Suva. The land was unsuitable for cotton, and the climate was too wet for sugar; so the speculators sold their property to the government, which moved the capital there from Levuka in 1882.

FIJI BECOMES A COLONY

The Polynesia Company's settlers were just a few of the several thousand European planters who came to Fiji in the 1860s and early 1870s. They bought land for plantations from the Fijians, sometimes fraudulently and often for whiskey and guns. Claims and counterclaims to

---

- **1917** German Raider Count Felix von Luckner captured at Wakaya.
- **1917–18** Fijian soldiers support Allies in World War I.
- **1942–45** Fijians serve as scouts with Allied units in World War II; failure of Indians to volunteer angers Fijians.
- **1956** First Legislative Council established, with Ratu Sir Lala Sukuna as speaker.

- **1966** Fijian-dominated Alliance Party wins first elections.
- **1969** Key compromises pave way for constitution and independence. Provision guarantees Fijian land ownership.
- **1970** Fiji becomes independent; Alliance party leader Ratu Sir Kamisese Mara chosen as first prime minister.
- **1987** Fijian-Indian coalition wins majority, names Dr. Timoci

Bavadra as prime minister with Indian-majority cabinet. Col. Sitiveni Rabuka leads two bloodless military coups, installs interim government.
- **1991** New constitution guaranteeing Fijian majority is promulgated.
- **1992** Rabuka's party wins election; he becomes prime minister.
- **1994** Second election cuts Rabuka's majority; he retains

continues

land ownership followed; and, with no legal mechanism to settle the disputes, Fiji was swept to the brink of race war. Things came to a head in 1870, when the bottom fell out of cotton prices, hurricanes destroyed the crops, and anarchy threatened. Within a year the Europeans established a national government at Levuka and named Cakobau king of Fiji. The situation continued to deteriorate, however, and 3 years later Cakobau was forced to cede the islands to Great Britain. This time there was no price tag attached, and the British accepted. The Deed of Cession was signed on October 10, 1874, at Nasovi village near Levuka.

Britain sent Sir Arthur Gordon to serve as the new colony's first governor. As the Americans were later to do in their part of Samoa, he allowed the Fijian chiefs to govern their villages and districts as they had done before (they were not, however, allowed to engage in tribal warfare) and to advise him through a Great Council of Chiefs. He declared that native Fijian lands could not be sold, only leased. That decision has to this day helped to protect the Fijians, their land, and their customs, but it has helped fuel the bitter animosity on the part of the land-deprived Indians.

Gordon prohibited the planters from using Fijians as laborers (not that many of them had the slightest inclination to work

for someone else). When the planters switched from profitless cotton to sugar cane in the early 1870s, Sir Arthur convinced them to import indentured servants from India. The first 463 East Indians arrived on May 14, 1879 (see "The Islanders," later in this chapter).

Following Gordon's example, the British governed "Fiji for the Fijians"— and the European planters, of course— leaving the Indians to struggle for their civil rights. The government exercised jurisdiction over all Europeans in the colony and assigned district officers (the "D.O.s" of British colonial lore) to administer various geographic areas. There was a large gulf between the appointed civil servants sent from Britain and the locals.

FIJI BECOMES INDEPENDENT

One of the highest-ranking Fijian chiefs, Ratu Sir Lala Sukuna, rose to prominence after World War I. (*Ratu* means "chief" in Fijian.) Born of high chiefly lineage, Ratu Sukuna was educated at Oxford, served in World War I, and worked his way up through the colonial bureaucracy to the post of chairman of the Native Land Trust Board. Although dealing in that position primarily with disputes over land and chiefly titles, he used it as a platform to educate his people and to lay the foundation for the independent state of Fiji.

power in coalition with mixed-race general electors.

■ **1995** Rabuka appoints constitutional review commission.

■ **1998** Parliament adopts new constitution with 25 open seats holding balance of power.

■ **1999** Labor union leader Mahendra Chaudhry is elected as Fiji's first Indian prime minister.

■ **2000** Failed businessman George Speight leads insurrection, holds Chaudhry and other parliamentarians hostage. Military disbands constitution, appoints interim Fijian-led government under Laisenia Qarase, arrests Speight.

■ **2001** Fiji's supreme court upholds 1998 constitution; Qarase's Fijian nationalist party wins parliamentary majority in new elections.

■ **2002–04** Qarase releases some coup participants from prison, proposes "reconciliation" bill seen by others as amnesty.

■ **2006** Citing corruption and racism, Commodore Frank Bainimarama overthrows Qarase, installs interim government with Chaudhry as finance minister.

■ **2007** Bainimarama promises new elections by 2009.

(*Fun Fact* **The Count Confounded**

In 1917 Count Felix von Luckner arrived at Wakaya Island off eastern Viti Levu in search of a replacement for his infamous World War I German raider, the *Seeadler,* which had gone aground in the Cook Islands after shelling Papeete on Tahiti. A local constable became suspicious of the armed foreigners and notified the district police inspector. Only Europeans—not Fijians or Indians—could use firearms, so the inspector took a band of unarmed Fijians to Wakaya in a small cattle trading boat. Thinking he was up against a much larger armed force, von Luckner unwittingly surrendered.

As much as anyone, Sukuna was the father of modern, independent Fiji.

After the attack on Pearl Harbor began the Pacific War in 1941, the Allies turned Fiji into a vast training base. They built the airstrip at Nadi, and several coastal gun emplacements still stand along the coast. Thousands of Fijians fought with great distinction as scouts and infantrymen in the Solomon Islands campaigns. Their knowledge of tropical jungles and their skill at the ambush made them much feared by the Japanese. The Fijians were, said one war correspondent, "death with velvet gloves."

Although many Indo-Fijians at first volunteered to join, they also demanded pay equal to that of the European members of the Fiji Military Forces. When the colonial administrators refused, they disbanded their platoon. Their military contribution was one officer and 70 enlisted men of a reserve transport section, and they were promised that they would not have to go overseas. Many Fijians to this day begrudge the Indo-Fijians for not doing more to aid the war effort.

Ratu Sukuna continued to push the colony toward independence until his death in 1958, and although Fiji made halting steps in that direction during the 1960s, the road was rocky. The Indo-Fijians by then were highly organized, in both political parties and trade unions, and they objected to a constitution that would institutionalize Fijian control of

the government and Fijian ownership of most of the new nation's land. Key compromises were made in 1969, however, and on October 10, 1970—exactly 96 years after Cakobau signed the Deed of Cession—the Dominion of Fiji became an independent member of the British Commonwealth of Nations.

Under the 1970 constitution, Fiji had a Westminster-style Parliament consisting of an elected House of Representatives and a Senate composed of Fijian chiefs. For the first 17 years of independence, the Fijians maintained a majority—albeit a tenuous one—in the House of Representatives and control of the government under the leadership of Ratu Sir Kamisese Mara, the country's first prime minister.

Then, in a general election held in April 1987, a coalition of Indians and liberal Fijians voted Ratu Mara and his Alliance party out of power. Dr. Timoci Bavadra, a Fijian, took over as prime minister, but his cabinet was composed of more Indians than Fijians. Animosity immediately flared between some Fijians and Indians.

RAMBO'S COUPS
Within little more than a month of the election, members of the predominantly Fijian army stormed into Parliament and arrested Dr. Bavadra and his cabinet. It was the South Pacific's first military coup, and although peaceful, it took nearly everyone by complete surprise.

The coup leader was Col. Sitiveni Rabuka (pronounced "Ram-*bu*-ka"), whom local wags quickly nicknamed "Rambo." A career soldier trained at Britain's Royal Military Academy Sandhurst, the then 38-year-old Rabuka was third in command of the army. A Fijian of non-chiefly lineage, he immediately became a hero to his "commoner" fellow Fijians. Rabuka at first installed a caretaker government, but in September 1987 he staged another bloodless coup. A few weeks later he abrogated the 1970 constitution, declared Fiji to be an independent republic, and set up a new interim government with himself as minister of home affairs and army commander.

In 1990 the interim government promulgated a new constitution guaranteeing Fijians a parliamentary majority—and rankling the Indians. Rabuka's pro-Fijian party won the initial election, but he barely hung onto power in fresh elections in 1994 by forming a coalition with the European, Chinese, and mixed-race general-elector parliamentarians.

Rabuka also appointed a three-person Constitutional Review Commission, which proposed the constitution that parliament adopted in 1998. It created a parliamentary house of 65 seats, with 19 held by Fijians, 17 by Indians, 3 by general-electors, 1 by a Rotuman, and 25 open to all races.

THE 2000 INSURRECTION & COUP

A year later, with support from many Fijians who were unsettled over the country's poor economy, rising crime, and deteriorating roads, labor union leader Mahendra Chaudhry's party won an outright majority of parliament, and he became Fiji's first Indian prime minister. Chaudhry had been minister of finance in the Bavadra government toppled by Rabuka's coup in 1987.

Chaudhry appointed several well-known Fijians to his cabinet, and the revered Ratu Mara encouraged his fellow Fijians to support the new administration. It didn't work, and in May 2000 a disgruntled Fijian businessman named George Speight led a gang of armed henchmen into parliament. Demanding the appointment of an all-Fijian government, they held Chaudhry and several members of parliament hostage for the next 56 days. While negotiating with Speight, the military under Commodore Frank Bainimarama disbanded the constitution and appointed an interim government headed by Laisenia Qarase, a Fijian banker. Speight released his hostages after being promised amnesty, but the army arrested him 2 weeks later and charged him with treason. His death sentence was later commuted to life in prison.

Fiji's supreme court then ruled that the 1998 constitution was still in effect and ordered fresh parliamentary elections to be held in 2001. Under the watchful eye of international observers, the Fijians won an outright majority, and caretaker leader Qarase became the legal prime minister. Chaudhry also was returned to parliament.

A Fiji nationalist, Qarase proposed a "Reconciliation, Tolerance, and Unity" bill, which opponents—including Bainimarama—claimed would grant amnesty to Speight and other participants in the 2000 insurrection. The proposed legislation was the most contentious issue in the general elections of May 2006, which returned Qarase's party to power.

THE 2006 COUP

Qarase further incensed the military by releasing some 200 coup participants from prison, and he continued to push his controversial reconciliation bill. He also proposed transferring ownership of Fiji's foreshore and lagoons from the government to indigenous seaside tribes, who would then be free to charge resorts, dive operators, fishers, and others to use their lagoons and coastal waters. This proposal created a firestorm of protest from the tourism industry as well as from Fijians who do not live by the sea—and thus presumably would have to pay to go fishing.

Bainimarama warned Qarase for most of 2006 that the military would take power if he did not abandon the proposals. On December 5—a date Fijians refer to as "5/12"—the military drove from Queen Elizabeth Barracks into downtown Suva and staged an entirely peaceful coup. Despite some protestors being taken to the barracks for a bit of persuasion, life outside tourism returned to normal relatively quickly. The initial military roadblocks and checkpoints markedly reduced Fiji's crime rate (it went back up when the soldiers were withdrawn, prompting some merchants to call for permanent checkpoints).

The interim regime has been surprisingly progressive. In addition to abandoning overtly racist government policies, Bainimarama has cracked down on corruption and uncontrolled government spending, which had become rampant under Qarase. Among actions with long-lasting consequences, he has opened Fiji's formerly monopolized communications industry to competition, which promises more over-the-air television channels (instead of one) and lower prices for phone and Internet services. He also has encouraged the thousands of Indian professionals who had fled the country to return home by letting them be permanent residents of Fiji as well as citizens of other countries (Fiji does not recognize dual citizenship).

3 The Lay of the Land & the Sea

A somewhat less-than-pious wag once remarked that God made the South Pacific islands on the 6th day of creation so He would have an extraordinarily beautiful place to rest on the 7th day. Modern geologists have a different view, but the fact remains that the islands and the surrounding sea are possessed of heavenly beauty and a plethora of life forms.

From its strategic position in the southwestern Pacific some 5,152km (3,200 miles) southwest of Honolulu and 3,175km (1,972 miles) northeast of Sydney, Fiji is the transportation and economic hub of the South Pacific islands. **Nadi International Airport** is the main connection point for flights going to the other island countries, and Fiji's capital city, **Suva,** is one of the region's prime shipping ports and headquarters of many regional organizations.

The Fiji archipelago forms a horseshoe around the shallow, reef-strewn **Koro Sea,** much of which was dry land some 18,000 years ago during the last Ice Age. More than 300 islands and islets range in size from Viti Levu (10 times the size of Tahiti) to tiny atolls that barely break the surface of the sea. The total land area is 18,187 sq. km (7,022 sq. miles).

The islands were created by volcanic eruptions along the collision of the Indo-Australian and Pacific tectonic plates. Although the main islands are quiet today, they are part of the volcanically active and earthquake-prone "Ring of Fire" around the Pacific Ocean.

FLORA & FAUNA

Most species of plants and animals now native to Fiji originated in Southeast Asia and worked their way eastward across the Pacific, by natural distribution or in the company of humans. The number of indigenous species diminishes the farther east one goes. Very few local plants or animals came from the Americas, the one notable exception being the sweet potato, which may have been brought back from South America by voyaging Polynesians.

PLANTS

In addition to the west-to-east differences, flora changes according to each island's topography. The mountainous islands make rain from the moist trade winds and thus possess a greater variety of plants. Their interior highlands are covered with ferns, native bush, or grass. The low atolls, by contrast, get sparse rainfall and support little other than scrub bush and coconut palms.

Ancient settlers brought coconut palms, breadfruit, taro, paper mulberry, pepper (*kava*, or *yaqona* in Fijian), and bananas to the isolated midocean islands because of their usefulness as food or fiber. Accordingly, they are generally found in the inhabited areas of the islands and not so often in the interior bush.

With a few exceptions, such as the *tagimaucia* found on Taveuni, tropical flowers also worked their way east in the company of humans. Bougainvillea, hibiscus, allamanda, poinsettia, *poinciana* (flame tree), croton, frangipani (plumeria), ixora, canna, and water lilies all give colorful testament to the islanders's love for flowers of every hue in the rainbow. The aroma of the white, yellow, or pink frangipani is so sweet it's used as perfume on many islands.

ANIMALS & BIRDS

The fruit bat, or "flying fox," and some species of insect-eating bats are the only mammals native to the South Pacific islands. The early settlers introduced dogs, chickens, pigs, rats, and mice. Fiji has one type of poisonous snake, but it lives in the mountains and is seldom seen. You will see lots of geckos and skinks, those little lizards that seem to be everywhere in Fiji. With their ability to walk upside-down across the ceiling at night, geckos are adept at scaring the devil out of unsuspecting tourists. They are harmless, however, and actually perform a valuable service by eating mosquitoes and other insects.

Most land birds live in the bush away from settlements and the accompanying cats, dogs, rats, and ubiquitous Indian myna birds. Mynas were brought to Fiji early in the 20th century to control insects and are now nuisances themselves (these fearless, aggressive creatures will steal the toast right off your breakfast table!). For this reason, the birds most likely to be seen are terns, boobies, herons, petrels, noddies, and others that earn their livelihoods from the sea. But if you keep your eyes and ears at the ready, you may see and hear some of the 26 species of birds that are endemic to Fiji, such as the barking pigeon, red-headed parrotfinch, and giant forest honeyeater. Taveuni is famous among birders for its orange dove, while Kadavu has its shining musk parrot, fantail, honeyeater, and whistling dove.

Tips **Be Careful What You Touch**

Fiji has laws protecting the environment, so *do not deface the reef.* You could land in the slammer for breaking off a gorgeous chunk of live coral to take home as a souvenir. The locals know what they can and cannot legally take from under the water, so buy your souvenir coral in a handicraft shop.

THE SEA

The tropical South Pacific Ocean teems with sea life, from colorful reef fish to the horrific Great White sharks featured in *Jaws,* from the paua clams that make tasty chowders to the deep-sea tuna that keep the cannery going at Levuka.

More than 600 species of coral—10 times the number found in the Caribbean—form the great reefs that make this a divers' mecca. Billions of tiny coral polyps build their own skeletons on top of those left by their ancestors, until they reach the level of low tide. Then they grow outward, extending the edge of the reef. The old skeletons are white, while the living polyps present a rainbow of colors. Corals grow best and are most colorful in the clear, salty water on the outer edge or in channels, where the tides and waves wash fresh seawater along and across the reef. A reef can grow as much as 5 centimeters (2 in.) a year in ideal conditions.

A plethora of tropical fish and other marine life fills most of the lagoons, which are like gigantic aquariums. Bookstores in the main towns sell pamphlets with photographs and descriptions of the creatures that will peer into your face mask.

Humpback whales migrate to the islands from June to October, and sea turtles lay their eggs on some beaches from November through February.

THE ENVIRONMENT TODAY

Although pollution, rising seawater temperature, and a proliferation of crown-of-thorns starfish have greatly hampered reef growth—and beauty—in parts of Fiji, many areas are unmatched in their color and variety of corals.

Fiji has allowed some resort owners to blast away parts of the reef to create marinas and swimming areas, but it has laws protecting its lagoons, which are a major source of food for the locals. Fiji allows but restricts the use of spear guns, so ask before you go in search of the catch of your life.

Sea turtle meat is considered a delicacy in the islands, and Fijians are not above making a meal of turtles despite laws that make it illegal. Do not even think of bringing home one of their shells: Both sea turtles and whales are on the list of endangered species. Many countries, including the United States, prohibit the importation of their shells, bones, and teeth.

You can collect empty sea shells on the beach, but not if they still have live animals inside. Likewise, you can make a souvenir of a dead piece of coral lying on the shore, but you cannot take coral directly from a reef.

4 The Islanders

Early European explorers were astounded to find the far-flung South Pacific islands inhabited by peoples who apparently had been there for thousands of years. How

had these people—who lived a late Stone Age existence and had no written languages—crossed the Pacific long before Christopher Columbus had the courage to sail out of sight of land? Where had they come from? The questions that baffled European explorers continue to intrigue scientists and scholars today.

THE FIRST FIJIANS

The late Thor Heyerdahl drifted in his raft *Kon Tiki* from South America to French Polynesia in 1947, to prove his theory that the Pacific Islanders came from the Americas. Bolstered by linguistic and DNA studies linking the Polynesians to Taiwan, however, experts now believe the Pacific Islanders have their roots in eastern Asia.

The accepted view is that during the Ice Age a race of humans known as Australoids migrated from Southeast Asia to Papua New Guinea and Australia, when those two countries were joined by dry land. Another group, the Papuans, arrived from Southeast Asia between 5,000 and 10,000 years ago. Later, a lighter-skinned race known as Austronesians pushed the Papuans out into the more eastern South Pacific islands. They became the Polynesians, whom archaeologists now believe settled in Samoa more than 3,000 years ago and then slowly fanned out to colonize the vast Polynesian triangle stretching from Hawaii to Easter Island to New Zealand.

The most tangible remains of the early Austronesians are remnants of pottery, the first shards of which were found during the 1970s in Lapita, in New Caledonia. Probably originating in Papua New Guinea, Lapita pottery spread east as far as Tonga. Throughout the area it was decorated with geometric designs similar to those used today on tapa cloth, known in Fijian as *masi*. Apparently the Lapita culture died out in Polynesia some 2,500 years ago, for by the time European explorers arrived in the 1770s, only the

---

Fun Fact **"Fiji Time"**

There's an old story about a 19th-century planter who promised a South Pacific islander a weekly wage and a pension if he would come to work on his copra plantation. *Copra* is dried coconut meat, from which oil is pressed for use in soaps, cosmetics, and other products. Hours of backbreaking labor are required to chop open the coconuts and extract the meat by hand.

The islander was sitting by the lagoon, eating fruit he had picked from nearby trees while hauling in one fish after another. "Let me make sure I understand you," said the islander. "You want me to break my back working for you for 30 years. Then you'll pay me a pension so I can come back here and spend the rest of my life sitting by the lagoon, eating fruit from my trees and the fish I catch? I may not be sophisticated, but I am not stupid."

The islander's response reflects an attitude still prevalent in Fiji, where many people don't have to work in the Western sense. Here life moves at a slow pace, which the locals call "Fiji Time."

Consequently, do not expect the same level of service rendered in most hotels and restaurants back home. The slowness is not slothful inattention; it's just the way things are done here. Your drink will come in due course. If you must have it immediately, order it at the bar. Otherwise, relax with your friendly hosts and enjoy their charming company.

A Holy Meal

When meeting and talking to the smiling Fijians, it's difficult to imagine that hardly more than a century ago their ancestors were among the world's most ferocious cannibals. Today the only vestiges of this past are the four-pronged wooden cannibal forks sold in handicraft shops (they make interesting conversation pieces when used at home to serve hors d'oeuvres).

Yet in the early 1800s, the Fijians were so fierce that Europeans were slow to settle in the islands for fear of literally being turned into a meal. Back then, Fijian society was organized by tribes, which constantly warred with each other, usually with brutal vengeance. The winners hung captured enemy children by their feet from the rigging of their canoes, and they sometimes consecrated new buildings by burying live adult prisoners in holes dug for the support posts.

The ultimate insult, however, was to eat the enemy's flesh. Victorious chiefs were even said to cook and nibble on the fingers or tongues of the vanquished, relishing each bite while the victims watched in agony. "One man actually stood by my side and ate the very eyes out of a roasted skull he had, saying, *'Venaca, venaca,'* that is, very good," wrote William Speiden, the purser on the U.S. exploring expedition that charted Fiji in 1840.

More than 100 white-skinned individuals ended up with their skulls smashed and their bodies baked in an earth oven, including the Rev. Thomas Baker, who attempted to convert the Viti Levu highlanders in 1867. Instead of converting, they killed the reverend, tossed his body into an oven, and made a meal of him.

Fijians still made pottery using Lapita methods. And they still do.

The islands settled by the Papuans and Austronesians are known collectively as *Melanesia,* which includes Papua New Guinea, the Solomon Islands, Vanuatu, New Caledonia, and Fiji. More specifically, Fiji is the melting pot of the Melanesians to the west and the Polynesians to the east.

The name Melanesia is derived from the Greek words *melas,* "black," and *nesos,* "island." The Melanesians in general have features more akin to sub-Saharan Africans, but interbreeding among the successive waves of migrants resulted in many subgroups with varying physical characteristics. Among them, the mountain tribes tend to have darker skin than the coastal dwellers, who interbred with the lighter-skinned Austronesians. The Fijian culture, on the other hand, has many Polynesian elements, brought by interbreeding and conquest.

FIJI'S MIXED POPULATION

Adding to the mix are Fiji Indians, most of whom are descendants of laborers brought to work the country's sugar-cane fields (see "The Fiji Indians," below). The official 2007 census found that of Fiji's total population of 827,900, indigenous Fijians made up 57%, Fiji Indians 38%, and other Pacific islanders, Chinese, Europeans, and persons of mixed race the other 5%. Thanks to a high Fijian birthrate, the overall population has been rising slightly despite the country's losing thousands of Fiji Indians since the first military coup in 1987.

It's difficult to imagine peoples of two more contrasting cultures living side by side than the indigenous Fijians and the Fiji Indians. "Fijians generally perceive Indians as mean and stingy, crafty and demanding to the extent of being considered greedy, inconsiderate, grasping, uncooperative, egotistic, and calculating," wrote Professor Asesela Ravuvu of the University of the South Pacific. On the other hand, he said, Indians see Fijians as *"jungalis"*—poor, backward, naive, foolish, and living on land they will not sell.

Given that these attitudes are not likely to change anytime soon, it is remarkable that Fijians and Fiji Indians actually manage to coexist. Politically correct Americans may take offense at things they overhear in Fiji, where racial distinctions are a fact of life—as you will notice on the country's immigration entry form.

From a visitor's standpoint, the famously friendly Fijians give the country its laid-back South Seas charm while providing relatively good service at the hotels. For their part, the Fiji Indians make this an easy country to visit by providing excellent maintenance of facilities and efficient and inexpensive services, such as transportation.

The 1998 constitution makes everyone, regardless of his or her race, a Fiji Islander.

THE INDIGENOUS FIJIANS

Today's indigenous Fijians are descended from a Melanesian people who came from the west and began settling here around 500 B.C. Legend says they arrived at Viseisei village, at Vuda Point on Viti Levu. Over time they replaced the Polynesians, whose ancestors had arrived some 1,000 years beforehand, but not before adopting much of Polynesian culture and intermarrying enough to give many Fijians lighter skin than that of most other Melanesians, especially in the islands of eastern Fiji near the Polynesian Kingdom of Tonga. (This is less the case in the west and among the hill dwellers, whose ancestors had less contact with Polynesians in ancient times.) Similar differences occur in terms of culture. For example, whereas Melanesians traditionally pick their chiefs by popular consensus, Fijian chiefs hold titles by heredity, in the Polynesian (or more precisely, Tongan) fashion.

Most Fijians still live in small villages along the coast and riverbanks or in the hills, and you will see some traditional thatch *bures,* or houses, scattered in the countryside away from the main roads. As in the old days, every Fijian belongs to a clan, or *matangali,* that was originally based on skills such as canoe making and farming. Clan elders meet in each village to chose a *ratu,* or chief. Charged with caring for their land, villagers still grow food crops in small "bush gardens" on plots assigned to their families. More than 80% of the land in Fiji is communally owned by Fijians and managed for them by the Native Lands Trust Board.

A majority of Fijians are Methodists, their forebears having been converted by Wesleyan missionaries who came to the islands from Tonga in the 19th century.

Impressions

A hundred years of prodding by the British has failed to make the Fijians see why they should work for money.

—James A. Michener, *Return to Paradise,* 1951

"Grog" Etiquette

Known as *kava* elsewhere in the South Pacific, the slightly narcotic drink Fijians call *yaqona* (yon-*gon*-na) or "grog" rivals Fiji Bitter beer as the national drink. In fact, Fiji has more "grog shops" than bars. You will likely have half a coconut shell of grog offered—if not shoved in your face— beginning at your hotel's reception desk.

And thanks to the promotion of *kavalactone,* the active ingredient, as a health-food answer to stress and insomnia in the United States and else- where, growing the root is an important part of the South Pacific's econ- omy. When fears surfaced a few years ago that kava could be linked to liver disease, locals commented that if that was true, there would be few healthy livers in Fiji.

Yaqona has always played an important ceremonial role in Fijian life. No significant occasion takes place without it, and a *sevusevu* (welcoming) cer- emony is usually held for tour groups visiting Fijian villages. Mats are placed on the floor, the participants gather around in a circle, and the yaqona roots are mixed with water and strained through coconut husks into a large carved wooden bowl, called a *tanoa.*

The ranking chief sits next to the tanoa during the welcoming ceremony. He extends in the direction of the guest of honor a cowrie shell attached to one leg of the bowl by a cord of woven coconut fiber. It's extremely impo- lite to cross the plane of the cord once it has been extended.

The guest of honor (in this case your tour guide) then offers a gift to the village (a kilogram or two of dried grog roots will do these days) and makes a speech explaining the purpose of his visit. The chief then passes the first cup of yaqona to the guest of honor, who claps once, takes the cup in both hands, and gulps down the entire cup of sawdust-tasting liquid in one swal- low. Everyone else then claps three times.

Next, each chief drinks a cup, clapping once before bolting it down. Again, everyone else claps three times after each cup is drained. Except for the clapping and formal speech, everyone remains silent throughout the ceremony, a tradition easily understood considering kava's numbing effect on the lips and tongue.

The Methodist Church is a powerful, pro-Fijian political force.

THE TABUA

The highest symbol of respect among Fijians is the tooth of the sperm whale, known as a *tabua* (pronounced "tam-*bu*- a"). Like large mother-of-pearl shells used in other parts of Melanesia, tabuas in ancient times played a role similar to that of money in modern society and still have various ceremonial uses. They are pre- sented to chiefs as a sign of respect, given as gifts to arrange marriages, offered to friends to show sympathy after the death of a family member, and used as a means to seal a contract or another agreement. It is illegal to export a tabua out of Fiji, and even if you did, the international conven- tions on endangered species prohibit your bringing it into the United States and most other Western countries.

FIRE WALKING

Legend says that a Fijian god once repaid a favor to a warrior on Beqa island by giving him the ability to walk unharmed on fire. His descendants, all members of the Sawau tribe on Beqa, still walk across stones heated to white-hot by a bonfire—but usually for the entertainment of tourists at the hotels rather than for a particular religious purpose.

Traditionally, the participants—all male—had to abstain from women and coconuts for 2 weeks before the ceremony. If they partook of either, they would suffer burns to their feet. Naturally a priest (some would call him a witch doctor) would recite certain incantations to make sure the coals were hot and the gods were at bay and not angry enough to scorch the soles.

Today's fire walking is a bit touristy but still worth seeing. If you don't believe the stones are hot, go ahead and touch one of them—but do it gingerly.

Some Fiji Indians engage in fire walking for religious purposes during an annual Hindu soul-cleansing festival (see "Fiji Calendar of Events," in chapter 3.

FIJIAN VILLAGE ETIQUETTE

Fijian villages are easy to visit, but keep in mind that to the people who live in them, the entire village—not just an individual's house—is home. In your native land, you wouldn't walk into a stranger's living room without being invited, so find someone and ask permission before traipsing into a Fijian village. The Fijians are accommodating people, and it's unlikely they will say no; in fact, they may ask you to stay for a meal or stage a small yaqona ceremony in your honor (see "'Grog' Etiquette" box, above).

If you are invited to stay or eat in the village, a small gift to the chief is appropriate; F$10 (US$6.50/£3.30) per person or a handful of dried kava root from the local market will do. The gift should be given to the chief or highest-ranking person present to accept it. Sometimes it helps to explain that it is a gift to the village and not payment for services rendered, especially if it's money you're giving.

Only chiefs are allowed to wear hats and sunglasses in Fijian villages, so it's good manners for visitors to take theirs off. Shoulders must be covered at all times. Fijians go barefoot and walk slightly stooped in their bures. Men sit cross-legged on the floor; women sit with their legs to the side. They don't point at one another with hands, fingers, or feet, nor do they touch each other's heads or hair. They greet each other and strangers with a big smile and a sincere *"Bula."*

THE FIJI INDIANS

The *Leonidas,* a labor transport ship, arrived at Levuka from Calcutta on May 14, 1879, and landed 463 indentured servants destined to work Fiji's sugar-cane fields. As more than 60,000 Indians would do over the next 37 years, these first immigrants signed agreements (*girmits,* they called them) requiring that they work in Fiji for 5 years; they would be free to return to India after 5 more years. Most of them labored in the cane

Impressions

It is doubtful if anyone but an Indian can dislike Fijians . . . They are one of the happiest peoples on earth and laugh constantly. Their joy in things is infectious; they love practical jokes, and in warfare they are without fear.
　　　　　　　　　　　　　　　—James A. Michener, *Return to Paradise,* 1951

> ⌒ *Moments* **Meeting the Friendly Fijians**
>
> The indigenous Fijians are justly renowned for their friendliness to strangers, and many Fiji Indians are as well educated and informed as anyone in the South Pacific. Together, these two peoples are fun to meet, whether it be over a hotel desk or while riding with them in one of their fume-belching buses.

fields for the initial term of their girmits, living in "coolie lines" of squalid shacks hardly better than the poverty-stricken conditions most left behind in India.

After the initial 5 years, however, they were free to seek work on their own. Many leased plots of land from the Fijians and began planting sugar cane or raising cattle. To this day most of Fiji's sugar crop, the country's most important agricultural export, is produced on small leased plots. Other Fiji Indians went into business in the growing cities and towns; joined in the early 1900s by an influx of business-oriented Indians, they thereby founded Fiji's modern merchant and professional classes.

Of the immigrants who came from India between 1879 and 1916, when the indenturing system ended, some 85% were Hindus, 14% were Muslims, and the remaining 1% were Sikhs and Christians. Fiji offered these adventurers far more opportunities than caste-controlled India. In fact, the caste system was scrapped very quickly by the Hindus in Fiji, and, for the most part, the violent relations between Hindus and Muslims that racked India were put aside on the islands.

Only a small minority of the Fiji Indians went home after their girmits expired. They tended then—as now—to live in the towns and villages, and in the "Sugar Belt" along the drier north and west coasts of Viti Levu and Vanua Levu. Hindu and Sikh temples and Muslim mosques abound in these areas, and places such as Ba and Tavua resemble small towns on the Indian subcontinent. On the southern coasts and in the mountains, the population is overwhelmingly Fijian. Fiji Indians constituted more than half of Fiji's population prior to the 1987 coup, but emigration (not to India but to Australia, New Zealand, Canada, and the U.S.) reduced their share to 38% by 2007.

5 Fiji in Popular Culture: Books, Film & TV

BOOKS

The National Geographic Society's book *The Isles of the South Pacific* (1971), by Maurice Shadbolt and Olaf Ruhen, and Ian Todd's *Island Realm* (1974), are out-of-date coffee-table books but have lovely color photographs. *Living Corals* (1979), by Douglas Faulkner and Richard Chesher, shows what you will see underwater.

HISTORY, POLITICS & CULTURE

Fiji-based writer Kim Gravelle has written several books about the country's history and culture. *Fiji's Times: a History of* *Fiji* (1980) is a compilation of his articles from the pages of the *Fiji Times* newspaper. *The Fiji Explorer's Handbook* (1980) is a dated guide to the country, but the maps are still excellent. Gravelle travels from Fiji to other South Pacific countries in *Romancing the Islands* (1977).

Noted conservationist Joana McIntyre Varawa married Fijian Male Varawa, who was half her age, and moved from Hawaii to his home village. In *Changes in Latitude* (1989), she writes of her experiences, providing many insights into modern Fijian culture.

Impressions

The question of what to do with these clever Indians of Fiji is the most acute problem in the Pacific today. Within 10 years it will become a world concern.
—James A. Michener, *Return to Paradise,* 1951

TRAVELOGUES

Sir David Attenborough, the British documentary film producer, traveled to Papua New Guinea, Vanuatu, Fiji, and Tonga in the late 1950s. Sir David entertainingly tells of his trips in *Journeys to the Past* (1983).

Travel writer and novelist Paul Theroux took his kayak along for a tour of Fiji and several other South Pacific islands and reported on what he found in *The Happy Isles of Oceania: Paddling the Pacific* (1992). The book is a fascinatingly frank yarn, full of island characters and out-of-the-way places.

Ronald Wright's enjoyable book *On Fiji Islands* (1986) is packed with insights about the Fijians and Indians.

John Dyson rode inter-island trading boats throughout the South Pacific and wrote about his experiences in *The South Seas Dream* (1982). It's an entertaining account of the islands and their more colorful inhabitants. Julian Evans tells of a more recent trading-boat trip to Fiji, the Samoas, and Tonga in *Transit of Venus* (1992).

More recently, J. Maarten Troost tells some hilarious tales in *Getting Stoned with Savages: A Trip Through the Islands of Fiji and Vanuatu* (2006). He spins similar yarns about Micronesia in *The Sex Lives of Cannibals* (2004).

FICTION

Starting with Herman Melville's *Typee* (1846) and *Omoo* (1847), the South Pacific has spawned a wealth of fiction. (Though set in the South Pacific Ocean, Melville's 1851 classic, *Moby Dick,* does not tell of the islands.)

W. Somerset Maugham's produced a volume of South Pacific short stories, *The Trembling of a Leaf* (1921; Mutual, 1985). Next on the scene were Charles Nordhoff and James Norman Hall, two young Americans who together wrote the most famous of all South Pacific novels, *Mutiny on the Bounty* (1932). They followed that enormous success with two other novels: *Men Against the Sea* (1934), based on Capt. Bligh's epic longboat voyage (including their narrow escape in Fiji), and *Pitcairn's Island* (1935), about Lt. Fletcher Christian's demise on the mutineers' remote hideaway.

For a nonfiction retelling of the great tale, see Caroline Alexander's *The Bounty: The True Story of the Mutiny on the Bounty* (2003).

The second most famous South Pacific novel appeared just after World War II—James A. Michener's *Tales of the South Pacific* (1947), which Richard Rodgers and Oscar Hammerstein turned into the musical *South Pacific,* a huge Broadway hit and blockbuster movie. Michener toured the islands a few years later and wrote *Return to Paradise* (1951), a collection of essays and short stories that capture the islands as they were after World War II but before tourists began to arrive. In it, he predicted today's Fijian-Indian conflict.

FILM & TV

Fiji has provided the backdrop for several movies and television shows, the most recent being a season of CBS's *Survivor: Fiji,* which took place on the northern coast of Vanua Levu in 2007.

In the movies, Jean Simmons played a teenage girl shipwrecked with a boy on a deserted island in the 1949 version of *The Blue Lagoon.* The 1980 remake helped launch the career of Brooke Shields, then 14 years old. Both were shot in the Yasawa Islands, the Brooke Shields version on Nanuya Levu, home of Turtle Island Resort. It inspired Richard Evanson, the resort's owner, to rename the surrounding waters "The Blue Lagoon." A 1991 sequel, *Return to the Blue Lagoon,* was made on Taveuni.

Tom Hanks starred in 2000 as a FedEx employee marooned on Modriki Island in the Mamanucas in *Castaway.* Hanks lost 55 pounds while making the movie, but not by roughing it on Modriki; he reportedly stayed in a suite at the Sheraton Fiji Resort and rode a helicopter out to the deserted island each morning.

Anacondas: The Hunt for the Blood Orchid was filmed in the winding, muddy waterways of Pacific Harbour in 2004. It was the sequel to 1997's *Anacondas,* which was shot in Brazil. Fiji, of course, has no real anacondas.

6 Eating & Drinking in Fiji

Fiji's dining scene was pretty bleak when I first visited in the 1970s. There was tasty food to be had at the country's numerous curry houses, which catered to the local Indian population; but other restaurants offered bland fare of the roast and grilled steak variety that predominated in Australia and New Zealand in those days. What a world of difference 3 decades make: Fiji today has some very good restaurants serving food from around the globe—although I never come here without also partaking of a native Fijian feast.

LOVOS AND MEKES

Like most South Pacific islanders, the Fijians in pre-European days steamed their food in an earth oven, known here as a *lovo.* They would use their fingers to eat the huge feasts *(mekes)* that emerged, then would settle down to watch traditional dancing and perhaps polish off a few cups of yaqona.

The ingredients of a lovo meal are *buaka* (pig), *doa* (chicken), *ika* (fish), *mana* (lobster), *moci* (river shrimp), *kai* (freshwater mussels), and various vegetables, such as dense *dalo* (taro root), spinachlike *rourou* (taro leaves), and *lumi* (seaweed). Most dishes are cooked in sweet *lolo* (coconut milk). The most plentiful fish is the *walu,* or Spanish mackerel.

Fijians also make delicious *kokoda* (ko-kon-da), their version of fresh fish marinated in lime juice and mixed with fresh vegetables and coconut milk. Another Fijian specialty is *palusami,* a rich combination of meat or fish baked in banana leaves or foil with onions, taro leaves, and coconut milk.

Most resort hotels have mekes on their schedule of weekly events. Traditional Fijian dance shows follow the meals. Unlike the fast, hip-swinging, suggestive dancing of Tahiti and the Cook Islands, Fijians follow the custom of the Samoas and Tonga, with gentle movements taking second place to the harmony of their voices. The spear-waving war dances have more action.

CURRY IN FIJI

While not all menus include Fijian-style dishes, they all offer at least one Indian curry, which bodes well for vegetarians, since most Hindus eat no meat or seafood.

Fijian curries traditionally are on the mild side, but you can ask for it spicy. Curries are easy to figure out from the menu: lamb, goat, beef, chicken, vegetarian. If in doubt, ask the waiter or waitress. *Roti* is the round, lightly fried bread normally used to pick up your food (it is a hybrid of the round breads of India and

Tips The Best Fijian Chow

You'll be offered Fijian food during meke nights at the resorts, but I join the locals for the best Fijian chow at:

- **Nadina Authentic Fijian Restaurant**, Nadi (☎ **672 7313**; p. 124).
- **Vilisite's Seafood Restaurant**, Korovou, Coral Coast (☎ **653 0054**; p. 162).
- **Hare Krishna Restaurant**, 16 Pratt St., Suva (☎ **331 4154**; p. 193)
- **Old Mill Cottage**, 47–49 Carnavon St., Suva (☎ **331 2134**; p. 194)
- **Surf 'n' Turf**, the Copra Shed, Savusavu (☎ **881 0966**; p. 227)
- **Vunibokoi Restaurant**, Matei, Taveuni (☎ **888 0560**; p. 242)

Pakistan). *Puri* is a soft, puffy bread, and *papadam* is thin and crispy.

The entire meal may come on a round steel plate, with the curries, condiments, and rice in their own dishes arranged on the larger plate. The authentic method of dining is to dump the rice in the middle of the plate, add the smaller portions around it, and then mix them all together.

WINE, BEER & SPIRITS

Fiji does not produce wine, but connoisseurs will have ample opportunity to sample the vintages from nearby Australia, where abundant sunshine produces renowned full-bodied, fruit-driven varieties, such as chardonnay, semillon, Riesling, shiraz, Hermitage, cabernet sauvignon, and merlot. New Zealand wines are also widely available, including distinctive whites, such as chenin blanc, sauvignon blanc, and soft merlot.

The country does brew the robust Fiji Bitter beer—or "Stubbie" to locals because of its distinctive short-neck bottles. Fiji Gold is a somewhat lighter version.

With all those sugar-cane fields, it's not surprising that Fiji produces a decent dark rum known as Bounty. A gin is produced here, too, but it's best used as paint thinner.

Freight and import duties drive up the cost of other spirits and all wines, so expect higher prices than at home. I always bring my two allowed bottles of spirits from the duty-free shops at the airport.

COFFEE LINGO

Coffee lovers are in for a treat, for excellent beans are grown in Fiji's mountains. The robust product is darkly roasted and served throughout the country. The **Bulaccino** and **Esquires** outlets in Nadi and Suva will satisfy your daily caffeine needs.

The coffee lingo spoken in Fiji is different than the North American version. Over here, a **short black** is an espresso. A **long black** is two shots of espresso with extra hot water. A **flat white** is what we call a latte (half espresso, half steamed milk), while a **trimmed flat white** is a flat white with skim milk.

I owe a debt of gratitude to my Kiwi friend Maggie Kerrigan for translating; otherwise, I would still be shaking from caffeine withdrawal.

3

Planning Your Trip to Fiji

Drawn by Fiji's beauty and charm—as well as its reputation as a safe haven in this time of international terrorism—record numbers of visitors are discovering this vast and varied paradise. Although many of them stayed away in the months following the December 2006 coup, Australians and New Zealanders—for whom Fiji is as convenient as the Caribbean is to Americans and Canadians, or the Greek Isles are to Europeans—are especially prevalent in Fiji.

A pre-coup tourism boom brought numerous new resorts and other facilities, but the country's overall tourism business dropped off significantly immediately following the coup. With fewer tourists and more competition from the new properties, the local travel industry has been luring visitors with reduced prices for hotel rooms, cruises, and airfares. As a result, this is an excellent time to visit Fiji—and save money while you're at it.

No single clearinghouse markets specials, but many show up on the Australian-oriented **www.etravelblackboard.com**. Also check with the Fiji Visitors Bureau and contact travel agents who specialize in package tours and independent travel to Fiji (see "Packages for the Independent Traveler," later in this chapter).

With Australian and New Zealand business down significantly, it has been easier to find a hotel room on the dates you want to travel. That was not always the case during Fiji's recent tourism boom.

For additional help in planning your trip and for more on-the-ground resources in Fiji, please turn to the "Fast Facts, Toll-Free Numbers & Websites" appendix A on p. 244.

1 Visitor Information & Maps

The **Fiji Visitors Bureau (FVB)**, P.O. Box 9217, Nadi Airport, Fiji Islands (© **672 2433**; fax 672 0141; www.bula fiji.com), sends out maps, brochures, and other materials from its head office in the Colonial Plaza shopping center, on the Queen's Road in Namaka, about halfway between Nadi Airport and Nadi Town. It also has an information desk (© **330 2433**) in a historic colonial house at the corner of Thomson and Scott streets in the heart of Suva.

The FVB's award-winning website is a trove of up-to-date information and is linked to the home pages of the country's airlines, tour operators, attractions, and hotels. It also has a directory of e-mail addresses.

Other FVB office locations are:

- **United States and Canada:** 5777 West Century Blvd., Ste. 220, Los Angeles, CA 90045 (© **800/932-3454** or 310/568-1616; fax 310/670-2318; www.bulafijinow.com)
- **Australia:** Level 12, St. Martins Tower, 31 Market St., Sydney, NSW 2000 (© **02/9264-3399**; fax 02/9264-3060; www.bulafiji-au.com)

> *Tips* **Beware of Unofficial "Tourist Information Centres"**
>
> When you see "Tourist Information Centre" in Nadi or elsewhere, it is most likely a travel agent or tour operator, whose staff will invariably steer you to its own products. The only official, nonprofit tourist information centers are operated by the Fiji Visitors Bureau, at the Nadi and Suva locations listed on p. 37.

- **New Zealand:** 33 Scanlon St., Grey Lynn (P.O. Box 1179), Auckland (© **09/373-2533;** fax 09/376-4720; info@bulafiji.co.nz)
- **Germany:** Petersburger Strasse 94, 10247 Berlin (© **30/4225-6026;** fax 30/4225-6287; www.bulafiji.de)
- **Japan:** Noa Building, 14th Floor, 3–5, 2 Chome, Azabuudai, Minato-Ku, Tokyo 106 (© **03/3587-2038;** fax 03/3587-2563; www.bulafiji-jp.com)
- **United Kingdom:** Lion House, 111 Hare Lane, Claygate, Surrey K1 0QF (© **0800 652 2158** or 1372 469818; fax 1372 470057; fiji@ihml.com)

You can tune many hotel room TVs to the advertiser-supported **Visitor Information Network (VIN),** usually on channel 10, for tips about what to do and where to dine.

The Fiji government's website is at **www.fiji.gov.fj**. See "Newspapers & Magazines" in the "Fast Facts, Toll-Free Numbers & Websites" appendix A (p. 247), for other useful sites. Other online venues for regional news are posted by the Hawaii-based *Pacific Magazine* (www.pacificmagazine.net) and Fiji-based *Islands Business Magazine* (www.islandsbusiness.com).

Many bookstores and hotel gift shops in Fiji sell maps, and the Fiji telephone directory has colorful city and town maps in the front.

The best place to order quality maps of the region is from **Maptown Ltd.** (www.maptown.com). The **Perry-Castañeda Library** at the University of Texas at Austin posts free maps of the region on its website at www.lib.utexas.edu/maps/australia.html. Other free sources are **www.mapsouthpacific.com**, **www.maps-pacific.com**, and **www.worldatlas.com**.

2 Entry Requirements

PASSPORTS & VISAS

All visitors must have a passport valid for 6 months beyond their visits and an onward or return airline ticket. See "Passports" in the "Fast Facts: Fiji" section in appendix A for information on how to get a passport.

Visitor permits good for stays of up to 4 months are issued upon arrival to citizens of the United States; all Commonwealth countries; most European, South American, and South Pacific island nations; and Mexico, Japan, Israel, Pakistan, South Korea, Thailand, Tunisia, and Turkey.

Citizens of all other countries must apply for visas in advance from the Fiji embassies or consulates. In the United States, contact the **Embassy of Fiji,** Ste. 710, 2000 M St. NW, Washington, DC 20007 (© **202/466-8320;** fax 202/466-8325; www.fijiembassy.org). Other Fiji embassies or high commissions are in Canberra and Sydney, Australia; Wellington, New Zealand; London, England; Brussels, Belgium; Tokyo, Japan; Kuala

Cut the Airport Security Line as a Registered Traveler

In 2003, the **Transportation Security Administration (TSA;** www.tsa.gov) approved a pilot program to help ease the time spent in line for airport security screenings. In exchange for information and a fee, persons can be pre-screened as registered travelers, granting them a front-of-the-line position when they fly. The program is run through private firms—the largest and most well-known is Steven Brill's **Clear** (www.flyclear.com), and it works like this: Travelers complete an online application providing specific points of personal information including name, addresses for the previous 5 years, birth date, social security number, driver's license number, and a valid credit card (you're not charged the **$99 fee** until your application is approved). Print out the completed form and take it, along with proper ID, with you to an "enrollment station" (this can be found in over 20 participating airports and in a growing number of American Express offices around the country, for example). It's at this point where it gets seemingly sci-fi. At the enrollment station, a Clear representative will record your biometrics necessary for clearance; in this case, your fingerprints and your irises will be digitally recorded.

Once your application has been screened against no-fly lists, outstanding warrants, and other security measures, you'll be issued a clear plastic card that holds a chip containing your information. Each time you fly through participating airports (and the numbers are steadily growing), go to the Clear Pass station located next to the standard TSA screening line. Here you'll insert your card into a slot and place your finger on a scanner to read your print—when the information matches up, you're cleared to cut to the front of the security line. You'll still have to follow all the procedures of the day like removing your shoes and walking through the X-ray machine, but Clear promises to cut 30 minutes off your wait time at the airport.

On a personal note: Each time I've used my Clear Pass, my travel companions are still waiting to go through security while I'm already sitting down, reading the paper and sipping my overpriced smoothie. Granted, registered traveler programs are not for the infrequent traveler, but for those of us who fly on a regular basis, it's a perk I'm willing to pay for.

—David A. Lytle

Lumpur, Malaysia; Port Moresby, Papua New Guinea; New Delhi, India; and Beijing, China. Check your local phone book, or go to www.fiji.gov.fj and click on "Fiji Missions Overseas."

Persons wishing to remain longer than their initial permits must apply for extensions from the **Immigration Department,** whose primary offices are at the Nadi International Airport terminal (© **672 2454;** www.fiji.gov.fj) and in the Labour Department building on Victoria Parade in downtown Suva (© **321 1775**).

MEDICAL REQUIREMENTS

Vaccinations are not required unless you have been in a yellow fever or cholera area shortly before arriving in Fiji.

CUSTOMS
WHAT YOU CAN BRING INTO FIJI

Fiji's **Customs allowances** are 200 cigarettes; 2 liters of liquor, beer, or wine; and F$400 (US$260/£132) worth of other goods in addition to personal belongings. Pornography is prohibited. Firearms and nonprescription narcotic drugs are strictly prohibited and subject to heavy fines and jail terms. Any fresh fruits and vegetables must be declared and are subject to inspection and fumigation. You will need advance permission to bring any animal into Fiji; if not, your pet will be quarantined.

Note: Customs will X-ray *all* of your luggage upon arrival.

WHAT YOU CAN TAKE HOME FROM FIJI

U.S. citizens who have been in Fiji for at least 48 hours are allowed to bring back, once every 30 days, US$800 worth of merchandise duty-free. For specifics on what you can bring back and the corresponding fees, download the invaluable free pamphlet *Know Before You Go* online at **www.cbp.gov**. (Click on "Travel," and then click on "Know Before You Go! Online Brochure.") Or contact the **U.S. Customs & Border Protection (CBP),** 1300 Pennsylvania Ave., NW, Washington, DC 20229 (© 877/287-8667), and request the pamphlet.

Canadian Citizens: For a clear summary of Canadian rules, write for the booklet *I Declare,* issued by the Canada Border Services Agency (© 800/461-9999 in Canada, or 204/983-3500; www.cbsa-asfc.gc.ca).

U.K. Citizens: For information, contact **HM Customs & Excise** at © 0845/010-9000 (from outside the U.K., 020/8929-0152), or consult their website at **www.hmce.gov.uk**.

Australian Citizens: A helpful brochure available from Australian consulates or Customs offices is *Know Before You Go.* For more information, call the **Australian Customs Service** at © 1300/363-263, or log on to **www.customs.gov.au**.

New Zealand Citizens: Most questions are answered in a free pamphlet available at New Zealand consulates and Customs offices: *New Zealand Customs Guide for Travellers, Notice no. 4.* For more information, contact **New Zealand Customs,** The Customhouse, 17–21 Whitmore St., Box 2218, Wellington (© 04/473-6099 or 0800/428-786; **www.customs.govt.nz**).

3 When to Go

THE CLIMATE

Although local weather patterns have changed in the past 20 years, making conditions less predictable, local residents recognize a cooler and more comfortable **dry season** during the austral winter, from June to September. The winter trade wind blows fairly steadily during these months, bringing generally fine tropical weather.

The austral summer from November through April is the warmer and more humid **wet season.** Low-pressure troughs and tropical depressions can bring several days of rain at a time, but usually heavy rain showers are followed by periods of very intense sunshine. An air-conditioned hotel room or bungalow will feel like heaven during this humid time of year. This is also the season for tropical cyclones (hurricanes), which can be devastating and should never be taken lightly. Fortunately, they usually move fast enough that their major effect on visitors is a day or two of heavy rain and wind. If you're caught in one, the hotel employees are experts on what to do to ensure your safety.

Another factor to consider is the part of an island that you'll visit. Because moist trade winds often blow from the east, the eastern sides of the high, mountainous islands tend to be wetter all year than the western sides. On the southeastern shore of Viti Levu, Suva gets considerably more rain than Nadi, on the island's dryer side. Consequently, most of Fiji's resorts are on the western side of Viti Levu.

Also bear in mind that the higher the altitude, the lower the temperature. If you're going up in the mountains, be prepared for much cooler weather than you'd have on the coast.

Fiji's average high temperatures range from 83°F (28°C) during the austral winter (June–Sept) to 88°F (31°C) during the summer months, which are December through March. Evenings average a warm and comfortable 70°F to 82°F (21°C–28°C) throughout the year.

The Fiji Meteorological Service (**www.met.gov.fj**) gives the current forecast.

Average Maximum Daytime Temperatures at Nadi

	Jan	Feb	Mar	Apr	May	June	July	Aug	Sept	Oct	Nov	Dec
Temp °F	89	89	88	87	86	85	83	84	85	86	88	89
Temp °C	32	32	31	31	30	29	28	29	29	30	31	32

THE BUSY SEASON

July and August are the busiest tourist season in Fiji. That's when Australians and New Zealanders visit the islands to escape the cold back home.

There also are busy miniseasons when it is school holiday time in Australia and New Zealand. These periods vary, but in general they are from the end of March through the middle of April, 2 weeks in late May, 2 weeks at the beginning of July, 2 weeks in the middle of September, and from mid-December until mid-January. You can get a list of Australian holidays at **www.oztourism.com.au** (click on the "Holiday dates" link); for New Zealand holiday schedules go to **www.tourism.org.nz** (the "Utilities and Holidays" link).

Some hoteliers raise their rates during the busy periods.

From Christmas through the middle of January is a good time to get a hotel reservation, but airline seats can be hard to come by, since thousands of islanders fly home from overseas.

FIJI CALENDAR OF EVENTS

Fiji has no grand nationwide festival around which to plan a visit, but there are local events that will enrich your time here. Many are Hindu festivals, whose timing changes from year to year.

February/March

Hindu Holi, nationwide. Hindus throughout Fiji often squirt each other with colored water during Hindu Holi, their Festival of Colors. February or March.

July

Bula Festival, Nadi. The town goes all out in July for its annual big bash, with parades, music, and cultural demonstrations. Mid-July.

Hindu Fire Walking, nationwide. Some Hindus engage in fire walking during soul-cleansing rituals, but unlike Fijian fire walkers, they do not perform for tourists at hotels. July or August.

August

Hibiscus Festival, Suva. The capital city's Hibiscus Festival is as close to a national festival as Fiji has. A carnival atmosphere prevails as thousands gather in Albert Park. Mid-August.

Moments   When the Moon Is Full

The islands are extraordinarily beautiful anytime, especially so at solstice time in late September and late March, when the sun's rays hit the lagoons at just the right angle to highlight the gorgeous colors in the waters. The play of moonlight on the surface, and the black silhouettes the mountains cast against the sky, are even more magical when the moon is full. Keep that in mind when planning your trip—especially if it's your honeymoon.

September

Sugar Festival Lautoka. Viti Levu's "Sugar City" gets into the act with its annual Sugar Festival. September.

Fiji Regatta Week, Mamanuca Islands. Cruising yachts from around the region gather at Musket Cove Island Resort in the Mamanucas for races, bikini contests, and the consumption of many thousands of Fiji Bitters. Some yachts then race to Port Vila in Vanuatu. Mid-September.

November

South Pacific World Music Festival. Regional artists converge on Savusavu for 3 days of music making. Go to www.fiji-savusavu.com for details. Early November.

Diwali Festival, nationwide. Although it's the Hindu festival of lights, every Fiji resident seems to put candles in their yards and set off fireworks during this holiday. October 30, 2008, and November 15, 2009.

HOLIDAYS

All banks, government offices, and most private businesses are closed for New Year's Day, Good Friday, Easter Saturday, Easter Monday, Ratu Sukuna Day (May 30 or the Mon closest thereto), the Prophet Mohammed's Birthday (a Mon in mid-July), Fiji Day (the Mon closest to Oct 10), Deepawali (the Indian festival of lights in late Oct or early Nov), Christmas Day, and December 26 (Boxing Day).

Banks take an additional holiday on the first Monday in August, and some businesses also close for various Hindu and Muslim holy days.

And if Fiji wins a seven-man rugby tournament, don't expect anyone to be at work the next day!

4 Getting to Fiji

GETTING TO FIJI

The only practical way to Fiji is by air. Even though Australians and New Zealanders can be in Fiji in a few hours, the distances for the rest of us run into the many thousands of miles. So be prepared to fly 11 hours or more from Los Angeles to Fiji, much longer from the U.K. and Europe.

Because populations are small in this part of the world, flights are not nearly as frequent to and among the islands as we Westerners are used to with destinations around home. The local airlines have relatively few planes, so mechanical problems as well as the weather can cause delays.

Most international flights arrive at **Nadi International Airport (NAN),** on the western side of Viti Levu about 11km (7 miles) north of Nadi Town. A few flights arrive from Samoa and Tonga at **Nausori Airport (SUV),** some 19km (12 miles) from Suva. Nadi and Nausori are the only lighted airstrips in the country, which means you don't fly domestically after dark. Many international flights arrive during the night, so a 1-night stay-over in Nadi may be necessary before you leave for another island.

THE AIRLINES

Here in alphabetical order are the airlines with service to Fiji (see appendix A for their telephone numbers in the U.K. and elsewhere):

- **Air New Zealand** (© **800/262-1234** or 310/615-1111; www.airnewzealand.com) flies between Auckland and Nadi. It serves many other New Zealand cities and several in Australia, so Kiwis and Aussies can reach the islands either nonstop or by changing planes in Auckland. It has service from Los Angeles to Fiji, although the planes are flown by Air Pacific (see below), on a code-share basis. It links the U.K. and Europe to Los Angeles, where passengers connect to Fiji. It also flies from Japan, Hong Kong, Singapore, Seoul, Taipei, and Beijing to Auckland, with connections from there to Fiji. It is a member of the Star Alliance (www.staralliance.com), which includes United Airlines, Air Canada, and several European and Asian carriers.

- **Air Pacific** (© **800/227-4446;** www.airpacific.com), Fiji's international airline, has extensive service to Nadi from Sydney, Brisbane, and Melbourne in Australia, and Auckland, Wellington, and Christchurch in New Zealand. It flies its own planes 6 days a week between Nadi and Los Angeles, a service it code-shares with Air New Zealand (see above) and Qantas Airways (see below), and once weekly between Vancouver, BC, and Nadi via Honolulu. One of its Nadi-Honolulu flights stops in Christmas Island in the central Pacific. It code-shares with American Airlines, which provides feeder service from many U.S. and Canadian cities to Los Angeles. Within the region, Air Pacific links Nadi to Samoa and Tonga, and it goes west to Vanuatu and Solomon Islands. It also provides nonstop service between Fiji and Japan.

- **Korean Air** (© **800/438-5000;** www.koreanair.com) has service between Seoul and Fiji. Although it's a longer distance, a connection through Seoul can be quicker from the U.K. and Europe than flying through Los Angeles.

- **Pacific Blue** (© **13 16 45** in Australia; 0800 67 0000 in New Zealand; www.flypacificblue.com), the international subsidiary of the Australian cut-rate domestic airline Virgin Blue (itself an offshoot of Sir Richard Branson's Virgin Atlantic), has low-fare service from Australia and New Zealand to Fiji.

- **Qantas Airways** (© **800/227-4500;** www.qantas.com), the Australian carrier, has flights from several Australian cities and Fiji, and between Los Angeles and Fiji, although its Los Angeles–Fiji passengers fly on Air Pacific planes.

FLYING FOR LESS: TIPS FOR GETTING THE BEST AIRFARE

The Pacific Ocean hasn't shrunk since 1928, when Australian aviator Charles Kingsford Smith spent 10 days and more than 83 hours in the air becoming the first person to fly from Los Angeles to Fiji. With distances running into the many thousands of miles, transportation costs may be the largest single expense of your trip to the South Pacific.

Many tour operators specializing in Fiji will sell discounted airfare with or without hotel accommodations. I list some of the best under "Packages for the Independent Traveler," later in this chapter. Always check with them.

Fiji & the South Pacific

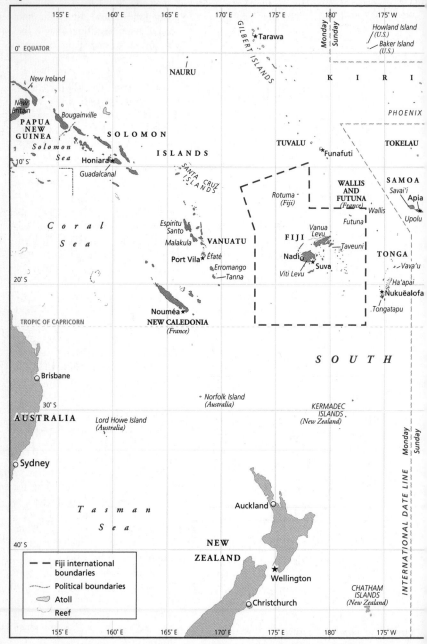

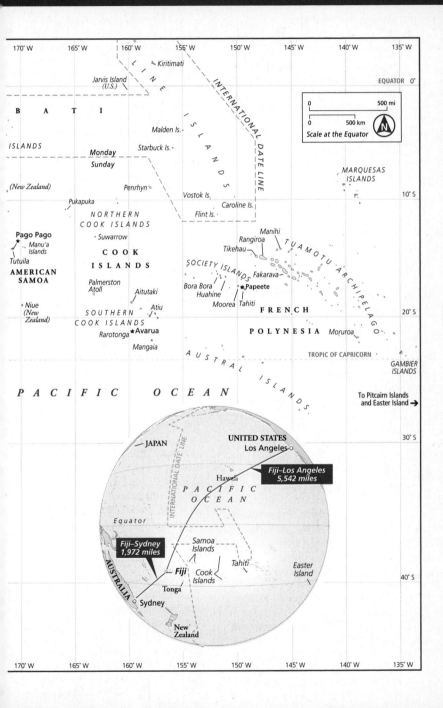

170° W   165° W   160° W   155° W   150° W   145° W   140° W   135° W

Kiritimati

Jarvis Island
(U.S.)

EQUATOR 0°

0   500 mi

0   500 km

Scale at the Equator

B   A   T   I

ISLANDS

Malden Is.

Monday

Starbuck Is.

MARQUESAS
ISLANDS

Sunday

(New Zealand)

Penrhyn

Vostok Is.

Caroline Is.

10° S

Pukapuka

NORTHERN
COOK ISLANDS

Flint Is.

Manihi

Rangiroa

TUAMOTU ARCHIPELAGO

Pago Pago

Manu'a
Islands

Suwarrow

COOK

Tikehau

SOCIETY ISLANDS

Fakarava

Tutuila

ISLANDS

Bora Bora

Papeete

AMERICAN
SAMOA

Palmerston
Atoll

Aitutaki

Huahine

Moorea   Tahiti

FRENCH

Niue
(New
Zealand)

SOUTHERN
COOK ISLANDS

Atiu

20° S

Rarotonga

Avarua

POLYNESIA   Moruroa

Mangaia

AUSTRAL ISLANDS

TROPIC OF CAPRICORN

GAMBIER
ISLANDS

PACIFIC   OCEAN

To Pitcairn Islands
and Easter Island →

30° S

JAPAN

UNITED STATES

Los Angeles

Fiji–Los Angeles
5,542 miles

INTERNATIONAL DATE LINE

Hawaii

PACIFIC
OCEAN

Equator

Fiji–Sydney
1,972 miles

Samoa
Islands

AUSTRALIA

Fiji

Tahiti

Easter
Island

Cook
Islands

40° S

Tonga

Sydney

New
Zealand

170° W   165° W   160° W   155° W   150° W   145° W   140° W   135° W

Here are some other tips:

- You may pay a fraction of the full fare passengers if you can book your ticket either **long in advance or at the last minute,** or **fly midweek** or **at less-trafficked times.** If your schedule is flexible, say so, and ask if you can secure a cheaper fare by changing your flight plans.

- Search **the Internet** for cheap fares. The most popular online travel agencies are **Travelocity** (www.travelocity. co.uk); **Expedia** (www.expedia.co.uk and www.expedia.ca); and **Orbitz**. In the U.K., go to **Travelsupermarket** (© **0845/345-5708;** www.travelsuper market.com), a flight search engine that offers flight comparisons for the budget airlines whose seats often end up in bucket-shop sales. Other websites for booking airline tickets online include **Cheapflights.com, Smarter-Travel.com, Priceline.com**, and **Opodo** (www.opodo.co.uk). Meta search sites (which find and then direct you to airline and hotel websites for booking) include **Sidestep.com** and **Kayak.com**—the latter includes fares for budget carriers like Jet Blue and Spirit as well as the major airlines. **LastMinute.com** is a great source for last-minute flights and getaways. In addition, most **airlines** offer online-only fares that even their phone agents know nothing about. British travelers should check **Flights International** (© **0800/0187050;** www.flights-international.com) for deals on flights all over the world.

- Keep an eye on local newspapers for **promotional specials** or **fare wars,** when airlines lower prices on their most popular routes.

- Try to book a ticket **in its country of origin.** If you're planning a one-way flight from London to Fiji, a U.K.-based travel agent will probably have the lowest fares. For foreign travelers on multi-leg trips, book in the country of the first leg; for example, book New York–Fiji–Sydney–New York in the U.S.

- **Consolidators,** also known as bucket shops, are wholesale brokers in the airline-ticket game. Consolidators buy deeply discounted tickets ("distressed" inventories of unsold seats) from airlines and sell them to online ticket agencies, travel agents, tour operators, corporations, and, to a lesser degree, the general public. Consolidators advertise in Sunday newspaper travel sections (often in small ads with tiny type), both in the U.S. and the U.K. They can be great sources for cheap international tickets. On the downside, bucket shop tickets are often rigged with restrictions, such as stiff cancellation penalties (as high as 50%–75% of the ticket price). And keep in mind that most of what you see advertised is of limited availability. Several reliable consolidators are worldwide and available online. **STA Travel** (www.statravel.com) has been the world's leading consolidator for students since purchasing Council Travel, but their fares are competitive for travelers of all ages. **Flights.com** (© **800/TRAV-800** [872-8800]; www.flights.com) has excellent fares worldwide, particularly to Europe. They also have "local" websites in 12 countries. **FlyCheap** (www.1800fly cheap.com) has especially good fares to sunny destinations. **Air Tickets Direct** (© **800/778-3447;** www. airticketsdirect.com) is based in Montreal and leverages the currently weak Canadian dollar for low fares; they also book trips to places that U.S. travel agents won't touch, such as Cuba.

- **Join frequent-flier clubs.** Frequent-flier membership doesn't cost a cent, but it does entitle you to free tickets or upgrades when you amass the airline's required number of frequent-flier points. You don't even have to fly to earn points; **frequent-flier credit cards** can earn you thousands of miles for doing your everyday shopping. Frankly, credit card miles have very low priority, so good luck trying to cash them in. Also keep in mind that award seats are limited, seats on popular routes are hard to snag, and more and more major airlines are cutting their expiration periods for mileage points—so check your airline's frequent-flier program so you don't lose your miles before you use them. *Inside tip:* Award seats are offered almost a year in advance, but seats also open up at the last minute, so if your travel plans are flexible, you may strike gold. To play the frequent-flier game to your best advantage, consult the community bulletin boards on **FlyerTalk** (www.flyertalk.com) or go to Randy Petersen's **Inside Flyer** (www.insideflyer.com). Petersen and friends review all the programs in detail and post regular updates on changes in policies and trends.

BAGGAGE ALLOWANCES

How many bags you can carry on board and check (and how much they can weigh) varies somewhat by airline, so always check with your chosen carrier before packing.

Only one rule is set in stone: Passengers on flights to or from the continental United States may check two bags each weighing up to 30 kilograms (66 lb.), with total dimensions (height, width, and length) of both not exceeding 158 centimeters (62 in.). The allowance on flights to and from Hawaii and the South Pacific may be limited to 30 kilograms (66 lb.) per economy class passengers, 32 kilograms (70 lb.) for first and business class.

Although domestic U.S. allowances may be less, you can check this much baggage if you're connecting to an international flight. United Airlines, US Airways, and other U.S. carriers now charge extra for more than one checked bag, so make sure they know you're connecting to an international flight.

In general, first-class passengers on other international flights are entitled to 40 kilograms (88 lb.) of checked luggage, business-class passengers to 30 kilograms (66 lb.), and economy-class passengers to 20 kilograms (44 lb.). Some airlines, including Air New Zealand and Air Pacific, strictly enforce these limits and make you pay extra for each kilogram over the maximum. So does Air Tahiti on its flights between Papeete and the Cook Islands.

In addition to a small handbag or purse, most international passengers are permitted one carry-on bag with total measurements not exceeding 115 centimeters (45 in.). Carry-on hoarders can stuff all sorts of things into a laptop bag; as long as it has a laptop in it, it's still considered a personal item (remember, however, you must remove your laptop and pass it through security separately).

Note: The domestic air carriers in Fiji limit their baggage allowance to 10 kilograms (22 lb.), which I point out in "Getting Around Fiji," below. Check with the individual airlines to avoid showing up at the check-in counter with too much luggage. A baggage storage facility is available at Nadi airport, and most hotels have storage facilities where you can leave your extra bags during side trips.

LONG-HAUL FLIGHTS: HOW TO STAY COMFORTABLE

Australians and New Zealanders have relatively short flights up to the islands. The rest of us will spend considerable time flying. Here are some tips on how we can stay comfortable while cooped up in airplanes:

(Tips) Getting Through the Airport

- Arrive at the airport at least 1 hour before a domestic flight and 2 hours before an international flight. You can check the average wait times at your airport by going to the TSA **Security Checkpoint Wait Times** site (waittime/tsa.dhs.gov).
- Know what you can carry on and what you can't. For the latest updates on items you are prohibited to bring in carry-on luggage, go to **www.tsa. gov/travelers/airtravel**.
- Beat the ticket-counter lines by using the self-service electronic ticket kiosks at the airport or even printing out your boarding pass at home from the airline website. Using curbside check-in is also a smart way to avoid lines, although this may not work for international flights.
- Help speed up security before you're screened. Remove jackets, shoes, belt buckles, heavy jewelry, and watches and place them either in your carry-on luggage or the security bins provided. Place keys, coins, cell-phones, and pagers in a security bin. If you have metallic body parts, carry a note from your doctor. Each passenger can carry on a 1L (1-qt.) size clear plastic bag with zip-top containing 100mL (3-oz.) or less bottles of liquids. Otherwise, keep liquids in checked baggage.
- Make sure the batteries in your camera, iPod, laptop, and other electronic gear are charged, in case you are asked to turn them on.
- Use a TSA-approved lock for your checked luggage. Travel Sentry certified locks are widely available at luggage or travel shops, at Brookstone stores (or online at www.brookstone.com), and at office supply stores such as Staples, Office Depot, and OfficeMax.

- Your choice of airline and airplane will definitely affect your leg room. Find more details about U.S. airlines at **www.seatguru.com**. For international airlines, the research firm Skytrax has posted a list of average seat pitches at **www.airlinequality.com**.
- Emergency exit seats and bulkhead seats typically have the most legroom. Emergency exit seats are usually left unassigned until the day of a flight (to ensure that someone able-bodied fills the seats); it's worth getting to the ticket counter early to snag one of these spots for a long flight. Many passengers find that bulkhead seating (the row facing the wall at the front of the cabin) offers more legroom, but keep in mind that bulkhead seats have no storage space on the floor in front of you.
- To have two seats for yourself in a three-seat row, try for an aisle seat in a center section toward the back of coach. If you're traveling with a companion, book an aisle and a window seat. Middle seats are usually booked last, so chances are good you'll end up with three seats to yourselves. And in the event that a third passenger is assigned the middle seat, he or she will probably be more than happy to trade for a window or an aisle.
- Ask about entertainment options. Many airlines offer seat-back video systems where you get to choose your

movies or play video games—but only on some of their planes. (Boeing 777s are your best bet.)

- To sleep, avoid the last row of any section or the row in front of an emergency exit, as these seats are the least likely to recline. Avoid seats near highly trafficked toilet areas. Avoid seats in the back of many jets—these can be narrower than those in the rest of coach. Or reserve a window seat so you can rest your head and avoid being bumped in the aisle.

- Get up, walk around, and stretch every 60 to 90 minutes to keep your blood flowing. This helps avoid **deep vein thrombosis,** or "economy-class syndrome." See the box "Avoiding 'Economy-Class Syndrome,'" p. 62.

- Drink water before, during, and after your flight to combat the lack of humidity in airplane cabins. Avoid alcohol, which will dehydrate you.

- When flying with kids, don't forget to carry on toys, books, pacifiers, and snacks and chewing gum to help them relieve ear pressure buildup during ascent and descent.

ARRIVING & DEPARTING
ARRIVING AT NADI

Arriving passengers can purchase duty-free items at two shops in the baggage claim area before clearing Customs (they are in fierce competition, so it will pay to shop between them and ask for discounts). Imported liquor is expensive in Fiji, so if you drink, don't hesitate to buy two bottles here.

After Customs runs your bags through an X-ray machine, you emerge onto an air-conditioned concourse lined on both sides by airline offices, travel and tour companies, car-rental firms, and a 24-hour-a-day branch of the **ANZ Bank** (see "Money & Costs," later in this chapter).

The Left Luggage counter at the far end of the departures concourse provides **baggage storage** for about F$3 to F$6 (US$1.95–US$3.90/90p–£1.80) a day, depending on the size of the baggage. The counter is open 24 hours daily. The hotels all have baggage-storage rooms and will keep your extra stuff for free. The Left Luggage also has **showers** and rents towels.

A **post office,** in a separate building across the entry road from the main ter-

---

Tips   Coping with Jet Lag

Flights from North America, including connecting flights from the U.K. and Europe, leave Los Angeles after dark, which means you will fly overnight and cross several time zones. For those of us traveling from the Northern Hemisphere, this invariably translates into jet lag. Here are some tips for combating this malady:

- **Reset your watch** to your destination time before you board the plane.
- **Drink lots of water** before, during, and after your flight. Avoid alcohol.
- **Exercise and sleep well** for a few days before your trip.
- Daylight is the key to resetting your body clock. At the website for Outside In (www.bodyclock.com), you can get a customized plan of when to seek and avoid light.
- If you need help getting to sleep and staying asleep, some doctors recommend taking either the hormone melatonin or the sleeping pill Ambien—but not together. Take 2 to 5 milligrams of melatonin about 2 hours before your planned bedtime.

minal, is open Monday to Friday from 8am to 4pm.

GETTING TO YOUR HOTEL FROM NADI AIRPORT

Representatives of the hotels and tour companies meet arriving visitors and provide free transportation to the hotels for those with reservations.

Taxis line up to the right outside the concourse. See the table under "Getting Around Fiji," below, for typical fares to the hotels. Only taxis painted yellow are allowed to take passengers from the airport. They have been inspected by the airport authority and are required to have air conditioning, which most drivers will not voluntarily turn on.

Local buses to Nadi and Lautoka pass the airport on the Queen's Road every day. Walk straight out of the concourse, across the parking lot, and through the gate to the road. Driving in Fiji is on the left, so buses heading for Nadi and its hotels stop on the opposite side, next to Raffle's Gateway Hotel; those going to Lautoka stop on the airport side of the road. See "Getting Around Nadi" in chapter 5 for details.

DEPARTING FROM NADI

The Nadi domestic terminal and the international check-in counters are to the right of the arrival concourse as you exit Customs (or to the left, if you are arriving from the main road). Several **snack bars** are near the domestic counters, including the excellent **Republic of Cappuccino,** the local version of Starbucks.

Fiji has no **departure tax** for either international or domestic flights.

Nadi Airport has a modern, air-conditioned international departure lounge with a currency exchange counter, snack bar, showers, and the largest duty-free shops in the South Pacific. Duty-free prices, however, are higher here than you'll pay elsewhere in the country, and haggling won't change the set prices.

ARRIVING AT SUVA

Nausori Airport is on the flat plains of the Rewa River delta about 19km (12 miles) from downtown Suva. The small terminal has a snack bar and an ATM but few other amenities. Taxis between Nausori and downtown Suva cost about F$25 (US$16/£8.25) each way.

DEPARTING FROM SUVA

Nausori Airport has a small duty-free shop in its departure lounge but no currency exchange facility. Some of Air Pacific's flights between Nadi and Samoa and Tonga stop first at Nausori, where you will deplane and clear Immigration and Customs.

5 Getting Around Fiji

Fiji has an extensive and reliable transportation network of airlines, rental cars, taxis, ferries, and both long-distance and local buses. This section deals primarily with getting from one island or major area to another; see "Getting Around" in chapter 5 and "Getting to the Islands" in chapter 6 for details on transportation within the local areas.

BY PLANE & HELICOPTER

The easiest way to get around the country is to fly with **Pacific Sun** (© **800/294-4864** in the U.S. or 672 0888 in Nadi, 331 5755 in Suva; www.pacificsun. com.fj) or **Air Fiji** (© **877/247-3454** in the U.S., 0800 347 3624 in Fiji or 672 2521 in Nadi, 331 3666 in Suva; www. airfiji.com.fj). Both fly small planes from Nadi to the tourist destinations and have offices in the international arrivals concourse at Nadi International Airport and on Victoria Parade in Suva.

Pacific Sun is the domestic subsidiary of Air Pacific, Fiji's international airline (see "Getting to Fiji," earlier in this chapter). The same offices handle both Air Pacific and Pacific Sun reservations.

The Fiji Islands

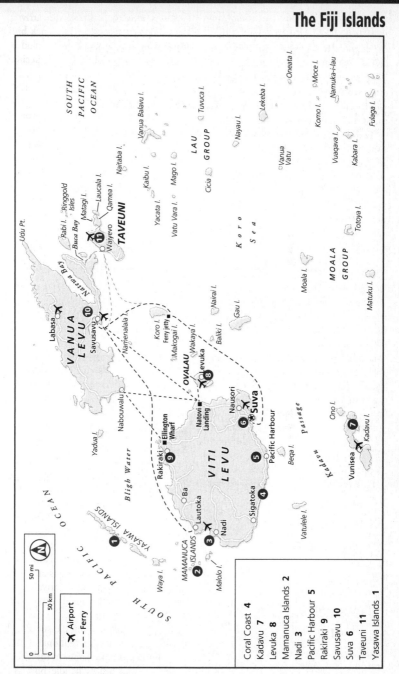

SOUTH PACIFIC OCEAN

SOUTH PACIFIC OCEAN

Udu Pt.

Natewa Bay

Buca Bay

Rabi I.
Ringgold Isles
Matagi I.
Laucala I.
Waiyevo
Qamea I.
TAVEUNI

Vanua Balavu I.

Naitaba I.

Kaibu I.
Mago I.
Vatu Vara I.
Yacata I.

LAU GROUP

Oneata I.
Moce I.
Namuka-i-lau
Lekeba I.

Tuvuca I.
Nayau I.

Vanua Vatu

Cicia

Vuaqava I.
Kabara I.

Fulaga I.

Labasa
VANUA LEVU
Savusavu

Nukubalavu

Koro I.
Ferry jetty
Makogai I.
Wakaya I.
OVALAU
Levuka

Nairai I.

Baliki I.

K o r o   S e a

Gau I.

Moala I.

MOALA GROUP

Matuku I.

Totoya I.

Udu Pt.

OCEAN

YASAWA ISLANDS

Waya I.

Yadua I.

Bligh Water

Nabouwalu

Rakiraki
Ellington Wharf
Ba
Lautoka

MAMANUCA ISLANDS

Malolo I.

Nadi

Vatulele I.

Sigatoka

VITI LEVU

Natovi Landing
Nausori
Suva
Pacific Harbour
Beqa I.

Kadavu Passage

Ono I.

Vunisea
Kadavu I.

SOUTH PACIFIC

50 mi
50 km

N

✈ Airport
- - - Ferry

Coral Coast **4**
Kadavu **7**
Levuka **8**
Mamanuca Islands **2**
Nadi **3**
Pacific Harbour **5**
Rakiraki **9**
Savusavu **10**
Suva **6**
Taveuni **11**
Yasawa Islands **1**

> ### Tips   How to Fly Smoothly in Fiji
>
> Here are few tips to help make flying in Fiji a smooth experience:
>
> - Book your domestic inter-island flights well in advance. You may not get on a plane at all if you wait until you arrive in Fiji to take care of this important chore.
> - Although it's unnecessary for international flights, **always reconfirm** your return inter-island flight as soon as you arrive on an outer island within Fiji. That way the local airlines will know how to reach you if there's a schedule change or cancellation.
> - Air Fiji's flights from Nadi and Suva to Taveuni stop in Savusavu going or coming (Pacific Sun's do not), so don't let an uninformed travel agent book you back to Nadi or Suva in order to get from Taveuni to Savusavu.
> - Weigh your bag, since **baggage allowances** on domestic flights may be 10 kilograms (22 lb.) instead of the 20 kilograms (44 lb.) allowed on international flights. Usually you can check 20 kilograms if you're connecting from or to an international flight, but inquire with the airlines to avoid showing up with too much luggage.

One-way fares from Nadi as I write are about F$61 (US$40/£20) to Malololailai Island (Plantation Island and Musket Cove Island resorts); F$77 (US$50/£25) to Mana Island; F$135 (US$88/£44) to Suva; F$200 (US$130/£65) to Savusavu; and F$250 (US$163/£82) to Taveuni. Suva-Taveuni costs about F$250 (US$163/£82). You can save by booking round-trip fares; ask the airlines for specifics. It also may pay to shop for the airlines' Internet specials (Pacific Sun often offers up to 40% discounts on its website). And always compare their fares, which can differ over the same route.

You can also save with the four-flight **Air Pass** from Air Fiji. Any four flights cost US$270 if purchased in North America, F$517 (US$336/£171) elsewhere. The passes are not available to buy once you are in Fiji. Call or go to Air Fiji's website for details.

Pacific Islands Seaplanes (© 672 5644; www.fijiseaplanes.com) provides charter service throughout Fiji in its small, Canadian-built floatplanes, which use wheels to take off from Nadi airport

and then use floats to land on water at the offshore.

Island Hoppers (© 672 0140; www.helicopters.com.fj) also will whisk you to the Mamanucas in one of its helicopters. If you have to ask how much these rides cost, you can't afford them. I would let my choice of resort arrange my transfers and tell me how much it will cost.

BY RENTAL CAR

Rental cars are widely available in Fiji. Each company has its own pricing policy, and you can frequently find discounts, special deals, and some give-and-take bargaining over long-term and long-distance use. All major companies, and a few not so major, have offices in the commercial concourse at Nadi International Airport, so it's easy to shop around. Most are open 7 days a week, some for 24 hours a day. Give careful consideration to how far you will drive; it's 197km (122 miles) from Nadi Airport to Suva, so an unlimited kilometer rate could work to your advantage if you plan to drive to Suva.

Avis (© 800/331-1212, or 672 2233 in Nadi; www.avis.com.fj) has more than

50% of the business here, and for good reason: The Toyota dealer is the local agent, so it has the newest and best-maintained fleet. In addition to the office at Nadi Airport, Avis can be found in Suva (© 331 3833), in Korolevu on the Coral Coast (© 653 0176), and at several hotels.

Thrifty Car Rental (© 800/367-2277, or 672 2935 in Nadi; www.thrifty.com), which is handled by Rosie the Travel Service, is my second choice, with rates and cars comparable to Avis's.

Other international agencies here are **Budget Rent A Car** (© 800/527-0700 or 672 2735; www.budget.com); **Hertz** (© 800/654-3131 or 672 3466; www.hertz.com), and **Europcar** (© 800/227-7368 or 672 5957; www.europcar.com).

The most reliable local companies are **Carpenters Rentals** (© 672 2772, or 332 8628 in Suva; rentals@carpenters.com.fj) and **Khan's Rental Cars** (© 679 0617 or 338 5033 in Suva; www.khansrental.com.fj). I do not rent from other "kick-the-tires" local companies.

Rates at all agencies range from F$100 (US$65/£33) and upward per day with unlimited kilometers. Add about F$22 (US$15/£8) a day to reduce your collision damage liability. Your home **insurance** policy might cover any damages that occur in Fiji, but I recommend getting local coverage when you rent a car. Even if you do, the local policies require you to pay the first F$500 (US$325/£163) or more of damages in any event. Underbody and overhead damage is not covered, so go slow when crossing Fiji's innumerable "road humps"—and do not park under coconut trees!

All renters must be at least 21 years old, and a few companies require them to be at least 25 or have at least 2 years driving experience.

Gasoline (petrol) is readily available at service stations in all the main towns. Expect to pay about twice what you would pay in the United States and Canada, about the same as elsewhere.

DRIVING RULES

Driving is on the left-hand side of the road throughout Fiji. Your valid home driver's license will be honored in the islands. **Seat belts** are mandatory. **Speed limits** are 80kmph (48 mph) on the open road and 50kmph (30 mph) in the towns and other built-up areas. It's illegal to drive while talking on a **cellphone.** You must **stop for pedestrians** in all marked crosswalks.

Driving under the influence of alcohol or other drugs is a criminal offense in Fiji, and the police frequently throw up roadblocks and administer Breathalyzer tests to all drivers. Even if I have a rental car, I take a taxi home after a session with friends at a local bar.

BY BUS

Appealing to backpackers and other cost-conscious travelers, **Feejee Experience** (© 672 5959; www.feejeeexperience.com) runs a bus counterclockwise around Viti Levu 4 days a week. The vehicles have local guides and stop for sightseeing and activities such as village visits, hiking, and river rafting. You buy a pass, which allows you to get on and off the bus at will for up to 6 months. The "Hula Hoop" pass costs F$396 (US$257/£129) and includes the bus around Viti Levu. The "Lei Low" pass for F$558 (US$363/£182) adds a night in a dorm on Beachcomber Island Resort in the Mamanuca Islands off Nadi (see chapter 6). The "Hotel Lei" adds hotel accommodations for F$710 (US$462/£231) double occupancy, F$1,013 (US$658/£329) single occupancy. Otherwise you must pay for your accommodations, although Feejee Experience will book and hold rooms or dorm beds at its preferred hostels, including Mango Bay Resort on the Coral Coast, Raintree Lodge in Suva, and Volivoli Beach Resort in Rakiraki. You can get around by bus for a lot less money, but you won't have the guides,

(Tips **Watch Out for Cows, Horses & Road Humps!**

Most roads in Fiji are narrow, poorly maintained, and crooked. Not all local drivers are well trained, experienced, or skilled, and some of them (including bus drivers) go much too fast for the conditions. Consequently, you should **drive defensively** at all times. Constantly be alert for potholes, landslides, hair-pin curves, and various stray animals—cows and horses are a very real danger, especially at night.

Also keep an eye out for speed bumps known in Fiji as **road humps.** Most Fijian villages have them. Although big signs made to resemble traditional Fijian war clubs announce when you're entering and leaving villages on the Queen's Road, road humps are usually positioned between the clubs, so slow down! The humps are large enough to do serious damage to the bottom of a car, and no local rental insurance covers that.

the activities, or the companionship of youthful fellow travelers.

Public buses are plentiful and inexpensive in Fiji, and it's possible to go all the way around Viti Levu on them. I did it once by taking the Fiji Express (see below) from Nadi to Suva one morning, a local express to Rakiraki the next morning, and then another express to Lautoka and a local back to Nadi.

The most comfortable bus between Nadi airport and Suva is the air-conditioned **Fiji Express** (© 672 3105 in Nadi, 331 2287 in Suva). One bus leaves Nadi airport daily at 7:30am and stops at the major hotels along the Queen's Road before arriving at Suva about 11:30am. It departs Suva at 4pm and returns to Nadi at 8pm. Another bus begins its daily runs at 7:30am from the Holiday Inn Suva and arrives in Nadi about 11:30am. It begins its return to Suva at 1pm, arriving in the capital about 5pm. One-way fares run up to F$20 (US$13/£6.50), depending on how far you go. You can book at any hotel tour desk.

Sunbeam Transport Ltd. (© 666 2822 in Lautoka, or 338 2704 in Suva) and **Pacific Transport Ltd.** (© 670 0044 in Nadi, or 330 4366 in Suva) operate express and regular buses that go all the way around Viti Levu. They stop

at the domestic terminal at Nadi Airport and the markets at Nadi Town, Sigatoka, and Navua. Express buses take about 4 hours between Nadi and Suva, compared to 5 hours on the local "stages." These buses cater to local residents, do not take reservations, and have no air conditioning. The Nadi-Suva fare is about F$10 (US$6.50/£3.30), express or local.

In addition to Sunbeam Transport Ltd., **Reliance Transport Bus Service** (© **666 3059** in Lautoka, or 338 2296 in Suva) and **Akbar Buses Ltd.** (© **669 4760** in Rakiraki) have express and local service between Lautoka and Suva via the King's Road. The Lautoka-Suva fare is about F$13 (US$8.50/£4.30).

Fume-belching **local buses** use the produce markets as their terminals. The older buses have side windows made of canvas panels that are rolled down during inclement weather (they usually fly out the sides and flap in the wind like great skirts). They run every few minutes along the Queen's Road between Lautoka and Nadi Town, passing the airport and most of the hotels and restaurants along the way (see "Getting Around Nadi," in chapter 5).

Minivans scoot along the Queen's Road between the Nadi Town market and the Suva Municipal Market. Those with yellow license tags with the prefix "LM" (licensed

---

Tips It Never Hurts to Bargain

In Nadi and on the Coral Coast, you will see the same taxi drivers stationed outside your hotel every day. Usually they are paid on a salaried rather than a fare basis, so they may be willing to spend more time than usual showing you around. Also, they might charge you less than the government-regulated fares for long-distance trips, such as from Nadi to the Coral Coast or Suva, because many would rather earn one big fare a day than several small ones. It never hurts to bargain politely.

---

minivan) are regulated by the government. I avoid the others, which can be unsafe, and strongly suggest you do the same.

BY TAXI

Taxis are as abundant in Fiji as taxi meters are scarce. The Nadi Airport taxis are now required to have both meters and air-conditioners, but the drivers do not always turn them on. Always settle on a fare to your destination before striking out (see the distance and fare chart below). Some drivers will complain about short fares and will badger you for more business later on during your stay; politely ignore these entreaties.

Not to be confused with minibuses, **"share taxis"** or "rolling taxis"—those not otherwise occupied—pick up passengers at bus stops and charge the bus fare. They are particularly good value on long-distance trips. A taxi returning to Suva, for example, will stop by the Nadi Town market and pick up a load of passengers at the bus fare rather than drive back to the capital empty. Ask around the local market bus stops if share taxis are available. You'll meet some wonderful Fijians that way.

Although the government sets all taxi fares, it has not raised them for several years despite skyrocketing fuel prices. They may be higher by the time you arrive. In the meantime, many drivers will ask for a few dollars more than the official fare. Even if they don't, I usually give them a small tip anyway—provided they haven't pestered me, refused to turn on the air-conditioner, or blared music from their radios. The following are distances from Nadi International Airport via the Queen's Road and the official government-regulated taxi fares at press time.

From Nadi Airport to:	km	Miles	Approx. Taxi Fare		
Tanoa/Novotel Hotels	1.3	0.8	F$3.00	US$1.95	£1.00
Nomads Skylodge Hotel	3.3	2.0	F$4.00	US$2.60	£1.32
Mercure/Sandalwood Inn	5.2	3.1	F$5.00	US$3.25	£1.65
Denarau Island	15	9.3	F$20.00	US$13.00	£6.60
Nadi Town	9.0	5.4	F$10.00	US$6.50	£3.30
Shangri-la's Fijian Resort and Spa	60	37	F$55.00	US$36.00	£18.00
Sigatoka	70	43	F$60.00	US$39.00	£20.00
Outrigger on the Lagoon Fiji	78	48	F$65.00	US$42.00	£21.50
Hideaway Resort	92	57	F$68.00	US$44.00	£22.40
The Warwick Fiji Resort & Spa	104	64	F$80.00	US$52.00	£26.40
Pacific Harbour	148	92	F$145.00	US$94.00	£48.00
Suva	197	122	F$165.00	US$107.00	£54.50

BY FERRY

Three reliable shuttle boats operated by Nadi-based **South Sea Cruises** (✆ **675 0500;** www.ssc.com.fj) connect the Mamanuca and Yasawa islands to Denarau Island and Nadi. The *Tiger IV* and the *Cougar* make three runs daily through the Mamanucas, while the *Yasawa Express* goes to the Yasawas and back once a day. See chapter 6, "The Mamanuca & Yasawa Islands," for details.

Vehicle- and passenger-carrying ferries also run between the main islands. Their schedules can change abruptly depending on the weather and the condition of the ships, however, so I don't recommend them unless you have unlimited time. Call the operators below for the latest information.

Bligh Water Shipping Ltd. (✆ **331 8247** in Suva; 990 2032 in Lautoka; www.blighwatershipping.com.fj) operates the cleanest and most reliable ferries between Suva, Savusavu, and Taveuni, and between Lautoka and Savusavu. Its ferries are fully air-conditioned and have both economy and first-class cabins. One departs Suva for Savusavu and Taveuni thrice weekly. Adult economy fare for the 11-hour run to Savusavu starts at F$63 (US$41/£21). Another ferry runs between Lautoka and Savusavu via the north coast of Viti Levu, going in one direction one day, the opposite way the next. Adult economy fares are F$60 (US$39/£20).

Patterson Shipping Services (✆ **331 5644** in Suva; patterson@connect.com.fj) has bus-ferry connections from Natovi Wharf (north of Suva on eastern Viti Levu) to Buresala Landing on Ovalau and to Nabouwalu on Vanua Levu. You connect by bus from Suva to Natovi, from Buresala to Levuka, and from Nabouwalu to Labasa (local buses connect Labasa to Savusavu). The Suva-Levuka fare costs about F$30 (US$20/£10), while the Suva-Labasa fare is about F$60 (US$39/£20). Patterson's office is in Ste. 1–2, Epworth House, Nina Street in Suva.

Based at Taveuni, the small ferry *Amazing Grace* (✆ **888 0320** on Taveuni, 927 1372 in Savusavu) crosses the Somosomo Strait between Buca Bay on Vanua Levu and Waiyevo on Taveuni. The one-way fare is F$25 (US$16/£8), including a bus ride from Savusavu to Buca Bay.

6 Money & Costs

Fiji is a moderately priced destination— cheaper than big cities such as New York and London, more expensive than some Southeast Asian countries. But it also has a wide range of prices. Domestic airfares are relatively high, but taxi and bus fares are cheap. Some luxury resorts charge more than F$3,000 (US$2,000/£1,000) a night, but you can get a clean, comfortable hotel room for F$75 (US$50/£25).

Much of the country's tourism infrastructure is oriented toward backpackers, with reasonable prices to attract young travelers on a budget.

Tips Small Change

When I change money (or after I've withdrawn local currency from an ATM), I ask for some small bills since petty cash comes in handy for public transportation (Fiji taxi drivers never seem to have change for large bills). I keep my small money separate from my larger bills, so that it's readily accessible while my big notes are less of a target for thieves. I also go first to WestPac Bank's ATMs, which usually dispense smaller notes than those at ANZ Bank.

What Things Cost in Fiji	U.S.$/C$	U.K. £
Taxi from airport to Nadi Town	6.50	3.30
Bus from airport to Nadi Town	0.43	0.21
Moderate hotel room for two	250.00	125.00
Inexpensive hotel room for two	52.00	26.50
Moderate lunch for two, without alcohol	26.00	13.00
Moderate three-course meal for two, without alcohol	25.00	12.50
Bottle of Fiji Bitter Beer in a bar	2.30	1.15
Cup of regular coffee	2.50	1.25

CURRENCY

The national currency is the Fiji dollar, which is divided into 100 cents. The Fiji dollar trades independently on the foreign exchange markets and is abbreviated "FID" by the banks and airlines, although I use **F$** in this book. Some hotels and resorts quote their rates in U.S. dollars, indicated here by **US$**.

HOW TO GET LOCAL CURRENCY

An **ANZ Bank** branch in the international arrivals concourse at Nadi International Airport is open 24 hours a day, 7 days a week. There's an ATM on the wall outside the branch, where you can draw Fijian currency by using MasterCard or Visa credit or debit cards. **GlobalEX** has exchange counters (but no ATMs) in the arrivals concourse and near the departures door.

ANZ Bank, Westpac Bank, and **Colonial National Bank** have offices throughout the country where currency and traveler's checks can be exchanged.

They all have ATMs at their Nadi and Suva offices and at their branches in Savusavu, and Colonial National Bank has an ATM on Taveuni. There's an ATM at the Nausori Airport terminal near Suva. Several large hotels on Viti Levu have ATMs in their lobbies. Elsewhere bring credit cards, cash, and traveler's checks. **Banking hours** nationwide are Monday to Thursday from 9:30am to 3pm and Friday from 9:30am to 4pm.

You can get a better rate for traveler's checks at **GlobalEX** offices at Nadi Airport and in Nadi Town and Suva. See the "Fast Facts: Nadi" section in chapter 5 for specific currency exchange locations.

CREDIT CARDS

American Express, MasterCard, and Visa are widely accepted by the hotels, car-rental firms, travel and tour companies, large stores, and most restaurants. Don't count on using a Diners Club card outside the hotels, and leave your Discover card at home.

Tips **Credit Card Add-Ons**

Many Fiji businesses add 3% to 5% to your bill if you use a credit card, while others may offer a similar discount for cash payments. Credit card issuers frown on the add-ons, but the locals do it anyway. Always ask if an add-on or discount will be assessed.

The Fiji Dollar, the U.S. and Canadian Dollar & the British Pound

At this writing, US$1 and the Canadian dollar (C$) = approximately F$1.54 (or, the other way around, F$1 = US65¢), which is the exchange rate I used to calculate the dollar values given in this book. **For British readers:** At this writing, £1 = approximately F$3 (or, F$1 = 33p), the rate used to calculate the pound values in this book. **Note:** International exchange rates fluctuate depending on economic and political factors. Thus, the values given in this table may not be the same when you travel to Fiji. Use the following table only as a guide. Find the current rates at **www.xe.com**.

F$	US$/C$	UK£	F$	US$/C$	UK£
.25	0.16	0.08	15	9.75	4.88
.50	0.33	0.16	20	13.00	6.50
.75	0.49	0.24	25	16.25	8.13
1	0.65	0.33	30	19.50	9.75
2	1.30	0.65	35	22.75	11.38
3	1.95	0.98	40	26.00	13.00
4	2.60	1.30	45	29.25	14.63
5	3.25	1.63	50	32.50	16.25
6	3.90	1.95	75	48.75	24.38
7	4.55	2.28	100	65.00	32.50
8	5.20	2.60	125	81.25	40.63
9	5.85	2.93	150	97.50	48.75
10	6.50	3.25	200	130.00	65.00

TRAVELER'S CHECKS

I seldom use them these days, but I carry a few hundred U.S. dollars in traveler's checks just in case the local ATM runs out of cash or is on the blink. You can get traveler's checks at most banks in denominations of US$20, US$50, US$100, US$500, and sometimes US$1,000. Generally, you'll pay a service charge ranging from 1% to 4%.

The most popular traveler's checks are offered by **American Express** (© 800/807-6233 or © 800/221-7282 for card holders—this number accepts collect calls, offers service in several foreign languages, and exempts Amex gold and platinum cardholders from the 1% fee); **Visa** (© 800/732-1322)—AAA members can obtain Visa checks for a $9.95 fee (for checks up to $1,500) at most AAA offices

---

Tips Getting Rid of Your Left-Over Currency

Use your left-over currency to pay part of your hotel bill when leaving Fiji. Put the rest on your credit card. It will save you the trouble of having to change money at the airport.

or by calling ✆ **866/339-3378;** and **MasterCard** (✆ **800/223-9920).**

Be sure to keep a record of the traveler's checks serial numbers separate from your checks in the event that they are stolen or lost. You'll get a refund faster if you know the numbers.

7 Health

STAYING HEALTHY
Fiji poses no major health problems for most travelers, although it's a good idea to have your tetanus, hepatitis-A, and hepatitis-B vaccinations up-to-date.

If you have a chronic condition, check with your doctor before visiting the islands. For conditions like epilepsy, diabetes, or heart problems, wear a **MedicAlert Identification Tag** (✆ **800/825-3785;** www.medicalert.org), which will alert doctors to your condition and give them access to your records through MedicAlert's 24-hour hot line.

Don't forget **sunglasses** and an extra pair of **contact lenses** or **prescription glasses,** though you can easily replace your contacts and prescription lenses in Nadi, Lautoka, and Suva.

Contact the **International Association for Medical Assistance to Travelers (IAMAT)** (✆ **716/754-4883** or, in Canada, 416/652-0137; www.iamat.org) for tips on travel and health concerns in the countries you're visiting, and for lists of local, English-speaking doctors. The United States **Centers for Disease Control and Prevention** (✆ **800/311-3435;** www.cdc.gov) provides up-to-date information on health hazards by region or country and offers tips on food safety. **Travel Health Online** (www.tripprep. com), sponsored by a consortium of travel medicine practitioners, may also offer helpful advice on traveling abroad. You can find listings of reliable medical clinics overseas at the **International Society of Travel Medicine** (www.istm.org).

COMMON AILMENTS
Among minor illnesses, Fiji has the common cold and occasional outbreaks of influenza and conjunctivitis (pink eye).

TROPICAL ILLNESSES
Fiji has plenty of mosquitoes but they do not carry deadly endemic diseases such as malaria. From time to time the islands will experience an outbreak of **dengue fever,** a viral disease borne by the *Adës aegypti* mosquito, which lives indoors and bites only during daylight hours. Dengue seldom is fatal in adults, but you should take extra precautions to keep children from being bitten by mosquitoes if the disease is present during your visit. (Other precautions should be taken if you are traveling with **children;** see "Specialized Travel Resources," below.)

BUGS, BITES & OTHER WILDLIFE CONCERNS
Living among the friendly Fijians are some of the world's friendliest creatures, including the likes of ants, roaches, geckos, crabs, and insects.

Indeed, the Fijian islands have multitudes of mosquitoes, roaches, ants, houseflies, and other insects. **Ants** are

---

⌒*Tips* **Band-Aids**
Cuts, scratches, and all open sores should be treated promptly in the Tropics to avoid infection. I always carry a tube of antibacterial ointment and a small package of adhesive bandages such as Band-Aids.

> ## ⎛Tips⎞ Multitudes of Animals
>
> Don't bother complaining to me about the multitude of dogs, chickens, pigs, and squawking myna birds running loose out here, even in the finest restaurants. They are as much a part of life as the islanders themselves. And don't be frightened by those little **geckos** (lizards) crawling around the rafters of even the most expensive bungalows. They're harmless to us humans but lethal to insects.

omnipresent here, so don't leave crumbs or dirty dishes lying around your room. A few beaches and swampy areas also have invisible **sand flies**—the dreaded "no-see-ums" or "no-nos"—which bite the ankles around daybreak and dusk.

Insect repellent is widely available in most drug stores and groceries. The most effective contain a high percentage of "DEET" (N,N-diethyl-m-toluamide).

I light a mosquito coil in my non-air-conditioned rooms at dusk in order to keep the pests from flying in, and I start another one at bedtime. Grocery stores throughout the islands carry these inexpensive coils. I have found the Fish brand coils, made by the appropriately named Blood Protection Company, to work best.

SUN EXPOSURE

The tropical sun in the islands can be brutal, even on what seems like an overcast day. Accordingly, it's important to use sunscreen whenever you're outdoors, especially at midday. This is particularly true for children.

HIV/AIDS

Sexual relations before marriage—heterosexual, homosexual, and bisexual—are more or less accepted in Fiji (abstinence campaigns fall on deaf ears here). Both male and female prostitution is common in Nadi and Suva. HIV is present in the islands, so if you intend to engage in sex with strangers, you should exercise *at least* the same caution in choosing them, and in practicing safe sex, as you would at home.

WHAT TO DO IF YOU GET SICK AWAY FROM HOME

Hospitals and clinics are widespread in Fiji, but the quality varies a great deal from place to place. You can get a broken bone set and a coral scrape tended, but treating more serious ailments likely will be beyond the capability of the local hospital. I list hospitals and emergency numbers under the "Fast Facts" in the following chapters.

You may have to pay all medical costs upfront and be reimbursed later. Medicare and Medicaid do not provide coverage for medical costs outside the U.S. Before leaving home, find out what medical services your health insurance covers. To protect yourself, consider buying medical travel insurance (see "Medical Insurance," under "Insurance" in the "Fast Facts: Fiji" section in appendix A).

Very few health insurance plans pay for medical evacuation back to the U.S., the U.K., or Europe (which can cost $10,000 and up). A number of companies offer medical evacuation services anywhere in the world. If you're ever hospitalized more than 150 miles from home, **MedjetAssist** (© **800/527-7478;** www.medjetassistance. com) will pick you up and fly you to the hospital of your choice virtually anywhere in the world in a medically equipped and staffed aircraft 24 hours day, 7 days a week. Annual memberships are $225 individual, $350 family; you can also purchase short-term memberships.

U.K. nationals will need a **European Health Insurance Card (EHIC)** to receive free or reduced-costs health benefits

Tips   Be Careful in the Water

Most of Fiji's marine creatures are harmless to humans, but you need to avoid some. Always **seek local advice** before snorkeling or swimming in a lagoon away from the hotel beaches. Many diving operators conduct snorkeling tours; if you don't know what you're doing, go with them.

Wash and apply a good antiseptic or antibacterial ointment to all **coral cuts and scrapes** as soon as possible.

Because coral cannot grow in fresh water, the flow of rivers and streams into the lagoon creates narrow channels known as **passes** through the reef. Currents can be very strong in the passes, so stay in the protected, shallow water of the inner lagoons.

Sharks are curious beasts that are attracted by bright objects such as watches and knives, so be careful what you wear in the water. Don't swim in areas where sewage or edible wastes are dumped, and never swim alone if you have any suspicion that sharks might be present. If you do see a shark, don't splash in the water or urinate. Calmly retreat and get out of the water as quickly as you can, without creating a disturbance.

Those round things on the rocks and reefs that look like pincushions are **sea urchins,** and their calcium spikes can be more painful than needles. A sea-urchin puncture can result in burning, aching, swelling, and discoloration (black or purple) around the area where the spines entered your skin. The best thing to do is to pull any protruding spines out. The body will absorb the spines within 24 hours to 3 weeks, or the remainder of the spines will work themselves out. In the meantime, take aspirin or other pain killers. Contrary to popular advice, do not urinate or pour vinegar on the embedded spines—this will not help.

Jellyfish stings can hurt like the devil but are seldom life-threatening. You need to get any visible tentacles off your body right away, but not with your hands, unless you are wearing gloves. Use a stick or anything else that is handy. Then rinse the sting with salt- or fresh water, and apply ice to prevent swelling and to help control the pain. If you can find it at an island grocery store, Adolph's Meat Tenderizer is a great antidote.

The **stone fish** is so named because it looks like a piece of stone or coral as it lies buried in the sand on the lagoon bottom with only its back and 13 venomous spikes sticking out. Its venom can cause paralysis and even death. You'll know by the intense pain if you're stuck. Serum is available, so get to a hospital at once. **Sea snakes, cone shells, crown-of-thorns starfish, moray eels, lionfish,** and **demon stingers** also can be painful, if not deadly. The last thing any of these creatures wants to do is to tangle with a human, so keep your hands to yourself.

during a visit to a European Economic Area (EEA) country (European Union countries plus Iceland, Liechtenstein, and Norway) or Switzerland. The European Health Insurance Card replaces the E111 form, which is no longer valid. For advice, ask at your local post office or see www.dh.gov.uk/travellers.

Avoiding "Economy-Class Syndrome"

Deep vein thrombosis, or as it's known in the world of flying, "economy-class syndrome," is a blood clot that develops in a deep vein. It's a potentially deadly condition that can be caused by sitting in cramped conditions—such as an airplane cabin—for too long. During a flight (especially a long-haul flight), get up, walk around, and stretch your legs every 60 to 90 minutes to keep your blood flowing. Other preventative measures include frequent flexing of the legs while sitting, drinking lots of water, and avoiding alcohol and sleeping pills. If you have a history of deep vein thrombosis, heart disease, or another condition that puts you at high risk, some experts recommend wearing compression stockings or taking anticoagulants when you fly; always ask your physician about the best course for you. Symptoms of deep vein thrombosis include leg pain or swelling, or even shortness of breath.

Fiji's main islands have drug stores that carry over-the-counter and **prescription medications.** Most medications can be purchased without a local prescription, but bring your own medications (in your carry-on luggage), in their original containers. Carry the generic name of medicines, since local pharmacies primarily carry medications manufactured in Australia, New Zealand, and the U.K.

8 Safety

While international terrorism is still a threat throughout the world, Fiji is among the planet's safest destinations. Security procedures are in effect at Nadi International Airport, but once you're on the outer islands, you are unlikely to see a metal detector, nor is anyone likely to inspect your carry-on.

Although its military coups brought Fiji to the world's attention and caused great consternation on the part of the New Zealand and Australian governments, I saw little impact of the takeover during my recent visit. From a traveler's point of view, everything was working normally.

Although the December 2006 coup put a dent in crime, Fiji still has a serious problem with robberies and home invasions. Street crimes against tourists have been infrequent, but friends of mine who live here don't stroll off the busy streets after dark, especially in Suva, and they keep a sharp eye peeled everywhere in Fiji. For that matter, you should stay alert wherever you are after dusk.

Don't leave valuable items in your hotel room, in your rental car, or unattended anywhere.

Women should not wander alone on deserted beaches any time, since some Polynesian men may consider such behavior to be an invitation for instant amorous activity.

When heading outdoors, keep in mind that injuries often occur when people fail to follow instructions. Hike only in designated areas, swim and snorkel only where you see other people swimming and snorkeling, follow the marine charts if piloting your own boat, carry rain gear, and wear a life jacket when canoeing or rafting. Mountain weather can be fickle at any time. Watch out for sudden storms that can leave you drenched and send bolts of lightning your way.

9 Specialized Travel Resources

TRAVELERS WITH DISABILITIES

Most disabilities shouldn't stop anyone from traveling, even in Fiji, where ramps, handles, accessible toilets, automatic opening doors, telephones at convenient heights, and other helpful aids such as those found in Western countries are just beginning to appear.

Some hotels provide rooms specially equipped for people with disabilities. Such improvements are ongoing; inquire when making a reservation whether such rooms are available.

The major international airlines make special arrangements for travelers with disabilities. Be sure to tell them of your needs when you reserve. Although most local airlines use small planes that are not equipped for those with disabilities, their staffs go out of their way to help everyone get in and out of the craft.

Organizations that offer a vast range of resources and assistance to travelers with disabilities include **MossRehab** (© 800/ **CALL-MOSS** (225-5667); www.moss resourcenet.org); the **American Foundation for the Blind (AFB)** (© 800/ **232-5463;** www.afb.org); and **SATH** (Society for Accessible Travel & Hospitality) (© 212/447-7284; www.sath.org). **AirAmbulanceCard.com** is now partnered with SATH and allows you to pre-select top-notch hospitals in case of an emergency.

Access-Able Travel Source (© 303/ **232-2979;** www.access-able.com) offers a comprehensive database on travel agents from around the world with experience in accessible travel; destination-specific access information; and links to such resources as service animals, equipment rentals, and access guides.

Many travel agencies offer customized tours and itineraries for travelers with disabilities. Among them are **Flying Wheels Travel** (© 507/451-5005; www.flying wheelstravel.com); and **Accessible Journeys** (© 800/846-4537 or 610/521-0339; www.disabilitytravel.com).

Flying with Disability (www.flying-with-disability.org) is a comprehensive information source on airplane travel. **Avis Rent a Car** (© 888/879-4273) has an "Avis Access" program that offers services for customers with special travel needs. These include specially outfitted vehicles with swivel seats, spinner knobs, and hand controls; mobility scooter rentals; and accessible bus service. Be sure to reserve well in advance.

Also check out the quarterly magazine *Emerging Horizons* (www.emerging horizons.com), available by subscription ($16.95 year U.S.; $21.95 outside U.S).

The "Accessible Travel" link at **Mobility-Advisor.com** (www.mobility-advisor. com) offers a variety of travel resources to travelers with disabilities.

British travelers should contact **Holiday Care** (© 0845-124-9971 in U.K. only; www.holidaycare.org.uk) to access a wide range of travel information and resources for travelers with disabilities and the elderly.

Healthy Travels to You

The following government websites offer up-to-date health-related travel advice.

- **Australia:** www.dfat.gov.au/travel
- **Canada:** www.hc-sc.gc.ca/index_e.html
- **U.K.:** www.dh.gov.uk/en/index.htm
- **U.S.:** www.cdc.gov/travel

GAY & LESBIAN TRAVELERS

Although homosexuality is officially frowned upon by local laws and by some local religious leaders, an old Fiji custom makes this a relatively friendly destination for gay men with one proviso: **Stay away from gay prostitutes.**

In the Pacific islands, many families with a shortage of female offspring literally rear young boys as girls, or at least relegate them to female chores around the home and village. Some of them grow up to live a heterosexual existence; others choose a homosexual or bisexual lifestyle and, often appearing publicly in women's attire, actively seek the company of tourists. Some dance the female parts in traditional island night shows. You'll see them throughout Fiji; many hold jobs in hotels and restaurants.

On the other hand, women were not considered equal in this respect in ancient times; thus, "choosing" lesbianism was discouraged.

The International Gay & Lesbian Travel Association (IGLTA) (© 800/448-8550 or 954/776-2626; fax 954/776-3303; www.iglta.org) is the trade association for the gay and lesbian travel industry, and offers an online directory of gay- and lesbian-friendly travel businesses; go to their website and click on "Members."

Many agencies offer tours and travel itineraries specifically for gay and lesbian travelers. **MIM Travel** (© **877/844-8055;** www.gay-travel-by-mim.com) recently had a gay cruise aboard the *Tahitian Princess,* while **Now, Voyager** (© **800/255-6951;** www.nowvoyager.com) had one on the *Star Flyer.* Also check out **Above and Beyond Tours** (© **800/397-2681;** www.abovebeyondtours.com), a gay Australia tour specialist, and **Olivia** (© **800/631-6277;** www.olivia.com), offering lesbian cruises and resort vacations.

Gay.com Travel (© **800/929-2268** or 415/644-8044; www.gay.com/travel or www.outandabout.com), is an excellent online successor to the popular *Out & About* print magazine. It provides regularly updated information about gay-owned, gay-oriented, and gay-friendly lodging, dining, sightseeing, nightlife, and shopping establishments in every important destination worldwide. British travelers should click on the "Travel" link at **www.uk.gay.com** for advice and gay-friendly trip ideas.

The Canadian website **GayTraveler** (**gaytraveler.ca**) offers ideas and advice for gay travel all over the world.

The following travel guides are available at many bookstores, or you can order them from any online bookseller: *Spartacus International Gay Guide, 35th Edition* (Bruno Gmünder Verlag; www.spartacusworld.com/gayguide) and *Odysseus: The International Gay Travel Planner, 17th Edition;* and the *Damron* guides (www.damron.com), with separate, annual books for gay men and lesbians.

SENIOR TRAVEL

Children are cared for communally in the Fiji's extended family systems, and so are seniors. Most Fijians live with their families from birth to death. Consequently, the local governments don't provide extensive programs and other benefits for persons of retirement age. You won't find many senior discounts. Children get them; seniors don't.

Nevertheless, mention the fact that you're a senior when you first make your travel reservations. All major airlines and many chain hotels offer discounts for seniors.

Elderhostel, 75 Federal St., Boston, MA 02110-1941 (© **877/426-8056;** www.elderhostel.org), occasionally has study programs to Fiji for those 55 and over (and a spouse or companion of any age) in the United States and in more than 80 countries. Most include airfare, accommodations in university dorms or modest inns, meals, and tuition.

Members of **AARP,** 601 E St. NW, Washington, DC 20049 (© **888/687-2277** or 202/434-2277; www.aarp.org), get discounts on hotels, airfares, and car rentals. AARP offers members a wide range of benefits, including *AARP The Magazine* and a monthly newsletter. Anyone over 50 can join.

FAMILY TRAVEL

Fijians adore infants and young children, but childhood does not last as long here as it does in Western societies. As soon as they are capable, children are put to work, first caring for their younger siblings and cousins and helping out with household chores, later tending the village gardens. It's only as teenagers—and then only if they leave their villages for town—that they cannot find jobs and thus know unemployment in the Western sense. Accordingly, few towns and villages have children's facilities, such as playgrounds, outside school property.

On the other hand, the Fijians invariably love children and are extraordinarily good at babysitting. The hotels can take care of this for you.

The larger hotels in Fiji cater to Australian and New Zealander families with ample activities to keep everyone occupied. **Jean-Michel Cousteau Fiji Islands Resort** in Savusavu is one of the top family resorts in all of the South Pacific islands (see chapter 13), and several others have excellent kids programs.

Some resorts do not accept children at all; I point those out in the establishment listings, but you should ask to make sure. Even if they are able to accommodate young visitors, check whether the hotel can provide cribs and other needs, and if they have children's menus.

Disposable diapers, cotton swabs (known as Buds, not Q-Tips), and baby food are sold in many main-town stores, but you should take along a supply of such items as children's aspirin, a thermometer, adhesive bandages (plasters), and special medications. Make sure your children's vaccinations are up-to-date before you leave home. If your children are very small, perhaps you should discuss your travel plans with your family doctor.

Remember to protect youngsters with ample sunscreen.

Other tips: Some tropical plants and animals may resemble rocks or vegetation, so teach your youngsters to avoid touching or brushing up against rocks, seaweed, and other objects. If your children are prone to swimmer's ear, use vinegar or preventive drops before they go swimming in freshwater streams or lakes. Having them shower soon after swimming or suffering cuts or abrasions will help reduce the chance of infection.

Rascals in Paradise, One Daniel Burnham Court, Ste. 105-C, San Francisco, CA 94107 (© **415/921-7000;** fax 415/921-7050; www.rascalsinparadise. com), specializes in organizing tours for families with kids, including visits with local families and children.

Adventures Abroad (© **800/665-3998;** www.adventures-abroad.com) organizes 1-week family sightseeing tours around Viti Levu, including village and market village visits.

For a list of more family-friendly travel resources, turn to the experts at frommers.com.

WOMEN TRAVELERS

Fiji is relatively safe for women traveling alone, but don't let the charm of warm nights and smiling faces lull you into any less caution than you would exercise at home. *Do not* wander alone on deserted beaches. In the old days this was an invitation for sex. If that's what you want today, then that's what you're likely to get. Otherwise, it could result in your being sexually assaulted.

And don't ever hitchhike alone, either.

Check out the award-winning website **Journeywoman** (www.journeywoman. com), a "real life" women's travel-information network where you can sign up for a free e-mail newsletter and get advice on everything from etiquette and dress to safety. The travel guide *Safety and Security for Women Who Travel* by Sheila Swan and Peter Laufer (Travelers' Tales Guides), offering common-sense tips on safe travel, was updated in 2004.

AFRICAN-AMERICAN TRAVELERS

Among general sources for African-American travelers, **Black Travel Online** (www.blacktravelonline.com) posts news on upcoming events and includes links to articles and travel-booking sites. **Soul of America** (www.soulofamerica.com) is a comprehensive website, with travel tips, event and family-reunion postings, and sections on historically black beach resorts and active vacations.

Agencies and organizations that provide resources for black travelers include: **Rodgers Travel** (© 800/825-1775; www.rodgerstravel.com); the **African American Association of Innkeepers International** (© 877/422-5777; www. africanamericaninns.com); and **Henderson Travel & Tours** (© 800/327-2309 or 301/650-5700; www.henderson travel.com), which has specialized in trips to Africa since 1957.

Go Girl: The Black Woman's Guide to Travel & Adventure (Eighth Mountain Press) is a compilation of travel essays by writers including Jill Nelson and Audre Lorde. *The African-American Travel Guide* by Wayne C. Robinson (Hunter Publishing; www.hunterpublishing.com)

was published in 1997, so it may be somewhat dated. *Travel and Enjoy Magazine* (© 866/266-6211) is a travel magazine and guide. The well-done *Pathfinders Magazine* (© 877/977-PATH (977-7284); www.pathfinders travel.com) includes articles on everything from Rio de Janeiro to Ghana to upcoming ski, diving, golf, and tennis trips.

STUDENT TRAVEL

Although Fiji has one of the most developed backpacker industries in the world, you won't find any student discounts here. If you're going on to New Zealand and Australia, you'd be wise to get an **international student ID card** from the **International Student Travel Confederation (ISTC)** (www.istc.org), which offers savings on plane tickets. It also provides basic health and life insurance and a 24-hour help line. You can apply for the card online or in person at **STA Travel** (© 800/781-4040 in North America; www.statravel. com), the biggest student travel agency in the world; check out the website to locate STA Travel offices worldwide.

If you're no longer a student but are still under 26, you can get an **International Youth Travel Card (IYTC)** for the same price from the same people. The card offers some discounts (but not on museum admissions).

Travel CUTS (© 800/667-2887 or 416/614-2887; www.travelcuts.com) offers similar services for both Canadians and U.S. residents. Irish students may prefer to turn to USIT (© 01/602-1904; www.usit now.ie), an Ireland-based specialist in student, youth, and independent travel.

Both high school and university students can participate in summer community service programs in Fiji organized by

---

Tips **Leave Fido at Home**

Don't even think about bringing your pet to Fiji. Fido will be quarantined until you are ready to fly home.

Rustic Pathways (© 800/321-4353; www.rusticpathways.com).

SINGLE TRAVELERS

Having traveled alone through the South Pacific for more years than I care to admit, I can tell you Fiji is a great place to be unattached. After all, this is the land of smiles and genuine warmth toward strangers. The attitude soon infects visitors: All I've ever had to do to meet my fellow travelers is wander into a hotel bar, order a beer, and ask the persons next to me where they are from and what they have done on their vacations.

And with its backpacker industry, Fiji seems to be crawling with young singles at all times.

Unfortunately, the solo traveler outside backpacker hostels is often forced to pay a "single supplement" charged by many resorts, cruise lines, and tours for the privilege of sleeping alone.

TravelChums (© 212/799-6464; www.travelchums.com) is an Internet-only travel-companion matching service hosted by respected New York–based Shaw Guides travel service.

Based in Canada, **Travel Buddies Singles Travel Club** (© 800/998-9099; www.travelbuddiesworldwide.com) runs small, intimate, single-friendly group trips and will match you with a roommate free of charge and save you the cost of single supplements.

10 Sustainable Tourism

Climate change and rising sea levels resulting from global warming are having a noticeable impact on all the South Pacific islands. Fijians I have known for more than 30 years tell me the seasons are now unpredictable (it's more likely to rain in the dry season, and vice versa), and the tides are higher than ever (in some places the lagoons lap directly on shore at high tide rather than on the beach). Indeed, most islanders don't want to hear any corporate-induced spin about the lack of evidence of global warming and its consequences. They know it's true from firsthand experience.

Although Fiji has been slack in allowing some resort owners to remove parts of the reef to create marinas and swimming holes, it has laws protecting its lagoons, reefs, and sea life. To the Fijians, lagoons are not just places where you swim around and look at beautiful corals and sea life; they are major sources of food. Protecting their lagoons and reefs is a matter of survival.

Consequently, it's up to us visitors to practice **sustainable tourism,** which means being careful with the environments we explore, and respecting the communities we visit.

Two overlapping components of sustainable travel are **ecotourism** and **ethical tourism.** The **International Ecotourism Society (TIES)** defines ecotourism as responsible travel to natural areas that conserves the environment and improves the well-being of local people. TIES suggests that ecotourists follow these principles:

- Minimize environmental impact.
- Build environmental and cultural awareness and respect.
- Provide positive experiences for both visitors and hosts.
- Provide direct financial benefits for conservation and for local people.
- Raise sensitivity to host countries' political, environmental, and social climates.
- Support international human rights and labor agreements.

You can find some eco-friendly travel tips and statistics, as well as touring companies and associations—listed by destination under "Travel Choice"—at the

Tips It's Easy Being Green

Here are a few simple ways you can help conserve fuel and energy when you travel:

- Each time you take a flight or drive a car greenhouse gases release into the atmosphere. You can help neutralize this danger to the planet through "carbon offsetting"—paying someone to invest your money in programs that reduce your greenhouse gas emissions by the same amount you've added. Before buying carbon offset credits, just make sure that you're using a reputable company, one with a proven program that invests in renewable energy. Reliable carbon offset companies include **Carbonfund** (www.carbonfund.org), **TerraPass** (www.terrapass.org), and **Carbon Neutral** (www.carbonneutral.org).
- Whenever possible, choose nonstop flights; they generally require less fuel than indirect flights that stop and take off again. Try to fly during the day—some scientists estimate that nighttime flights are twice as harmful to the environment. And pack light—each 15 pounds of luggage on a 5,000-mile flight adds up to 50 pounds of carbon dioxide emitted.
- Where you stay during your travels can have a major environmental impact. To determine the green credentials of a property, ask about trash disposal and recycling, water conservation, and energy use; also question if sustainable materials were used in the construction of the property. The website **www.greenhotels.com** recommends green-rated member hotels around the world that fulfill the company's stringent environmental requirements. Also consult **www.environmentallyfriendlyhotels.com** for more green accommodations ratings.
- At hotels, request that your sheets and towels not be changed daily. (Many hotels already have programs like this in place.) Turn off the lights and air-conditioner (or heater) when you leave your room.
- Use public transport where possible—trains, buses, and even taxis are more energy-efficient forms of transport than driving. Even better is to walk or cycle; you'll produce zero emissions and stay fit and healthy on your travels.
- If renting a car is necessary, ask the rental agent for a hybrid, or rent the most fuel-efficient car available. You'll use less gas and save money at the tank.

TIES website, www.ecotourism.org. Also check out **Ecotravel.com**, which lets you search for sustainable touring companies in several categories (water-based, land-based, spiritually oriented, and so on).

While much of the focus of ecotourism is about reducing impacts on the natural environment, ethical tourism concentrates on ways to preserve and enhance local economies and communities, regardless of location. You can embrace ethical tourism by staying at a locally owned hotel or shopping at a store that employs local workers and sells locally produced goods.

Responsible Travel (www.responsible travel.com) is a great source of sustainable travel ideas; the site is run by a spokesperson for ethical tourism in the travel industry. **Sustainable Travel International** (www.sustainabletravelinternational.org) promotes ethical tourism practices, and manages an extensive directory of sustainable properties and tour operators around the world.

In the U.K., **Tourism Concern** (www.tourismconcern.org.uk) works to reduce social and environmental problems connected to tourism. The **Association of Independent Tour Operators (AITO)** (www.aito.co.uk) is a group of specialist operators leading the field in making holidays sustainable.

Volunteer travel has become increasingly popular among those who want to venture beyond the standard group-tour experience to learn languages, interact with locals, and make a positive difference while on vacation. Volunteer travel usually doesn't require special skills—just a willingness to work hard—and programs vary in length from a few days to a number of weeks. Some programs provide free housing and food, but many require volunteers to pay for travel expenses, which can add up quickly.

For general info on volunteer travel, visit **www.volunteerabroad.org** and **www.idealist.org**. Specific volunteer options in Fiji are listed under "Special-Interest Trips," below.

Before you commit to a volunteer program, it's important to make sure any money you're giving is truly going back to the local community, and that the work you'll be doing will be a good fit for you. **Volunteer International** (www.volunteer international.org) has a helpful list of questions to ask to determine the intentions and the nature of a volunteer program.

11 Packages for the Independent Traveler

In addition to searching for the lowest airfare, you may want to consider booking your flight as part of a travel package. Buying a package tour is simply a way to get the airfare, accommodations, and other elements of your trip (such as car rentals, airport transfers, and sometimes even meals and activities) at the same time and often at discounted prices—kind of like one-stop shopping. In fact, package tours usually provide the best bargains available.

Package tours are not the same thing as escorted tours, which are structured tours with a group leader. Scant few escorted tours go to Fiji except as add-ons to tours primarily of Australia and New Zealand.

The costs are kept down because wholesale tour operators (known as wholesalers in the travel industry) can make volume bookings on the airlines and at the hotels. Packages traditionally were then sold through retail travel agents, but many wholesalers now deal directly with the public, thus passing savings along to you, rather than part of their commissions to retail agents.

Travel packages are listed in the travel section of many Sunday newspapers. Or check ads in magazines such as *Arthur Frommer's Budget Travel Magazine, Travel + Leisure, National Geographic Traveler,* and *Condé Nast Traveler.*

Airlines frequently offer air-and-hotel packages, so be sure to check the websites of **Air New Zealand** (www.airnew zealand.com/vacations) and **Air Pacific** (www.airpacific.com). See "The Airlines," earlier in this chapter.

Following in alphabetical order are some reputable companies selling package tours. Some will discount air tickets and hotel rooms separately; that is, not as part of a package. Be sure to shop for the best deal among them.

Frommers.com: The Complete Travel Resource

Planning a trip or just returned? Head to **Frommers.com,** voted Best Travel Site by *PC Magazine*. We think you'll find our site indispensable before, during and after your travels—with expert advice and tips; independent reviews of hotels, restaurants, attractions, and preferred shopping and nightlife venues; vacation giveaways; and an online booking tool. We publish the complete contents of over 135 travel guides in our **Destinations** section, covering over 4,000 places worldwide. Each weekday, we publish original articles that report on **Deals and News** via our free **Frommers.com Newsletters**. What's more, **Arthur Frommer** himself blogs five days a week, with cutting opinions about the state of travel in the modern world. We're betting you'll find our **Events** listings an invaluable resource; it's an up-to-the-minute roster of what's happening in cities everywhere—including concerts, festivals, lectures, and more. We've also added weekly **podcasts, interactive maps,** and hundreds of new images across the site. Finally, don't forget to visit our **Message Boards,** where you can join in conversations with thousands of fellow Frommer's travelers and post your trip report once you return.

- **Brendan Worldwide Vacations** (℃ **800/421-8446** or 818/785-9696; www.brendanvacations.com) provides packages to Fiji.
- **Costco Travel** (℃ **877/849-2730;** www.costco.com) sells island packages to Costco members. The agency was a South Pacific specialist before Costco bought it.
- **Go-Today** (℃ **800/227-3235;** www.go-today.com), based in Washington State, offers discount-priced packages to Fiji.
- **Impulse Fiji** (℃ **800/953-7595** in the U.S.; www.impulsefiji.com) is a Nadi-based firm owned by American Dick Beaulieu, who has lived in Fiji since 1980. He and his staff arrange personalized travel to Fiji, including money-saving last-minute deals.
- **Islands in the Sun** (℃ **800/828-6877** or 310/536-0051; www.islandsinthesun.com), the largest and oldest South Pacific specialist, offers packages to Fiji.

- **Jetabout Island Vacations** (℃ **800/348-8145;** www.jetabouttahitivacations.com) of El Segundo, California, offers a wide variety of packages to Fiji. It's the U.S. representative of Qantas Vacations, an arm of the Australian airline.
- **Journey Pacific** (℃ **800/704-7094;** www.journeypacific.com) is a Las Vegas–based agency offering Fiji packages.
- **Newmans South Pacific Vacations** (℃ **800/421-3326;** www.newmansvacations.com) offers packages to Fiji. It's a long-established New Zealand company.
- **Pacific Destination Center** (℃ **800/227-5317;** www.pacific-destinations.com) is owned and operated by Australian-born Janette Ryan, who offers some good deals to the islands.
- **Pacific for Less** (℃ **800/915-2776;** www.pacific-for-less.com), based in Hawaii, specializes in high-end honeymoons.

- **Pleasant Holidays** (© 800/742-9244; www.pleasantholidays.com), a huge company best known for its Pleasant Hawaiian and Pleasant Mexico operations, offers packages to Fiji.
- **South Pacific Direct** (www.south pacificdirect.com) is an Internet-only firm offering deals to Fiji.
- **South Seas Adventures** (© 800/576-7327; www.south-seas-adventures. com) has adventure travel packages to Fiji.
- **Sunspots International** (© 800/334-5623 or 503/666-3893; www.sun spotsintl.com), based in Portland, Oregon, has trips specifically tailored to Fiji.
- **Swain Tahiti Tours** (© 800/22-SWAIN (227-9246); www.swaintours. com) obviously knows a lot about

Tahiti and French Polynesia but it also sells packages to Fiji.
- **Travel Arrangements Ltd.** (© 800/392-8213; www.southpacific reservations.com) is operated by Fiji-born Ron Hunt, a veteran South Pacific travel agent who now lives in California. He sells packages and specializes in designing itineraries (and weddings) to suit your whims and pocketbook.
- **Travelwizard** (© 800/330-8820; www.travelwizard.com) specializes in designing luxury travel packages but also has less expensive offerings. Among its offerings are adventure, diving, and surfing trips to Fiji.

Other companies have adventure travel packages combining outdoor activities with accommodations. See "The Active Traveler," below.

12 Escorted General-Interest Tours

Escorted tours are structured group tours, with a group leader (I prefer the old-fashion term "tour guide"). The price usually includes everything from airfare to hotels, meals, tours, admission costs, and local transportation.

Escorted tours are not a big part of the business in Fiji, where it's easy to find your way around and book local tours and activities. Most of the travel agents I mention under "Packages for the Independent Traveler," above, will have someone meet and greet you at the airport upon arrival, take you to your hotel, and make sure you get on any prearranged tours and activities; but you will not have a tour guide.

Some tour companies add a short stopover in Fiji to their escorted tours of Australia and New Zealand, but these may not include a guide for the island portion. Leaders in this add-on feature include **Tauck Tours** (© 800/788-7885; www.tauck.com), **Qantas Vacations**

(© 800/641-8772; www.qantasvacations. com), **Australia Escorted Tours** (© 888/333-6607; www.australia-escorted-tours. com), and **Abercrombie & Kent** (© 800/652-7986; www.abercrombiekent.com), which adds Fiji to its high-end escorted tours. Otherwise, I recommend getting a travel agent to track down an escorted tour.

Despite the fact that escorted tours require big deposits and predetermine hotels, restaurants, and itineraries, many people derive security and peace of mind from the structure they offer. Escorted tours let travelers sit back and enjoy the trip without having to drive or worry about details. They're particularly convenient for people with limited mobility, and they can be a great way to make new friends.

On the downside, you'll have little opportunity for serendipitous interactions with locals. The tours can be jam-packed with activities, leaving little room

> **Tips Ask Before You Go**
>
> Before you invest in a package deal or an escorted tour:
> - Always ask about the **cancellation policy.** Can you get your money back? Is a deposit required?
> - Ask about the **accommodations choices and prices** for each. Then look up the hotels' reviews in a Frommer's guide and check their rates online for your specific dates of travel. Also find out what types of rooms are offered.
> - Request a complete **schedule.** (Escorted tours only.)
> - Ask about the **size** and demographics of the group. (Escorted tours only.)
> - Discuss what is included in the **price** (transportation, meals, tips, airport transfers, and so on). (Escorted tours only.)
> - Finally, look for **hidden expenses.** Ask whether airport departure fees and taxes, for example, are included in the total cost—they rarely are.

for individual sightseeing, whim, or adventure—plus they often focus on the heavily touristed sites, so you miss out on many a lesser-known gem.

13 Special-Interest Trips

Although outdoor activities take first place in the islands (see "The Active Traveler," below), you can also spend your time learning a new craft, exploring the reefs as part of a conservation project, and whale- and dolphin-watching.

BIRD-WATCHING

Avid bird-watchers are likely to see terns, boobies, herons, petrols, noddies, and many other seabirds throughout the islands. Land birds, on the other hand, live in the bush away from settlements and the accompanying cats, dogs, and rats, so you will need to head into the bush for the best watching.

With 26 endemic species of land birds, Fiji has more diversity than any other South Pacific island country. Many are on display in **Kula Eco Park** (© 650 0505; www.fijiwild.com), on Fiji's Coral Coast (see chapter 7). **Taveuni** island is best for bird-watching in Fiji, with more than 100 species including the rare orange dove, which lives high on Des Veoux Peak. **Savusavu** on Vanua Levu is also good, especially the nearby Waisali Rainforest Reserve. **Daku Resort** in Savusavu

(© **885 0046;** www.dakuresort.com) hosts bird-watching tours run by veteran Fiji watcher Robin Mercer. See chapter 13.

A few companies have bird-watching tours to Fiji, including the U.K.-based **Bird Quest** (© **44/1254 826317;** www. birdquest.co.uk) and **Birdwatching Breaks** (© **44/1381 610495;** www.bird watchingbreaks.com).

EDUCATIONAL COURSES

In addition to bird-watching, **Daku Resort,** in northern Fiji (© **885 0046;** www.dakuresort.com), hosts weeklong courses in such subjects as novel writing, sketching, painting, quilting, and gospel singing. The courses are organized by creative writing teacher Delia Rothnie-Jones (she and her husband John own the resort). They have special package rates for the courses and will help you arrange air transportation to Fiji as well. See chapter 13.

ECOTRAVEL TOURS

The **Oceanic Society** (© **800/326-7491;** www.oceanic-society.org), an award-winning organization based in California, has natural history and ecotourism expeditions to Fiji. A marine naturalist accompanies its annual 11-day snorkeling to the colorful, pristine reefs off Namena and Taveuni islands in northern Fiji (see chapters 13 and 14, respectively). The trip includes village visits and bird-watching excursions.

Seacology (© 510/559-3505; www.seacology.org), a California-based organization dedicated to preserving island cultures and environments, has an annual trip to Jean-Michel Cousteau Fiji Islands Resort and occasionally to Samoa.

Fiji Adventures (© 888/418-4461; www.fijiadventures.com) offers several packages, one of which combines several cultural activities offered in Fiji such as river rafting, cave and waterfall visits, and a trip into Viti Levu's interior. The packages do not include airfare, but they save you from having to arrange each activity after you arrive in Fiji.

Formerly known as Tui Tai Adventure Cruises, the environmentally and culturally friendly **Active Fiji** (www.activefiji.com) uses a 42m (140-ft.) sailing schooner to explore out-of-the-way islands in northern Fiji. The boat goes to Fijian villages and carries mountain bikes as well snorkeling and diving gear. See chapter 13.

Based in London but with an office in the U.S., the nonprofit **Greenforce** (© 0207 470 8888 in London, 740/416 4016 in the U.S.; www.greenforce.org) sends expeditions to help survey Fiji's coral reefs for the World Conservation Society. They'll even teach you to dive while you're there. The trips last from 6 to 10 weeks. Check the website for prices.

14 The Active Traveler

Fiji is a dream for active travelers who are into diving, snorkeling, swimming, boating, and other watersports. You can also play golf and tennis, or hike into the jungle-clad mountainous interiors of the islands. Kayaking is popular everywhere, and Fiji has river rafting. Good biking can be had along the many roads skirting colorful lagoons. Here's a brief rundown of my favorite active pursuits.

ACTIVE VACATION PACKAGES

Some travel companies have tours combing several outdoor activities in one trip. For example, Colorado-based the **World Outdoors** (© 800/488-8483; www.theworldoutdoors.com) includes mountain biking, hiking, river rafting, sea kayaking, snorkeling, and sailing in its "Fiji Multi-Sport" tour. **Travelwizard** (© 800/330-8820; www.travelwizard.com) sells diving and surfing packages to Fiji and French Polynesia. Likewise **Fiji Adventures** © 888/418-4461; www.fijiadventures.com) has diving, surfing, river rafting, and windsurfing expeditions to Fiji.

On the Web, **Gordon's Guide** (www.gordonsguide.com) compiles adventure tours from around the world. It's a good place to search for Fiji-specific adventure trips in a variety of categories.

BIKING

Bicycles are one of my favorite means of getting around. Most of the coastal roads are relatively flat and fabulously scenic. It's simple and inexpensive to rent bikes, and many hotels and resorts provide either rental or complimentary bikes for their guests to use.

Active Fiji (www.activefiji.com), formerly known as Tui Tai Adventure Cruises, carries mountain bikes on its ecocruises. See chapter 13.

DIVING & SNORKELING

Fiji is famous among divers as being the "Soft Coral Capital of the World" because of its enormous number and variety of colorful corals, which attract a host of fish: More than 35 species of angelfish and butterfly fish swim in these waters.

Live-Aboard Diving

The best way to dive a lot of reefs in Fiji, especially in Bligh Water between Viti Levu and Vanua Levu—its famous E6 and Mount Mutiny rise some 1,000m (3,000 ft.) from the bottom—is on a live-aboard dive boat. Most luxurious is the *NAI'A* (© 888/510-1593 in North America or 345 0382 in Fiji; www.naia.com.fj), a 36m (120-ft.) motor-sailing yacht which can carry 18 persons in nine staterooms. It's the favorite of every diver I know who lives in Fiji. Rates start at F$4,528 (US$2,940/£1,494) per person double occupancy for a 7-day cruise. Others are the two catamarans *Fiji Aggressor I* and *Fiji Aggressor II*, both operated by the U.S.-based Aggressor Fleet (© **800/348-2628** or 985/385-2628; www.aggressor.com). Rates begin at F$3,850 (US$2,500/£1,270) per person double occupancy.

All but a few resorts in Fiji have dive operations on-site, as I point out in the following chapters. Most of them have equipment for rent, but ask before coming out here what they have available. Preferably bring your own, including a spare mask.

Even the heavily visited **Mamanuca Islands** off Nadi have their share of good sites, including the **Pinnacle,** a coral head rising 18m (60 ft.) from the lagoon floor, and a W-shaped protrusion from the outer reef. A drawback for some divers is that they don't have the Mamanuca sites all to themselves. See chapter 6.

In Beqa Lagoon, the soft corals of **Frigate Passage** seem like cascades falling over one another, and **Side Streets** has unusual orange coral. The nearby southern coast of Viti Levu has mostly hard corals, but you can go **shark diving** off Pacific Harbour; that is, the dive masters attract sharks by feeding them. See chapter 8.

South of Viti Levu, **Kadavu** island is skirted by the **Great Astrolabe Reef,** known for its steep outside walls dotted with both soft and hard corals. The Astrolabe attracts Fiji's largest concentration of manta rays. See chapter 9.

The reefs off **Rakiraki and northern Viti Levu** offer many tunnels and canyons plus golden soft corals growing on the sides of coral pinnacles ("bommies" in this part of the world). See chapter 11.

Ovalau Island and the historic town of Levuka aren't beach destinations, but good dive sites are nearby, including at the shipwrecks in and near Levuka harbor, and soft coral spots off nearby Wakaya Island, home of the fabulous but very expensive Wakaya Club. See chapter 12.

Off Savusavu, the barrier reef around Namenalala Island, home to Moody's Namena resort, is officially the **Namena Marine Protected Reserve.** Both hard and soft corals attract an enormous number of small fish and their predators. See chapter 13.

Fiji's best and most famous site for soft corals is **Somosomo Strait** between Vanua Levu and Taveuni in northern Fiji, home of the **Great White Wall** and its **Rainbow Reef** (see chapter 14). The Great White Wall is covered from between 23 and 60m (75–200 ft.) deep with pale lavender corals, which appear almost snow-white underwater. Near Qamea and Matagi, off Taveuni, are the appropriately named **Purple Wall,** a straight drop from 9 to 24m (30–80 ft.), and **Mariah's Cove,** a small wall as colorful as the Rainbow Reef.

Just in case, the **Fiji Recompression Chamber Facility** (© **336 2172**) is in Suva near Colonial War Memorial Hospital.

And remember, you will need at least 12 hours—longer after multiple dives—between your last dive and flying, so plan accordingly.

GOLF & TENNIS

Denarau Golf & Racquet Club is a modern complex with an 18-hole resort course and 10 tennis courts near Nadi. Nearby is the **Nadi Airport Golf Club**, where Vijay Singh took his first swings See chapter 5.

Malololailai Island, home of Plantation Island Resort and Musket Cove Resort & Spa, has a flat 9 holes (see chapter 6). The **Naviti Resort** has a course on the Coral Coast (see chapter 7). The country's most picturesque links are at the **Pearl Championship Golf Course & Country Club,** in Pacific Harbour. See chapter 8. You can also play at **Koro Sun Resort** in Savusavu (see chapter 13) and at **Taveuni Estates** on Taveuni (see chapter 14).

HIKING

These aren't the Rocky Mountains, nor are there blazed trails out here, but hiking in the islands is a lot of fun.

In Fiji you can trek into the mountains and stop at—or stay in—native Fijian villages. **Adventure Fiji,** an arm of Fiji's Rosie the Travel Service (www.rosiefiji. com), has guided hikes ranging from 1 to 10 days into the mountains of Viti Levu, with meals and accommodations provided by Fijian villagers. See chapter 5.

On Taveuni island, you can hike a spectacular **Lavena Coastal Walk** to a waterfall or up to **Lake Tagimaucia,** in a crater at an altitude of more than 800m (2,700 ft.). It's home of the rare *tagimaucia* flower. See chapter 14.

HORSEBACK RIDING

Although I prefer sipping a cold drink, a great way to experience a South Pacific sunset is from the back of a horse while riding along a beach. You can do just that on Nadi's **Wailoaloa Beach** and at **Sonaisali Island Resort** (see chapter 5).

Some resorts on the Coral Coast have riding in their stable of activities (see chapter 7). In Pacific Harbour, **Uprising Beach Resort** lets you go "horse-boarding"—a horse running along the beach pulls you and your boogie board across the lagoon (see chapter 8).

KAYAKING

All but a few beachfront resorts have canoes, kayaks, small sailboats, sailboards, and other toys for their guests' amusement. Since most of these properties sit beside lagoons, using these craft is not only fun, it's relatively safe.

Sea kayaking is popular among Fiji's many small islands. **Tamarillo Tropical Expeditions** (② 877/682-5433 in the U.S., 4/2399 855 in New Zealand; www. tamarillo.co.nz) has guided 5- to 9-day kayak expeditions along the shore of Kadavu island. See chapter 9.

RIVER RAFTING

Fiji has rivers long enough and swift enough for white-water rafting. The best is the Navua River on Viti Levu, which starts in the mountainous interior and flows swiftly down to a flat delta on the island's south coast. Local companies offer trips using traditional *bilibilis* (bamboo rafts) on the lower, slow-flowing section of the river. The outstanding **Rivers Fiji** (② 800/446-2411; www.riversfiji. com) uses inflatable rafts for white-water trips up in the highlands. See chapter 8.

SURFING

Fiji has some popular surfer-dude hangouts such as **Tavarua Island Resort** (② 805/687-4551 in the U.S.; www. tavarua.com), in the Mamanuca Islands near the main pass through the Great Sea Reef (see chapter 6).

Its most famous surfing spots are **Frigate Passage** in the Beqa Lagoon and at **Cape Washington** on Kadavu (see chapters 8 and 9, respectively).

All the best are reef breaks; that is, the surf crashes out on coral reefs instead of on sandy beaches. These are no places for beginners, since you could suffer serious injury by landing on a razor-sharp coral reef—or as one of my island friends puts it, "You'll become hamburger in a hurry."

15 Staying Connected

TELEPHONES
Land-line telephone service is provided throughout the country by **Telecom Fiji Limited,** or **TFL** (℗ **112 233;** www.tfl. com.fj). Although calls are relatively expensive, it's a modern system.

TO CALL FIJI
To call into Fiji, first dial the international access code (011 from the U.S.; 00 from the U.K., Ireland, or New Zealand; or 0011 from Australia), then Fiji's country code **679,** and the local number (Fiji has no area codes).

TO CALL FROM WITHIN FIJI
To make an international call from within Fiji, first dial **00,** then the country code (U.S. or Canada 1, U.K. 44, Ireland 353, Australia 61, New Zealand 64), then the area code and phone number. Calls to most countries cost F60¢ (US40¢/20p) a minute when dialed directly. Frequent TFL promotions cut the price by 20% or more on nights and weekends.

LOCAL ACCESS NUMBERS
You cannot use a credit card to make calls in Fiji, but several international long-distance carriers have local access numbers their customers can call to access their international networks and use their company cards: **AT&T USA** (℗ 004 890 1001); **AT&T Canada** (℗ 004 890 1009); **Australia Telstra** (℗ 004 890 6101); **Australia Octopus** (℗ 004 890 6102); **Bell South** (℗ 004 890 1008); **BT** (℗ 004 890 4401); **BT Prepaid** (℗ 004 890 4402); **MCI** (℗ 004 890 1002); **New Zealand Telecom** (℗ 004 890 6401); **Sprint** (℗ 004 890 1003); **Teleglobe Canada** (℗ 004 890 1005); and **Verizon** (℗ 004 890 1007). These numbers can be dialed toll-free from any land-line phone.

TO CALL WITHIN FIJI
No prefix or area code is required for domestic long-distance calls, so dial the local number.

DIRECTORY ASSISTANCE
Dial ℗ **011** for domestic information, ℗ **022** for international numbers. (On the Web you can look up local numbers at **www.whitepages.com.fj** and **www. yellowpages.com.fj**.)

OPERATOR ASSISTANCE
Dial ℗ **010** for operator assistance in making a call.

TOLL-FREE NUMBERS
Local numbers beginning with **0800** are toll-free within Fiji, but calling a 1-800 number in the U.S. or Canada from Fiji is not toll-free. In fact, it costs the same as an overseas call.

PAY PHONES
Public phones are located at all post offices and in many other locations (look for Fijian war spears sticking out from plastic booths). You can make local, domestic long-distance ("trunk"), or international calls without operator assistance from any of them. They accept only prepaid Fiji Telecom **Telecards,** not coins. Post offices and many shops (including the gift shops in the Nadi Airport terminal) sell Telecards in denominations up to F$50 (US$33/£17). Scratch the tape off the back of the card to reveal your personal identification number (PIN), which you must enter prior to placing a call.

CELLPHONES

Known as "mobiles" over here, cellphones are prevalent throughout Fiji. No international wireless company operates here, and many American phones won't work since Fiji uses the Global System for Mobiles (GSM) technology. Although the technology is gaining in popularity worldwide, only T-Mobile and AT&T Wireless use this quasi-universal system in the U.S. In Canada, Microcell and some Rogers customers are GSM. All Europeans and most Australians use GSM. Call your wireless company to see if your phone is GSM.

If you do have a GSM phone, you may be able to use it in Fiji if your home provider has a roaming agreement with the local phone companies. Call your wireless operator and ask if it has roaming in Fiji, and if so, ask that "international roaming" be activated on your account.

If it doesn't, you may still use your phone (1) if it transmits and receives on the 900 mHz band; (2) it has been "unlocked" from its SIM card, the removable computer chip which stores your and your provider's information; and (3) you rent or buy a local SIM card.

The Travel Insider (www.thetravel insider.info) has an excellent explanation of all this as well as a phone unlocking service. Click on "Road Warrior Resources" and "International Cellphone Service."

At press time, **Digicel Pacific** (www.digicelpacific.com) had been awarded a license to operate in Fiji, thus bringing competition to **Vodaphone Fiji** (© 672 6226; www.vodafone.com.fj), which had previously held a monopoly and was able to charge near exorbitant rates. Digicel has brought much lower cellphone prices to Samoa and Tonga, and hopefully it will do so in Fiji by the time you arrive.

In the meantime, Vodaphone rents both cellphones and GSM-compatible SIM cards for unlocked phones. It has a desk in the arrivals concourse at **Nadi airport,** which is staffed daily from 5am to 11pm and for major international flights, and offices in Nadi Town and Suva. Phones cost F$6 (US$4/£2) a day to rent, while SIM cards are F$2 (US$1.30/70p) per day, plus F95¢ (US60¢/30p) per minute for outgoing calls to land lines, F50¢ (US35¢/20p) to other mobile phones. Incoming calls are free. Vodaphone will pre-authorize a credit of F$200 (US$130/£66) on your credit card, to which it will bill your rental and usage fees.

An Australian firm, **Inkk Mobile,** sells phones and slightly discounted prepaid airtime over Vodaphone's network. The Tappoo department stores sell Inkk's phones and SIM cards.

You can also buy or rent cellphones to take to Fiji. **Mobal** (© 888/399-2418; www.mobal.com) sells GSM phones that work in Fiji and about 150 other countries for as little US$49 (£25), with no monthly fees or minimum usage requirements. Calls are billed to your credit card as you make them—US$1.95 (£1) per minute for both incoming and outgoing calls within Fiji, US$3.95 (£2) from Fiji to the U.S. and Canada, US$5.95 (£3) from Fiji to other countries. Mobal gave me a U.K. cellphone number. Frankly, I found it less expensive to rent a phone or SIM during a short vacation in Fiji, but I carry my Mobal phone for emergencies, and I can use it when I am traveling in other countries.

SKYPE—VOICE OVER INTERNET PROTOCOL (VOIP)

I use my laptop to call internationally using **Skype** (www.skype.com), a broadband-based telephone service (in technical terms, **Voice over Internet protocol,** or **VoIP**), which allows you to make free international calls from your laptop or in some cybercafes. Talking worldwide on Skype is free if the people you're calling also have it (that is, computer-to-computer calls). You can also make calls

Online Traveler's Toolbox

Veteran travelers usually carry some essential items to make their trips easier. Following is a selection of handy online tools to bookmark and use.

- **Airplane Food** (www.airlinemeals.net)
- **Airplane Seating** (www.seatguru.com; www.airlinequality.com)
- **Foreign Languages for Travelers** (www.travlang.com)
- **Maps** (www.mapsouthpacific.com; www.maps-pacific.com; www.worldatlas.com)
- **Time and Date** (www.timeanddate.com)
- **Travel Warnings** (http://travel.state.gov; www.fco.gov.uk/travel; www.voyage.gc.ca; www.smartraveller.gov.au)
- **Universal Currency Converter** (www.xe.com/ucc)
- **Visa ATM Locator** (www.visa.com), **MasterCard ATM Locator** (www.mastercard.com)
- **Weather** (www.met.gov.fj; www.intellicast.com; www.weather.com; www.accuweather.com; www.wunderground.com)

to land-line phones for a fee, which is based on the country you are calling, not where you are calling from. Skype calls to land-line phones in most Western countries cost about US2¢ (1p) per minute. Check Skype's website for details.

INTERNET & E-MAIL

E-mail is as much a part of life in Fiji as it is anywhere else these days, but most Internet connections here are relatively slow. High-speed access is growing, but at best, the ADSL systems operate at 512 kilo bauds per second. That's a snail's pace compared to the 3 mega bauds per second or more in most Western countries.

WITHOUT YOUR OWN COMPUTER

All but a few hotels and resorts have computers from which guests can send and receive e-mail and surf the Web, and cybercafes are widespread in Nadi and Suva, and present in Savusavu. See the "Fast Facts" sections in chapters 5, 10, and 13.

WITH YOUR OWN COMPUTER

Some hotels now have wireless Internet connections, or wired high-speed Internet connections in their rooms, which I point out in the hotel listings in this book.

You can find wireless hot spots at some coffee shops in Nadi and Suva. See the "Fast Facts" in chapters 5 and 10.

No international Internet service provider has a local access number in Fiji, but you can sign up for temporary dial-up access through **Connect Internet Services** (© **670 7359** in Nadi, 330 0100 in Suva; www.connect.com.fj), which as I write is Fiji's primary Internet service provider (the interim government was moving to allow competition). See the "Fast Facts" in chapters 5 and 10 for Connect's locations in Nadi Town and Suva, respectively. Connect charges F$15 (US$9.75/£5) 1 month's access, plus F8¢ (US5¢/3p) a minute, which will be billed to your hotel room. (*Be careful:* Some hotels add a whopping service fee on top of these charges.)

Configuring Your Laptop

Once you have purchased a temporary dial-up account from Connect, here's how to set up your computer in Windows XP and 2000:

- Double click on **Control Panel.**
- Double click **Network Connections.**
- Double click **Create a New Connection.**
- Name the new connection anything you want.
- Click **Configure** and set the maximum speed of your modem to not more 57,600kbps. Click **OK.**
- Leave the Area Code box blank and in Telephone Number box type (with no spaces) the number you must dial to reach an outside line (0 in Fiji), a comma, and the local access number. Don't change the Country box. Click **OK.**
- After you have created your new connection, double-click **Network Connections** in XP, and the icon for your new connection. Click **Connect.** When the connection is made, enter *both* your name and your password.
- From then on, you can double-click **My Computer, Dial-Up Networking,** your local connection icon, and **Connect.** After the connection is made, load your browser, and you're online.

16 Tips on Accommodations

Fiji has a wide range of accommodations, from deluxe resort hotels on their own islands to dormitories with bunk beds.

TYPES OF ROOMS

My favorite type of hotel accommodates its guests in individual bungalows set in a coconut grove beside a sandy beach and quiet lagoon. If that's not the quintessential definition of the South Seas, then I don't know what is!

Hotels of this style are widespread in Fiji. **Likuliku Lagoon Resort** is the first in Fiji with romantic bungalows actually standing on stilts out over the reef (see chapter 6). Others are as basic as camping out. In between they vary in size, furnishings, and comfort. In all, however, you enjoy your own space and a certain degree of privacy. The bungalows are usually built or accented with thatch and other native materials but they contain most of the modern conveniences.

An increasing number of these accommodations are air-conditioned, which is a definite plus during the humid summer months from November through March. All but a few bungalows have ceiling fans, which usually will keep you comfortable during the rest of the year.

Fiji's major tourist markets for the island countries are Australia and New Zealand. Accordingly, the vast majority of hotels are tailored to Aussie and Kiwi tastes, expectations, and uses of the English language.

The standard Down Under room has a double or queen-size bed and a single bed that also serves as a settee. The room may or may not have a bathtub but always has a shower. There will be tea, instant coffee, sugar, creamer, and an electric jug to heat water (that's usually what I mean by "coffeemaker" in my hotel descriptions). Televisions and telephones are numerous but are not yet universal; and most hotels have radios whose selections are limited to the one, two, or three stations on the island.

Rooms are known to Fiji reservation desks as "singles" if one person books them, regardless of the number and size of beds they have. Singles are slightly less expensive than other rooms. A unit is a "double" if it has a double bed and is reserved for two persons who intend to

> **Tips It Could Pay to Ask**
>
> It never hurts to ask politely for a discounted or local hotel rate. Many Fiji hotels have **local rates** for islanders, which they may extend to visitors if business is slow. Most pay travel agents and wholesalers 20% or more of their rates for sending clients their way, and some may give you the benefit of at least part of this commission if you book directly instead of going through an airline or travel agent. Some wholesale travel agents reduce the commission and sell directly to the public; see my list under "Packages for the Independent Traveler," earlier in this chapter.

sleep together in that bed. On the other hand, a "twin" has two twin beds; it is known as a "shared twin" if two unmarried people book them and don't intend to sleep together. Third and fourth occupants of any room are usually charged a few dollars on top of the double or shared twin rates.

Some hotel rooms have kitchenettes equipped with a small refrigerator (the "fridge"), hot plates (the "cooker"), pots, pans, crockery, silverware, and utensils. Having a kitchenette can result in quite a saving on breakfasts and light meals.

SURFING FOR HOTELS

In addition to the online travel booking sites **Travelocity, Expedia, Orbitz, Priceline,** and **Hotwire,** you can book hotels through **Hotels.com; Quikbook** (www.quikbook.com); and **Travelaxe** (www.travelaxe.net). Frankly, I always go to the hotels' own sites before booking, since many now offer their own Internet specials, which often beat the big-site prices.

The best independent website for Fiji hotel discount shopping is **www.Travelmaxia.com,** where properties post their specials. You can search for resorts, hotels, bed-and-breakfasts, dive operators, and cruises.

The Australian-based **Whotif.com** (© **300/88 7979,** 866/514-3281 in the U.S., 0845 458 4567 in the U.K.; www.whotif.com) discounts rooms in Fiji.

Headquartered in London, **www.Pacific-Resorts.com** often slashes rates for Fiji resorts.

Backpackers and other budget travelers can book inexpensive rooms and dorm beds at hostels in most island countries at **www.hostelworld.com**.

Other websites have reviews and comments about accommodations worldwide. **HotelChatter.com** is a daily webzine offering coverage and critiques. Go to **TripAdvisor.com** or **HotelShark.com** for independent consumer reviews of hotels and resort properties. (Anyone can post reviews on these sites, including hotel owners themselves and "guests" who have never stayed at a property, so I read them with a proverbial grain of salt.)

It's a good idea to **get a confirmation number** and **make a printout** of any online booking transaction.

SAVING ON YOUR HOTEL ROOM

The rate ranges quoted in this book are known as **rack rates,** or published rates; that is, the maximum a property charges for a room. Rack rates remain the best way of comparing prices, but they are becoming less meaningful as more and more hotels change their rates almost daily depending on how many people are booked in for a particular night. They change so frequently, in fact, that many hotels refuse to divulge their rack rates to travel writers like me. In other words, you may not know what the price of a room is until you call the hotel or book online for a particular date.

Another tactic is to check with **inbound tour operators.** In addition to selling tours and day trips to visitors already in the islands (that is, at hotel activities desks), these companies put together the local elements of tour packages—such as hotel rooms and airport transfers—for overseas wholesalers. They have the advantage of being on the scene and thus familiar with the properties. Some sell directly to inbound visitors as well as other tour companies.

In Fiji, two small companies specialize in discount travel arrangements, including hotel rooms: **Impulse Fiji** (© **800/ 953-7595** in the U.S., 672 0600 in Fiji; www.impulsefiji.com) and **Sun Vacations** (© **672 4273** in Fiji; www.sunvacations fiji.com). See "Packages for the Independent Traveler," earlier in this chapter.

Here some other money-saving tips:

- **Ask about special rates or other discounts.** At international chain motels, you may qualify for corporate, student, military, senior, frequent flier, trade union, or other discounts.
- **Dial direct.** When booking a room in a chain hotel, you'll often get a better deal by calling the individual hotel's reservation desk rather than the chain's main number.
- **Book online.** Many hotels offer Internet-only discounts, or supply rooms to Priceline, Hotwire, or Expedia at rates much lower than the ones you can get through the hotel itself.

Be sure to check the individual hotel's site for discounts and specials.

- **Remember the law of supply and demand.** You can save big on hotel rooms by traveling in a destination's off-season or shoulder seasons, when rates typically drop, even at luxury properties.
- **Look into group or long-stay discounts.** If you come as part of a large group, you should be able to negotiate a bargain rate. Likewise, if you're planning a long stay (at least 5 days), you might qualify for a discount. As a general rule, expect 1 night free after a 7-night stay.
- **Sidestep excess surcharges and hidden costs.** Many hotels have adopted the unpleasant practice of nickel-and-diming its guests with opaque surcharges. When you book a room, ask what is included in the room rate, and what is extra. Avoid dialing direct from hotel phones, which can have exorbitant rates. And don't be tempted by the room's minibar offerings: Most hotels charge through the nose for water, soda, and snacks. Finally, ask about local taxes and service charges, which can increase the cost of a room by 15% or more.
- **Carefully consider your hotel's meal plan.** You will have no choice but to buy a plan at a remote offshore resort, from which it's impossible to stroll over to a nearby restaurant. Unless you're staying out on such a rock, it makes sense to choose a **Continental Plan (CP),** which includes breakfast only, or a **European Plan (EP),** which

---

(*Tips* **Bring a Face Cloth**

All South Pacific hotels and resorts supply bath and hand towels, but many do not have face towels (or wash cloths) in their bathrooms. Just in case, bring your own.

doesn't include any meals and allows you maximum flexibility. A **Modified American Plan (MAP)** includes breakfast and one meal. I thoroughly enjoy dining out and sampling local cuisine, so I usually avoid the **American Plan (AP),** which includes three meals.

- **Book an efficiency,** or a "self-contained unit," as rooms with cooking facilities are known in this part of the world. A kitchenette allows you to shop for groceries and cook your own meals. This is a big money saver, especially for families on long stays.

- **Consider enrolling in hotel chains' "frequent-stay" programs,** which are upping the ante lately to win the loyalty of repeat customers. Frequent guests can now accumulate points or credits to earn free hotel nights, airline miles, in-room amenities, merchandise, tickets to concerts and events, and discounts on sporting facilities. Many chain hotels partner with other hotel chains, car-rental firms, airlines, and credit card companies to give consumers additional incentive to do repeat business.

LANDING THE BEST ROOM

Somebody has to get the best room in the house. It might as well be you. You can start by joining the hotel's frequent-guest program, which may make you eligible for upgrades. A hotel-branded credit card usually gives its owner "silver" or "gold" status in frequent-guest programs for free. Always ask about a corner room. They're often larger and quieter, with more windows and light, and they often cost the

same as standard rooms. When you make your reservation, ask if the hotel is renovating; if it is, request a room away from the construction. Ask about nonsmoking rooms and rooms with views. Be sure to request your choice of twin, queen- or king-size beds. If you're a light sleeper, ask for a quiet room away from vending or ice machines, elevators, restaurants, bars, and discos. Ask for a room that has been recently renovated or refurbished.

If you aren't happy with your room when you arrive, ask for another one. Most lodgings will be willing to accommodate you.

Here are some other questions to ask before you book a room:

- What's the view like? If you're a cost-conscious traveler, you might be willing to pay less for a bungalow in the garden, especially if you don't plan to spend much time in the room.
- Does the room have air conditioning or ceiling fans? An important consideration between November and March.
- What's included in the price? Your room may be moderately priced, but if you're charged for beach chairs, towels, sports equipment, and other amenities, you could end up spending more than you bargained for. Also ask if airport transfers and local hotel taxes are included in the quoted rate.
- How far is the room from the beach and other amenities, especially the bar if the hotel has nighttime entertainment?
- What is the cancellation policy?

4

Suggested Fiji Itineraries

People often ask me where they should go and what they should do in Fiji. While I cannot plan their vacations for them, I can in this chapter give some recommendations to help you personalize your own visit to Fiji. The end result will depend on what you want to see and do, how much time you have, and how much money you want to spend.

For a majority of its visitors, especially those from nearby Australia and New Zealand, Fiji is one of those "3-S" tropical destinations—as in, sun, sea, and sand. For those relaxing diversions, I think you should choose one resort in your price range and stay there for the better part of your vacation.

You could spend your entire vacation in Nadi or one of the nearby islands, but you will miss what I consider to be the best parts of Fiji. This is a country of more than 300 gorgeous islands, and—in order to get a sense of this diversity—I would try to experience more than one.

By that I do not mean island hopping in the Mamanuca or Yasawa islands off

Nadi. Those islands and their resorts are variations on the same theme, and you would waste valuable time jumping from one similar environment to another.

While Aussies and Kiwis can fly up here for a weekend, the long flights coming and going mean the rest of us burn a whole day getting to Fiji and another day returning home. Consequently, we Northern Hemisphere folk should certainly spend at least 1 week here, or more if we can.

When planning your trip, first find out both the international and domestic airlines' schedules, and try to book all domestic inter-island flights at the same time as your international flights. Do not wait until you arrive in Fiji to take care of this important chore. See the "Getting to Fiji" and "Getting Around Fiji" sections in chapter 3.

And remember the travel agent's classic advice: Never stay at the most luxurious property first. Anything after that will seem inferior, and you will likely come home disappointed.

1 Fiji's Regions in Brief

First let's review Fiji's regions and the differences among them. I present them here in the order in which they appear in this book.

Everyone starts on **Viti Levu.** Known locally as the "mainland," Viti Levu is actually Fiji's largest island. **Suva,** the capital city, lies 197km (122 miles) from Nadi airport, or about halfway around the island. With a few exceptions, Viti Levu does not have the best beaches in Fiji. Where it does have good sands, the reef offshore is more walkable than swimmable, especially at low tide. In other words, plan to look beyond Nadi and Viti Levu for good beaches and the best diving.

THE NADI AREA

Nadi International Airport is located among sugar-cane fields on Viti Levu's dry western side. To locals, the name **Nadi** applies to this area, which is the focal point of much of Fiji's tourism industry. Many tourists on package deals spend all their time here, and there is, in fact, plenty to do, including day trips out to the Mamanuca Islands. Nadi also is a convenient base from which to explore the nearby areas. Unless I have only a few days to spend in Fiji, however, I make it a stopover on the way to another destination.

A variety of hotels are concentrated between the airport and the predominately Indian-populated **Nadi Town,** whose main industries are tourism and farming. Here you will find numerous handicraft, electronics, and clothing merchants.

Fiji has some spectacular beaches, but don't expect to find any in the Nadi area. None of the airport hotels are on the beach, and even at **Denarau Island,** where the country's major resort development boasts half a dozen large beachfront hotels, coastal mangrove forests make the sand gray and the lagoon murky.

THE MAMANUCA ISLANDS

Beckoning just off Nadi, the **Mamanuca Islands** are popular among day cruisers. Off-shore resorts of various sizes and prices appeal to a broad spectrum of travelers, from swinging singles to quieter couples and families. Generally speaking, this is the driest part of Fiji, which means it is sunny most of the time. Some of the Mamanucas are flat atolls so small you can walk around them in 5 minutes. Others are hilly, grassy islands reminiscent of the Virgin Islands in the Caribbean or the Whitsundays in Australia. Since the islands lie relatively close together, most offer excursions to the others. They also are conveniently close to Nadi, so you don't have to spend much extra money or time to get there.

THE YASAWA ISLANDS

A chain of gorgeous and relatively unspoiled islands stretching to the north of the Mamanucas, the hilly **Yasawas** are blessed with the best collection of beaches in Fiji. Two versions of *The Blue Lagoon* movie were filmed here: the 1949 original, and the 1980s remake starring Brooke Shields as the castaway schoolgirl. Young backpackers turned the Yasawas into one of the country's hottest destinations, but the islands now have resorts to fit every pocketbook. The Yasawas are easy to reach from Nadi by daily high-speed ferry service, and you can visit them on **Blue Lagoon Cruises** or **Captain Cook Cruises** (p. 131).

THE CORAL COAST

The **Queen's Road** runs around the south coast of Viti Levu through the area known as the **Coral Coast.** This was Fiji's first resort area, developed even before the international airport opened in Nadi in the early 1960s. You'll find big resorts, comfortable small hotels, fire-walking Fijians, and a host of things to see and do, such as a collection of Fiji's native fauna in the excellent **Kula Eco Park.** Most of the beaches along the Coral Coast lead into lagoons that are very shallow, especially at low tide. Most visitors staying on the Coast these days are tourists on package holidays, but it's still a good choice for anyone who wants beachfront resort living while being able to conveniently explore the country.

Impressions
There is no part of Fiji which is not civilized, although bush natives prefer a more naked kind of life.

—James A. Michener, *Return to Paradise,* 1951

PACIFIC HARBOUR & BEQA ISLAND

About 48km (30 miles) west of Suva, Pacific Harbour was developed in the early 1970s as a resort complex with a golf course, private residences, shopping center, cultural center, and a seaside hotel (in other words, a real-estate development). Because this area is on the edge of Viti Levu's rain belt, the project never reached its full potential. Nevertheless, it has the country's best cultural center, most scenic golf course, and excellent deep-sea fishing. It's also the most central location for river rafting on the **Navua River,** kayaking along the coast, and diving in marvelous **Beqa Lagoon** (pronounced *Beng*-ga)—all of which make Pacific Harbour the self-anointed "Adventure Capital of Fiji."

A 30-minute boat ride off Pacific Harbour, rugged **Beqa** is best known for its surrounding lagoon. Here you'll also find **Frigate Passage,** one of the world's best surfing spots (but not for novices, since the curling breakers slam onto the reef). Beqa has a bevy of comfortable hotels.

KADAVU ISLAND

Fiji's third-largest island, **Kadavu** lies about 100km (60 miles) south of Viti Levu. It's a long skinny island whose south shore is skirted by the **Great Astrolabe Reef,** another of Fiji's top diving destinations. On the north coast is beautiful **Long Beach,** which—at several kilometers in length—lives up to its name and is one of Fiji's finest. Ashore, its lack of mongooses, iguanas, and other imported predators make it a heaven for indigenous wildlife and birds, including the endemic musk parrot, fantail, honeyeater, and whistling dove.

SUVA

The Queen's Road runs between Nadi Airport and **Suva,** Fiji's busy capital and one of the South Pacific's most cosmopolitan cities. Suva city has a population of 86,178, according to the 2007 census, but more than 300,000 are believed to live in the metropolitan area. The country's history is on display at the excellent **Fiji Museum,** Suva's top attraction. Remnants of Fiji's century as a British possession and the presence of so many Indians give downtown Suva a certain air of the colonial "Raj"—as if this were Madras or Bombay, instead of the boundary between Polynesia and Melanesia. On the other hand, Suva has modern high-rise buildings and lives at a fast pace—not surprising because Suva is in many respects the bustling economic center of the South Pacific islands and is the home of many regional organizations. The streets are filled with a melting-pot blend of Indians, Chinese, Fijians, other South Pacific islanders, "Europeans" (a term used in Fiji to mean persons with white skin, regardless of geographic origin), and individuals of mixed race.

RAKIRAKI & NORTHERN VITI LEVU

An alternative to the Queen's Road driving route to Suva, the **King's Road** runs from Lautoka through the "Sugar Belt" of northern Viti Levu, passing through the predominately Indian towns of **Ba** and **Tavua** to **Rakiraki,** a Fijian village near the island's northernmost point and site of one of the country's few remaining colonial-era hotels. Jagged green mountains lend a gorgeous backdrop to the shoreline along the Rakiraki coast. At Viti Levu's northernmost point, **Volivoli Beach** is one of the country's most beautiful. Offshore, **Nananu-I-Ra Island** beckons windsurfers and budget-minded travelers, and the nearby reefs are among Fiji's best for diving.

East of Rakiraki, the King's Road hugs deep, mountain-bounded **Viti Levu Bay,** one of the most beautiful parts of Fiji. From the head of the bay, the road then twists through the mountains, following the Wainbuka River until it emerges near the east coast at Korovou. A left turn there takes you to Natovi Wharf, where ferries depart for northern Fiji. A right turn leads to Suva. In other words, it's possible to entirely circumnavigate Viti Levu via the Queen's and King's roads.

LEVUKA & OVALAU

East of Viti Levu in the central Lomaviti Group of islands, picturesque **Ovalau** is home to the historic town of **Levuka,** which has changed little in appearance since its days as a boisterous whaling port and the first capital of a united Fiji in the 1800s. No other place in Fiji has retained its frontier facade as has this living museum. Ovalau is an incredibly beautiful island, but its lack of beaches has deterred major tourism development; consequently, it remains in a time warp and is of interest mainly to those who want a taste of the way the South Seas used to be.

Within sight of Levuka, **Wakaya Island** is the home of Fiji's top resort, the Wakaya Club, an enclave for Hollywood stars and other well-heeled folk. It's the project of Canadian David Gilmour, who also is responsible for giving us Fiji Water.

SAVUSAVU

Vanua Levu, Taveuni, and their nearby islands are known collectively as "The North" because they lie northeast of Viti Levu and comprise Fiji's Northern Province.

The northern side of **Vanua Levu,** Fiji's second-largest island, is dedicated to sugar cane, and its main town of **Labasa** is like Nadi without the tourists—and without anything for tourists to do should they go there.

But on the south shore, the little town with the singsong name **Savusavu** lies nestled in one of the region's most protected deepwater bays, making it a favorite stop for cruising yachts. Tucked behind a small islet, the town is a throwback to the old days when schooners arrived from Suva to trade cloth and rum for cattle and *copra* (coconut oil).

Southern Vanua Levu has a considerable amount of freehold land; in fact, so many of my compatriots have bought parcels that Fijians now facetiously refer to Savusavu as "Little America." One of them is motivational speaker Anthony Robbins, who owns Namale Fiji Islands Resort & Spa and holds some of his seminars there. Another is environmentalist Jean-Michel Cousteau, son of Jacques Cousteau, who has lent his name to **Jean-Michel Cousteau Fiji Islands Resort,** the finest family resort in all of the South Pacific.

Savusavu also is the homeport of **Adventure Fiji,** which uses the 42m (140-ft.) sailing schooner *Tui Tai* to make 7- and 10-day soft-adventure voyages to Taveuni, Kioa, and Rabi islands in northern Fiji, and to the Lau Group on the eastern side of the archipelago.

TAVEUNI

Fiji's "Garden Isle" of **Taveuni** is another representation of the old South Seas, a land of copra plantations and small Fijian villages tucked away in the bush. Unlike Vanua Levu, Taveuni has some of Fiji's best beaches, especially near **Matei,** at the airstrip on its northern end. Matei is one of my favorite places in Fiji. It has several small hotels and surprisingly good restaurants within walking distance of each other, yet it seems a century removed from modern life. Taveuni is the best place in Fiji to visit a waterfall in **Bouma National Heritage Park** and go for a hike on the **Lavena Coastal Walk** along its wild eastern shore. Offshore lies the **Somosomo Strait,** Fiji's most famous diving destination. Two excellent resorts inhabit lovely **Matagi** and **Qamea** islands off Taveuni's northern coast.

2 Highlights of Fiji in 2 Weeks

This whirlwind trip whisks you through the highlights of Fiji. The Queen's Road, a two-lane highway, links Nadi, the Coral Coast, and Suva, so you'll make this part of the trip overland. Bus connections are available, but we recommend renting a car in order to have maximum flexibility. Ferries run from Suva to Taveuni and Savusavu, but flying is your best bet.

Days ❶–❷: Relaxing in Nadi

Take the first day to recover from your international flight by lounging around the pool, shopping in Nadi Town, or light sightseeing. Spend Day 2 on land-based excursions, such as to the late Raymond Burr's **Garden of the Sleeping Giant** (p. 104); **Lautoka,** Fiji's second-largest city (p. 104); and **Viseisei Village,** the country's oldest native Fijian village (p. 104). Finish off with some more shopping and dinner in Nadi.

Days ❸–❹: Exploring the Coral Coast ⟨★

Get up early and drive south to the Coral Coast, on the southern coast of Viti Levu, Fiji's "mainland." On the way stop at the **Momi Guns** (p. 104) for a look at the World War II battery and a gorgeous view across Nadi Bay; the **Kalevu South Pacific Cultural Centre** (p. 153) for a glimpse into Fijian culture; and at **Sigatoka Sand Dunes National Park** (p. 153) for an example of its more interesting geology. The next day, visit **Kula Eco Park** (p. 154) to meet Fiji's interesting wildlife, and hike to a waterfall with **Adventures in Paradise Fiji** (p. 154). Catch an evening show featuring the "fire walkers" from Beqa Island (p. 162).

Day ❺: Rafting on the Navua River ⟨★★★

One of our favorite Fiji excursions is on the **Navua River,** which carves a dramatic gorge through Viti Levu's mountainous interior before spilling into a flood plain west of Suva. The usual trip takes you upriver on a fast speedboat but brings you back on a *bilibili* (bamboo raft). Alternately, you can ride an inflatable boat over white waters with the excellent **Rivers Fiji** (p. 166).

Day ❻: Suva ⟨★

On the way to Suva, Fiji's humid capital city, stop in Pacific Harbour for a presentation of native arts, crafts, and traditions at the **Arts Village,** the country's best cultural center (p. 165). Once in Suva, take a walking tour of downtown, ending at the **Fiji Museum** (p. 182). Be sure to have a Fijian lunch at the **Old Mill Cottage** (p. 194) next to the U.S. Embassy.

Day ❼: A Trip Back in Time to Levuka

A day trip from Suva to **Levuka** always highlights a visit to Fiji. The country's original capital, the old town has retained its 19th-century appearance, and the backdrop of sheer cliffs makes it one of the South Pacific's most beautiful towns. Get **Ovalau Watersports** (p. 207) to

Fiji in 2 Weeks

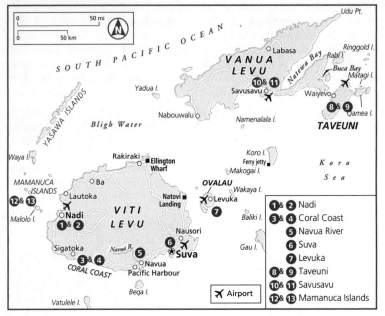

organize a morning walking tour and an afternoon excursion to Ovalau. Either catch the late afternoon flight back to Suva or plan an overnight at the charming **Levuka Homestay** (p. 211).

Days ⑧–⑨: Exploring Taveuni 𝒦𝒦𝒦
If you slept on Ovalau, take the early morning Air Fiji flight back to Nausori Airport near Suva. You can connect from there to **Taveuni,** Fiji's third-largest island. Famous for world-class diving on the nearby **Great White Wall** and its **Rainbow Reef,** Taveuni also is a hiker's paradise. Stay near the airport, from where it's an easy trip to the waterfalls in **Bouma National Heritage Park** and the scenic **Lavena Coastal Walk** (p. 233). The next day hike to the mountaintop **Lake Tagimaucia,** where you might see the rare flower of the same name.

Days ⑩–⑪: Savusavu: "Little America" 𝒦𝒦𝒦
A morning flight will land you at **Savusavu,** on Fiji's second-largest island,

Vanua Levu. Although it is rapidly developing, the town still recalls its days as a 19th-century copra port. Stroll along the harbor, have lunch at the **Bula-Re Cafe** (p. 227), and visit the famous **Savusavu Hot Springs** (p. 218), where Fijians still cook their evening meals. Stop by **Rock 'n Downunder Divers** (p. 216) to rent a kayak or arrange an excursion to a Fijian village. If you're traveling with children, stay at **Jean-Michel Cousteau Fiji Islands Resort** (p. 222), one of the South Pacific's top family resorts.

Days ⑫–⑬: An Island Retreat
Spending at least 1 night on a small island in the Mamanucas or Yasawas is almost an essential ingredient of any trip to Fiji, whether it's in one of Fiji's first overwater bungalows at **Likuliku Lagoon Resort** (p. 136), at the raucous **Beachcomber Island Resort** (p. 139), the family-oriented **Plantation Island Resort** (p. 135), a quiet couples-only hideaway like **Matamanoa Island Resort** (p. 138), the

charming **Navutu Stars Resort** in the Yasawas, or one of the dormitories dotting the islands. They all have much better beaches than you'll find on Viti Levu, and the stopover will give you a chance to rest up for your trip home.

Day ⓮: Last-Minute Shopping in Nadi

If your homeward flight departs late at night, you can stay in the islands for an extra day. Otherwise spend your last day catching up on shopping or any excursions you might have missed in and around Nadi.

3 Around Viti Levu in 1 Week

This trip will expose you to Fiji's diversity by taking you all the way around Viti Levu from Nadi to Coral Coast, Pacific Harbour, Suva, and Rakiraki. The most convenient means of traveling the island is by car, which allows maximum flexibility and lets you get off the beaten path. You can also ride the **Feejee Experience** (p. 197), a backpacker-oriented bus that circles the island daily with stops at attractions and inexpensive accommodations. Public buses also circle Viti Levu via the Queen's and King's roads, but you will have to change buses in Suva and Lautoka.

Days ❶–❷: Exploring the Coral Coast 👁

From Nadi drive south to the Coral Coast, stopping at the **Momi Guns** for a look at the World War II battery and a gorgeous view across Nadi Bay; the **Kalevu South Pacific Cultural Centre** (p. 153) for a glimpse into Fijian culture; and at **Sigatoka Sand Dunes National Park** (p. 153) for an example of its more interesting geology. On Day 2 visit **Kula Eco Park** (p. 154) to meet Fiji's interesting wildlife, and hike to a waterfall with **Adventures in Paradise Fiji** (p. 154). Catch an evening show featuring the "fire walkers" from Beqa Island (p. 162).

Days ❸–❹: Rafting the Navua River 👁👁👁

Pacific Harbour is the most convenient base from which to go rafting on the **Navua River,** either on a bilibili or over white waters in the gorges with the excellent **Rivers Fiji** (p. 166). On Day 4 visit the country's best cultural center at the **Arts Village** (p. 165), and go flying through a rainforest canopy with **ZIP Fiji** (p. 166).

Day ❺: Strolling Around Suva 👁

Once in Suva, take a walking tour of downtown, ending at the excellent **Fiji Museum** (p. 182). The lunchtime Fijian fare at the **Old Mill Cottage,** next to the U.S. Embassy (p. 194), is among the country's best.

Days ❻–❼: Rakiraki

You'll spend at least half of Day 6 driving or riding via the King's Road from Suva to Rakiraki, on the northern tip of Viti Levu. The road follows the **Wainbuka River** through the mountains and emerges on the north shore at picturesque **Viti Levu Bay.** Once in Rakiraki spend the afternoon exploring nearby **Vaileka,** the area's predominately Indian commercial center. Spend the afternoon at **Volivoli Beach,** one of Fiji's best and home to the inexpensive **Volivoli Beach Resort** (p. 201). Rakiraki itself is a small Fijian village where you can stay at the **Tanoa Rakiraki Hotel** (p. 200), Fiji's last remaining colonial-era accommodations. On Day 7 head back to Nadi. The central mountains will be off to your left as you pass through the **Yaqara Cattle Ranch,** home of the famous Fiji Water, and the predominately Indian towns of **Tavua** and **Ba.** See chapter 11.

Viti Levu in 1 Week

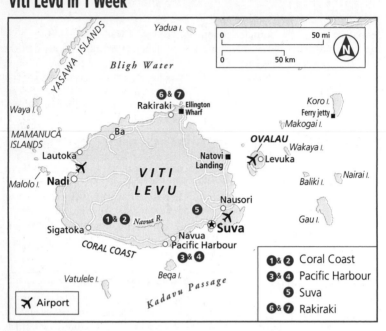

Bligh Water

YASAWA ISLANDS

Yadua I.

0 — 50 mi
0 — 50 km

Koro I.
Ferry jetty
Makogai I.

Waya I.

Rakiraki — Ellington Wharf **6** & **7**

MAMANUCA ISLANDS

Ba

OVALAU
Wakaya I.
Levuka

Lautoka

Natovi Landing

Malolo I. **Nadi**

*V I T I
L E V U*

Nairai I.
Baliki I.

Nausori

Sigatoka

5

Gau I.

1 & **2** *Navua R.*

Navua
Pacific Harbour

★ **Suva**

CORAL COAST

3 & **4**

Vatulele I.

Beqa I.

Kadavu Passage

✈ **Airport**

1 & **2** Coral Coast
3 & **4** Pacific Harbour
5 Suva
6 & **7** Rakiraki

4 Savusavu & Taveuni in 1 Week

Venturing to Savusavu and Taveuni islands in northern Fiji means paying for additional airfares, but this is my favorite part of the country. Children will love it up here, too, particularly at Savusavu's **Jean-Michel Cousteau Fiji Islands Resort** (p. 222), the best Fiji has to offer for children. Both Savusavu and Taveuni have other fine resorts and hotels, but tourism is minor in "The North," which is much more reminiscent of the Old South Seas than is Viti Levu. The country's best diving and snorkeling is up here, but this also is a fine place to explore the great outdoors ashore. *Note:* Remember when planning that Air Fiji flies between Savusavu and Taveuni, but Pacific Sun does not.

Day ❶: Exploring Savusavu
Take a morning flight from Nadi to Savusavu's little airstrip, on the southern side of Vanua Levu. Check in or leave your bags at your hotel and spend the rest of the morning and early afternoon seeing the scenery, examining the **hot springs,** and shopping for the orb of your dreams at **J. Hunter Pearls** (p. 221) in Savusavu town.

Day ❷: Waisali Rainforest Reserve
While most Fiji activities are at or near the seaside, spend this day in the jungly interior at **Waisali Rainforest Reserve** (p. 219), a national forest with a waterfall up in Vanua Levu's central mountains.

Day ❸: Boat Tour of Savusavu Bay
The bay at Savusavu is so large the U.S. navy made plans to hide the Pacific fleet there in case of a hurricane. Spend Day 3 exploring it on a boat tour organized by **Rock 'n Downunder Divers** (p. 219).

Day ❹: Straddling the 180° Meridian
Catch the morning Air Fiji flight to **Matei,** on the northern end of Taveuni. After settling into your hotel, hire a taxi and ride

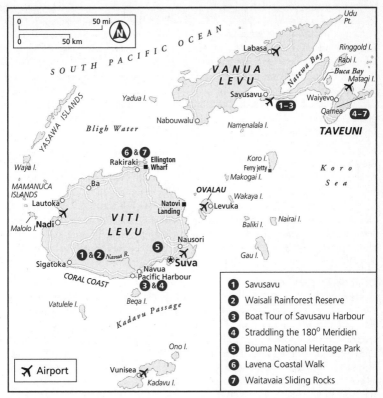

0   50 mi
0   50 km

SOUTH PACIFIC OCEAN

Udu Pt.

Labasa ✈

VANUA LEVU

Ringgold I.
Rabi I.
Buca Bay
Matagi I.

Natewa Bay

Yadua I.

Savusavu ✈
1–3

Waiyevo ✈

Qamea **4–7**

Nabouwalu

Namenalala I.

TAVEUNI

Bligh Water

YASAWA ISLANDS

Waya I.

MAMANUCA ISLANDS

Malolo I.

Lautoka ✈

Nadi ✈

Ba

Rakiraki **6 & 7**
Ellington Wharf

VITI LEVU

Natovi Landing

OVALAU
✈ Levuka

Nausori

5

Navua R. **1 & 2**

Sigatoka

Navua
Pacific Harbour **3 & 4**

✈ **Suva**

CORAL COAST

Vatulele I.

Beqa I.

Kadavu Passage

Koro I.
Ferry jetty
Makogai I.

Wakaya I.

Baliki I.

Nairai I.

Gau I.

Koro Sea

Ono I.

Vunisea

Kadavu I.

✈ **Airport**

1   Savusavu
2   Waisali Rainforest Reserve
3   Boat Tour of Savusavu Harbour
4   Straddling the 180° Meridien
5   Bouma National Heritage Park
6   Lavena Coastal Walk
7   Waitavaia Sliding Rocks

through **Somosomo** and **Waiyevo** villages to **Wairiki**, where the **180th meridian** passes through Fiji (p. 233). Although the international date line technically detours from the 180° longitude line to bypass Fiji, you can stand under a sign at the meridian, one foot in today, the other in "yesterday." On the way back, stop for a swim at **Prince Charles Beach**, which holds a place among Fiji's best (p. 236).

Day 5: Bouma National Heritage Park

Spend most of today in **Bouma National Heritage Park** (p. 233), Fiji's best national park. You will not need a guide for the short walk up to Bouma Falls, but you will on the longer **Vidawa Rainforest Walk,** which has great views of the islands

off northern Taveuni. Retire for a sunset drink at **Tramontu Bar & Grill,** on a clifftop high above the Somosomo Strait (p. 242).

Day 6: Lavena Coastal Walk

Plan on more hiking today, this time along the beautiful **Lavena Coastal Walk** on Taveuni's wild east coast. Be prepared to swim the last few yards to reach **Wainibau Falls.** If this is a Friday night, graze the buffet of Fijian foods at **Vunibokoi Restaurant** (p. 242).

Day 7: Waitavaia Sliding Rocks

You'll need to catch the afternoon flight back to Nadi, but can spend the morning cascading down the **Waitavaia Sliding Rocks** (p. 236) near Waiyevo village.

5 Fiji with a Family

Although it's not in the same league as Florida or other places with attractions like Disney World, Fiji is a fine place for families with children. My cousin Virginia Silverman and her then 9-year-old daughter, Eve, joined me for 10 days in Savusavu and Taveuni during my most recent trip, and Eve had a blast while learning a lot in the process (read their reports in chapter 13). Many Australian and New Zealand families take their annual holidays in Fiji, usually at one resort equipped with a children's program (see "The Best Family Resorts," in chapter 1). Or you can take your youngsters on the following 2-week educational tour around Fiji.

Day ❶: Recovering in Nadi

Spend your first day in Nadi recovering from your flight and getting acclimated to the heat and humidity. Kids will love frolicking in the pools at the **Radisson Resort Fiji Denarau Island** (p. 114) or the less expensive **Raffle's Gateway Hotel** opposite the airport (p. 118).

Days ❷–❸: Coral Coast: Culture & Wildlife 𝒜𝒜

On Day 2 move to the Coral Coast, stopping on the way at the **Kalevu South Pacific Cultural Centre** (p. 153) for a demonstration of traditional Fijian ways. Across the Queen's Road, **Shangri-La's Fijian Resort** (p. 155) is well equipped for families, but we prefer the more convenient **Outrigger on the Lagoon Fiji** (p. 156), which has another fine swimming pool complex. On Day 3 go across the road to **Kula Eco Park** (p. 154), where the kids can touch tame iguanas and admire Fiji birds and other wildlife. It's a bit of a hike, but you can take them to a Fijian village and either a cave or waterfall with **Adventures in Paradise Fiji** (p. 154). At night they will be mesmerized by a Fijian *meke* dance, especially if a firewalking demonstration is part of it.

Days ❹–❺: Pacific Harbour: River Rafting & Jungle Canopy Rides 𝒜

Moving on to Pacific Harbour, take the kids to the **Arts Village Cultural Centre** (p. 165), where they can ride a boat while learning about Fijian culture. That afternoon they can glide through a rainforest

canopy with **ZIP Fiji** (p. 166). You'll need all of Day 5 to take them on a bili-bili rafting trip on the Navua River with **Discover Fiji Tours** (p. 166). (*Note:* Kids must be 5 or over to go river rafting or canopy riding.) With a fine pool and beach, the **Pearl South Pacific** (p. 167) is aimed primarily at couples, but is also a lodging option for families.

Day ❻: Suva: The Fiji Museum 𝒜𝒜𝒜

Most children I know aren't particularly excited to tour new cities, but Fiji's capital does have the excellent **Fiji Museum** (p. 182), where kids can gape at actual war clubs the ancients used in real-life combat.

Days ❼–❾: Taveuni: Waterfalls & Rock Slides 𝒜𝒜𝒜

Take the morning flight from Nausori airport to Taveuni, where several outdoor adventures await. Spend the first afternoon cascading down the **Waitavaia Sliding Rocks** (p. 236), where your kids may pick up a few slight bruises but will have a grand time. On the morning of Day 8 take them to **Bouma National Heritage Park** (p. 233), where a short walk leads to a swimming hole beneath Bouma Falls. Fijian children love it here, so yours could make some local friends. The park also has the guided **Vidawa Rainforest Walk,** which leads to historic hill fortifications and great views. On Day 9, take them on a horseback riding excursion at **Maravu Plantation Beach Resort & Spa** (p. 238).

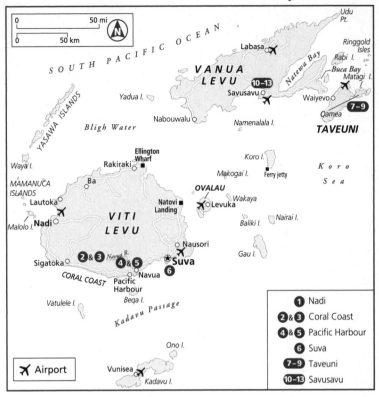

Legend:
1. Nadi
2. & 3. Coral Coast
4. & 5. Pacific Harbour
6. Suva
7.–9. Taveuni
10.–13. Savusavu

Days 10–13: Savusavu: Environmental Education ✿✿✿

On the morning of Day 10 take a 20-minute flight to Savusavu, and—assuming your broker agrees—check into **Jean-Michel Cousteau Fiji Islands Resort** (p. 222), whose Bula Club is the finest children's program in the South Pacific islands. It's both educational and fun for the youngsters, who are almost guaranteed to become friends with their assigned Fijian "buddy." Off campus, take them to **Waisali Rainforest Reserve** (p. 219), where gravel pathways lead to a waterfall.

Day 14: Back to Nadi

Flights back to Australia and New Zealand depart Nadi during the day, but those for North America and Europe leave just before midnight. Accordingly, fly back to Nadi today and spend your spare time lounging at a resort pool (see "Day 1," above).

6 Cruising in Fiji

Large cruise ships frequently visit Suva and Lautoka, usually from Sydney, Australia, but the country has three fine small-vessel operations based here all the time. **Captain Cook Cruises** sails in the Mamanuca and Yasawa islands, while my favorite, the excellent **Blue Lagoon Cruises,** primarily plies the Yasawas. See "Cruising Through the Islands," in chapter 6. Based at Savusavu, **Active Fiji** (p. 220) sends the luxurious

Cruising in Fiji

schooner *Tui Tai* on soft-adventure cruises through the seldom-explored islands of northern Fiji. This 2-week itinerary allows you to make cruises on both sides of the country, but I based it on their usual operations. Needless to say, check their sailing schedules to see when they're going during the time you want to be here.

Day **1**: Savusavu

Arrive at Nadi and take a flight to **Active Fiji's** homeport in Savusavu (p. 220). Kill the morning shopping for black pearls.

Days **2–8**: Adventure Cruise on the *Tui Tai* ✹✹✹

The typical 1-week cruise on the 42m (140-ft.) schooner *Tui Tai* will take you to Taveuni for a visit to **Bouma Falls** (p. 220), and then to the seldom visited islands of Kioa and Rabi. The boat carries dive equipment, snorkeling gear, and kayaks for exploring the reefs and shoreline.

Days **9–10**: Relaxing in the Mamanuca Islands

After the *Tui Tai* cruise, fly back to Nadi and catch a ferry from Denarau Island to a resort in the Mamanuca Islands (see chapter 6), where you can relax for 2 days prior to being picked up by Blue Lagoon Cruises. I normally would suggest finishing your visit in an overwater bungalow at **Likuliku Lagoon Resort** (p. 136), but Blue Lagoon Cruises will pick you up there at the start but not at the end of your voyage; plan for your own transportation if you stay at the resort.

Days ⓫–⓭: A Blue Lagoon Cruise ☆☆☆

Blue Lagoon's 3-night **Gold Club Cruise** will take you through the gorgeous Yasawa Islands, stopping during the day for snorkeling, beach picnics, and visits to Fijian villages. This is the best way to see several of the islands in a minimum amount of time.

Day ⓮: Departing from Nadi

Blue Lagoon Cruises will drop you at Lautoka in time to catch a flight back to Australia or New Zealand. The rest of us can kill the wait for our night flight by shopping in Nadi Town (p. 100) or lounging by the pool at **Raffle's Gateway Hotel** opposite the airport (p. 118).

7 Diving in Fiji

One could spend months in Fiji diving all its marvelous sites, and you will still miss a few. Not being a diver myself, I cannot speak from personal experience, but I've talked to hundreds of divers—and traveled with two of them—so I have a reasonably good idea of where you will find the best waters. This 2-week itinerary starts out with an exhilarating shark dive off Pacific Harbour and ends at the famous White Wall in the Somosomo Strait off Taveuni. *Note:* I built in the 12 hours or more you will need between diving and flying.

Day ❶: Nadi to Pacific Harbour

After arriving at Nadi, drive 2½ hours around the Coral Coast to Pacific Harbour. Kill the afternoon visiting the **Arts Village Cultural Centre** (p. 165) or flying through the jungle canopy with **ZIP Fiji** (p. 166).

Days ❷–❸: Shark Diving & the Beqa Lagoon ☆☆☆

Day 2 will test your mettle right away during a shark dive off Pacific Harbour with **Beqa Adventure Divers** (p. 167), whose masters will draw the attention of tiger, bull, and other sharks by feeding them, while you watch from behind a coral wall. Day 3 is spent out in the **Beqa Lagoon,** perhaps seeing the colorful walls of **Frigate Passage.** See chapter 8.

Days ❹–❼: The Great Astrolabe Reef

Day 4 is devoted to driving from Pacific Harbour to Suva's Nausori Airport, flying to Vunisea on **Kadavu Island,** and taking a boat to your new dive base from which to explore the **Great Astrolabe Reef,** skirting Kadavu's eastern and southern coasts. The rustic, eco-friendly **Matava—The Astrolabe Hideaway** (p. 176) is the closest resort to the so-called Manta Pass, which draws Fiji's largest congregation of manta rays. That will take Day 5, while days 6 and 7 can be spent diving the colorful passage between Kadavu and nearby Ono Island. See chapter 9.

Days ❽–⓭: The Somosomo Strait ☆☆☆

Assuming Air Fiji is punctual on Day 8, fly back to Nausori Airport at midday and connect from there to Taveuni. I have more fun staying near the airstrip at Matei, but the modest **Garden Island Resort** (p. 239) is nearest the **Great White Wall** and **Rainbow Reef,** which are on the reefs out in the Somosomo Strait. Spend the next few days here exploring Fiji's best collection of colorful soft corals. See chapter 14.

Day ⓮: Back to Nadi & Home

Your last day will be spent flying back to Nadi and connecting to your flight back home.

Diving in Fiji

1	Nadi–Pacific Harbour
2 & 3	Shark Diving & the Beqa Lagoon
4–7	Great Astrolabe Reef
8–13	Somosomo Strait

X Airport

The Nadi Area

You won't see much of the real Fiji if you spend your entire vacation in Nadi, but this area has more to keep you busy than any other part of the country. That's because the international airport and a dry climate combine to make it the country's main tourist center, with the multitude of activities that entails. The lagoon off Nadi is usually murky from mangrove forests and runoff coming from the area's sugar-cane fields, however, so this is not the ideal place in Fiji for a beach vacation. On the other hand, it is the most convenient base from which to explore the rest of the country, and a vacation here means you don't have to spend extra money to get elsewhere in Fiji.

Despite the cloudy waters, many visitors spend their entire holidays on pancake-flat **Denarau Island,** the country's largest tourist development with several resorts, a golf-and-tennis center, and a shopping complex at **Port Denarau,** the marina from whence shuttles and cruises depart to the Mamanuca and Yasawa islands. In a matter of seconds, the short bridge from the mainland onto Denarau whisks you from the Third World into the First World.

By "Nadi" the locals mean the entire area around the international airport. It's the fastest-growing part of Fiji. New homes, stores, shopping centers, and office buildings are popping up along the 9km (5½ miles) of traffic-heavy Queen's Road between the airport and **Nadi Town,** a farming community stocked with handicraft, souvenir, and other stores as well as some of the country's better restaurants.

Rather than fight for parking spaces in town, many locals now do their shopping in **Namaka,** a rapidly developing commercial strip between Nadi Town and the airport. **Martintar,** another Queen's Road suburb, has a number of hotels, restaurants, and bars. From Martintar, a paved road leads to **Wailoaloa Beach,** a 1.5km-long (1-mile) stretch of grayish sand, where a development known as **Newtown Beach** has several inexpensive hotels and hostels.

From Nadi, it's an easy 33km (20-mile) side trip to **Lautoka,** Fiji's second-largest city. Lautoka offers a genteel contrast to tourist-oriented Nadi Town.

1 Getting Around Nadi

All of Fiji's major international and local **car-rental** firms have offices in the international arrival concourse of Nadi International Airport. See "Getting Around Fiji," in chapter 3.

Westside Motorbike Rentals (© **672 6402;** www.motorbikerentalsfiji.com) in Namaka, Martintar, Denarau Island, and Sigatoka rents scooters for F$79 (US$51/£26) including helmets and third-party insurance. However, in my opinion, riding scooters in Fiji is not for novices.

Nadi Bay

Denarau Island **5**
Garden of the Sleeping Giant **4**
Lautoka **1**
Momi Battery Historical Park **7**
Nadi Town **6**
Viseisei Village **3**
Vuda Point **2**

Taxis gather outside the arrival concourse at the airport and are stationed at the larger hotels. Ask the reception desk to call one, or contact **Taxi 2000** (© **672 1350**), one of the more reliable companies whose cabs are radio dispatched. The aggressive drivers will find you in Nadi Town. See "Getting Around Fiji" in chapter 3 for a taxi fare chart.

I often take the **local buses** that ply the Queen's Road between the markets in Nadi Town and Lautoka frequently during daylight, every 30 minutes after dark. Tell the driver where you're going; he'll tell you how much to pay when you board. Fares vary according to the length of the trip. No more than F65¢ (US42¢/22p) will take you anywhere between the airport and Nadi Town.

Westbus (© **672 2917**) links the Nadi Town market to Denarau Island, where you can catch the free **Bula Bus** shuttle around the island from 7am to 11pm daily.

FAST FACTS: Nadi

The following facts apply specifically to Nadi and Lautoka. For more information, see "Fast Facts: Fiji" in appendix A.

Bookstores The best bookstore is in the departures area of Nadi International Airport; it's open 24/7. Hotel boutiques are also good places to buy magazines and books. Bookshops in town are actually stationery stores.

Camera & Film **Caines Photofast** (© **670 1608**) has a film and 1-hour processing shop on Queen's Road in Nadi Town, and you can also download and print your digital photos there. Most of the hotel gift shops also sell film.

Currency Exchange **ANZ Bank, Westpac Bank,** and **Colonial National Bank** have offices with cash machines in Namaka and on the Queen's Road in Nadi Town. ANZ and Westpac have ATMs at the Port Denarau marina on Denarau Island, and ANZ's airport office is open 24 hours a day. You'll get a better rate for currency and traveler's checks at the **GlobalEX** offices at the airport and on the Queen's Road in Nadi Town.

Drugstores There are drugstores on the Queen's Road in Nadi Town, but **Budget Pharmacy** (© **670 0064**) is the most well-stocked. It has a branch in Namaka (© **672 2533**), and it operates **Denarau Pharmacy** (© **675 0780**) in the Port Denarau complex.

Emergencies & Police The emergency phone number for **police** is © **917**. Dial © **911** for **fire** and **ambulance.** The Fiji **police** have stations at Nadi Town (© **670 0222**) and at the airport terminal (© **672 2222**).

Eyeglasses For optical needs, try **Eyesite,** on the Queen's Road in Nadi Town (© **670 7178**).

Healthcare The government-operated **Lautoka Hospital** (© **666 3337**) is the region's main facility. There is a **government medical clinic** (© **670 0362**) in Nadi Town. **Dr. Ram Raju,** 2 Lodhia St., Nadi Town (© **670 0240** or 976333 mobile), has treated many visitors, including me. The private **Namaka Medical Center** (© **672 2228**) is open 24 hours a day and has doctors on call. Ask your hotel staff to recommend a **dentist** in private practice.

Internet Access All hotels and hostels have computers for their guests to access the Internet. Internet kiosks are in the Nadi Airport terminal, and several cyber-cafes are on the Queen's Road in Nadi Town. On Denarau Island, the **Esquires** (© 675 0989), in front of the Sheraton Denarau Villas, has free wireless access for its customers. Fiji's major provider, **Connect Internet Services** (© 670 7359) has an office in Namaka where you can sign up for temporary dial-up access (see "Staying Connected" in chapter 3).

Laundry & Dry Cleaning **Flagstaff Laundry & Dry Cleaning** (© 672 2161), on Northern Press Road in Martintar, has 1-day laundry and dry-cleaning service.

Mail The **Nadi Town post office,** on Hospital Road near the south end of the market, is open Monday to Friday 8am to 4pm, Saturday 8am to noon. It has a well-stocked stationery store in the lobby. A small airport branch is across the main entry road from the terminal (go through the gates and turn left). It is open Monday to Friday 8am to 4pm, Saturday 8am to noon.

Visitor Information You can get brochures and other information from the tour companies in the arrivals concourse at Nadi Airport. Other so-called Tourist Information Centres are really travel agents or tour operators.

Water The tap water is safe to drink.

2 Exploring the Nadi Area

You can easily waste time driving around this area without seeing much of anything, so I recommend a half-day guided sightseeing tour with a reputable company. Round-trip bus transportation from Nadi area hotels is included in the price of the tours and outings; that is, a bus will pick you up within 30 minutes or so of the scheduled departure time for Nadi area trips, 1 hour or more for those on the Coral Coast. Children 11 and under years of age pay half fare on most activities. Most hotel and hostel activity desks, or the reception-desk staffs, will make reservations or arrangements for all activities.

NADI TOWN

Along the banks of the muddy Nadi River, the actual town of Nadi earns its livelihood by selling supplies to sugar-cane farmers and souvenirs to tourists. The Queen's Road passes through town as **Main Street,** an 8-block-long commercial strip lined with stores of every description. The biggest and best are on the north end of town near the river (see "Shopping in Nadi," p. 110). Many shop owners will beckon you to come into their stores and have a look. By contrast, the teeming **Nadi Market,** on Hospital Road inland, has a multitude of vendors purveying fresh local produce. It's not as large as the markets in Suva and Lautoka, but it's a fascinating glimpse into how Fijians—and Third World people in general, for that matter—buy their fruits and vegetables.

The town's other prime attraction is the **Sri Siva Subrahmaniya Swami Temple** (© 670 0016), on the south end of Main Street; the local Hindu community erected it in 1994. Artisans from India carved the images of the Hindu gods adorning the colorful building, itself dedicated to Lord Muruga, the mythical general said to have defeated evil. The temple is open daily from 8am to 5pm. Admission is F$3.50

The Nadi Area

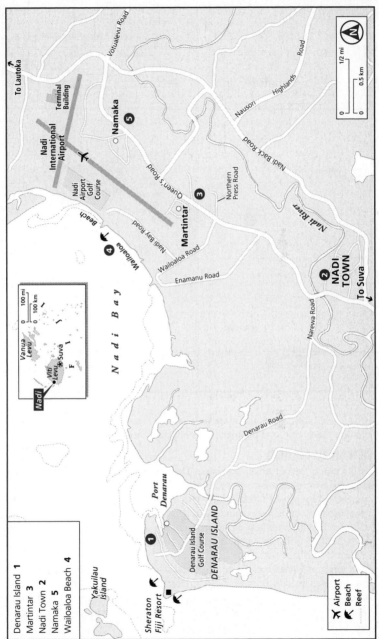

Denarau Island **1**
Martintar **3**
Nadi Town **2**
Namaka **5**
Wailoaloa Beach **4**

To Lautoka

Terminal Building

Namaka **5**

Nadi International Airport

Nadi Airport Golf Course

Voualevu Road

Nausori Highlands Road

Nadi Back Road

Queen's Road

Martintar **3**

Northern Press Road

Wailoaloa Beach

Nadi Bay Road

Wailoaloa Road

Enamanu Road

Nadi River

NADI TOWN **2**

To Suva

Narewa Road

N a d i   B a y

Vanua Levu

Viti Levu ★ Suva

FIJI

Nadi

100 mi
100 km

Denarau Road

Port Denarau

Denarau Island Golf Course

DENARAU ISLAND

1

Yakuilau Island

Sheraton Fiji Resort

✈ Airport
🏖 Beach
...... Reef

1/2 mi
0.5 km

Nadi Town

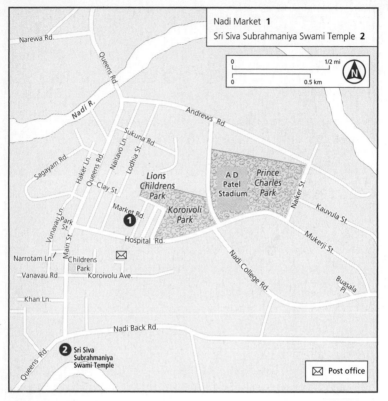

Nadi Market **1**
Sri Siva Subrahmaniya Swami Temple **2**

⊠ Post office

(US$2.30/£1.20). *Note:* You must wear modest dress and remove your shoes when entering the temple, and photography is not permitted inside.

DENARAU ISLAND

Only a muddy mangrove creek separates **Denarau Island,** about 7km (4⅓ miles) west of Nadi Town, from the mainland. Denarau is home to Fiji's largest real estate development, a huge project officially known in its entirety as **Denarau Island Resort Fiji** (www.denarau.com). To my mind—and that of many local folks—it's a generic tropical resort development bearing little resemblance to the rest of Fiji. It includes several resort hotels, a 150-unit timeshare complex, and numerous homes and condos (see "Where to Stay in Nadi," below).

As much as Denarau could be in Hawaii, Florida, or Australia's Gold Coast, it is still the place for play in Nadi. All the resorts have watersports and other activities, which both their guests and outsiders can use, and the **Denarau Golf & Racquet Club** has an 18-hole golf course as well as top-flight tennis courts (see "Boating, Golf, Hiking & Other Outdoor Activities," below).

Except for those paying extra to fly, everyone else heading out to the islands departs from **Port Denarau,** a modern shopping center and marina where most of the area's

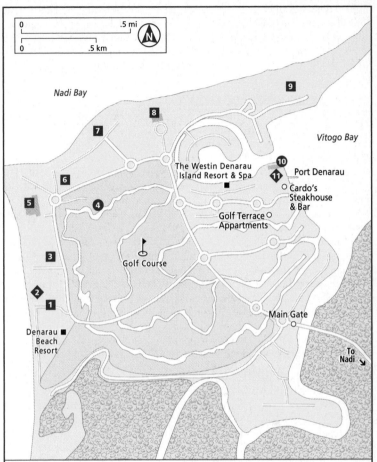

Nadi Bay

Vitogo Bay

The Westin Denarau
Island Resort & Spa

Port Denarau

Cardo's
Steakhouse
& Bar

Golf Terrace
Appartments

Golf Course

Main Gate

To
Nadi

Denarau
Beach
Resort

ATTRACTIONS ●
Port Denarau **10**
Denarau Golf & Racquet Club **4**

DINING ◆
Cardo's Steakhouse &
  Cocktail Bar **11**
Hard Rock Cafe **11**
Indigo **11**
Seafront Restaurant **2**

ACCOMMODATIONS ■
Fiji Beach Resort & Spa Managed
  by Hilton **9**
Radisson Resort Denarau Island **3**
Sheraton Denarau Villas **6**
Sheraton Fiji Resort **5**
Sofitel Fiji Resort & Spa **8**
Westin Denarau Island
  Resort & Spa **7**
WorldMark Denarau Island Fiji **1**

shuttle boats and cruises are based (see chapter 6). The shopping center has a number of retail outlets, two banks (with ATMs) and a money exchange, an ice-cream parlor, a Budget Rent A Car office, and several restaurants, including Fiji's best Indian restaurants and its first Hard Rock Cafe (see "Where to Dine in Nadi," below).

Anyone can ride the free **Bula Bus,** which runs around the island from 7am to 11pm daily.

ATTRACTIONS NORTH OF NADI

My favorite half-day tour goes north of Nadi Airport to the **Garden of the Sleeping Giant** *. In 1977, the late Raymond Burr, star of TV's *Perry Mason* and *Ironside,* started this lovely, 20-hectare (50-acre) orchid range north of the airport to house his private collection of tropical orchids (he once also owned Naitoba, a small island in the Lau Group). It sits at the base of "Sleeping Giant Mountain," whose profile forms the outline of a man fast asleep. There's much more here than orchids, however, and the guides will describe a variety of local plants and their uses.

You can get here on your own by rental car or taxi. Look for the sign at Wailoko Road off the Queen's Road between Nadi and Lautoka. It's open Monday to Saturday from 9am to 5pm. Entrance fees are F$12 (US$7.80/£4) for adults, F$6 (US$3.90/ £2) for children, including guided tour and a fruit drink.

From there the tour stops at historic **Viseisei Village,** on the Queen's Road about halfway between Nadi and Lautoka. One legend says that the first Fijians settled here. Today it's a typical, fairly prosperous Fijian village, with some modern houses and some shacks of concrete block and tin, a small handicraft shop, and the usual road humps that bring traffic to a crawl.

Coral Sun Fiji (© **672 3105;** www.coralsunfiji.com) charges about F$88 (US$57/ £29) for its "Orchids and Village" tour.

AN ATTRACTION SOUTH OF NADI

Installed during World War II to protect the main pass through the Great Sea Reef, the concrete bunkers and naval guns in **Momi Battery Historical Park** are now under the care of the National Trust of Fiji (© **330 1807**), which operates the country's national parks and historical sites. The drive to the park is worth it just for the splendid view over the lagoon and western coast of Viti Levu. It's open daily from 9am to 5pm. Admission is F$3 (US$1.90/£1) for adults, F$1 (US65¢/33p) for students. Turn west off the Queen's Road 16km (10 miles) south of Nadi Town toward **Momi Bay.** The road toward the coast is paved, since it leads to an on-again, off-again Marriott hotel project being developed on Momi Bay. Turn right at the signpost beside the school and follow a rough dirt track another 4km (2½ miles) to the park. *Note:* The park does not have toilets or drinking water.

LAUTOKA

Fiji's second-largest city, pleasant **Lautoka** has broad avenues, green parks, and a row of towering royal palms marching along the middle of **Vitogo Parade,** the main drag running from the harbor along the eastern side of downtown.

Tourism may rule Nadi, but sugar is king in Lautoka. The **Fiji Sugar Corporation**'s huge mill was built in 1903 and is one of the largest crushing operations in the Southern Hemisphere. At the industrial port you'll also see a mountain of wood chips ready for export; the chips are a prime product of the country's pine plantations.

Fun Fact The Dreaded Degei

Viseisei village between Nadi and Lautoka reputedly is where the great canoe *Kaunitoni* came out of the west and deposited the first Fijians some 3,000 years ago. From there, as the legend goes, they dispersed all over the islands. The yarn is encouraged by the local district name Vuda, which means "our origin" in Fijian, and Viseisei, which means "to scatter."

Although it's clear today that the Fijians did indeed migrate from the west, no one knows for sure whether they landed first at Viseisei; like all Pacific Islanders, the Fijians had no written language until the missionaries arrived in the mid–19th century.

The most common story has the great chiefs Lutunasobasoba and Degei arriving in the *Kaunitoni* on the northwest coast of Viti Levu. From there they moved inland along the Nakauvadra Range in Northern Viti Levu. Lutunasobasoba died on this trip, but Degei lived on to become a combination man, ancestor, and spirit—and an angry spirit at that: He is blamed for causing wars and a great flood that washed the Fijians to all parts of the islands.

The dreaded Degei supposedly still inhabits a mysterious cave in the mountains above Rakiraki.

The stores along Vitogo Parade mark the boundary of Lautoka's business district; behind them are several blocks of shops and the lively **Lautoka Market,** which doubles as the bus station and is second in size only to Suva's Municipal Market. Handicraft stalls at the front of the market offer a variety of goods, especially when cruise ships are in port. Shady residential streets trail off beyond the playing fields of **Churchill Park** on the other side of Vitogo Parade. The Hare Krishnas have their most important temple in the South Pacific on Tavewa Avenue.

GETTING TO LAUTOKA Local **buses** leave the market in Nadi Town every half-hour for the Lautoka Market from Monday to Saturday between 6am and 8pm. The fare is no more than F$3 (US$1.90/£1), depending on where you get on. The one-way **taxi** fare to Lautoka is about F$25 (US$16/£8) from Nadi. **Rosie the Travel Service** has a half-day Lautoka excursion from Nadi; book at any hotel activity desk.

When **driving** from Nadi, you will come to two traffic circles on the outskirts of Lautoka. Take the second exit off the first one and the first exit off the second. That will take you directly to the post office and the southern end of Vitogo Parade.

WHERE TO STAY & DINE IN LAUTOKA The southern end of downtown gives way to a large park and picturesque promenade along the harbor. Beside it are Lautoka's best digs, the moderately priced **Waterfront Hotel** (© **666 4777;** www.tanoahotels.com), which primarily attracts business travelers.

I usually stop for lunch at the **Chilli Tree Café** (© **655 1824**), a modern coffee shop at Tukani and Nede streets; it is open Monday to Saturday 7:30am to 7pm. My second choice is **Jolly Good** (© **666 9980**), at Naviti and Vakabale streets. This inexpensive outdoor cafeteria is operated by a family who resided in New Zealand before returning to Lautoka. Opening hours are daily from 8am to 10pm.

FLIGHTSEEING & SKY DIVING

Island Hoppers Fiji (✆ 672 0410; www.helicopters.com.fj) and **Pacific Islands Seaplanes** (✆ 672 5643; www.fijiseaplanes.com) both offer sightseeing flights over Denarau Island, Nadi Bay, the Mamanucas, and Vuda Point north of Nadi between Viseisei village and Lautoka. Call them or inquire at any hotel activities desk for prices and reservations.

I've never had the courage to put my life in someone's hands while falling to Denarau Island from 3,000m (10,000 ft.) up in the air, but you can with **Skydive Fiji** (✆ 672 8166; www.skydivefiji.com.fj). You'll pay at least F$350 (US$227/£116) for a tandem flight.

3 Exploring Viti Levu from Nadi

Although I wouldn't spend my entire vacation in Nadi, it does make a good base from which to explore Fiji. In fact, you can make day trips from Nadi to other parts of Viti Levu. Some Coral Coast and Pacific Harbour area tour operators provide transportation from the Nadi area hotels.

RAFTING ON THE NAVUA RIVER

The best of these excursions onto the water—in fact, it's one of Fiji's top experiences—is a full-day rafting trip on the **Navua River,** between Pacific Harbour and Suva on Viti Levu's south coast. The tour visits a Fijian village that puts on a *yaqona* (kava) welcoming ceremony, a lunch of local-style foods, and a traditional dance show. The cost is about F$150 (US$97/£50) from the Nadi hotels, less from those on the Coral Coast. Be sure to opt for the variation of this tour that includes a ride down the river on a *bilibili* (bamboo raft). See "River Rafting & Kayaking" in chapter 8.

EXCURSIONS TO THE CORAL COAST

Other fine outdoor excursions are the waterfall and cave tours offered by **Adventures in Paradise Fiji** (✆ 652 0833; www.adventuresinparadisefiji.com), on the Coral Coast. You can also go for a ride on the **Coral Coast Railway Co.** (✆ 652 0434), based outside Shangri-La's Fijian Resort. I'm most fond of the trip to lovely Natadola Beach, where you swim (bring your own towel) and have a barbecue lunch. Another Coral Coast tour visits the town of Sigatoka and the meandering river and fertile valley of the same name. For animal lovers, the best part of this trip is **Kula Eco Park.** These full-day trips cost about F$150 (US$97/£50) from Nadi.

Robinson Crusoe Island (✆ 628 1999; www.robinsoncrusoeislandfiji.com), on an islet off Natadola Beach, offers a day trip from Nadi including bus transportation to its jetty, a jungle river cruise (on the mainland), snorkeling trips, lunch, and an island dance show for F$89 (US$58/£30). **Jet Fiji** has one of its high-speed jet boats stationed

---

⟨Tips⟩ Take a Day Trip to a Small Island

No visit to Fiji is complete without exploring a small offshore island, so put at least a day trip to one of the Mamanuca or Yasawa islands high on your list of things to do while you're in Nadi. You'll find details under "Seeing the Islands on Day Trips from Nadi," in chapter 6.

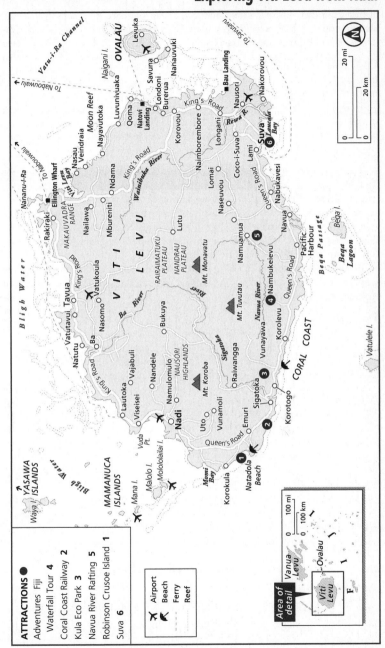

ATTRACTIONS ●
Adventures Fiji
Waterfall Tour **4**
Coral Coast Railway **2**
Kula Eco Park **3**
Navua River Rafting **5**
Robinson Crusoe Island **1**
Suva **6**

Airport ✈
Beach
Ferry ---
Reef

at the island (see "Boating, Golf, Hiking & Other Outdoor Activities," below). You also will pay extra for water-skiing, tube rides, hair braiding, and massages.

See "What to See & Do on the Coral Coast," in chapter 7.

DAY TRIPS TO SUVA

Full-day guided tours go from Nadi to Suva, picking up guests at the Coral Coast hotels in between. From Nadi you'll spend a total of 8 hours riding in the bus for 4 hours in Suva, half of which can easily be spent in the **Fiji Museum;** so think about staying overnight and riding the Fiji Express (p. 54) back to Nadi the next day. You'll pay about F$90 (US$58/£30) per person from Nadi, less from the Coral Coast hotels. See chapter 10.

4 Boating, Golf, Hiking & Other Outdoor Activities

The Nadi area offers a host of sporting and outdoor activities to suit almost every interest. Most of these excursions take place near Nadi, but some—such as white-water rafting on the Navua River (see "River Rafting & Kayaking" in "Pacific Harbour & Beqa Island," chapter 8)—require a boat trip to the Mamanuca Islands or a bus ride to other locations on Viti Levu.

Adrenalin Watersports (© **675 1288;** www.adrenalinfiji.com) provides diving, jet-skiing, wakeboarding, sailing, parasailing, game fishing, and other watersports at the resorts on Denarau Island.

FISHING 𝄞𝄞

The Denarau Island hotels and all the resorts in the Mamanucas offer sportfishing as a pay-extra activity for their guests. Based at Port Denarau, **Crystal Blue Adventures** (© **675 0950;** www.crystalbluefiji.com) has a fleet of fishing boats that ply the waters off the Manamucas for wahoo, giant trevally, mahimahi, tuna, and other game fish.

GOLF & TENNIS

The 18-hole, 7,150-yard, par-72 links at the **Denarau Golf & Racquet Club** 𝄞𝄞 (© **675 0477;** www.denaraugolf.com.fj) occupy most of Denarau Island, with the clubhouse opposite the Sheraton Fiji Resort. Its barbecue-style restaurant and bar serve breakfast, lunch, and dinner at moderate prices. It also has locker rooms with showers. Greens fees for 18 holes are F$110 (US$71/£36) for guests of the island's big resorts, and F$120 (US$78/£40) for those of us who can't afford to stay there. The course is open daily from 7am to dark, and lessons are available.

The club's six Wimbledon-standard grass tennis courts are open daily from 7am to dark, and its four all-weather courts stay open until 10pm. Fees are F$25 (US$16/£8)

⌐Fun Fact Where "V. Singh" Started Swinging

The Nadi Airport Golf Club plays second fiddle to the manicured links at the Denarau Golf & Racquet Club these days, but it was here that one V. Singh won the Grade A Open Championship in 1981. That would be Vijay Singh, one of the world's top professional golfers. Before he started playing, the Fiji native served as caddy for his father, who was club president. Vijay Singh now lives in Florida and is seldom seen around Fiji.

per person per hour on grass, or F$20 (US$13/£7) per hour on the hard courts. Lessons are available, and proper tennis attire is required.

The **Novotel Nadi Hotel** (© **672 2000**) has a 9-hole executive course, and the hotel tour desks can arrange for you to play at the 18-hole **Nadi Airport Golf Club** (© **672 2148**) near Newtown Beach, behind the airport. The latter is a 5,882-yard, par-70 course that isn't particularly challenging or well kept, but the setting, on the shores of Nadi Bay, is attractive.

HIKING

In addition to Adventures in Paradise's waterfall hikes on the Coral Coast (see earlier in this chapter), **Adventure Fiji** (© **672 2935** or 672 2755; www.rosiefiji.com), a branch of Rosie Holidays, takes trekkers (as hikers are known in these parts) on 1-day walks some 600m (2,000 ft.) up into the Nausori Highlands above Nadi. I found this hike to be fascinating but strenuous; in fact, you have to be between 10 and 45 years old to sign up. Wear high-traction walking shoes that you don't mind getting wet, because the sandy trail goes into and out of steep valleys and crosses streams. Most of this walk is through grasslands with no shade, so wear sunscreen. We had a long midday break in a Fijian village, where we shared a local-style lunch sitting cross-legged in a simple Fijian home. The cost is about F$95 (US$62/£32) per person. The company also has 4-, 6-, and 10-day hikes across the Sigatoka Valley and Nausori Highlands, ranging from about F$777 to F$1,739 (US$505–US$1,129/£259–£580), including transfers, guide, accommodations, and meals provided by Fijian villagers along the way.

I have never been up there, nor do I know anyone who has, but in the mountains 15km (9 miles) east of Lautoka is the **Koroyanitu National Heritage Park,** an eco-tourism project operated by Abaca (pronounced Am-*bar*-tha) village and funded by the Native Land Trust Board, the South Pacific Regional Environment Programme, and the New Zealand government. The park includes native forests, grasslands, water-falls, and magnificent mountain vistas. Admission is F$8 (US$5.20/£2.70). Before you set out call the **Ambaca Visitor Center** (© **666 6644** and dial 1234 after the second beep) to make sure the village has someone on hand to show you around.

HORSEBACK RIDING

You can ride along Wailoaloa Beach in Nadi with a local man known as **Babba** (© **679 3652**), who charges about F$25 (US$16/£8) an hour.

A 20-minute drive south of Nadi Town, **Sonaisali Island Resort** (© **670 6011;** www.sonaisali.com) has guided horseback rides through the tropical vegetation on its 42-hectare (105-acre) private island. Rides cost F$20 (US$13/£7) per hour. Reservations are required.

JET BOATS

For a thrill-a-minute carnival ride afloat, **Jet Fiji** (© **675 0400;** www.jetfiji.com) will take you twisting and turning through the mangrove-lined creeks behind Denarau Island. Heart-stopping 360-degree turns are guaranteed to get the adrenaline flowing and the clothes wet. The half-hour rides depart every 30 minutes daily from Port Denarau. A shuttle connects the nearby Sheratons; scheduled pickups are arranged from other Nadi area hotels, so call for reservations. The price is about F$80 (US$52/£27) for adults; children 14 and under ride for half-fare, and kids 5 and under ride for free. Jet Fiji also has a boat stationed at Robinson Crusoe Island, off Natadola Beach (see "Excursions to the Coral Coast," above).

SCUBA DIVING & SNORKELING

Serious divers head elsewhere in Fiji (see "The Active Traveler," in chapter 3), but you can go underwater with **Aqua Blue** (© 672 6111; www.aquabluefiji.com) on Wailoaloa Beach; they provide dive guides and teach courses. Expect to pay about F$130 (US$84/£42) for a single-tank dive. You can also go snorkeling with Aqua Blue for F$60 (US$39/£20). **Adrenalin Watersports** (© 675 1288; www.adrenalinfiji.com) provides diving on Denarau Island.

5 Shopping in Nadi

Haggling is not considered to be polite when dealing with Fijians, and the better stores now have fixed prices. Bargaining is still acceptable, however, when dealing with Indo-Fijian merchants in many small shops. They will start high, you will start low, and somewhere in between you will find a mutually agreeable price. I usually knock 40% off the asking price as an initial counteroffer and then suffer the merchants' indignant snickers, secure in the knowledge that they aren't about to kick me out of the store when the fun has just begun.

To avoid the hassles of bargaining, visit **Jack's of Fiji** (Fiji's largest merchant), **Prouds,** and **Tappoo,** all of which have branches on the Queen's Road in Nadi Town, at Port Denarau, and in Sigatoka, Suva, and the shopping arcades of the larger hotels. In Nadi Town, the upstairs rooms of Jack's of Fiji are filled with clothing and leather goods. Tappoo carries a broad range of merchandise, including electronics, cameras, and sporting goods. Prouds concentrates on perfumes, watches, and jewelry including Fiji's own J. Hunter black pearls (see "Savusavu," chapter 13).

In addition to being the shove-off point for cruises and transfers to the islands, **Port Denarau** is the shopping mecca on Denarau Island. This modern mall has a Jack's of Fiji branch, a surf shop, two banks and a FourEx currency exchange, a grocery and wine store, an ice-cream parlor, and several restaurants (see "Where to Dine in Nadi," later in this chapter).

"DUTY-FREE" SHOPPING

Fiji has the most developed shopping industry in the South Pacific, as will be very obvious when you walk along the main thoroughfare in Nadi Town. The Fiji government charges an import tax on merchandise brought into the country; so, despite their claims to the contrary, the stores aren't "duty-free." I have found much better prices and selections on the Internet and at large-volume dealers such as Best Buy and Circuit City in the United States, so shop around at home first so that you can compare the prices in Fiji. Also the models offered in the duty-free shops here are seldom the latest editions.

You should have no problems buying watches, cameras, and electronic gear from large merchants such as Prouds and Tappoo, but get receipts that accurately describe your purchases from small stores. Make sure all guarantee and warranty cards are properly completed and stamped by the merchant. Examine all items before making payment. If you later find that the item is not what you expected, return to the shop immediately with the item and your receipt. As a general rule, purchases are not returnable and deposits are not refundable. Always pay for your duty-free purchases by credit card. That way, if something goes wrong after you're back home, you can solicit help from the financial institution that issued the card.

If you missed anything, you'll get one last chance at the huge shops in the departure lounge at Nadi Airport.

Tips **Beware of Men Wielding Swords**

Fijians are extremely friendly people, but beware of so-called **sword sellers.** These are Fijian men who carry bags under their arms and approach you on the street. "Where you from, 'Stralia? States?" will be their opening line, followed by, "What's your name?" If you respond, they will quickly inscribe your name on a sloppily carved wooden sword. They expect you to buy the sword, whether you want it or not. They are numerous in Nadi, and they may even come up to you in Suva, though government efforts to discourage the practice have been more successful there. The easiest way to avoid this scam is to not tell any stranger your name and walk away as soon as you see the bag.

HANDICRAFTS

Fijians produce a wide variety of handicrafts, such as carved *tanoa* (kava) bowls, war clubs, and cannibal forks; woven baskets and mats; pottery (which has seen a renaissance of late); and *masi* (tapa) cloth. Although generally not of the quality of those produced in Tonga, they are made in prolific quantities. Be careful when buying souvenirs and some woodcarvings, however, for many of today's items are machine-made, and many smaller items are imported from Asia. Only with masi can you be sure of getting a genuine Fijian handicraft.

The larger shops sell some very fine face masks and *nguzunguzus* (pronounced noo-zoo-noo-zoos), the inlaid canoe prows carved in the Solomon Islands, and some primitive art from Papua New Guinea. (Although you will see plenty hanging in the shops, the Fijians never carved masks in the old days.)

The largest and best-stocked shop on Queen's Road is **Jack's of Fiji** 𝒜𝒜 (𝒞 670 0744). It has a wide selection of handicrafts, jewelry, T-shirts, clothing, and paintings by local artists. The prices are reasonable and the staff is helpful rather than pushy. The Chefs The Restaurant complex is on premises (see "Where to Dine in Nadi," later in this chapter). Jack's of Fiji has other outlets including the shopping arcade of the Sheraton Fiji Resort (𝒞 670 1777), at the Tokatoka Resort Hotel (𝒞 672 0400), and in Sigatoka (𝒞 650 0810).

Other places to look are **Nadi Handicraft Center** (𝒞 670 2357) and **Nad's Handicrafts** (𝒞 670 3588). Nadi Handicraft Center has an upstairs room carrying clothing, leather goods, jewelry, and black pearls. Nad's usually has a good selection of Fijian pottery. **Nadi Handicraft Market** (no phone) is a collection of stalls on the Queen's Road near the south end of Nadi Town. The best are operated by Fijian women who sell baskets and other goods woven of *pandanus,* a palm whose supple leaves are more durable than those of the coconut tree.

TROPICAL CLOTHING

You'll have innumerable choices of tropical clothing here, but for the most unusual items in the entire South Pacific, head out to **Michoutouchkine Creations** 𝒜𝒜𝒜 at the Sheraton Fiji (𝒞 675 0518). This little shop carries the colorful creations of Nicolai Michoutouchkine and Aloi Pilioki, two noted Vanuatu artists whose unique squiggly swirls and swooshes distinguish each of their shirts, blouses, pant suits, and beach towels.

6 Where to Stay in Nadi

Most Nadi area hotels are on or near the Queen's Road, either near the airport or in **Martintar,** a suburban area halfway between the airport and Nadi Town. An advantage of Martintar is that you can walk from your hotel to several restaurants and bars. Only the resorts on **Denarau Island** and beside **Wailoaloa Beach** actually sit beside a beach. Even if they do, runoff from the mountains, hills, cane fields, and coastal mangrove swamps perpetually leaves Nadi Bay less than clear and its beaches more gray than white.

This area has a host of backpacker hostels, all of them in fierce competition with each other. The **Fiji Backpackers Association** (www.fiji-backpacking.com) is an organization of reputable hostel owners.

ON DENARAU ISLAND

You timeshare owners can exchange your intervals at **WorldMark Denarau Island Fiji** (𝄐 **800/457-0103** or 675 0442; www.worldmarktheclub.com), a large complex on the beach next to the Radisson Resort Fiji Denarau Island. Known until 2007 as TrendWest Fiji, it has a huge rectangular pool with swim-up bar, a spa and fitness center, and the Seafront Restaurant, which is managed by noted chef Eugene Gomes (see "Where to Dine in Nadi," below).

Fiji Beach Resort & Spa Managed by Hilton 𝄐𝄐   Extending along the northeastern point of Denarau Island, this resort opened in 2007 and was still a work in progress during my recent visit—though a new central building and more units could be open by the time you arrive. Two-story buildings house the accommodations, which are two-bedroom, two-bathroom condos designed so that one bedroom and bathroom can be rented as a standard room. The remaining bedroom, bathroom, kitchen, and living area are known as "villas." High-tech prevails, including big flatscreen TVs and PlayStations in each unit. Sliding doors separate the bedrooms from the bathrooms, which have both showers and soaking tubs. Each villa has a gas barbecue grill on its balcony, most of which look out to a long, rectangular beachside pool divided into seven separate areas. The main restaurant is out by the pool, but the star here is **Lépicier,** a coffee shop–deli with superb, freshly baked breads and pastries.

P.O. Box 11185, Nadi Airport. 𝄐 **800/HILTONS** (445-8667) or 675 8000. Fax 675 6801. www.fijibeachresortby-hilton.com. 225 units. F$485–F$675 (US$315–US$438/£163–£219). AE, DC, MC, V. **Amenities:** 2 restaurants; 1 bar; activities desk; babysitting; car-rental desk; children's programs; concierge-level rooms; fitness center; game room; Jacuzzi; laundry service; 7 outdoor pools; room service; spa; free coin-op washers and dryers; watersports equipment rentals; Wi-Fi in public areas. *In room:* A/C, TV, coffeemaker, fridge, high-speed Internet access, iron, kitchen (in 1-bed-room villas), safe.

⌒*Tips*   Last-Minute Plans

If you're making last-minute plans, contact **Impulse Fiji,** P.O. Box 10000, Nadi Airport (𝄐 **800/953-7595;** 672 3952; fax 672 5064; www.impulsefiji.com), which sells "unused" hotel rooms at reduced rates. It saves you the trouble of asking the front desk for a discount on rooms that would otherwise go unused. You can also get discounts on airline tickets and hotel rooms if you book in advance on the company's website.

Where to Stay in Nadi

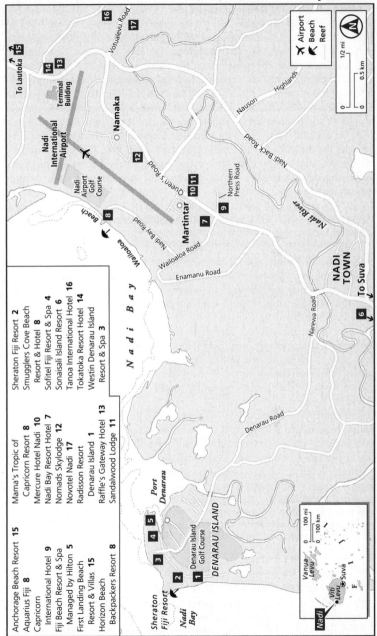

Anchorage Beach Resort **15**
Aquarius Fiji **8**
Capricorn International Hotel **9**
Fiji Beach Resort & Spa Managed by Hilton **5**
First Landing Beach Resort & Villas **15**
Horizon Beach Backpackers Resort **8**

Mama's Tropic of Capricorn Resort **8**
Mercure Hotel Nadi **10**
Nadi Bay Resort Hotel **7**
Nomads Skylodge **12**
Novotel Nadi **17**
Radisson Resort Denarau Island **1**
Raffle's Gateway Hotel **13**
Sandalwood Lodge **11**

Sheraton Fiji Resort **2**
Smugglers Cove Beach Resort & Hotel **8**
Sofitel Fiji Resort & Spa **4**
Sonaisali Island Resort **6**
Tanoa International Hotel **16**
Tokatoka Resort Hotel **14**
Westin Denarau Island Resort & Spa **3**

Radisson Resort Fiji Denarau Island ⚓⚓ Denarau Island's newest resort boasts a sophisticated and streamlined design. An extraordinary pool complex is the highlight here: The four pools are designed like lagoons—some sand-surrounded, others with waterfalls and green islands. An open and airy *bure-* (bungalow-) style lobby welcomes guests with an expansive view of the resort's lush grounds, the pool, and the South Pacific. Spagoers can request specialized wellness menus in addition to the offerings of the hotel's restaurants, which feature a pizza kitchen as well as traditional island fare and Western dishes. Individualized service is par for the course, as the staff is obliging and ready to help at a moment's notice. Decorated in calming colors, the guest rooms have white porcelain tiled floors, practical for back-and-forth activity between the pool, beach, and hotel rooms. Each room has a furnished patio or balcony where you can enjoy night views of the Southern Hemisphere skies. Families and large parties should consider renting the condolike suites, which offer kitchens with washers and dryers.

P.O. Box 9347, Nadi Airport. ℂ **888/201-1718** or 675 1264. Fax 675 1117. www.radisson.com/fiji. 270 units. F$180–F$500 (US$117–US$325/£60–£167). AE, DC, MC, V. **Amenities:** 3 restaurants; 3 bars; activities desk; babysitting; business center; car-rental desk; children's programs; concierge; fitness center; Jacuzzi; 4 pools; room service; spa; coin-op washers and dryers; watersports equipment rentals; Wi-Fi. *In room:* A/C, TV, coffeemaker, iron, minibar, safe.

Sheraton Fiji Resort ⚓⚓ This 1987-vintage hotel was scheduled to be closed between May and November 2008 for a thorough renovation, including installation of a new swimming pool complex and a state-of-the-art spa and workout center. The central building is strongly reminiscent of a U.S. shopping mall (it does indeed have some very fine shops). In contrast to the Fijian-style of its nearby sister, the Westin Denarau Island Resort & Spa (see below), it could be relocated to any tropical resort destination, not necessarily in the South Seas. In two-story buildings flanking the central complex, the large rooms here have ocean views from their private terraces or balconies. The food choices (none of them inexpensive) include fine dining in the swanky Ports O' Call. Guests can swim, snorkel, and sunbathe on a private island across the lagoon.

The resort also manages the 184 adjacent condos known as the **Sheraton Denarau Villas.** Built around a courtyard—one end of which opens to a beachside swimming pool and bar—these are among Nadi's fanciest digs. They come in various sizes, ranging from single rooms to three-bedroom apartments, and are appointed with all the comforts, including full kitchens and washers and dryers.

P.O. Box 9761, Nadi. ℂ **800/325-3535** or 675 0777. Fax 675 0818. www.sheraton.com/fiji. 292 hotel units, 184 condos. US$330–US$535 (£165–£267) double; US$435–US$1,065 (£217–£532) condo. AE, DC, MC, V. **Amenities:** 4 restaurants; 3 bars; activities desk; babysitting; bike rentals; business center; car-rental desk; children's programs; concierge; exercise room; laundry service; massage; outdoor pool; room service; salon; shopping arcade; watersports equipment rentals. *In room:* A/C, TV, coffeemaker, iron, kitchen (in condos), minibar, safe.

Sofitel Fiji Resort & Spa ⚓⚓⚓ One of Fiji's largest outdoor swimming pools and some of its best big-hotel dining highlight this luxury resort. The central building sports a gleaming open-air lobby overlooking the pool and beach. The spacious guest quarters are in three-story buildings lined up along the beach. Furnished and equipped in European style, they range from oceanview rooms to presidential suites. I prefer the "junior suites" with romantic Jacuzzis hidden behind louvered windows on their balconies. Under the direction of European chefs, the central kitchen provides excellent fare for three food outlets, including a fine-dining seafood restaurant. Although it lacks the Fijian charm of the Westin Denarau Island Resort & Spa—and

---

Tips Check Hotel Websites for Rates & Specials

Hotel room rates in Fiji have been in a state of serious flux since the coup in December 2006. Most resorts have been offering substantial discounts to lure business back to the country. The practice is so widespread that many large hotels were unwilling to tell me their rack rates. Therefore, the rates in these pages are useful primarily to tell if one hotel is more expensive than another. Frankly, you won't know what you will pay until you select a date and try to book a room. Be sure to check the hotel website to see if specials or Internet-only rates are being offered when you plan to visit.

---

the pool isn't as spectacular as the Radisson Fiji Denarau Island's—I admire the food and modern amenities here.

Private Mail Bag 396, Nadi Airport. © 800/763-4835 or 675 1111. Fax 675 1122. www.sofitel.com.fj. 296 units. F$430–F$2,000 (US$279–US$1,299/£143–£667). AE, DC, MC, V. **Amenities:** 3 restaurants; 5 bars; activities desk; babysitting; business center; children's programs; concierge; concierge-level rooms; fitness center; game room; Jacuzzi; laundry service; outdoor pool; room service; shopping arcade; spa; free washers and dryers; watersports equipment rentals; Wi-Fi throughout. *In room:* A/C, TV, coffeemaker, fridge, iron, minibar, safe.

The Westin Denarau Island Resort & Spa ✹✹✹   Originally known as the Regent of Fiji and more recently as the Sheraton Royal Denarau Resort, this venerable property first opened its doors in 1972. The Westin's new owners, Starwood Hotels (which also bought the nearby Sheraton Fiji),recently upgraded it to luxury status. Fortunately, the Westin still maintains more Fijian charm than any other large hotel here. Covered by a peaked wooden roof and laden with artifacts, the dark, breezy foyer opens to an irregularly shaped pool and the gray-sand beach. The rooms are in a series of two-story, motel-style blocks grouped in "villages" surrounded by thick, lush tropical gardens and linked by covered walkways to the central building. All but two of these buildings face the beach. With lots of varnished wood trim, exposed timbers, and masi cloth accents, the spacious units ooze tropical charm. Guests here can use the private island shared with the Sheraton Fiji, while guests there can use the fitness center and full-service spa at the Westin. While families will be at home here, this is the most tranquil resort on Denarau Island, which makes it more attractive to couples than its competition.

P.O. Box 9761, Nadi Airport. © 800/325-3535 or 675 0000. Fax 675 0259. www.westin.com. 274 units. US$475–US$600 (£237–£300) double; US$1,130 (£565) suite. AE, DC, MC, V. **Amenities:** 4 restaurants; 4 bars; activities desk; babysitting; car-rental desk; children's programs; concierge; exercise room; game room; 2 Jacuzzis; laundry service; massage; outdoor pool; room service; shopping arcade; watersports equipment rentals. *In room:* A/C, TV, coffeemaker, iron, high-speed Internet access, minibar, safe.

AT WAILOALOA BEACH

Wailoaloa Beach, about 3km (2 miles) off the Queen's Road, is a long strip of grayish-brown sand fringing Nadi Bay. Although it was originally built as a tract-housing project, the area known as **Newtown Beach** is now host to both suburban homes and several budget accommodations.

Aquarius Fiji ✹   Canadian Terrence Buckley merged these two beachside condos into Fiji's first "flashpacker" budget-priced resort. Although backpackers usually occupy the five downstairs rooms with 2, 6, or 10 bunk beds (each is air-conditioned and has its own bathroom), the eight spacious rooms upstairs are suitable for anyone searching for an inexpensive beachside stay. The four upstairs rooms facing the bay are particularly attractive since they have large balconies overlooking the beach and a small outdoor swimming pool. The other upstairs units have smaller balconies facing the mountains. Downstairs, a restaurant, bar, and TV lounge open to the pool.

P.O. Box 7, Nadi. © 672 6000. Fax 672 6001. www.aquarius.com.fj. 8 units (all with bathroom), 18 dorm beds. F$89–F$99 (US$58–US$64/£30–£33) double; F$28–F$30 (US$18–US$19/£9.30–£10) dorm bed. AE, MC, V. **Amenities:** Restaurant; bar; activities desk; laundry service; outdoor pool. In room: A/C, no phone.

Horizon Beach Backpackers Resort   Although it's not directly on the beach, this two-story clapboard house is a less expensive alternative to the nearby Aquarius Fiji and Smugglers Cove Beach Resort & Hotel and the Tropic of Capricorn Resort, both next-door. The rooms are spacious if not luxurious and have their own bathrooms with hot-water showers. Superior units are air-conditioned, while the others have fans. The dorm beds are in two rooms; the smaller one with eight bunks is air-conditioned. The open-air restaurant serves inexpensive meals, and Fijian musicians perform at night at the bar. Guests here can use the facilities at Smugglers Cove Beach Resort & Hotel, which has the same owners.

P.O. Box 1401, Nadi (Wasawasa Rd., Newtown Beach). © 672 2832. Fax 672 4578. www.horizonbeachfiji.com. 14 units (all with bathroom), 16 dorm beds. F$50–F$155 (US$32–US$101/£17–£52) double; F$15–F$22 (US$9.70–US$14/£5–£7) dorm bed. Rates include continental breakfast. AE, MC, V. **Amenities:** Restaurant; bar; activities desk; laundry service; outdoor pool. In room: A/C (all rooms and 8 dorm beds), no phone.

Mama's Tropic of Capricorn Resort   Owned by a well-traveled Fijian named Mama Salena, this hostel grew in 2007 to include a three-story building between the outdoor pool and the beach—meaning that, with the pool not beside the beach, Mama's is not as resorty as Aquarius and Smugglers Cove. The new wing includes a mix of air-conditioned and fan-cooled rooms and dorms. One rooftop unit has three walls of louvered windows, making it seem like a bungalow. It has the privilege of sharing the roof with a sunset bar.

P.O. Box 1736, Nadi. © 672 3089. Fax 672 3050. www.mamasfiji.com. 20 units (all with bathroom), 32 dorm beds. F$90 (US$58/£30) double; F$28 (US$18/£9) dorm bed. Rates include continental breakfast. AE, MC, V. **Amenities:** Restaurant; 2 bars; activities desk; laundry service; outdoor pool. In room: A/C (some units), no phone.

Smugglers Cove Beach Resort & Hotel ☆☆ Value   Opened in 2006, this three-story hotel is larger than Aquarius Fiji, and its medium-size rooms are equipped with amenities found at more expensive hotels. The family suite also has a kitchen, but best are the four rooms on the front of the building with balconies overlooking the swimming pool, the beach, and Nadi Bay. Arranged in four-bed coed cubicles, the 34 beds in the first-floor Pirates Dormitory are often full (overflow heads to the owners' Horizon Beach Backpackers Resort next-door). The young guests keep the restaurant and bar—which open to the deck-surrounded pool—busy and sometimes noisy at night. Another plus here is a large, air-conditioned Internet room.

P.O. Box 5401, Nadi. © 672 6578. Fax 672 8740. www.smugglersbeachfiji.com. 22 units (all with bathroom), 34 dorm beds. F$98–F$198 (US$64–US$129/£33–£66) double; F$28 (US$18/£9) dorm bed. Rates include continental breakfast. AE, MC, V. **Amenities:** Restaurant; bar; activities desk; laundry service; outdoor pool; coin-op washers and dryers. In room: A/C, TV, coffeemaker, fridge, kitchen (in family suite), safe.

IN THE MARTINTAR AREA

Capricorn International Hotel Value   Cleanliness and firm mattresses are trademarks at this budget property, along with its Suva sister, the Capricorn Apartment Hotel (see "Where to Stay in Suva," in chapter 10). Least expensive are the standard

rooms, which are entered from the rear and have window walls instead of balconies overlooking a lush tropical courtyard with a pool and a hot tub (they are the highlight here); but I would opt for a unit with a balcony or patio. Six family units have kitchens and two bedrooms. The fan-cooled dorm is an afterthought.

P.O. Box 9043, Nadi Airport. ℂ **672 0088.** Fax 672 0522. www.capricornfiji.com. 68 units, 14 dorm beds. F$100–F$170 (US$65–US$110/£33–£57) double; F$25 (US$16/£8) dorm bed. Rates include continental breakfast. AE, DC, MC, V. **Amenities:** Restaurant; bar; activities desk; babysitting; Jacuzzi; laundry service; massage; outdoor pool; room service; spa. *In room:* A/C, TV, coffeemaker, fridge, iron (family units), kitchen (family units), safe.

Mercure Hotel Nadi

Mercure Hotel Nadi   Formerly the Dominion International, this motel now sports modern European decor and furniture, thanks to a face-lift when it recently became a Mercure property. The spacious rooms are in two white, three-story buildings flanking a tropical garden surrounding a swimming pool and wooden deck. The rooms have desks, shower-only bathrooms with French-style "bowl" hand basins, and glass doors sliding open to patios or balconies. Some have king-size beds; others have both queen-size and single beds. A few units are equipped for guests with disabilities.

P.O. Box 9178, Nadi Airport. ℂ **800/637-2873** or 672 0272. Fax 672 0187. www.accorhotels.com.fj. 85 units. F$138–F$234 (US$90–US$152/£46–£78) double. AE, DC, MC, V. **Amenities:** Restaurant; bar; activities desk; babysitting; game room; laundry service; massage; outdoor pool; room service; spa; tennis court. *In room:* A/C, TV, coffeemaker, fridge.

Nadi Bay Resort Hotel

Nadi Bay Resort Hotel   Although suitable for any cost-conscious traveler, 110 dormitory beds make this Nadi's largest backpacker establishment. Behind its walls you'll find three bars, two sophisticated restaurants serving reasonably priced meals, an air-conditioned TV lounge, and courtyards with two swimming pools (usually surrounded by a multitude of nubile young bodies). The hotel even has a hair salon, a massage parlor, and a 70-seat theater for watching movies and sporting events on TV. In addition to the dormitories, its five buildings hold standard motel rooms and apartments. The property is directly under Nadi Airport's flight path, however, so jets occasionally roar overhead in the middle of the night. Lower-priced units and dorms are not air-conditioned.

NAP 0359, Nadi Airport. ℂ **672 3599.** Fax 672 0092. www.fijinadibayhotel.com. 42 units (19 with bathroom), 110 dorm beds. F$80–F$150 (US$52–US$97/£27–£50) double; F$25–F$28 (US$16–US$18/£8–£9) dorm bed. Room rates include continental breakfast; dormitory rates do not. AE, MC, V. **Amenities:** 2 restaurants; 3 bars; activities desk; laundry service; massage; 2 outdoor pools; salon. *In room:* A/C (most units), coffeemaker, fridge, no phone.

Nomads Skylodge

Nomads Skylodge   This sprawling, 4.4-hectare (11-acre) property is part of Nomads World, an Australian company specializing in accommodations and tours for backpackers and other budget-minded travelers, although it's expertly managed by Fiji's Tanoa hotels. Thirteen hotel rooms are air-conditioned dormitories, each with four or six bunk beds, private lockers (bring a lock), and its own bathroom but no other amenities such as TVs and phones. One unit has cooking facilities. Imported sand forms a small faux beach by the swimming pool, which has its own bar.

P.O. Box 9222, Nadi Airport. ℂ **672 2200.** Fax 671 4330. www.nomadsskylodge.com. 53 units. F$78–F$153 (US$52–US$99/£26–£51) double; F$25–F$31 (US$16–US$20/£8–£10) dorm bed. AE, DC, MC, V. **Amenities:** Restaurant; 2 bars; activities desk; game room; laundry service; outdoor pool; coin-op washers and dryers. *In room:* A/C, coffeemaker, fridge.

Sandalwood Lodge

Sandalwood Lodge 🌴 *Value*   "Clean and comfortable at a sensible price" is the appropriate motto at John and Ana Birch's establishment, which is now managed by their charming daughter, Angela. I have long considered the Sandalwood to be Nadi's best value—provided you don't need a restaurant on the premises. Quietly situated about 270m (900 ft.) off the Queen's Road behind the Mercure Hotel Nadi, the New Zealand–style motel consists of three two-story buildings flanking a nicely landscaped lawn with a rock-bordered pool. Units in the Orchid Wing are somewhat larger than the others and have queen-size beds instead of doubles. Every unit has a kitchen and sofa bed.

P.O. Box 9454, Nadi Airport. © 672 2044. Fax 672 0103. sandalwood@connect.com.fj. 34 units. F$80–F$96 (US$52–US$62/£26–£31) double. AE, DC, MC, V. **Amenities:** Babysitting; laundry service; outdoor pool; coin-op washer and dryer. *In room:* A/C, TV, coffeemaker, iron (in Orchid Wing), kitchen.

NEAR THE AIRPORT

Novotel Nadi   Formerly the Fiji Mocambo, this sprawling hotel atop a hill received a much-needed face-lift after being taken over by Accor Hotels in 2006 and is once again a fitting competitor to the nearby Tanoa International Hotel (see below). All rooms have excellent views across the cane fields to the mountains; the best are on the top floor, where their peaked ceilings give them the feel of bungalows. A main restaurant plus an open-air coffee shop are down by the swimming pool. You can practice your swing at the hotel's 9-hole executive golf course.

P.O. Box 9195, Nadi Airport. © 800/942-5050 or 672 2000. Fax 672 0324. www.novotel.com.fj. 117 units. F$201–F$276 (US$131–US$179/£66–£91) double. AE, DC, MC, V. **Amenities:** 2 restaurants; 2 bars; activities desk; babysitting; business center; game room; 9-hole golf course; laundry service; outdoor pool; room service; shopping arcade; spa; 2 tennis courts. *In room:* A/C, TV, coffeemaker, fridge, high-speed Internet access, iron.

Raffle's Gateway Hotel *Kids*   This older property (no connection whatsoever to Singapore's famous Raffles Hotel) is my favorite place to wait for a flight at the airport just across Queen's Road. As at the slipping Tokatoka Resort Hotel next-door (see below), you can whisk yourself down a water slide into a figure-8 swimming pool, the larger of two here. All units recently received a face-lift and now sport attractive tropical furniture and improved, shower-only bathrooms. The best have sitting areas and patios or balconies next to the large pool. The tiny, least expensive "standard" rooms can barely hold their double beds and are devoid of most amenities. The roadside main building houses an open-air, 24-hour coffee shop and an air-conditioned nighttime restaurant. Passengers departing on late-evening flights to Los Angeles can check out late without paying extra here.

P.O. Box 9891, Nadi Airport. © 672 2444. Fax 672 0620. www.rafflesgateway.com. 95 units. F$95–F$206 (US$62–US$134/£31–£67) double. AE, DC, MC, V. **Amenities:** 2 restaurants; bar; activities desk; babysitting; game room; Jacuzzi; laundry service; 2 outdoor pools; room service; tennis court. *In room:* A/C, TV, coffeemaker, fridge, safe.

Tanoa International Hotel *G*   This motel and the nearby Novotel Nadi are top places to stay near the airport. The bright public areas open onto a lush garden with a waterfall splashing into a modest swimming pool. Shingle-covered walkways lead to medium-size, motel-style rooms in two-story blocks. The Tanoa was built in the 1970s as a TraveLodge, so its rooms are somewhat smaller than the Novotel's. Most have a double and a single bed, combination tub-and-shower bathrooms, and balconies or patios. Superior rooms have king-size beds, large desks, sofas, and walk-in showers. Dignitaries often take the two luxurious one-bedroom suites. The open-air restaurant by the pool is open 24 hours.

P.O. Box 9203, Nadi Airport. © 800/835-7742 or 672 0277. Fax 672 0191. www.tanoahotels.com. 135 units. F$220–F$280 (US$143–US$182/£72–£91) double; F$350–F$500 (US$227–US$325/£114–£163) suite. AE, DC, MC, V. **Amenities:** Restaurant; bar; activities desk; babysitting; coffeemaker; exercise room; Jacuzzi; laundry service; outdoor pool; room service; salon; spa; 2 tennis courts; coin-op washers and dryers. *In room:* A/C, TV, fridge (stocked in suites), iron, safe.

Tokatoka Resort Hotel   The highlight at this modern complex, at the edge of sugar-cane fields across the Queen's Road from the airport, is an unusual combination swimming pool–restaurant-bar at the rear of the property. Unfortunately, it has had ownership problems of late and now lags behind the Raffle's Gateway next door. Nadi's most varied mix of accommodations are here, from hotel rooms to apartments to two-bedroom bungalows, many of them equipped with cooking facilities. The poolside restaurant is open 24 hours a day for snacks and a blackboard meal menu. Some units are equipped for guests with disabilities.

P.O. Box 9305, Nadi Airport. ☏ **672 0222.** Fax 672 0400. www.hexagonfiji.com. 112 units. F$189–F$395 (US$123–US$256/£62–£128) double. AE, DC, MC, V. **Amenities:** Restaurant; bar; babysitting; game room; laundry service; playground; outdoor pool; room service; spa; tour desk; coin-op washers and dryers. *In room:* A/C (except villa living rooms), TV, coffeemaker, fridge, kitchen (in some units).

SOUTH OF NADI

Sonaisali Island Resort   You drive through cane fields and ride a boat across a narrow muddy channel to this modern resort set on a flat, 42-hectare (105-acre) island. The lagoon is very shallow here at low tide, so imported sand held in place by a seawall serves as the main beach. You can also frolic in an attractive rock-lined pool with a swim-up bar. A large shingled roof covers all other common facilities, including an air-conditioned fine-dining restaurant. The tropically attired guest quarters include spacious hotel rooms, but the top choice are the airy duplex bungalows out in the lush gardens—some of the largest bures on Viti Levu. Beachside bungalows have small Jacuzzi tubs on their front porches (these are *duplex* units, however, so don't expect the ultimate in privacy). Three of the units have two bedrooms each and are attractive to families. I wouldn't spend my entire vacation here (as many Australians and New Zealanders do), but this is a viable alternative to the Denarau Island resorts for a bayside stopover. Getting into Nadi Town for shopping requires a rental or taxi ride.

P.O. Box 2544, Nadi (Sonaisali Island, 20 min. south of Nadi Town). ☏ **670 6011.** Fax 670 6092. www.sonaisali.com. 123 units. F$477 (US$310/£155) double; F$558–F$653 (US$362–US$424/£181–£212) bungalow. Rates include full breakfast. AE, DC, MC, V. **Amenities:** 2 restaurants; 4 bars; activities desk; babysitting; business center; game room; Jacuzzi; laundry service; massage; outdoor pool; room service; spa; tennis court; watersports equipment rentals. *In room:* A/C, TV, coffeemaker, iron, minibar, safe.

NORTH OF NADI

The two resorts below are on the paved Vuda Point Road, which runs from the Queen's Road west to Vuda Point, the promontory where the first legendary Fijians came ashore some 2,500 years ago. Today, this is where modern Fiji's oil is imported, so the landmarks are large petroleum storage tanks. This also is home to **Vuda Point Marina,** the best mainland stop for cruising yachts. The lagoon up here is so shallow it can turn into a mud flat at low tide, but both resorts have removed enough of the reef to make marinas and swimming holes. You can base your Fiji vacation here and not have to pay extra for transportation, but, to my mind, these two resorts (as well Sonaisali Island Resort, above) are best for lagoonside layovers. Getting into Nadi Town requires a rental or taxi.

Anchorage Beach Resort   Originally a motel with a gorgeous view of Nadi Bay from atop Vuda Point, Anchorage has been expanded to include a block of hotel rooms, a few duplex cottages, a massage bure, and a poolside restaurant and bar down by the lagoon. The resort has a bit of beach, and more white sand for sunning is held in place by a stone wall. The best views are from the original units atop the hill, but the spacious bungalows climbing the hill above the beach are the most luxurious accommodations here. The hotel rooms are rather typical except for their Jacuzzi tubs. The resort runs its own day trips from its marina to Beachcomber and Bounty island resorts (see chapter 6). Note that trains hauling sugar cane run on narrow gauge tracks between the restaurant and hotel rooms during the harvest season from June through November.

P.O. Box 10314, Nadi Airport (on Vuna Point Rd. 13km/8 miles north of Nadi Airport). ✆ **666 2099.** Fax 666 5571. www.anchoragefiji.com. 50 units. F$175–F$195 (US$114–US$127/£57–£64) double; F$345 (US$224/£112) bunga-low. AE, MC, V. **Amenities:** 2 restaurants; 2 bars; activities desk; complimentary canoes, kayaks, and snorkeling gear; laundry service; massage; outdoor pool; room service. *In room:* A/C, TV, coffeemaker, fridge, iron, safe.

First Landing Beach Resort & Villas   The creation of American Jim Dunn and Australian George Stock, this little resort sits beachside at Vuda Point, near where the first Fijians came ashore 3 millennia ago. Vuda Point Marina and the country's major oil storage tanks are nearby, but the grounds here are festooned with coconut palms and other tropical plants. The foliage and picturesque waterside setting make the resort's restaurant a favorite weekend lunch retreat for local residents. An outdoor swimming pool is an attractive option, and Jim and George have dredged the shallow reef to create a swimming hole and small islet offshore. The duplex guest bungalows are comfortably furnished with both king-size and single beds, and their bathrooms have whirlpool tubs. The bures also boast charming screened porches, and four beach-side bures also have decks. The resort also has three two-bedroom, two-bathroom vil-las with their own pools. Although not as spacious as Sonaisali Island Resort, this is a more charming choice for a layover.

P.O. Box 348, Lautoka (at Vuda Point, 15km/9 miles north of Nadi Airport). ✆ **666 6171.** Fax 666 8882. www.first-landingfiji.com. 39 units. F$325–F$820 (US$211–US$532/£106–£266) double. Rates include full breakfast. AE, DC, MC, V. **Amenities:** Restaurant; bar; activities desk; babysitting; car-rental desk; laundry service; outdoor pool; room service; spa. *In room:* A/C, coffeemaker, fridge (stocked on request), kitchen (in villas), safe.

7 Where to Dine in Nadi

ON DENARAU ISLAND

You will pay a relatively high price to dine in them, but all of the Denarau Island resorts have restaurants, most either on or near the beach. The island's best breads and pastries are at **Lépicier,** a coffee shop cum deli in the Fiji Beach Resort & Spa Man-aged by Hilton (✆ **675 8000;** daily 8am to 10pm).

An **Esquires** coffee shop with high-speed Wi-Fi is in front of the Sheraton Dena-rau Villas (✆ **675 0989**). It's open daily 7am to 10pm. Port Denarau has a branch of **Mama's Pizza** (✆ **675 0533;** daily 9am to 11pm), which has the same menu as the Nadi Town outlet (see below).

Cardo's Steakhouse & Cocktail Bar   STEAKS/SEAFOOD/PIZZA   Owner Cardo is known throughout Fiji for providing quality chargrilled steaks and fish, and they're his best offerings here, taken at a multitude of tables on the large deck beside the marina waterway—which can be problematic if it's raining. I usually have break-fast here before a cruise or a hair-raising ride on a Jet Fiji, or chill over a cold Stubbie afterward. Lunch specials like a chargrilled chicken salad are posted on a blackboard. The pizzas are wood-fired, but I go around the corner to Mama's Pizza for my pies.

Port Denarau. ✆ **675 0900.** Reservations accepted. Breakfast F$4.50–F$10 (US$2.90–US$6.50/£1.50–£3.30); pizza F$17–F$32 (US$11–US$21/£5.70–£11); main courses F$22–F$49 (US$14–US$32/£7–£16). AE, MC, V. Daily 7am–10:30pm.

Where to Dine in Nadi

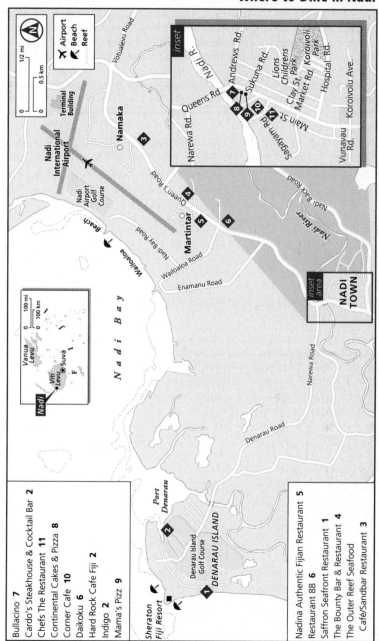

Bullacino **7**
Cardo's Steakhouse & Cocktail Bar **2**
Chefs The Restaurant **11**
Continental Cakes & Pizza **8**
Corner Cafe **10**
Daikoku **6**
Hard Rock Cafe Fiji **2**
Indigo **2**
Mama's Pizz **9**

Nadina Authentic Fijian Restaurant **5**
Restaurant 88 **6**
Saffron Seafront Restaurant **1**
The Bounty Bar & Restaurant **4**
The Outer Reef Seafood
Café/Sandbar Restaurant **3**

Hard Rock Cafe Fiji INTERNATIONAL   I am tempted to wear my earplugs to Fiji's first franchise of the famous chain because it's just like the others: loud, hip, relatively expensive, and adorned with autographed rock-'n'-roll memorabilia. In fact, you could be in a Hard Rock in Berlin or Beirut, New York or New Orleans. The menu offers the usual selection of nachos, blackened chicken pasta, huge burgers, and grilled steaks and fish. Unlike many restaurants in Fiji, where you'll get poor imitations, everything here is up to international standards. The fajitas really taste like Mexican fare, for example, and the pulled pork barbecue sandwiches could be from South Carolina.

Port Denarau. ℂ **675 0032**. Reservations accepted. Burgers and sandwiches F$13–F$27 (US$8.40–US$18/£4.30–£9); main courses F$18–F$48 (US$12–US$31/£6–£16). AE, MC, V. Daily 11am–10:45pm.

Indigo 🌟🌟🌟 *Value* INDIAN/ASIAN   This excellent restaurant with mostly outdoor tables is the latest creation of executive chef Eugene Gomes, who left the Sheraton Fiji to open the dining outlets at Jack's of Fiji in Nadi Town (see below). Along with his Saffron restaurant, Indigo serves the country's best and most authentic Indian cuisine. The top (and most expensive) offering is mangrove crab masala, but I prefer the Goan pork curry (an import from Eugene's home of Goa, a former Portuguese and predominately Catholic colony). The butter chicken is excellent, too. The Asian side of the menu features Thai-style crab and Rendang curry. Vegetarians can choose from among at least eight dishes.

Port Denarau. ℂ **675 0026**. Reservations recommended. Main courses F$11–F$48 (US$7.10–US$31/£3.70–£16). AE, MC, V. Daily 11am–9:30pm.

Seafront Restaurant INTERNATIONAL   Like Indigo, this sprawling restaurant at the WorldMark Denarau Island timeshare hotel is another project overseen by chef Eugene Gomes. Here he devises a wide-ranging menu, from simple chargrilled steaks, fish, and burgers to more refined fare such as smoked salmon with fettuccine and a watercress cream sauce. Light fare might include seared yellowfin tuna with Moroccan spices or vegetarian ravioli. This is a good spot for an open-air breakfast.

In WorldMark Denarau Island. ℂ **675 0722**. Reservations recommended. Breakfast F$5–F$14 (US$3.20–US$9/£1.70–£4.70); burgers F$16 (US$10/£5.30); main courses F$15–F$38 (US$9.70–US$25/£5–£13). AE, MC, V. Daily 7am–9:30pm.

IN NADI TOWN

Bullacino 🌟🌟🌟 *Value* COFFEE SHOP/DELI/BAKERY   Until this urbane establishment opened its doors in 2007, the Esquires shops (originally known as Republic of Cappuccino) had the corner on Fiji's coffee-shop business. Bullacino's coffee is rich and steamy, the pastries—including the best bagels in Fiji—are fresh from **Nutmeg & Tulips** bakery next-door, and the lunchtime offerings are among the finest I've had in Fiji: I am absolutely in love with the warm roasted chicken over a salad of mesclun greens with a lemony dressing. Grilled swordfish with Italian salsa, yellowfin tuna with wasabi mayonnaise, and vegetarian ratatouille are winners, too. You can dine at tables in the air-conditioned shop or under ceiling fans out on a deck overlooking the muddy Nadi River. I have only one problem: This exceptional restaurant is not open for dinner.

Queen's Rd. (at Nadi River bridge). ℂ **672 8638**. Reservations not accepted. Breakfast F$5–F$15 (US$3.20–US$9.70/£1.70–£5); lunch F$10–F$17 (US$6.50–US$11/£3.30–£5.70). MC, V. Daily 8am–6pm.

Chefs The Restaurant ★★★ *Value* INTERNATIONAL The first of executive chef Eugene Gomes's creations is still one of Fiji's top restaurants. The service is attentive, and the cuisine is very well presented. Menus vary with the season, but always include grilled beef tenderloin and rack of lamb to satisfy Australian and New Zealand patrons. Breakfast is served, and the lunch menu offers salads, burgers, curries, and fish and chips. You get a 10% discount if you purchase F$100 (US$65/£33) worth of merchandise from Jack's (bring your receipt).

Sangayam Rd. (behind Jack's of Fiji). ✆ 670 3131. Reservations recommended. Breakfast F$5.50–F$8 (US$3.60–US$5.20/£1.80–£2.70); lunch F$8.50–F$30 (US$5.50–US$19/£2.80–£10); dinner main courses F$29–F$69 (US$19–US$45/£9.70–£23). AE, DC, MC, V. Daily 9am–10pm.

Continental Cakes & Pizza BAKERY/PIZZA This storefront bakery isn't much to look at, but it supplies the major hotels with bread, cakes, and pastries. It's my favorite place in town for one of the crispiest croissants in the South Pacific (and that includes Tahiti). I'm a great fan of the toasted croissant sandwich with ham and cheese anytime of day. You can also order thin-crust pizzas and made-to-order submarine sandwiches on fresh bread. For an afternoon sugar high, try a slice of black forest cake.

Queen's Rd. (opposite Mobil station). ✆ 670 3595. Breakfast F$8–F$9.50 (US$5.20–US$6.20/£2.70–£3.20); sandwiches F$4–F$10 (US$2.60–US$6.50/£1.30–£3.30); pizzas F$9–F$24 (US$5.80–US$15.60/£3–£8). MC, V. Mon–Sat 8am–6pm.

Corner Cafe ★ *Value* CAFETERIA Another of chef Eugene Gomes's operations, this pleasant cafeteria that shares quarters in Jack's Handicrafts with Saffron (see below) is a fine place to stop for a snack, an ice cream, or a quick lunch in Nadi Town. The cafeteria menu is varied: pastries and coffee (you can get a latte here), hot dogs and hamburgers, sandwiches and salads, roast chicken, pastas, and fish and chips. I prefer the creamy Thai curry chicken. You can also order from the adjacent Saffron's menu (see below).

Queen's Rd. (in Jack's of Fiji building). ✆ 670 3131. Most items F$5–F$12 (US$3.20–US$7.80/£1.70–£4). AE, DC, MC, V. Mon–Sat 8am–6pm.

Mama's Pizza ITALIAN If you need a tomato sauce fix, follow the aroma of garlic to Robin O'Donnell's establishment. Her wood-fired pizzas range from a small plain model to a large deluxe version with all the toppings. Just remember that this is Nadi, not New York or Naples, so adjust your expectations accordingly. She also has spaghetti with tomato-and-meat sauce, lasagna, and fresh salads. Two other locations of Mama's Pizzas are at Port Denarau (✆ 675 0533) and in the Colonial Plaza shopping mall on the Queen's Road north of Martintar (✆ 672 0922).

Queen's Rd., Nadi Town, opposite Mobil Station. ✆ 670 0221. Pizzas F$7–F27 (US$4.50–US$18/£2.30–£9); pastas F$10–F$12 (US$6.50–US$7.80/£3.30–£4). MC, V. Daily 10am–11pm.

Saffron ★★★ NORTHERN INDIAN/VEGETARIAN This restaurant offering the best Indian cuisine in Fiji is executive chef Eugene Gomes's ode to the tandoori cooking of northern India and Pakistan, although his menu also features a number of vegetarian and other dishes from around the subcontinent. You'll be greeted with a complimentary basket of crispy *papadam* chips (made from an Indian flatbread) with dipping sauce. The Punjabi chicken *tikka* is great, although I'm addicted to the smooth butter chicken curry.

Queen's Rd., Nadi Town (in Jack's of Fiji building). ✆ 670 1233. Reservations accepted. Main courses F$11–F$42 (US$7.10–US$27/£3.70–£14). AE, DC, MC, V. Mon–Sat 11am–2:30pm and 5:30–9:30pm; Sun 5:30–9:30pm.

IN THE MARTINTAR AREA

The suburban version of **Mama's Pizza** resides in the rear of the Colonial Plaza shopping center on the Queen's Road between Martintar and Namaka (© **672 0922**). It has the same menu, prices, and hours as its Nadi Town mama (see above).

The local **McDonald's** is on the Queen's Road at Emananu Road, between Nadi Town and Martintar.

The Bounty Bar & Restaurant INTERNATIONAL/FIJIAN   Although not nearly as good as it used to be, this informal pub still draws imbibing tourists, resident expatriates, and parliamentarians, especially during happy hour (5–8pm) and on weekend evenings. The best menu items are the grilled steaks and large burgers. You usually can get a meal here after 10pm, when many other restaurants are closed.

Queen's Rd., Martintar. © **672 0840**. Reservations accepted. Main courses F$16–F$33 (US$10–US$21/£5.30–£11). AE, MC, V. Daily 9am–11pm.

Daikoku 𝓡𝓡 JAPANESE   There are two dining areas at this authentic restaurant, which was prefabricated in Japan and reconstructed here. Downstairs is the sushi bar, which uses only the freshest salmon, tuna, and lobster. Upstairs is the teppanyaki room, where the chef will stir-fry vegetables, shrimp, chicken, or extraordinarily tender beef as you watch. You can also order sukiyaki, udon, and other traditional Japanese dishes. Fiji's best Nipponese cuisine is here.

Queen's Rd., Martintar (at Northern Press Rd.). © **672 3622**. Reservations recommended. Sushi and sashimi F$5–F$26 (US$3.20–US$17/£1.70–£8.70); main courses F$12–F$33 (US$7.80–US$21/£4–£11). AE, DC, MC, V. Daily noon–2pm and 6–9:30pm.

Nadina Authentic Fijian Restaurant 𝓡𝓡𝓡 FIJIAN   Nadi lacked a really good Fijian restaurant until proprietor Amy Suvan opened this one in late 2007. In a small wooden cottage with wraparound porch, it excels in traditional fare such as *kokoda* (raw fish marinated in lime juice and served with fresh vegetables) and *kovu walu* (Spanish mackerel steamed with coconut milk in banana leaves). Nadina is the only place I know that regularly serves *miti*, the crunchy young shoots of the wood fern— delicious served with coconut milk. Some ordinarily bland Fijian dishes are spiced up for those with worldly tastes, and you can get a good curry here, too.

Queen's Rd., Martintar (opposite Capricorn International Hotel). © **672 7313**. Reservations recommended. Main courses F$18–F$22 (US$12–US$14/£6–£7.30). MC, V. Daily 7am–10pm.

The Outer Reef Seafood Café/Sandbar Restaurant 𝓡𝓡 SEAFOOD   Australian Allan Watters relocated to Fiji and opened this cafe and restaurant, for which he imports the same fresh seafood he used to sell back home. Open for lunch, his roadside store doubles as a fish market and the **Outer Reef Seafood Café,** serving sandwiches, sashimi, and fish and chips. Or, if you don't mind feeling like someone sneaking into a 1920s speak-easy, follow the narrow passage to the **Sandbar Restaurant,** an alfresco dining patio and trendy bar. The specialty under the stars is a two-level stack of hot or cold crab, shrimp, oysters, mussels, scallops, and the Australian crustaceans known as Balmain bugs; it's big enough to serve two adults. Thick steaks cooked over a gas grill are very good. The Sandbar has live music on weekend nights, but forget coming here if it's raining.

Queen's Rd. north of Nomads Skylodge, btw. Martintar and Namaka. © **672 7201**. Reservations recommended. Cafe items F$5–F$9 (US$3.20–US$5.80/£1.70–£3); main courses F$20–F$45 (US$13–US$29/£6.70–£15). MC, V. Cafe Mon–Sat 8am–7pm; Sun 11am–7pm. Restaurant daily 11am–11pm.

Restaurant 88 ASIAN   This large upstairs room was a garment factory until émigrés from Singapore converted it into this restaurant. A wall-size photo of the Singapore waterfront attests to their origins, as do their Singaporean-influenced Chinese dishes and choices from nearby countries in Southeast Asia. Peking ducks hanging in the glassed-in kitchen become very good meals here, and the Thai fired chicken in curry and coconut sauce is excellent. The service is attentive and efficient, but this is no place for romance since a playpen in one corner attracts local families with children.

Northern Press Rd., Martintary. © **672 6688.** Reservations accepted. Main courses F$10–F$70 (US$6.50–US$45/£3.30–£23). MC, V. Mon–Sat 11am–3pm and 6–10pm; Sun 9am–2pm and 6–10pm.

SPECIAL DINING EXPERIENCES

For a scenic dining experience, you can sail out on Nadi Bay with **Captain Cook Cruises** (© **670 1823;** www.captaincook.com.au). While you dine on rather ordinary Australian fare, Fijians serenade you with island music. The boat departs from Port Denarau Tuesday and Saturday at noon for lunch, daily at 5:30pm for dinner. The lunch cruises cost F$59 (US$38/£19) for adults, while dinner cruises are F$99 (US$64/£32), or F$133 (US$86/£43) including lobster. Children 3 to 15 pay half fare on either cruise, while those 2 and under eat for free. Reservations are required.

   First Landing Beach Resort & Villas (© **666 6171;** see "Where to Stay in Nadi," earlier in this chapter) offers dinner excursions by boat from Denarau Island to its pleasant outdoor dining area near Vuda Point for F$89 to F$129 (US$58–US$84/£29–£42) per person. The higher price includes lobster as the main course, instead of fish or steak. *Note:* You must make reservations.

8 Island Nights in Nadi

The large hotels usually have something going on every night. This might be a special meal followed by a Fijian dance show, and the large hotels also frequently offer live entertainment in their bars during the cocktail hour. Check with the hotel activities desk to see what's happening.

   With several pubs, Martintar is Nadi's nightlife center. The most civilized nightclub is the German-owned **Hamburg Bar** (no phone), on Northern Press Road just off the Queen's Road; it has sports TVs, billiard tables, and a DJ who provides music for a dance floor. The **Bounty Bar & Restaurant** (© **672 0840**) draws many expatriates and has live music on weekend nights (see "Where to Dine in Nadi," above). Across the Queen's Road, the outdoor tables at **Ed's Bar** (© **672 4650**) are popular with locals.

   Out on Denarau Island, **Cardo's Upstairs** is a sophisticated lounge, bar, and retro dance floor above Cardo's Steakhouse & Cocktail Bar (© **675 0900;** see "Where to Dine in Nadi," above).

Tips Keep an Eye on Your Beer Mug

Bartenders in Fiji are taught to keep your beer mug full and your pockets empty. That is, they don't ask if you want another beer: They keep pouring until you tell them emphatically to stop.

6

The Mamanuca & Yasawa Islands

by Valerie Haeder & Bill Goodwin

The Great Sea Reef off northwest Viti Levu encloses a huge lagoon where usually calm waters surround the nearby Mamanuca and Yasawa island groups with speckled shades of yellow, green, and blue. With ample sunshine and some of Fiji's best beaches, these little islands are great places to escape from the hustle of modern civilization.

The **Mamanuca Group,** as it's officially known, consists of small flat atolls and hilly islands ranging from 8 to 32km (5–20 miles) west of Nadi. Day cruises have made the Mamanucas a destination since the dawn of Fiji's modern tourism in the early 1960s; these islands are home to some of the country's oldest offshore resorts, which are still very popular among Australians and New Zealanders on 1- or 2-week holidays.

The Mamanucas generally are divided into two sections. To the north are a group of flat, tiny sand islands that barely break the lagoon's surface. Three of them are within virtual hailing distance, including **Tai Island,** better known for the rollicking Beachcomber Island Resort; **Elevuka,** home to family-oriented Treasure Island Resort; and **Kadavu,** shared by a nature preserve and Bounty Island Resort.

To the south, a row of hilly islands begins with **Malololailai,** which is nearly joined to the larger **Malolo.** Each has three resorts. Next to Malolo lie tiny **Wadigi Island,** home to an upscale get-away, and **Qalito Island,** which is better known as Castaway for its lone hotel, Castaway Island Resort. Beyond them, **Mana Island** has one of the group's larger resorts as well as low-budget properties, all sharing a great beach. The Mamanucas end to the west with **Matamanoa** and **Tokoriki** islands, both with resorts, and the beautiful, uninhabited **Monuriki,** where Tom Hanks starred in the movie *Castaway.*

North of the Mamanucas, the **Yasawa Islands** stretch as much as 100km (62 miles) from Nadi. Lt. Charles Wilkes, commander of the U.S. exploring expedition that charted Fiji in 1840, compared the Yasawa Islands to "a string of blue beads lying along the horizon."

For the most part, Fijians still live in small villages huddled among the curving coconut palms beside lagoons with excellent snorkeling and some of the country's most awesomely beautiful beaches. But the Yasawas are changing rapidly, with more than two dozen small resorts that span all price ranges. Particularly prolific are the low-budget establishments aimed at young backpackers, who now see a bit of beach time in the Yasawas as an essential part of their Fiji experience. In fact, rather than tour around Fiji, many backpackers today simply head for the Yasawas.

While accommodations are spread throughout the Yasawas chain, the largest concentration is on the shores of the so-called **Blue Lagoon,** a lovely baylike body of water nearly enclosed by **Matacawalevu, Nacula, Nanuya Lailai,** and **Nanuya Levu** islands.

1 Getting to the Islands

While a few run their own transfer boats, the Mamanuca and Yasawa resorts arrange third-party transfers for their guests. All of them require reservations, and most leave from the Port Denarau marina.

BY PLANE & HELICOPTER

The quickest, easiest, and most expensive way to the islands is via seaplane or helicopter. **Pacific Island Seaplanes** (© 672 5643; www.fijiseaplanes.com) provides seaplane service to the islands; the flights are on a charter basis arranged by the resorts, which will also quote you prices. Even more expensive, **Island Hoppers** (© 672 0140; www.helicopters.com.fj) flies its helicopters to most of the moderate and expensive resorts. Expect to pay about F$450 (US$292/£146) round-trip per person via helicopter, or F$350 (US$227/£114) by seaplane.

Only Malololailai and Mana islands have airstrips in the Mamanucas, both served by **Pacific Sun** (© 672 0888). See "Getting Around Fiji," in chapter 3. There is an airstrip on Yasawa Island, but it's a private affair for Yasawa Island Resort and Spa.

BY SHUTTLE BOAT

Most folks take one of the fast, air-conditioned catamarans providing daily shuttle service from Port Denarau to and from the islands. Only a few offshore resorts have piers, so be prepared to get your feet wet wading ashore.

The **Malolo Cat** (© 672 0774) is a catamaran that runs daily runs between Port Denarau and Malololailai, home to Musket Cove, Plantation Island, and Lomani resorts. One-way fares are about F$50 (US$32/£16).

Most travelers take one of three fast catamarans operated between Port Denarau and the islands by **South Sea Cruises** (© 675 0500; www.ssc.com.fj). The *Tiger IV* and the *Cougar* depart for most of the Mamanuca resorts three times daily, usually 9am, 12:15pm, and 3:15pm. The *Tiger IV* normally serves the closer islands to Nadi, while the *Cougar* goes to Matamanoa and Tokoriki islands.

The bright yellow *Yasawa Flyer* makes one voyage a day to the Yasawas and back, departing daily at 8:30am. It goes as far north as Nacula Island, a 4½-hour voyage from Port Denarau, then returns along the same route.

Round-trip fares range up to F$100 (US$65/£33) per person to the Mamanucas, F$120 (US$78/£39) to the Yasawas. For a bit extra you can ride up in the captain's lounge and have someone bring you refreshments.

A subsidiary of South Sea Cruises, **Awesome Adventures Fiji** (© 670 5006; www.awesomefiji.com) has a "Bula Pass" allowing unlimited island-hopping via the

---

Tips Take a Big Boat

Some inexpensive properties will offer to take you to the islands in their own small craft for less money than you would pay on the *Tiger IV*, the *Cougar,* or the *Yasawa Flyer.* These rides take at least an hour to the Mamanucas, several hours to the Yasawas, and the boats can be small, poorly equipped, and perhaps lacking covers to protect you from the elements. One of them sank a few years ago, fortunately without the loss of life. Take my advice and board one of the fast catamarans.

Yasawa Flyer for 7, 14, and 21 days. These cost F$270 (US$175/£88), F$390 (US$253/£127), and F$420 (US$273/£137) per person, respectively.

SeaFiji (© **672 5961;** www.seafiji.net) provides 24-hour water taxi service to the Mamanuca islands from Port Denarau.

2 Seeing the Islands on Day Trips from Nadi

Even if you're laying over in Fiji for just a short time, you should get out to the islands for a day from Nadi or the Coral Coast. Most of the trips mentioned below depart from the Port Denarau marina on Denarau Island. Bus transportation from the Nadi or Coral Coast hotels to the marina is included in their prices (you'll pay more from the Coral Coast). Children pay half fare on all the day trips.

My favorite is **Beachcomber Day Cruises** ☆☆☆ (© **666 1500;** www.beachcomberfiji.com), which goes to youth-oriented Beachcomber Island Resort (see "Resorts in the Mamanuca Islands," below). Despite the advent of so many inexpensive properties elsewhere, Beachcomber still is a most popular stop for young people seeking sand, sun, and suds—but beware if you have fundamentalist eyes: Young European women have been known to drop their tops at Beachcomber. You'll pay F$82 (US$53/£27) for bus transportation, the cruise, and an all-you-can-eat buffet lunch on Beachcomber Island. Swimming is free, but snorkeling gear, scuba diving, and other activities cost extra.

You can sightsee through the Mamanucas on the *Tiger IV* (see "Getting to the Islands," above). The half-day sightseeing-only voyage costs about F$90 (US$58/£29). I prefer taking the morning voyage, getting off at **South Sea Island, Malolo Island Resort, Castaway Island Resort, Mana Island Resort,** or **Bounty Island** (see "Resorts in the Mamanuca Islands," below, before making your decision). These sailings include a buffet lunch, swimming, and sunbathing. Depending on where you spend the day, these cost between F$120 and F$135 (US$78–US$88/£39–£44).

It's a long day (8:30am–6pm), but you can ride the *Yasawa Flyer* (© **675 0500;** www.ssc.com.fj) on its daily voyages through the Yasawas and back for about F$125 (US$81/£42) round-trip. You won't be able to luxuriate on any beaches—the boat stops at each property only long enough to put off and pick up passengers and their luggage—but it's the only way to take in the Yasawas in 1 day. Or you can get off at beautiful **Waya Island** in the southern Yasawas for lunch and a guided tour of a Fijian village, which will give you more of a glimpse into Fijian life than the Mamanuca day trips.

Malamala Island (© **670 2444**) is a 2.4-hectare (6-acre) islet studded with palm trees and circled with white-sand beaches. The only inhabitants will be you and your fellow passengers, who will use Malamala's big thatch *bure* (bungalow) for a barbecue

---

(*Moments* **Sand Between My Toes**

Nothing relaxes me more than digging my toes into the sand at one of Fiji's small get-away-from-it-all resorts. If I have a day to spare in Nadi, I head out to Beachcomber Island Resort, where the floor of the bar and dining room is nothing but sand. And with all those young folks running around out on the beach, I feel like I'm 25 again.

The Mamanuca & Yasawa Islands

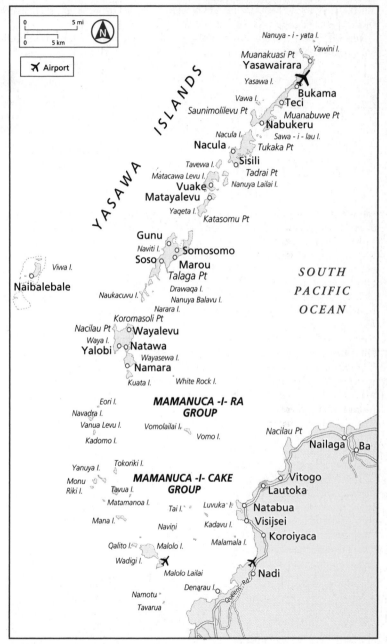

0   5 mi
0   5 km

✈ Airport

Nanuya - i - yata I.

Yawini I.

Muanakuasi Pt

Yasawairara

Yasawa I.

Bukama

Vawa I.

○**Teci**

Saunimolilevu Pt

Muanabuwe Pt

○**Nabukeru**

Nacula I.

Sawa - i - lau I.

Nacula

Tukaka Pt

Tavewa I.

○**Sisili**

Matacawa Levu I.

Tadrai Pt

Vuake

Nanuya Lailai I.

Matayalevu

Yaqeta I.

Katasomu Pt

Gunu

Naviti I.

○**Somosomo**

Soso○

Marou

Talaga Pt

Viwa I.

Drawaqa I.

Nanuya Balavu I.

Naibalebale

Naukacuvu I.

Narara I.

Koromasoli Pt

Nacilau Pt

○**Wayalevu**

Waya I.

○**Natawa**

Yalobi

Wayasewa I.

○**Namara**

Kuata I.

White Rock I.

Eori I.

MAMANUCA -I- RA GROUP

Navadra I.

Vanua Levu I.

Vomolailai I.

Nacilau Pt

Kadomo I.

Vomo I.

Nailaga○

Ba

Yanuya I.

Tokoriki I.

MAMANUCA -I- CAKE GROUP

○**Vitogo**

Monu

Riki I.

Tavua I.

○**Lautoka**

Matamanoa I.

Tai I.

Luvuka I.

○**Natabua**

Mana I.

○**Visijsei**

Navini

Kadavu I.

○**Koroiyaca**

Qalito I.

Malolo I.

Malamala I.

Wadigi I.

✈

Malolo Lailai

✈**Nadi**

Namotu

Denarau I.

Tavarua

YASAWA ISLANDS

SOUTH PACIFIC OCEAN

lunch. The F$89 (US$58/£29) price includes lunch, a beer or drink from the bar, snorkel gear, and coral viewing.

You will have more options on **Malololailai Island,** home of Plantation Island, Musket Cove, and Lomani resorts. You can visit them on a day cruise via the *Malololo Cat* (© **672 0744**) for about F$50 (US$32/£16) round-trip, or fly over on **Pacific Sun** (© **672 0888**) for F$122 (US$79/£40) round-trip. You can hang out at the two resorts, shop at Georgie Czukelter's **Art Gallery** (no phone) on the hill above Musket Cove, and dine at **Anandas Restaurant and Bar** (© **672 2333**) by the airstrip. You can book at the restaurant to play the island's short 9-hole **golf course;** fees are F$20 (US$13/£6.70).

Seafari Cruise is what South Sea Cruises (© **675 0500**) calls its rent-a-boat service at Port Denarau. You design your own cruise to the Mamanuca Islands, such as picnicking at a deserted beach or picking your own snorkeling spots. Prices depend on the size of the boat, with the largest holding up to 20 passengers.

3 Sailing Through the Islands

I hesitate to use such a well-worn cliché as "reef-strewn," but that's the most precise way to describe Fiji's waters—so strewn, in fact, that the government does not allow you to charter a "bareboat" yacht (without a skipper). It's just too dangerous. You can rent both boat and skipper or local guide for extended cruises through the islands. The marina at **Musket Cove Island Resort** (see "Resorts in the Mamanuca Islands," below) is a mecca for cruising yachts, some of whose skippers take charters for a living. Contact the resort for details.

On the other hand, you can easily get out on the lagoons under sail for a day. Most interesting to my mind is the **MV** *Seaspray* ✫✫ (© **675 0500;** www.ssc.com.fj), a 25m (83-ft.) schooner that starred in the 1960s TV series *Adventures in Paradise,* based on James A. Michener's short stories. Based at Mana Island, it sails through the outer Mamanucas and stops for swimming and snorkeling at the same beach on rocky **Monuriki Island** upon which Tom Hanks filmed the movie *Castaway* (Hanks, by the way, did *not* live on the islet all by himself during production). The cruises range from F$140 to F$175 (US$91–US$114/£46–£57), depending on where you board, including morning tea, lunch, beer, wine, and soft drinks. You pay more to come out from Port Denarau to Mana on the *Tiger IV,* less from the Mamanuca resorts.

The *Whale's Tale* (© **672 2455;** funcruises@connect.com.fj), a luxury, 30m (100-ft.) auxiliary sailboat, takes no more than 12 guests on day cruises from Port Denarau through the Mamanucas. The F$170 (US$110/£55) per person cost includes a continental breakfast with champagne on departure; a buffet lunch prepared on board; and all beverages, including beer, wine, liquor, and sunset cocktails. The *Whale's Tale* is also available for charters ranging from 1 day in the Mamanucas to 3 days and 2 nights in the Yasawas. Rates vary according to the length of the trip.

Captain Cook Cruises (© **670 1823;** www.captaincook.com.au) uses the *Ra Marama,* a 33m (110-ft.) square-rigged brigantine built in Singapore during the 1950s and once the official yacht of Fiji's colonial governors-general, for the 1-hour sail out to Tivua Island, an uninhabited 1.6-hectare (4-acre) islet in the Mamanucas. A traditional Fijian welcoming ceremony greets you at the island, where you can swim, snorkel, and canoe over 200 hectares (500 acres) of surrounding coral gardens (or see the colors from a glass-bottom boat). Lunch and drinks are included in the F$97 (US$63/£32) charge. I've never done it, but you can stay overnight on Tivua for

---

Fun Fact **Drop-Dead Good Looks**

The late actor Gardner McKay, who sailed around on the MV *Seaspray* while starring as Capt. Adam Troy, walked away from the boob tube after the popular TV series *Adventures in Paradise* bit the dust in the 1960s. At first he opted for real dust—as in riding across the Sahara Desert with the Egyptian Camel Corps. He went on to crew on yachts in the Caribbean and hike the Amazonian jungles before settling down as a novelist, poet, playwright, and newspaper drama critic. Despite his drop-dead good looks, he never acted again.

---

about F$300 (US$195/£98) per person, double occupancy, including meals. Accommodations are in two bures with cool freshwater showers.

A subsidiary of Captain Cook Cruises, **Fiji Windjammer Barefoot Cruises** (© 670 1823; www.fijisailingsafari.com.fj) has 3- and 4-day "sailing safaris" to the Yasawas on its tall-ship *Spirit of the Pacific.* It sails during daylight but deposits you ashore at its Barefoot Lodge at night. Safaris start at F$535 (US$347/£179) per person, with a double-occupancy room.

4 Cruising Through the Islands

Blue Lagoon Cruises ★★★ (© 818/554-5000 or 666 1622; www.bluelagoon-cruises.com) is one of the South Pacific's best small cruise lines. Captain Trevor Withers—who had worked on the original 1949 *Blue Lagoon* movie starring Jean Simmons—started the company in the 1950s with a converted American crash vessel.

Newest of Blue Lagoon's vessels is the *Fijian Princess,* a 60m (196-ft.) catamaran with 34 air-conditioned cabins and a spa. The 47m (155-ft.) *Nanuya Princess,* carries up to 66 passengers in 33 staterooms, while the sleek 56m (185-ft.) *Mystique Princess,* looks as if it should belong to a Greek shipping magnate; the 35 staterooms do indeed approach tycoon standards. Oldest is the 38m-long (126-ft.) *Lycianda,* which carries 54 passengers in 26 air-conditioned cabins.

Most cruises range from 3 to 7 nights through the Yasawas, with one of the 7-night voyages designed especially for scuba divers. Trips depart Lautoka and arrive in the Yasawas in time for a welcoming cocktail party and dinner on board. They then proceed to explore the islands, stopping in little bays for snorkeling, picnics, or *lovo* feasts (featuring food cooked underground in a freshly dug pit oven) on sandy beaches, and visits with the Yasawans in their villages. The ships anchor in peaceful coves at night, and even when they cruise from island to island, the water is usually so calm that only incurable landlubbers get seasick. In the one major variation from this theme, the weeklong "historical and cultural" cruises go to Northern Fiji, with stops at Levuka, Savusavu, Taveuni, and several remote islands.

Rates range from about F$2,000 to F$5,200 (US$1,299–US$3,377/£650–£1,689) per cabin for double occupancy, depending on the length of the voyage, the season, and the cabin's location. Diving cruises cost more. All meals, activities, and taxes are included. Singles and children staying in their parents' cabins pay supplements.

A less expensive alternative is **Captain Cook Cruises** (© 670 1823; www.captaincook.com.fj). This Australian-based firm uses the 120-passenger MV *Reef Escape* for most of its 3- to 7-night cruises from Port Denarau to the Mamanucas and Yasawas.

Tips **Pickups by Blue Lagoon Cruises**

Blue Lagoon Cruises picks up passengers from some Mamanuca resorts at the beginning of each trip, but the ships always return directly to Lautoka at the end. In other words, you can stay at one of the resorts and depart on your cruise directly from there. If you do it the other way around, you have to get from Lautoka back to Denarau Island to catch a ferry to the resort, thus wasting money and valuable time.

The *Reef Escape* has a swimming pool, spa, and sauna. Compared to the sleek vessels in the *Blue Lagoon Cruises* fleet, it's more like a floating hotel. Prices begin at F$1,450 (US$942/£471) per person double occupancy.

5 Resorts in the Mamanuca Islands

The **Mamanuca Hotel Association,** Private Mail Bag, Nadi Airport (*©* **670 0144;** fax 670 2336; www.fijiresorts.com), has information about all the resorts.

They all have watersports and scuba dive operators on premises. **Subsurface Fiji Diving and Watersports** (*©* **666 6738;** www.subsurfacefiji.com), a PADI five-star operation, staffs more than a dozen of the resorts, while **Awesome Adventures Fiji** (*©* **670 5006;** www.awesomefiji.com) is at Mana Island Resort.

Also here is **South Sea Island** (*©* **675 0500;** www.ssc.com.fj), which like Beachcomber Island Resort (see below) occupies a tiny islet. It has accommodations, but it is primarily a day-trip destination.

Near the main pass through the Great Sea Reef, the American-operated **Tavarua Island Resort** (*©* **805/687-4551** in the U.S., or 670 6513; www.tavarua.com) caters to anyone but is still Fiji's best-known surf camp. Tavarua has enjoyed recent upgrades, including the addition of an outdoor pool, so "surfing widows" can enjoy reasonable luxuries while their other halves are out riding the waves.

Another small islet off Lautoka is home to the 10-unit **Navini Island Resort** (*©* **666 2188;** www.navinifiji.com.fj), which does its own transfers rather than rely on the *Tiger IV.* It's on a small sand islet.

We are organizing the resorts by the islands on which they reside, in alphabetical order. Consult the map to see which resorts are closest to Viti Levu.

ELUVUKA (TREASURE) ISLAND

This tiny atoll-like islet is nearly surrounded by a white-sand beach (a stroll of 15 min. or less brings you back to your starting point). The name Eluvuka is seldom used, since locals call it simply "Treasure" because it is completely occupied by one resort.

Treasure Island Resort *(Kids)*   This venerable resort is geared to couples and families rather than to the sometimes-raucous singles who frequent its neighbor, Beachcomber Island Resort (see later in this chapter). Pathways through tropical shrubs pass playgrounds for both adults and children, a sea turtle breeding pool, and a minigolf course—all of which, along with the kids' program, makes this a good choice for families. For those wishing to start one, the resort has a glass-wall wedding chapel with a lagoon view. Treasure's 33 duplex bungalows hold 66 bright rooms. All face the beach and have bright furniture, shower-only bathrooms, both a queen-size and single bed,

Where to Stay in the Mamanuca Islands

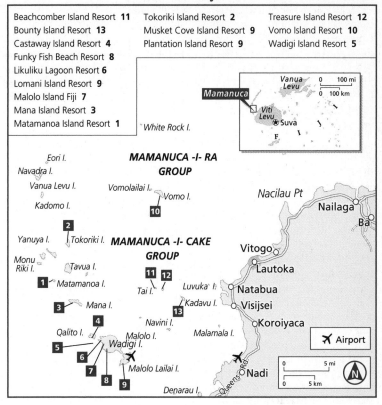

Beachcomber Island Resort **11**
Bounty Island Resort **13**
Castaway Island Resort **4**
Funky Fish Beach Resort **8**
Likuliku Lagoon Resort **6**
Lomani Island Resort **9**
Malolo Island Fiji **7**
Mana Island Resort **3**
Matamanoa Island Resort **1**

Tokoriki Island Resort **2**
Musket Cove Island Resort **9**
Plantation Island Resort **9**

Treasure Island Resort **12**
Vomo Island Resort **10**
Wadigi Island Resort **5**

and a porch facing the lagoon. An airy beachside building houses the restaurant and bar; it opens to the swimming pool (which plans are afloat to improve). Guests pay extra for motorized activities and to visit Beachcomber Island Resort.

P.O. Box 2210, Lautoka. ℂ **666 6999.** Fax 666 6955. www.treasure.com.fj. 67 units. F$545 (US$354/£177) double. AE, MC, V. **Amenities:** Restaurant; bar; children's program; laundry service; outdoor pool; room service; spa; tennis court; coin-op washers and dryers; watersports equipment. *In room:* A/C, coffeemaker, fridge.

KADAVU (BOUNTY) ISLAND

Not to be confused with the larger Kadavu Island south of Viti Levu (see chapter 9), this one is near Treasure Island and Beachcomber Island resorts. It's a flat, 19-hectare (48-acre) island, of which 14 hectares (35 acres) are a nature preserve with ample birdlife, a sea turtle nursery, and the remains of an ancient Fijian village.

Bounty Island Resort While Beachcomber Island continues to be the most popular Mamanuca resort among budget-minded travelers, you can get away from the crowds without paying a fortune at this Fijian-owned and -managed hotel. A main building with a restaurant and bar opens to a swimming pool beside a very good beach. The 22 beachside bungalows are rather simple, but they all have bathrooms and are clean and comfortable. Electric fans and screened, louvered windows compensate for the lack of air-conditioners, which are seldom needed since the resort benefits from the prevailing southeast trade winds. The dormitory that is air-conditioned is more expensive than the two fan-equipped dorms.

P.O. Box 2210, Lautoka. ℂ 666 6999 or 666 7461. Fax 666 6955. www.fiji-bounty.com. 22 units, 60 dorm beds. F$170 (US$110/£57) double; F$30–F$35 (US$19–US$23/£10–£12) dorm bed. MC, V. **Amenities:** Restaurant; bar; game room; free kayaks, snorkeling gear, and Hobie Cats; outdoor pool; free washers and dryers. *In room:* A/C (extra fee applies); fridge; no phone.

MALOLOLAILAI ISLAND

The closest island to Nadi, boomerang-shape Malololailai faces a shallow bay. This is the one Mamanuca island where you can stay at one resort and wander over to another for dinner or drinks. As I noted under "Seeing the Islands on Day Trips from Nadi," above, you can also shop at Georgie Czukelter's **Art Gallery,** dine at the barbecue-oriented **Anandas Restaurant and Bar** (ℂ 672 2333) near the airport, and play a short 9-hole golf course. The dirt airstrip divides the island into two, with Musket Cove Island Resort on one end, and Lomani Island Resort and Plantation Island Resort on the other. Lomani and Plantation resorts share one of Fiji's best beaches (shallow though the lagoon may be at low tide), while scores of cruising yachts put into Musket Cove from April into October.

Lomani Island Resort 🐟   This small boutique hotel is next door to Plantation Island Resort and shares its long, picturesque beach. The main building formerly was a private residence but now houses a comfy guest lounge, restaurant, and bar in an innlike atmosphere. Serving good international fare, the dining room opens to a 35m-long (115-ft.) pool—plenty of room to swim your laps. You can also dine poolside or by the beach. The accommodations are all spacious and amply appointed, but they are not individual bungalows. My choice would be one of the Hibiscus Suites, which are in duplex buildings. The Deluxe Suites are in two-story motel-like buildings, but they do have separate bedrooms, which the Hibiscus Suites do not. This is the most intimate resort on Malololailai Island.

P.O. Box 9732, Nadi Airport. ℂ 666 8212. Fax 666 8523. www.lomaniisland.com. 12 units. F$590–F$640 (US$383–US$416/£192–£208) double. Rates include full breakfast. AE, MC, V. **Amenities:** Restaurant; bar exercise room; laundry service; outdoor pool; room service; spa; watersports equipment. *In room:* A/C, TV (DVD movies only), coffeemaker, fridge (stocked on request), iron, safe.

Musket Cove Island Resort   One of three Australians who own Malololailai Island, Dick Smith founded this retreat in 1977. It has grown considerably since then, and it now has a marina where cruising yachties call from June to September. They congregate at an open-air bar under a thatched roof out on a tiny man-made island reached by the marina's pontoons. "Dick's Place" has been retained as the name of the pleasant bar and restaurant next to two swimming pools, one with a real yacht protruding from its side, as if it has run aground. Although a broad mud bank appears

---

⸤Tips⸥ **Ask About Meal Plans**

Except on Malololailai Island, where you can walk among Musket Cove, Plantation, and Lomani resorts, you will have no choice but to dine in your resort's or hostel's restaurant. Be sure to ask if it has meal packages available, which usually are less expensive than paying separately for each meal.

here at low tide, Dick has dredged out a swimmable beach area. Accommodations range from charming one-room bures to luxury villas with living rooms, full kitchens, master bedrooms downstairs, and two bedrooms upstairs, each with its own private bathroom. Musket Cove also manages Armstrong Villas at Musket Cove, a group of two-bedroom condo bungalows on a man-made island; the units have kitchens and phones. Check the website and consult with the reservationist when booking your unit to make sure you'll have the in-room amenities you desire.

Private Mail Bag, Nadi Airport. ℂ 877/313-1464 or 672 2371. Fax 672 0378. www.musketcovefiji.com. 55 units. F$474–F$551 (US$308–US$358/£154–£179) bungalow; F$680 (US$442/£221) villa. AE, DC, MC, V. **Amenities:** 2 restaurants; 2 bars; activities desk; babysitting; bike rentals; laundry service; massage; 3 outdoor pools; spa; coin-op washers and dryers; watersports equipment rentals. *In room:* A/C (in villas only), coffeemaker, fridge, iron, kitchen (villas only), safe, no phone (in bungalows).

Plantation Island Resort *Kids*

The oldest, largest and most diverse of the Mamanuca resorts, Plantation primarily attracts Australian couples and families, plus day-trippers from Nadi. Like Mana Island Resort & Spa (see below), it has a Club Med–style atmosphere of nonstop activity. The resort has several types of accommodations: duplex bures suitable for singles or couples, two-bedroom bungalows for families, and motel-style rooms. Some are next to the beach, others surround a swimming pool, and the rest are removed from the resort action. A large central building beside the beach has a bar, dance floor, lounge area, restaurant, and coffee shop. A children's playroom with a full-time babysitter makes this another good choice for families.

P.O. Box 9176, Nadi Airport. ℂ 666 9333. Fax 666 9200. www.plantationisland.com. 192 units. F$250–F$375 (US$162–US$244/£81–£122) double; F$375–F$550 (US$244–US$357/£122–£179) bungalow. AE, DC, MC, V. **Amenities:** 2 restaurants; 2 bars; activities desk; babysitting; children's programs; game room; 9-hole golf course; laundry service; massage; 3 outdoor pools; salon; tennis courts; coin-op washers and dryers; watersports equipment rentals. *In room:* A/C (in hotel rooms), coffeemaker, fridge.

MALOLO ISLAND

Joined at low tide to its smaller sister, Malololailai (Little Malolo), this island is one of the largest of the Mamanucas. Malolo is a hilly island with a serrated coastline dotted with beaches. Fijians live in traditional villages on the eastern side, while the west coast is occupied by resorts in all price ranges. You can hike into the hills but not from one resort to the other to have a meal or drink.

Funky Fish Beach Resort

A former New Zealand All Black rugby star and coach of the Fijian and Italian national teams, Brad Johnstone decided he was tired of cold weather and so, with his wife, Rosemary, created this "flashpacker" resort—flashpackers being backpackers looking for more than cheap hostels. They put their main building with casual, sand-floor restaurant and bar up on a hill to take advantage of a fine sea view. The outdoor pool and accommodations are down beside the beach. They do have a regular dorm (the coed, 12-bunk "Octopussy Lodge"), but they also have five "Thorny Oyster" private dorm rooms with ceiling fans. Each of their 10 "Rock Lobster" bures has a bedroom and private bathroom with outdoor shower. Atop the heap, each of the "Grand Grouper" units has two bedrooms and a private bathroom, also with outdoor shower. Although its guest rooms are spacious enough for families, the resort has no children's program.

P.O. Box 11053, Nadi Airport. ℂ 651 3180. Fax 651 6180. www.funkyfishresort.com. 17 units (12 with bathroom), 12 dorm beds. F$156–F$311 (US$101–US$202/£51–£101) bungalow; F$99 (US$64/£32) dorm room; F$35 (US$23/£12) dorm bed. MC, V. **Amenities:** Restaurant; bar; free kayaks and snorkeling gear; laundry service; outdoor pool. *In room:* Fridge (2 units), no phone.

How to Choose Your Offshore Resort

Fiji has one of the world's finest collections of offshore resorts—small establishments with islands all to themselves. They have lovely beach settings and modern facilities, and are excellent places to get away from it all. The major drawback of any offshore resort, of course, is that you've done just that. You won't see much of Fiji while you're basking in the sun on a tiny rock some 40km (25 miles) at sea. Consider them for what they have to offer but not as bases from which to explore the country.

You can check your e-mail, but you're unlikely to have a television in your bungalow at Fiji's offshore resorts, and you may not get a telephone, either. If you must be in touch with the world every minute of every day, stay on the mainland of Viti Levu. Come out here with one goal in mind: relaxation.

Although the Mamanuca and Yasawas have more offshore resorts than anywhere else in Fiji, others are on Vatulele Island off the Coral Coast, Beqa Island off Pacific Harbour, Wakaya Island off Suva, Namenalala Island off Savusavu, and Qamea and Matagi islands off Taveuni. If you decide to stay at one of them, I suggest you read all my descriptions before making your choice.

Pay attention to what I say about the resorts' styles. For example, if you don't enjoy getting to know fellow guests at sometimes raucous parties, you might not like Vatulele Island or Turtle Island resorts, but you might love the Wakaya Club or Yasawa Island Resort and Spa. If you like a large establishment with lively, Club Med–like ambience, you might prefer Mana Island and Plantation Island resorts. Many other resorts offer peace, quiet, and few fellow guests—and no children. In other words, choosing carefully could mean the difference between a miserable week or a slice of heaven.

In most cases, you'll have no place to dine other than your resort's restaurants. Be sure to inquire about meal plans if food is not already included in the rates. All but a few of the island resorts provide free snorkeling gear, kayaks, and other nonmotorized watersports equipment. They charge extra for scuba diving and motorized sports.

Likuliku Lagoon Resort 𝄞𝄞𝄞   Opened in 2007, this exquisitely designed resort is the first in Fiji to have overwater bungalows, and is thus the first here to compete directly with Bora Bora and other French Polynesian islands for honeymooners and others seeking these romantic cottages built on stilts over the lagoon. Looking out at Castaway Island from a half-moon, beach-fringed bay on the northwestern corner of Malolo Island, Likuliku shows intricate Fijian touches throughout, with *magimagi* (sennit, or coconut rope) lashing the log beams under the natural thatched roofs of its buildings. Likuliku was built and is owned by the Fiji-bred Whitten family, who made sure it reflects their country's indigenous culture. The 10 overwater bures aren't nearly as large as the new humongous units at Bora Bora, but they have glass fish-viewing floor panels flanking their coffee tables, and more glass behind the sinks in their airy bathrooms. Each unit has a deck with steps leading down into the lagoon, which can be very shallow at low tide—during which the average depth is 1.5m (5 ft.), compared to a few centimeters in French Polynesia. The overwaters are close to a reef edge, however, so you can easily reach deep water at all tides. The split-level bungalows ashore all face the beach and are identical except for plunge pools set in the front decks of the deluxe models. Overlooking the sea and a large swimming pool, the restaurant serves very good (and sometimes exotic) Pacific Rim fare. The service is attentive, efficient, and friendly; in fact, I met several veteran staffers who came here from other top-end Fijian resorts. Only the overwater bures have TVs; the rest of you can watch a big screen while chilling in the air-conditioned library lounge. You can pamper yourself in Likuliku's full-service adults-only spa.

P.O. Box 10044, Nadi Airport. ☎ **672 4275** or 666 3344. Fax 664 0014. www.likulikulagoon.com. 45 units. F$1,300–F$1,950 (US$844–US$1,266/£422–£633) bungalow. Rates include all meals and nonmotorized watersports. AE, DC, MC, V. Children 16 and under not accepted. **Amenities:** Restaurant; 2 bars; activities desk; concierge; fitness center; laundry service; massage; outdoor pool; room service; spa; watersports equipment; Wi-Fi in public areas. *In room:* A/C, TV (in overwater bungalows), coffeemaker, fridge (stocked on request), iron, safe.

Malolo Island Fiji *Kids*   Although it draws mostly couples, this resort is a good choice for families with children. Among adults it's notable for having an outdoor spa, a grown-ups-only lounge, and one of the best beachside bars in Fiji—a thatched-roof building with a lagoonside deck and a lunchtime dining area under a sprawling shade tree. Two other restaurants and bars occupy a two-story building at the base of a hill at the rear of the property. They open to two swimming pools, one especially suited for children since it has a walk-in sand bottom under a tarp to provide shade, the other good for grown-ups since it sports a swim-up bar. Most of the guest bungalows are duplexes. Of these, 18 have separate bedrooms; the others are studios. In addition, an upstairs family unit can sleep eight persons. Malolo is around a headland from its sister, Likuliku Lagoon Resort.

P.O. Box 10044, Nadi Airport. ☎ **666 9192**. Fax 666 9197. www.maloloisland.com. 49 units. F$556–F$649 (US$361–US$421/£181–£211) double; F$1,082 (US$703/£352) family unit. AE, DC, MC, V. **Amenities:** 3 restaurants; 3 bars; activities desk; babysitting; children's programs; laundry service; massage; 2 outdoor pools; spa; watersports equipment rentals. *In room:* A/C, coffeemaker, fridge, iron, no phone.

MANA ISLAND

A long, rectangular island, Mana is half occupied by Mana Island Resort and half by Fijians, who operate backpacker-oriented accommodations. All of them share one of Fiji's best beaches, which runs along the island's southern side. A barrier reef offshore creates a safe lagoon for watersports.

The backpacker lodges include **Mana Island Lodge** (☎ **620 7030;** manalodge2@ yahoo.com), on the beach about 180m (600 ft.) south of Mana Island Resort. Rooms in simple bungalows cost F$180 to F$250 (US$117–US$162/£59–£81), and dorm beds are F$60 (US$39/£20), including meals.

Next door is **Ratu Kini Backpackers** (☎ **672 1959;** www.ratukini.com), offering dormitories (F$38/US$25/£13 per person), units with bathrooms (F$100/US$65/£33), and rooms with shared facilities (F$85/US$55/£28); prices include breakfast. Ratu Kini's restaurant virtually hangs over the beach. Guests at these accommodations cannot use Mana Island Resort's watersports facilities, but both hostels have their own dive shops. Facilities are much more basic than at Funky Fish Beach Resort, Beachcomber Island Resort, and Bounty Island Resort.

Mana Island Resort *Kids*   One of the largest off Nadi, this lively resort attracts Japanese singles and honeymooners, plus Australian and New Zealand couples and families. It's a popular day-trip destination from Nadi (see "Seeing the Islands on Day

Trips from Nadi," earlier in this chapter). Seaplanes, planes, and helicopters also land here. In other words, you'll have a *lot* of company on Mana. Accommodations include varied bungalows, town houses, and hotel rooms. Least expensive are the few original "island" bures, which have been upgraded and air-conditioned. Situated by themselves on the beach north of the airstrip, seven honeymoon bures feature Jacuzzis and butler service. Six executive beachfront bures have their own hot tubs. Two-story, town house–style oceanfront suites feature mezzanine bedrooms and two bathrooms, one with claw-foot tub. A good children's program makes Mana a fine family choice.

P.O. Box 610, Lautoka. © **665 0423**. Fax 665 0788. www.manafiji.com. 160 units. F$400 (US$260/£130) double room; F$270–F$1,200 (US$175–US$779/£88–£390) bungalow. Rates include full buffet breakfast. AE, DC, MC, V. **Amenities:** 3 restaurants; 3 bars; activities desk; babysitting; business center; children's programs; game room; Jacuzzi; laundry service; massage; outdoor pool; spa; 2 tennis courts; coin-op washers and dryers; watersports equipment rentals. *In room:* A/C, coffeemaker, fridge, iron, safe.

MATAMANOA ISLAND

A small rocky island with two steep hills, Matamanoa is the westernmost—and thus the most remote—of the Mamanuca resorts. The island terminates in a small flat point with a beach of deep, white sand, one of Fiji's best. The reef shelf falls away steeply here, resulting in great snorkeling even at low tide. For scuba divers, this is the closest of all Mamanuca resorts to the outer reef.

Matamanoa Island Resort *Value*   This intimate, adults-oriented complex (no kids 11 and under) sits beside the great beach on Matamanoa's southwestern end. The horizon-edge pool and a central building with bar and open-air dining room overlook the beach and lagoon. They aren't the most luxurious in Fiji, but each of the rectangular bungalows is spacious and comfortable. The 13 motel rooms are much smaller than the bungalows and do not face the beach. Because this well-managed resort is one of the better values in the Mamanucas, Australian, American, and European couples keep it busy year-round; book as early as possible.

P.O. Box 9729, Nadi Airport. © **666 0511**. Fax 666 0069. www.matamanoa.com. 33 units. F$375 (US$244/£122) double room; F$565 (US$367/£184) bungalow. Rates include breakfast. AE, DC, MC, V. Children 11 and under not accepted. **Amenities:** Restaurant; bar; activities desk; laundry service; massage; outdoor pool; tennis court; watersports equipment rentals. *In room:* A/C, fridge, coffeemaker, iron, safe.

QALITO (CASTAWAY) ISLAND

Off the northwestern corner of Malolo, Qalito is usually referred to as Castaway because of its resident resort. Its northern point is flanked by a very good beach.

Castaway Island Resort *Kids*   Built in the mid-1960s of logs and thatch, Castaway maintains its rustic, Fijian-style charm despite many improvements over the years. The central activities building, perched on the beach-flanked point, has a thatch-covered roof, and the ceilings of it and the guest bures are lined with genuine masi cloth. Although the bures sit relatively close together in a coconut grove, their roofs sweep low enough to provide some privacy. Located upstairs at the beachside

---

Impressions

Every resort seemed to have a platoon of insanely friendly Fijians.

—Scott L. Malcolmson, *Tuturani*, 1990

(Tips) Keeping You Entertained

Don't worry about staying busy at the offshore resorts in the Mamanucas and Yasawas. The range of activities depends on the resort, and you can participate in as much or as little as you like.

Not surprisingly, most resort activities center around, on, and in the ocean. In addition to snorkeling, kayaking, and fishing, most resorts offer PADI-certified scuba classes. Snorkeling itself offers incredible glimpses of electric blue starfish, zebra-striped fish, and underwater plant life.

Cultural activities include village visits and church services. Many resorts partner with local villages, providing jobs for the villagers and money for their families. The visits usually include a stop at a school where children will sing and teachers explain the children's daily activities. Toward the end of the visit and depending on the village, women lay out homemade wares for tourists to purchase. Worship services are always at a Methodist church, the predominate religion here. *Remember:* Female visitors must wear clothing that covers shoulders and knees, and no one wears a hat in a Fijian village.

Most resorts have a Fijian *meke* night, usually on Friday. The resort staff performs traditional Fijian song and dance, and guests are asked to join in later in the show.

---

watersports shack, the Sundowner Bar appropriately faces west toward the Great Sea Reef. Guests have wood-fired pizzas there or dine in the central building, usually at umbrella tables on a stone beachside patio. This is a very good family resort, with a nurse on duty and the staff providing a wide range of activities, from learning Fijian to sack races. Consequently, couples seeking a quiet romantic retreat should look elsewhere during school holiday periods. Australian restaurateur Geoff Shaw owns both this resort and the Outrigger on the Lagoon Fiji on the Coral Coast (see chapter 7, "The Coral Coast"), and the two often have attractive joint packages including helicopter transfers between them.

Private Mail Bag, Nadi Airport. © **800/888-0120** or 666 1233. Fax 666 5753. www.castawayfiji.com. 66 units. F$625–F$1,690 (US$406–US$1,097/£203–£549) bungalow. AE, DC, MC, V. **Amenities:** 2 restaurants; 3 bars; activities desk; babysitting; children's programs; game room; laundry service; massage; outdoor pool; tennis court; watersports equipment rentals. *In room:* A/C, coffeemaker, fridge, iron, no phone.

TAI (BEACHCOMBER) ISLAND

Back in 1963, Fiji-born Dan Costello bought an old Colonial Sugar Refining Company tugboat, converted it into a day cruiser, and started carrying tourists on day trips out to a tiny piece of sand and coconut palms known as Tai Island, which he renamed Beachcomber Island. The visitors liked it so much that some of them didn't want to leave. Some of their grandchildren still love it.

Beachcomber Island Resort ★★ (Value) Although the Yasawa Islands have stolen some of its thunder, Beachcomber still attracts the young, young-at-heart, and other like-minded souls in search of fun, members of the opposite sex, and a relatively inexpensive vacation (considering that all-you-can-eat meals are included in the rates). The youngest-at-heart cram into the coed dormitories. If you want more room, you can have or share a semiprivate lodge. And if you want your own charming bure, you can have that, too—just don't expect luxury. Rates also include a wide range of activities, though you pay extra for sailboats, canoes, windsurfing, scuba diving, water-skiing, and fishing trips.

P.O. Box 364, Lautoka. (©) 800/521-7242 or 666 1500. Fax 666 4496. www.beachcomberfiji.com. 36 units, 102 dorm beds. F$391–F$436 (US$254–US$283/£127–£142) double bure; F$300 (US$195–£98) double lodge; F$83 (US$54/£28) dorm bed. Rates include all meals. AE, DC, MC, V. **Amenities:** Restaurant; bar; activities desk; laundry service; massage; miniature golf; outdoor pool; watersports equipment rentals. *In room:* Coffeemaker, fridge, no phone.

TOKORIKI ISLAND

At the end of the line for the ferry shuttles from Port Denarau, Tokoriki is another hilly island with two good beaches. *Heads up:* I must point out that it sporadically has a problem with seaweed creating an unpleasant odor, though hopefully this will not be the case when you visit.

Tokoriki Island Resort   This adults-only property sits beside a wide beach stretching 1.5km (1 mile) on Tokoriki's northern side Although it doesn't have deep sand, once you get past rock shelves along the shoreline, the bottom slopes gradually into a safe lagoon with colorful coral gardens protected by a barrier reef. The resort itself sits on a flat shelf of land backed by a steep hill (a 4km/2½-mile hiking trail leads up to the ridgeline). Lined up along the beach, most of the spacious units have separate sleeping and living areas equipped with wet-bars, and both indoor and outdoor showers. Five much more luxurious Sunset Pool units have daybeds under thatched roofs next to their own plunge pools. A central thatch-topped bar divides the one-room central building into lounge and dining areas. Unless you count scuba diving, there are no motorized watersports here.

P.O. Box 10547, Nadi Airport. (©) **666 1999.** Fax 666 5295. www.tokoriki.com. 34 units. F$848–F$1,130 (US$551–US$734/£276–£367) bungalow. AE, MC, V. No children 11 and under accepted. **Amenities:** Restaurant; bar; game room; laundry service; massage; 2 outdoor pools; spa; tennis court; watersports equipment rentals. *In room:* A/C, coffeemaker, iron, minibar, safe.

VOMO ISLAND

An unusual clump of land, Vomo features a steep, 165m-high (550-ft.) hill on one end and a perfectly flat, 80-hectare (200-acre) shelf surrounded by a reef edged by brilliantly colorful corals on the other. Offshore, **Vomolailai (Little Vomo)** is a rocky islet with its own little beach. Vomo is the northernmost of the Mamanuca Islands and is almost on the border with the Yasawa Islands.

Vomo Island Resort   This upmarket resort occupies all of Vomo Island. The restaurant is adjacent to the beach, a deck-surrounded pool, and a stylish bar. Some of the luxurious guest bungalows climb the hill to provide views of the reef and sea, although I prefer those along a fine stretch of beach. Some of the beach bures are in duplex buildings, so ask for a self-standing one if you don't want next-door neighbors. Honeymooners, take note: About half of the duplex units interconnect, making them popular choices for well-heeled families with young children, especially during Australian school holidays, likewise the two-bedroom, two-bathroom Royal Deluxe Villa. All of the well-equipped units have sitting areas with sofas, and their large bathrooms have both showers and two-person Jacuzzis. Vomo is served by the *Yasawa Flyer* as well as by seaplane and helicopter.

P.O. Box 5650, Lautoka. (©) **666 7955.** Fax 666 7997. www.vomofiji.com. 29 units. F$1,500–F$2,000 (US$974–US$1,299/£487–£650) bungalow. Rates include meals, soft drinks, and activities except scuba diving and deep-sea fishing. AE, DC, MC, V. **Amenities:** Restaurant; bar; babysitting; children's program (during Australian school holidays); pitch-and-put golf course; laundry service; massage; outdoor pool; room service; spa; tennis court; watersports equipment. *In room:* A/C, coffeemaker, minibar, safe.

WADIGI ISLAND

Off Malolo's northwestern side, 1.2-hectare (3-acre) Wadigi (Wah-*ding*-ee) appears like a single hill precipitously protruding from the colorful lagoon. It and its two beaches are owned by Australians Jim and Tracey Johnston, who allow no one to set foot on Wadigi without advance permission, making it one of the best places in Fiji to get away from it all—as certain celebrities can testify.

Wadigi Island Resort 🐠🐠🐠   Staying with the Johnstons on Wadigi is more like having your own private island than staying at a resort. Jim and Tracey live here, and in a way you'll be their guests (although they and the staff will leave you absolutely alone if that's your desire). You will stay in a villa built on top of the island with spectacular views of the nearby islands and reefs, from the rooms as well as from an infinity-edge swimming pool. A central lounge and three bedrooms are like separate bungalows linked by walkways (the bedrooms can be rented separately or all together, thus giving you the entire island). A short walk downhill leads to the dining room and bar, or you can be served excellent fare in your room, by the pool, down by the beach, or wherever else you can imagine. Every unit has a satellite-fed TV with DVD player (you actors can pick out your own from an extensive library of movies) and a large veranda with daybed. The honeymoon unit comes equipped with an outdoor shower and two king-size beds that can be pushed together to form one humongous bed. This outstanding choice is the most private retreat in Fiji.

P.O. Box 10134, Nadi Airport. © **672 0901.** www.wadigi.com. 3 units. US$1,990 (£995) double. Rates include all meals, beverages, and activities except scuba diving, surfing, and sportfishing. AE, MC, V. Minimum stay 3 nights. **Amenities:** Restaurant; bar; laundry service; massage; outdoor pool; room service. *In room:* A/C, TV, coffeemaker, iron, minibar, safe.

6 Resorts in the Yasawa Islands

Once quiet, sleepy, and devoid of most tourists except a few backpackers and well-heeled guests at Turtle Island and Yasawa Island Resort and Spa, this gorgeous chain of islands has seen an explosion of accommodations in recent years, many of them owned by villagers and aimed at backpackers and other cost-conscious travelers. In fact, the Yasawas are one of the hottest backpacker destinations, not just in Fiji but the entire South Pacific.

West Side Waters Sports (© **666 1462;** westside@connect.com.fj) provides daily dive trips for all of the northern Yasawa retreats and teaches introductory and PADI certification courses. **Reef Safari** (© **675 0950;** www.reefsafari.com.fj) does the same for those on Naviti and nearby islands.

We have organized the islands below in the order in which you will come to them on the *Yasawa Flyer,* that is, from south to north.

WAYA ISLAND

Near the southern end of the Yasawas chain, Waya is one of the most beautiful islands in Fiji. You can see the jagged outline of Mount Batinareba soaring over Yalobi Bay from as far away as the Viti Levu mainland. Trails over the mountains link Waya's four Fijian villages and make it the best place in the Yasawas for hiking.

Octopus Resort 🐠🐠   Of all the resorts in the Yasawas, Octopus has the broadest appeal across all age groups. Typically, the Yasawas are couples and singles friendly, attracting honeymooners and backpackers (and generally not children), but Octopus welcomes everyone and provides activities for singles and families alike. Many visitors island-hop throughout the Yasawas, but for the traveler who wants to stay in one place for a more relaxed vacation, Octopus is our clear choice. You don't have to spend a fortune to eat good food, relax on a long, beautiful beach, and stay in comfortable accommodations. A mix of accommodations include a 14-bed dorm room, private en suite bures, bungalow-style rooms with shared facilities, and deluxe private hotel-style rooms decorated with fresh flowers from the resort's gorgeous gardens. Octopus is one of the few resorts in the Yasawas that has a swimming pool. Right in the center of the resort, it's used for training in its PADI-certified dive course. With the choice of activities including the likes of movies under the stars, Octopus offers plenty to do over the course of a week, while you get in as much sun and sand as you like. Rare among the Yasawas, Octopus offers a free guided visit to a traditional Fijian village where you can buy homemade crafts and experience life among the locals. Take part in quiz night, held every Thursday evening, snack on homemade pastries and delicious Fijian fare, and snorkel in the turquoise waters. Don't miss a full hour's massage on the beach (book early—appointments fill up fast). It's the best F$30 (US$20/£10) you'll ever spend!

P.O. Box 1861, Lautoka. ℂ **666 6442** or 666 6337. Fax 666 6210. www.octopusresort.com. 14 units (all with bathroom), 13 dorm beds, 2 tents. US$104–F$175 (£52–£83) bungalow; US$25 (£13) dorm bed. 2-night minimum stay required. MC, V. **Amenities:** Restaurant; bar; laundry service; massage; outdoor pool; watersports equipment rentals. *In room:* TV (hotel rooms), no phone.

NAVITI & NEARBY ISLANDS

About halfway up the chain, Naviti is one of the largest and highest of the Yasawas. Soso, an important Fijian village, is on the east coast, while three basic backpacker establishments—**Korovou Eco-Tour Resort** (ℂ **665 1001**), **Coconut Bay Resort** (ℂ **666 6644,** ext. 1300), and **White Sandy Beach Resort** (ℂ **666 6644,** ext. 1360)—share a long beach and shallow lagoon on the western side. Korovou Eco-Tour Resort is the pick.

Also on the west coast, the midrange **Botaira Resort** (ℂ **666 2266;** www.botaira.com) has 13 modern Fijian-style bures, all with bathrooms.

South of Naviti, the small islands of **Nanuya Balavu** and **Drawaqa** islands are a favorite gathering ground for manta rays between March and November.

Mantaray Island Resort 𝄫   On small Nanuya Balavu Island, Mantaray gets its name from the manta rays that converge offshore. It is a backpacker's hangout, with good dorm accommodations and a selection of private rooms. The 32-bed dorm room clusters four beds to a group, affording quite a lot of privacy in an otherwise open area. The private bures—three of which have private facilities—are bare-bones, with only a bed with mosquito netting and a chair. All three meals are served buffet-style in an open-air lodge amid the treetops. It's a trek to climb up, but once you get there, you're treated to a good meal and one of the best views the Yasawas can offer. Mantaray's waters offer great snorkeling, but the beach is a bit pebbly with pumicelike rocks; be sure to walk around in flip-flops.

P.O. Box 405, Lautoka. ℂ **664 0520.** www.mantarayisland.com. 13 units (3 with bathroom), 32 dorm beds, 20 tent sites. F$115–F$175 (US$75–US$114/£38–£57); F$40 (US$26/£13) dorm bed; F$35 (US$23/£12) per person camping. MC, V. **Amenities:** Restaurant; bar; massage; watersports equipment rentals. *In room:* No phone.

YAQETA ISLAND

Navutu Stars Resort 𝄫𝄫𝄫   If you're longing for a luxury get-away, you can't go wrong with Navutu Stars. Owned and operated by a young Italian couple, Manfredi

Where to Stay in the Yasawa Islands

de Lucia and Maddalena Morandi, it provides a relaxing Fijian atmosphere with laid-back Mediterranean elegance. For years, Turtle Island set the standard for luxury in the Yasawas, but many staff defected in favor of signing on here at Navutu. Guests receive individualized, focused yet discreet attention. From the frangipani welcome and departure leis to a personalized flower petal greeting placed on your bed, no detail is overlooked. A complimentary 30-minute massage is offered to all guests, but if you stay at Navutu any longer than a day, it's a safe bet you'll return to the masseuse with the softest hands anywhere. The beach here isn't as welcoming as at other Yasawa resorts, but a saltwater swimming pool gives a great view of an inlet that can be crossed on foot at low tide. Six of the nine bures are beachfront. They all are exquisitely decorated, painted a stark white, with bedding and cushions providing splashes of color throughout the spacious rooms. Two grand bures have in-room soaking tubs. Enjoy laying out on bedlike chaise longues on your own patio as you watch the dramatic ebb and flow of the tide. Dinner is a gastronomic delight of Italian and Fijian dishes (don't miss the homemade fish ravioli in garlic butter sauce). Navutu Stars lives up to any vision of paradise and will haunt your dreams for years to come.

P.O. Box 1838 Lautoka. ℭ **664 0553.** Fax 679 666 0807. www.navutustarsfiji.com. 9 units. F$500–F$850 (US$325–US$552/£163–£276) double. MC, V. **Amenities:** Restaurant; bar; massage; spa; watersports. *In room:* No phone.

Tips How to Travel in the Yasawa Islands

You might think you're a time traveler to the 1980s as you lounge on the top deck of the *Yasawa Flyer,* listening to a strange mix of hair bands and Paul Simon (if you don't know the lyrics to "You Can Call Me Al" before heading to Fiji, you can be sure you'll have them down pat by the time you depart). Even with these songs running through your head, you'll be inspired to burst into song, belting out "Bali Ha'i" as you sail past tall, skinny mountains shooting out of tropical waters, scenery straight out of *South Pacific.* Travelers immediately pull out cameras to the sounds of oohs and ahhs as they get a first glimpse of breathtaking tropical islands bordered by white-sand beaches giving way to a patchwork quilt of variegated blue water.

For someone who wants to escape from it all, the Yasawa Islands are the place to do it. In the fast-paced modern world, where Blackberries and iPhones buzz constantly and people are linked-in 24/7, the Yasawas are a stark contrast. While many resorts provide Internet access and some have phones, there's very little reason to bother logging on because connection speed is slow, computers are in offices tucked away from the ocean—which is why you are here in the first place—and it's sometimes difficult to buy Fiji Telecom cards.

On that note, beware of hotels selling **phone cards** for more than their face value. That's illegal but almost impossible to enforce because these little islands are far removed from the center of government. You should stock up on phone cards while in Nadi.

A convivial atmosphere usually prevails on the *Yasawa Flyer,* and your fellow travelers can be valuable tour guides by suggesting things to do and warning you against resorts based on their own experiences.

Because you'll find many young backpackers throughout the Yasawas, the atmosphere on the catamarans and throughout the inexpensive resorts is casual. A swimsuit and cover-up are entirely appropriate for traveling within the Yasawas. There's plenty of time to lay out when you reach your resort. On your way there, though, keep your hat and sunblock close by. You don't want to be burned to a crisp before the adventure has even begun.

The *Yasawa Flyer* has **restrooms** on board, and a **concession stand** sells beer, soda, and ice cream. If you're prone to seasickness, bring your own medicine before boarding. Staff announce resort stops about 15 minutes before arrival time, and you can follow along with a schedule, which is usually on time. The resorts and the cruise company handle luggage, which you won't be able to access while traveling.

When you **arrive at your resort or hostel,** the staff will orient you and often serve a fresh, tropical drink. Meals are served during set hours, either buffet style or by waitstaff. The better resorts serve a variety of dishes, including vegetarian fare; but if you have strict dietary restrictions, notify the resort, which can likely accommodate. Depending on the resort, guests will pay a mandatory per diem food charge, which includes breakfast, lunch, and dinner. Other resorts charge a la carte for lunch and dinner but usually include a continental breakfast with the room fee.

Yaqona (welcoming) ceremonies are held each night for guests who have arrived earlier that day. If you're uncomfortable participating, simply forgo the ceremony of introductions and lots of clapping.

Tropical escapes conjure up images of calm, still waters, but the South Seas can be surprisingly choppy. Keep that in mind when deciding where to stay. If you're looking for a steady stream of ocean swimming and laying out, choose a resort like Nanuya, where waters are calm and beach chairs are comfy. Navutu Stars doesn't have the best beach, but it has a saltwater swimming pool that gives a great view of an inlet that can be crossed on foot at low tide. Mantaray Island Resort, while more of a budget place, has another great beach, but the sand is a bit pebbly.

Travelers hitting only the higher-end places don't need to worry about packing shampoo, soap, and towels. Even Octopus Resort—a combination budget/midrange property—provides plush towels, soap, shampoo, and lotions. Otherwise, bring your own towel because they are a big part of vacationing in the Yasawas. Some resorts don't provide lounge chairs, and a towel is all you have between your body and the sand.

Tap water at the mid-to-upper range resorts is purified, and guests don't need to worry about drinking it. But think twice about drinking nonpurified water at the inexpensive places, since it can cause diarrhea and general malaise. Stock up on bottled water before leaving Nadi, or avoid the low-budget places altogether.

Postal service on the islands is nearly nonexistent. Wait and mail your postcards from Nadi.

There is no electrical system in the Yasawas, and while midrange to upscale resorts generate power round-the-clock, the inexpensive resorts shut theirs off when night falls. You'll want to pack a flashlight regardless of the resort.

The resorts are self-contained, and while you will be able to buy personal supplies, it's best to prepare in advance and pack what you need, rather than expecting to find necessities here. You'll definitely pay a premium for them. In fact, all prices in the Yasawas are a little higher than on Viti Levu because so many supplies must be shipped to and from the resorts, including fuel. Similarly, you won't find much to buy for friends back home; purchase your souvenirs on the mainland.

If you have only a week in the Yasawas, spend it on one island. Otherwise you'll waste valuable time planning, packing, riding the boat, and unpacking instead of using it to really enjoy all these beautiful islands offer.

—Valerie Haeder

NANUYA LEVU ISLAND

San Franciscan Richard Evanson graduated from Harvard Business School, made a bundle in cable television, got divorced, ran away to Fiji, and in 1972 bought Nanuya Levu Island. Growing lonely and bored, he decided to build Turtle Island (see below) on his hilly, 200-hectare (500-acre) retreat. He had completed three bures by 1980, when a Hollywood producer leased the entire island as a set for a second version of *The Blue Lagoon,* starring the then-teenage Brooke Shields. Clocks were set ahead 1 hour to maximize daylight, and the resort still operates on "Turtle Time," an hour ahead of the rest of Fiji. The movie's most familiar scenes were shot on Devil's Beach, one of Nanuya Levu's dozen gorgeous little stretches of sand wedged between rocky headlands.

Turtle Island 𝒜𝒜𝒜   Enjoying one of the most picturesque settings of any resort in Fiji, this venerable little getaway nestles beside an idyllic, half-moon-shaped beach and looks out on a nearly landlocked body of water. Supplied by the resort's own garden, the kitchen serves excellent meals dinner-party fashion in the beachside dining room. If you don't want company, you can dine alone on the beach or on a pontoon floating on the lagoon. The beach turns into a sandbar at low tide, but you can swim and snorkel off a long pier. Everything is included in the rates except the Hawaiian-style therapeutic massage. A dozen of the superluxe, widely spaced bungalows have two-person spa tubs embedded in the floors of their enormous bedrooms or bathrooms. In a few bungalows, the front porch has a lily pond on one side and a queen-size bed under a roof on the other. A few are more modest (no spa tubs), but one of these, on a headland with a 360-degree view of the lagoon and surrounding islands, is the most private of all. Every unit has its own kayaks and a hammock strung between shade trees by the beach. Only couples and singles are accepted here, except during certain family weeks in July and at Christmas. Instead of a phone in your bungalow, you will have a two-way radio to call for room service.

P.O. Box 9317, Nadi Airport. ☎ **877/288-7853** or 672 2921 for reservations, 666 3889 on the island. Fax 672 0007. www.turtlefiji.com. 14 units. US$1,632–US$2,390 (£816–£1,195) per couple. Rates include meals, drinks, all activities including game fishing and 1 scuba dive per day. 6-night stay required. AE, DE, MC, V. Children 11 and under not accepted except during family weeks in July and at Christmas. **Amenities:** Restaurant; bar; laundry service; massage; room service. *In room:* Coffeemaker, iron, minibar, safe, no phone.

NANUYA LAILAI ISLAND

Sitting next to the Blue Lagoon, Nanuya Lailai Island has a fantastic beach on its southern and eastern sides. Nanuya Island Resort sits on the western end of the beach, which then wraps around a point draped with coconut palms. Blue Lagoon Cruises expeditions stop around the point to let passengers enjoy the sand and sea.

Nanuya Island Resort 𝒜   This resort sits amid clear, calm waters, on what is by far the best beach in the Yasawas, a long stretch of white sand wrapping around a narrow point. Next to the resort is West Side Water Sports' headquarters, which offers any number of water activities from kayaking to diving to caving to snorkeling—just be careful of nibbling fish! Upscale bures are nestled in the wooded hills, requiring a hike but offering stunning views of the ocean; you can't beat waking up to views of the South Pacific just a few feet away! No children under 7 years old are accepted here.

P.O. Box 7136, Lautoka. ☎ **666 7633.** Fax 666 1462. www.nanuyafiji.com. 12 units. F$235–F$402 (US$153–US$261/£77–£132) double. MC, V. No children under 7 years old. **Amenities:** Restaurant; bar; massage; watersports equipment rentals. *In room:* Coffeemaker, fridge, no phone.

Tips A Package Deal Worth Your Money

Awesome Adventures Fiji (© 670 5006; www.awesomefiji.com) has packages including transportation on the *Yasawa Flyer* and accommodations at several Yasawa Islands resorts and hostels, which are thoroughly inspected for cleanliness and safety. Frankly, several Yasawa hostels are operated by Fijian families and can be very basic. One of us became ill when staying and eating at one such Yasawa establishment, and we have heard similar stories about others. We like to recommend Fijian-owned businesses whenever possible, but we would stick to those approved by Awesome Adventures Fiji. The packages are easily arranged at any Nadi area hotel or hostel, but since the choices are many and complicated, check the website or pick up a current Awesome Adventures Fiji brochure (they're widely available at the airport tour offices and at many hotel activities desks).

TAVEWA ISLAND

Before storms and tides took away much of its sand, Tavewa had a long, gorgeous beach facing the Blue Lagoon and was a favorite backpacker hangout. Two of its hostels, **David's Place** (© 672 1820) and **Otto & Fanny's** (© 666 6481), have been around since the 1980s. Both are basic by even backpacker standards, and we do not recommend them. Their lodging is uncomfortable, the food is mediocre, and the wind often sweeps over the grounds so fiercely that guests must watch out for falling coconuts. Better is **Coral View Resort** (© 922 2575), on a small beach on the other side of a headland. It has two hotel rooms with bathrooms and several thatched bures without, plus a dorm and campsites.

NACULA ISLAND

On the northeastern edge of the Blue Lagoon, Nacula possesses one of Fiji's finest beaches, a dreamy stretch of deep white sand bordering a lagoon that is deep enough for swimming at all tides. Oarsmans Bay Lodge shares this magnificent setting with **Nalova Bay Resort** (© 672 8276; www.nalovabayresortfiji.com), which we do not recommend.

Oarsmans Bay Lodge 🐠 *Value*   Although owned by Fijians, Oarsman Bay Lodge was designed and built by Richard Evanson, owner of Turtle Island (see above); so, in some respects, this is an inexpensive version of that super-luxury resort. A live tree helps support the central building with a sand-floor dining room and bar (no communal kitchen here). Steep stairs lead up a floor to a one-room coed dorm, whose residents share toilets and warm-water showers with guests camping on the grounds. Although the tin-roof guest bungalows are a bit cramped, they are nicely appointed with wooden cabinets, full-length mirrors, reading lights over their double beds, porches with hammocks and chairs, screened louvered windows, and bathrooms with solar-heated showers. Paddle boats and canoes are available, plus gear for fabulous snorkeling off the magnificent beach. Backpacking or not, you'll find this no-frills resort to be a very good bargain.

P.O. Box 9317, Nadi Airport. © 672 2921. Fax 672 0007. www.fijibudget.com. 6 units, 13 dorm beds. F$132–F$265 (US$86–US$172/£43–£86) double; F$23 (US$15/£7.70) dorm bed; F$36 (US$23/£12) per person campsite with tent rental; F$25 (US$16/£8) per person campsite without tent. MC, V. **Amenities:** Restaurant; bar; watersports equipment rentals. *In room:* No phone.

Fun Fact **Running Away to a Famous Cave**

In the 1980 version of the *Blue Lagoon* movie, actress Brooke Shields runs away to a cave on **Sawa-i-Lau Island,** a small rocky islet between Nacula and Yawawa Islands. Carved out of limestone by rainwater, the cave has a hole at the top, which lets in light, and you can swim underwater into a smaller, dark cave. The resorts often run trips to Sawa-i-Lau, and some cruise ships stop here.

YASAWA ISLAND

Long, skinny Yasawa Island stretches from the Blue Lagoon area all the way to the top of the chain. Its north end forms a hook bordered by a long beach, one of Fiji's best. Big black rocks break the beach in two parts and separate two Fijian villages. It's worth taking a Blue Lagoon Cruise just to see this beach, because that's the only way you can get there.

Yasawa Island Resort and Spa ✸✸✸   This luxurious resort sits in a small indention among steep cliffs about midway up Yasawa Island. The Great Sea Reef is far enough offshore here that surf can slap against shelves of black rock just off a terrific beach of deep white sand. Or you can dip in a saltwater swimming pool. Most of the large, air-conditioned guest bures are long, 93 sq. m (1,000 sq. ft.) rectangular models with thatched roofs over white stucco walls. A door leads from the bathroom, which has an indoor shower, to an outdoor shower and a private sunbathing patio. A few other one- and two-bedroom models are less appealing but are better arranged for families (although children 11 and under are allowed here only during Jan, mid-June to mid-July, and Dec) and have fine views from the side of the hill backing the property. Best of all is the remote, extremely private Lomolagi honeymoon bure, which has its own beach and pool. Guests all dine together for once-weekly Fijian-style lovos; otherwise, they can choose their own spacious seating arrangements or dine in their bungalows on the beach. This is the only Yasawa resort with an airstrip.

P.O. Box 10128, Nadi Airport. ✆ **672 2266.** Fax 672 4456. www.yasawa.com. 18 units. US$900–US$1,800 (£450–£900) double. Rates include room, all meals, and nonmotorized watersports, but no drinks. AE, DC, MC, V. Children 11 and under not accepted except in Jan, mid-June to mid-July, Dec. **Amenities:** Restaurant; bar; laundry service; massage; outdoor pool; room service; spa; tennis court. *In room:* A/C, coffeemaker, iron, kitchen (2 units), minibar, safe.

7

The Coral Coast

Long before big jets began bringing visitors to Fiji, many affluent local residents built cottages on the dry southwestern shore of Viti Levu as sunny retreats from the rain and high humidity of Suva. When visitors started arriving in big numbers during the early 1960s, resorts sprang up among the cottages, and promoters gave a new, more appealing name to the 70km (43-mile) stretch of beaches and reef on either side of the town of Sigatoka: the Coral Coast.

The appellation was apt, for coral reefs jut out like wide shelves from the white beaches that run between mountain ridges all along this picturesque coastline. In most spots the lagoon just reaches snorkeling depth at high tide, and when the water retreats, you can put on your reef sandals or a pair of old sneakers and walk out nearly to the surf pounding on the outer edge of the shelf.

Frankly, the Coral Coast is now overshadowed by other parts of Fiji. Its large hotels cater primarily to meetings, groups, and families from Australia and New Zealand on 1-week holidays. Nevertheless, it has dramatic scenery and some of the country's better historical sites, and it's a central location from which to see both the Suva and Nadi sides of Viti Levu. Pacific Harbour's river rafting and other adventures are relatively close at hand.

The Coral Coast is divided into three natural regions. Its only town, **Sigatoka** serves as both commercial and administrative headquarters. A primarily Indian settlement, it earns its living trading with farmers in the **Sigatoka Valley,** Fiji's breadbasket.

The area west of Sigatoka is dominated by Shangri-La's Fijian Resort & Spa, the country's largest hotel. Across the road are the Coral Coast Railway and the Kalevu South Pacific Cultural Centre.

East of Sigatoka, the central area is anchored by the village of **Korotogo,** where several hotels, restaurants, and the Kula Eco Park are grouped around the Outrigger on the Lagoon Fiji, another major hotel. Many of the properties are on Sunset Strip, a dead-end section of the highway that was rerouted inland around the Outrigger.

To the far east, more resorts and hotels are dispersed on either side of **Korolevu** village.

The Coral Coast beaches aren't the best in Fiji, but they get better the farther east you go.

1 Getting to & Getting Around the Coral Coast

The Coral Coast doesn't have an airport, so you must get here from Nadi International Airport by taxi, bus, or rental car along the Queen's Road (see "Getting Around Fiji" in chapter 3).

The drive from Nadi to Shangri-La's Fijian Resort & Spa takes about 45 minutes. After a sharp right turn at the south end of Nadi Town, the highway runs well inland,

Impressions

They passed the kava cups around and drank deep of the milky, slightly stupefying grog. They chatted quietly under the starlight. They laughed, one would propose a song, and then they would break into chorus after chorus, in perfect harmony, of some of the great Fijian folk songs, songs that told of sagas of long ago and far away, and always of war and peace, of love, and of triumph over disaster.

—Simon Winchester (author and travel writer), 1990

first through sugar-cane fields undulating in the wind and then past acre after acre of pine trees planted in orderly rows, part of Fiji's national forestry program. The blue-green mountains lie off to the left; the deep-blue sea occasionally comes into view off to the right.

Since the Coral Coast essentially is a strip running for 70km (43 miles), a rental car is by far the easiest way to get around. The large hotels have car-rental desks as well as taxis waiting outside their main entrances. Express buses between Nadi and Suva stop at Shangri-La's Fijian Resort & Spa, the Outrigger on the Lagoon Fiji, the Hideaway Resort, the Naviti Resort, and the Warwick Fiji Resort & Spa.

Local buses ply the Queen's Road and will stop for anyone who flags them down. **Westside Motorbike Rentals** (© 672 6402; www.motorbikerentalsfiji.com) has an outlet on the Queen's Road at the Korotonga traffic circle. See "Getting Around Nadi," in chapter 5 for more information.

FAST FACTS: The Coral Coast

The following information applies to the Coral Coast. If you don't see an item here, see "Fast Facts: Fiji," in appendix A, and "Fast Facts: Nadi," in chapter 5.

Camera & Film **Caines Photofast** (© 650 0877) has a shop on Market Road in Sigatoka. Most hotel boutiques sell film and provide 1-day processing.

Currency Exchange **ANZ Bank, Westpac Bank,** and **Colonial National Bank** all have branches with ATMs on the riverfront in Sigatoka. The Outrigger on the Lagoon Fiji, the Warwick Fiji Resort & Spa, and the Naviti resorts have ATMs in their lobbies (see "Where to Stay on the Coral Coast," below).

Drugstores **Patel Pharmacy** (© 650 0213) is on Market Road in Sigatoka.

Emergencies The emergency phone number for **police** is © 917; for **fire** and **ambulance** dial © 911. The Fiji **police** has posts at Sigatoka (© 650 0222) and at Korolevu (653 0322).

Healthcare The government-run **Sigatoka Hospital** (© 650 0455) can handle minor problems.

Post Office Post offices are on the Queen's Road in Sigatoka and Korolevu.

The Coral Coast

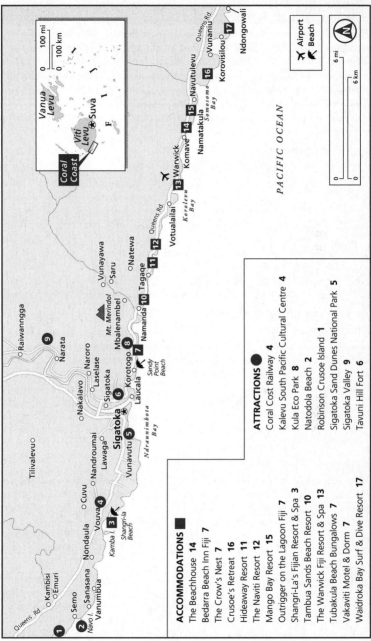

ATTRACTIONS

Coral Cost Railway **4**
Kalevu South Pacific Cultural Centre **4**
Kula Eco Park **8**
Natodola Beach **2**
Robinson Crusoe Island **1**
Sigatoka Sand Dunes National Park **5**
Sigatoka Valley **9**
Tavuni Hill Fort **6**

ACCOMMODATIONS

The Beachhouse **14**
Bedarra Beach Inn Fiji **7**
The Crow's Nest **7**
Crusoe's Retreat **16**
Hideaway Resort **11**
The Naviti Resort **12**
Mango Bay Resort **15**
Outrigger on the Lagoon Fiji **7**
Shangri-La's Fijian Resort & Spa **3**
Tambua Sands Beach Resort **10**
The Warwick Fiji Resort & Spa **13**
Tubakula Beach Bungalows **7**
Vakaviti Motel & Dorm **7**
Waidroka Bay Surf & Dive Resort **17**

2 What to See & Do on the Coral Coast

Hotel reception or tour desks can make reservations for most of the Nadi activities and Mamanuca Islands day cruises mentioned in chapters 5 and 6, respectively. You will likely pay slightly more for Nadi-based activities than if you were staying on the west coast. On the other hand, you are closer to such activities as the rafting trips on the Navua River (see chapter 8). You also can easily take advantage of the golf, fishing, and diving at Pacific Harbour and see the sights in Suva.

I have organized the attractions below from west to east; that is, in the order in which you will come to them from Nadi.

NATADOLA BEACH 🛪🛪🛪

Off the Queen's Road 35km (22 miles) south of Nadi, the paved Maro Road runs down to **Natadola Beach** 🛪🛪🛪, the only exceptionally beautiful beach on Viti Levu. A big resort is going up here, although land disputes and other setbacks had stopped construction during my recent visit. It was to have included a golf course designed by Fiji-native Vijay Singh, but he reportedly has backed out. There's no telling what will be going on here by the time you arrive. One thing is for sure: A gap in the reef allows some surf to break on Natadola Beach, especially on the south end. Already here is **Natadola Beach Resort** (© 672 1001; www.natadola.com), a small Spanish-style hotel with a dining room and bar in a shady courtyard. Rather than drive here, I would take the Coral Coast Railway train from Shangri-La's Fijian Resort & Spa (see below).

ROBINSON CRUSOE ISLAND

On Likuri, a small islet north of Natadola Beach, the backpacker-oriented **Robinson Crusoe Island** (© 628 1999; www.robinsoncrusoeislandfiji.com) has a lovely beach, a swimming pool, restaurant, bar, small *bures* (bungalows), and two dorms. It's a relaxing stop on the low-budget trail around Viti Levu. Jet Fiji has one of its high-speed jet boats stationed at the island (see "Boating, Golf, Hiking & Other Outdoor Activities," in chapter 5). Snorkeling, water-skiing, tube rides, hair braiding, and massages are available to both overnight guests and day-trippers. Accommodations range from F$82 (US$53/£27) for a dorm bed to F$120 (US$78/£39) for a bure, double occupancy. Rates include all meals.

CORAL COAST RAILWAY 🛪

Based on the Queen's Road outside Shangri-La's Fijian Resort & Spa, the **Coral Coast Railway Co.** (© 652 0434) uses two restored sugar-cane locomotives for a variety of tours on narrow-gauge railroads through the cane fields, across bridges, and along the coast. The best destination is lovely Natadola Beach, where you swim (bring your own towel) and have a barbecue lunch at the beach. "Natadola BBQ Bash" trips (F$115/US$75/£38 including lunch) run daily, departing Shangri-La's Fijian resort at 10am and returning at 4pm.

A variation of the Natadola Beach trip includes a boat ride out to Robinson Crusoe Island (see above) for swimming, snorkeling, and a picnic lunch. These excursions cost about F$135 (US$88/£44), and water-skiing is extra. The boat doesn't run every day, so call ahead.

The other locomotive makes trips east to Sigatoka on the Coral Coast. A half-day version (F$59/US$38/£19) takes you to Sigatoka town for shopping and sightseeing. The train also makes all-day "Ratu's Scenic Inland" tours into the Sigatoka Valley

(F$125/US$81/£42) and sundown tours (F$75/US$49/£25), which include a kava welcoming ceremony and dinner.

Children pay half fare, and all fares are somewhat more expensive if you are staying at a Nadi area hotel.

KALEVU SOUTH PACIFIC CULTURAL CENTRE ✿

Well worth a visit if you're interested in island life and history, the **Kalevu South Pacific Cultural Centre** (© **652 0200;** www.fijiculturalcentre.com), on the Queen's Road opposite Shangri-La's Fijian Resort & Spa, presents demonstrations of traditional kava processing, handicraft making, *lovo* (in a hand-dug pit) cooking, and fishing. The cultural exhibits include not just Fiji but Samoa, Kiribati (in the central Pacific), and New Zealand. The center offers 3-hour tours of the complex daily at 9am and 1pm for F$45 (US$29/£15), including a traditional island lunch cooked in an earth oven. Or you can take a 1-hour tour of the grounds and Fiji historical museum for F$15 (US$9.70/£5). Call for schedules and reservations. The center is open daily from 9am to 4pm. You can also get refreshments here, or attend a Fijian *meke* (traditional feast and dance performance) nightly, at Gecko's Restaurant (see "Where to Dine on the Coral Coast," later).

SIGATOKA SAND DUNES NATIONAL PARK

The pine forests on either side of the Queen's Road soon give way to rolling fields of mission grass before the sea emerges at a viewpoint above Shangri-La's Fijian Resort & Spa on Yanuca Island. After you pass the resort, watch on the right for the visitor center for **Sigatoka Sand Dunes National Park** (© **652 0243**). Fiji's first national park protects high sand hills, which extend for several miles along the coast. About two-thirds of them are stabilized with grass, but some along the shore are still shifting sand (the surf crashing on them is dangerous). Ancient burial grounds and pieces of pottery dating from 5 B.C. to A.D. 240 have been found among the dunes, but be warned: Removing them is against the law. Exhibits in the visitor center explain the dunes and their history. Rangers are on duty daily from 8am to 5pm. Admission to the visitor center is free, but adults pay F$8 (US$5.20/£2.70), students F$3 (US$1.90/£1) to visit the actual dunes. Call ahead for a free guided tour. *Note:* You *must* go to the visitor center before visiting the dunes.

SIGATOKA TOWN

About 3km (2 miles) from the sand dunes visitor center, the Queen's Road enters **Sigatoka** (pop. 2,000), the commercial center of the Coral Coast. This quiet, predominantly Indo-Fijian town is perched along the west bank of the **Sigatoka River,** Fiji's longest waterway. The broad, muddy river lies on one side of the main street; on the other is a row of stores. The river is crossed by the Melrose Bridge, built in 1997 and named in honor of Fiji's winning the Melrose Cup at the Hong Kong Sevens rugby matches. The old bridge it replaced is now for pedestrians only.

SIGATOKA VALLEY

From Sigatoka, you can go inland along the west bank of the meandering river, flanked on both sides by a patchwork of flat green fields of vegetables that give the **Sigatoka Valley** its nickname: "Fiji's Salad Bowl." The pavement ends about 1km (½ mile) from the town; after that, the road surface is poorly graded and covered with loose stones.

The residents of **Lawai** village (1.5km/1 mile from town) offer Fijian handicrafts for sale. Two kilometers (1¼ miles) farther on, a small dirt track branches off to the left and runs down a hill to **Nakabuta,** the "Pottery Village," where the residents make and sell authentic Fijian pottery. This art has seen a renaissance of late, and you will find Nakabuta-made bowls, plates, and other items in handicraft shops elsewhere. Tour buses from Nadi and the Coral Coast stop there most days.

Unless you're subject to vertigo, you can look forward to driving past Nakabuta: The road climbs steeply along a narrow ridge, commanding panoramic views across the winding Sigatoka Valley with its quiltlike fields to the right and much smaller, more rugged ravine to the left. It then winds its way down to the valley floor and the **Sigatoka Agricultural Research Station,** on whose shady grounds some tour groups stop for picnic lunches. The road climbs into the interior and eventually to Ba on the northwest coast; it intersects the **Nausori Highlands Road** leading back to Nadi, but it can be rough or even washed out during periods of heavy rain. Unless you have a four-wheel-drive vehicle or are on an organized tour with a guide, I would turn around at the research station and head back to Sigatoka.

JET BOAT TOURS

An alternative to driving up the Sigatoka Valley is a thrill ride in a jet boat operated by **Sigatoka River Safari** (© **0800 650 1721** in Fiji or 650 1721; www.sigatokariver.com). Similar to Jet Fiji in Nadi (see above), these half-day rides cost F$179 (US$116/£58) for adults, F$89 (US$58/£29) for children 4 to 15. Add F$20 (US$13/£7) for departures from Nadi.

TAVUNI HILL FORT

A dirt road runs from Queen's Road at the eastern end of the Sigatoka River bridge inland 5km (3 miles) to the **Tavuni Hill Fort,** built by an exiled Tongan chief as a safe haven from the ferocious Fijian hill tribes living up the valley. Those highlanders constantly fought wars with the coastal Fijians, and they were the last to give up cannibalism and convert to Christianity. When they rebelled against the Deed of Cession to Great Britain in 1875, the colonial administration sent a force of 1,000 men up the Sigatoka River. They destroyed all the hill forts lining the river, including Tavuni. Part of the fort has been restored as a Fiji Heritage Project. The visitor center (© **650 0818**) has exhibits explaining the history, and park rangers will lead 30-minute tours if you ask. The fort is open to the public Monday to Saturday 8am to 4pm. Admission is F$12 (US$7.80/£4) for adults and F$6 (US$3.90/£2) for children.

KULA ECO PARK 👭

Off the Queen's Road opposite the Outrigger on the Lagoon Fiji, **Kula Eco Park** (© **650 0505;** www.fijiwild.com) is Fiji's only wildlife park. Along the banks of a stream in a tropical forest, it has a fine collection of rainbow-feathered tropical birds and an aquarium stocked with examples of local sea life. Allow 2 hours here, since this is one of the South Pacific's best places to view local flora and fauna in a natural setting. Children will love it. It's open daily 10am to 4pm. Admission is F$20 (US$13/£6.70) for adults, F$10 (US$6.50/£3.30) for children 11 and under.

WATERFALL & CAVE TOURS 👭

You won't soon forget the waterfall and cave tours offered by **Adventures in Paradise Fiji** (© **652 0833;** www.adventuresinparadisefiji.com), near the Outrigger on the Lagoon Fiji. The waterfall tour goes to Biausevu village in the Korolevu Valley. A tour bus takes you to the village, where you'll be welcomed at a traditional *yaqona* (kava) ceremony. Then comes a 30-minute hike along a rocky stream to the falls, which plunge straight over a cliff into a swimming hole. The sometimes slippery trail fords the stream seven times, so wear canvas or reef shoes or a pair of strap-on sandals. Wear a bathing suit and bring a towel if you want to take a very cool and refreshing dip after the sweaty hike. You'll be treated to a barbecue lunch.

On the other excursion, you'll spend 45 minutes inside the Naihehe Cave, which was used as a fortress by Fiji's last cannibal tribe. After a picnic lunch, you'll return via a *bilibili* (bamboo) raft on the Sigatoka River (the cave is a 35-min. drive up the Sigatoka Valley).

The cost is F$99 (US$64/£32) per person for either tour; they run on alternate days and can be booked at any hotel activities desk. Add F$20 (US$13/£6.50) from Nadi.

SHOPPING ON THE CORAL COAST

In Sigatoka Town, you can do some serious hunting at **Sigatoka Indigenous Women's Handicraft Centre** (no phone), in a tin-roof shack on the main street beside the river. Operated by local women, it has carvings, shell jewelry, *masi* (bark) cloth, and other items made in Fiji. **Jack's of Fiji** (© 650 0744), **Prouds** (© 650 0707), and **Tappoo** (© 650 0199) have large stores across the street.

Prices at relaxed, "browse-in-peace" **Baravi Handicrafts** 𝒜𝒜 (© 652 0364) in Vatukarasa village, 13km (8 miles) east of Sigatoka, are somewhat lower than you'll find at the larger stores, and it has a snack bar that sells excellent coffee made from Fijian-grown beans (you will be offered a freebie cup). The shop buys woodcarvings and pottery directly from village artisans. It's open Monday to Saturday 7:30am to 6pm, Sunday 8:30am to 5pm. Vatukarasa also has a **roadside stall** where you might find unusual seashells.

3 Where to Stay on the Coral Coast

Most hotels have abundant sports facilities, including diving, and those that don't will arrange activities for you. Outsiders are welcome to use the facilities at most resorts—for a fee, of course.

Although Shangri-La's Fijian Resort & Spa is west of Sigatoka town, most accommodations are in two areas: Near **Korotogo,** a small village about 8km (5 miles) east of Sigatoka, and spread out on either side of **Korolevu,** another village some 30km (19 miles) east of Sigatoka. The greatest concentration is at Korolevu, where the Outrigger on the Lagoon Fiji and several other hotels are within walking distance of each other, as are restaurants on **Sunset Strip,** which leaves the Queen's Road at a traffic circle and skirts the lagoon until it dead-ends at the Outrigger. In other words, you can easily walk among the Korotogo hotels and restaurants. Elsewhere you will need transportation to go out to dinner or visit another resort.

I have organized the accommodations below by area, from west to east.

WEST OF SIGATOKA

Shangri-La's Fijian Resort & Spa 𝒜𝒜𝒜   Fiji's largest hotel, "The Fijian" occupies all 42 hectares (105 acres) of flat Yanuca Island, which is joined to the mainland by a short, one-lane causeway. Yanuca is bordered by a crystal clear lagoon and a coral-colored sand beach, both superior to those at Denarau Island near Nadi. Needless to say, there are a host of watersports activities here, including diving, or you can play tennis or knock around the 9-hole golf course. Covered walkways wander through thick tropical foliage to link the hotel blocks to three main restaurant-and-bar buildings, both adjacent to swimming pools. The spacious rooms and suites occupy two- and three-story buildings, all on the shore of the island. Each room has a view of the lagoon and sea from its own private balcony or patio. The suites have separate bedrooms and two bathroom sinks. While the Fijian draws many families, its Ocean Premier units on one end of the sprawling property are reserved exclusively for couples. The Fijian's restaurants have something for everyone's taste, if not necessarily for everyone's pocketbook, and four bars are ready to quench any thirst. Away from the throngs at the end of the island, the **Chi Spa Village** is a knockout, with bungalow-like treatment rooms where you can spend the night after being pampered. The half-dozen luxurious Premier Ocean bures—between the spa and the resort's glass-walled wedding chapel—are great for honeymooners.

Private Mail Bag (NAPO 353), Nadi Airport (Yanuca Island, 10km/6¼ miles west of Sigatoka). ℂ **866/565-5050** or 652 0155. Fax 652 0402. www.shangri-la.com. 442 units. F$400–F$520 (US$260–US$338/£130–£169) double; F$650–F$750 (US$422–US$487/£211–£244) suite; F$950 (US$617/£309) bungalow. AE, DC, MC, V. **Amenities:** 4 restaurants; 4 bars; activities desk; babysitting; bike rentals; business center; car-rental desk; children's programs; concierge; fitness center; game room; 9-hole golf course; laundry service; massage; 3 outdoor pools; room service; salon; shopping arcade; 4 tennis courts; watersports equipment rentals. In room: A/C, TV, coffeemaker, fridge, iron, safe.

NEAR KOROTOGO

Bedarra Beach Inn Fiji 𝄞 ⟨Value⟩   This comfortable inn began life as a private home with bedrooms on either end of a two-story central hall, which opened to a veranda overlooking a swimming pool and the lagoon. The beach is across a dead-end road known as Sunset Strip, which was the main drag before the Queen's Road was diverted around the Outrigger on the Lagoon Fiji, a short walk from here. Today, a bar, lounge furniture, and potted palms occupy the great hall, and two restaurants have taken over the verandas (see "Where to Dine on the Coral Coast," below). Upstairs, four rooms open to another veranda wrapping around the house. Inside, guests can opt for two-bedroom family rooms capable of sleeping up to four persons. To the side of the house, a two-story motel block holds 16 air-conditioned rooms, all sporting large bathrooms with walk-in showers. Four of these also have cooking facilities.

P.O. Box 1213, Sigatoka (Sunset Strip, 8km/5 miles east of Sigatoka). ℂ **650 0476.** Fax 652 0166. www.bedarrafiji.com. 24 units, all with bathroom. F$145–F$180 (US$94–US$117/£47–£59) double. AE, MC, V. **Amenities:** 2 restaurants; bar; babysitting; laundry service; outdoor pool. In room: A/C, coffeemaker, fridge, no phone.

The Crow's Nest   Although it's far from being my favorite, this hotel enjoys a convenient location on Sunset Strip within walking distance of restaurants and the Outrigger on the Lagoon Fiji. Accommodations are in two rows of duplex buildings, the first sitting in a coconut grove across the road from the beach. Behind is a second row up on a terraced hillside. The outdoor pool, bar, and pedestrian restaurant are even higher up, which gives them fine views over the lagoon to the sea. The split-level units have queen-size beds on their mezzanine level and two single beds down in the lounge area. Executive units add a kitchen, which makes them money-saving options for families or two couples sharing a room. All have balconies.

P.O. Box 270, Sigatoka (Sunset Strip, 8km/5 miles east of Sigatoka). ℂ **650 0230.** Fax 650 0513. 25 units. F$99–F$145 (US$64–US$94/£32–£47) double. AE, MC, V. **Amenities:** Restaurant; bar; laundry service; outdoor pool; rental kayaks and snorkeling gear; room service. In room: A/C, TV, coffeemaker, fridge, kitchen (some units).

Outrigger on the Lagoon Fiji 𝄞𝄞 ⟨Kids⟩   This fine lagoonside resort compensates for Mother Nature's having robbed its beach of most of the sand with one of the most attractive swimming pools in Fiji. You can still go kayaking, *spy boarding* (riding face-down on a board with a plastic window for fish-viewing), and snorkeling at high tide, but the gorgeous pool is the center of attention here. In a way, the Outrigger is two hotels in one. A majority of the accommodations are hotel rooms in five-story hillside buildings at the rear of the property. They all have balconies, with spectacular views from the upper floor units. In a coconut grove down by the lagoon, a stand of thatched-roof guest bungalows and restaurants resembles a traditional Fijian village. Hotel rooms in the Reef Wing, a three-story lagoonside building (and the last remnant of the Reef Resort which once stood here), are smaller than their hillside counterparts and better suited to couples than families. You'll have butler service down in the comfortable guest bures, which have masi-lined peaked ceilings. The beachfront bungalows are the pick of the litter. A few others are joined as family units. Australian restaurateur Geoff Shaw, who owns both this resort and Castaway Island Resort (see "Resorts in the Mamanuca Islands," in chapter 6), sees to it that everyone is well-fed in an intimate fine-dining restaurant, a large open-air, buffet-style dining room, and a midday restaurant by the pool. The wedding chapel here sits high on a hill with a stunning lagoon and sea view.

P.O. Box 173, Sigatoka (Queen's Rd., 8km/5 miles east of Sigatoka). ℂ **800/688-7444** or 650 0044. Fax 652 0074. www.outrigger.com. 254 units. F$340–F$425 (US$221–US$276/£111–£138) double; F$500–F$1,000 (US$325–US$649/£163–£325) bungalow. AE, DC, MC, V. **Amenities:** 3 restaurants; 4 bars; activities desk; babysitting; business center; car-rental desk; children's programs; exercise room; game room; Jacuzzi; laundry service; massage; outdoor pool; salon; shopping arcade; spa; 2 tennis courts; coin-op washers and dryers; watersports equipment rentals. *In room:* A/C, TV, coffeemaker, fridge (stocked in bures), high-speed Internet access, iron, safe.

Tubakula Beach Bungalows   Although not nearly as charming as the Beachouse or as well equipped as Mango Bay Resort, this simple, almost staid property (whose name is pronounced *Toomb*-a-koola) sits in a lagoonside coconut grove near the Outrigger on the Lagoon Fiji; the restaurants on Sunset Strip are within walking distance along the beach. The lower level of each A-frame bungalow has a lounge, kitchen, bathroom, bedroom, and front porch; upstairs is a sleeping loft, which can be hot in the midday sun. Each can sleep six persons, so sharing one will save you some money. The dorms are in European-style houses; no more than four beds are in any one room, and guests share communal kitchens, showers, and toilets. A minimart sells beer, soft drinks, and basic groceries.

P.O. Box 2, Sigatoka (Queen's Road, 79km/49 miles from Nadi Airport, 13km/8 miles east of Sigatoka). ℂ **500 097.** Fax 340 236. www.fiji4less.com.fj. 23 bungalows (all with bathroom), 24 dorm beds. F$109–F$156 (US$71–US$101/£36–£51) bungalow; F$25 (US$16/£8) dorm bed. AE, MC, V. **Amenities:** Restaurant; bar; game room; outdoor pool. *In room:* Kitchen, no phone.

Vakaviti Motel & Dorm (*Value*   This basic but clean little motel next to the Crow's Nest offers one of the Coral Coast's better values for the money. It's a bit of climb up a steep driveway, but you'll be rewarded with fine lagoon views through towering coconut palms. A concrete-block structure houses four motel-style rooms. They all have small kitchenettes, ample bathrooms with showers, tile floors, ceiling fans, and louvered windows and doors looking out over a long patio and small swimming pool. Vakaviti also has a family bure down by the road. It has a kitchen, bathroom, and a double bed and three singles. One room and a bure are used as dormitories.

P.O. Box 5, Sigatoka (Sunset Strip, 8km/5 miles east of Sigatoka). ℂ **650 0526.** Fax 652 0424. www.vakaviti.com. 6 units, 10 dorm beds. F$80–F$90 (US$52–US$58/£26–£29) double; F$20–F$25 (US$13–US$16/£6.70–£8) dorm bed. MC, V. **Amenities:** Bar; bicycle and kayak rentals; laundry service; outdoor pool. *In room:* Kitchen, no phone.

BETWEEN KOROTOGO & KOROLEVU

Hideaway Resort ★★ *Value*   Brothers Robert and Kelvin Wade bought this beach-side property about the time I started writing about Fiji in the mid-1980s and have been enlarging and improving it ever since; today, it is the best all-bungalow resort on the Coral Coast. During their early years it was famous as a young persons' hangout, with a large dormitory and mile-a-minute entertainment. The dormitory belongs to history now, but lively evening entertainment still features a Fijian meke feast once a week, Beqa island fire walking, and Club Med–style cabaret shows. The resort occupies a narrow strip of land between the Queen's Road and the lagoon that's long enough so that families, singles, and couples don't get in each other's way or disturb each other's sleep (or lack thereof). For optimum peace and quiet, choose a duplex "deluxe villa" on the far western end of the property. They have dual indoor showers as well as outdoor showers. The 16 original, A-frame bungalows here are much closer to the action. Other units are in modern, duplex bungalows with tropical furnishings and shower-only bathrooms. A few larger family units here can sleep up to five persons. The main building opens to a beachside pool with a waterfall and a water slide. As has happened at the Outrigger on the Lagoon Fiji (see above), most of the beach is obscured at high tide, but you can follow a trail out on the reef and observe a coral restoration project being undertaken in cooperation with local villagers. Ashore, you can keep busy with tennis, horseback tours, trips to the mountains and waterfalls, minigolf, and pumping iron in an exercise bure, where you can catch the news on TV.

P.O. Box 233, Sigatoka (Queen's Rd., 21km/13 miles east of Sigatoka). © **650 0177.** Fax 652 0025. www.hideaway-fiji.com. 112 units. F$340–F$540 (US$221–US$351/£111–£176) bungalow. Rates include full breakfast buffet. AE, DC, MC, V. **Amenities:** 2 restaurants; 2 bars; miniature golf; outdoor pool; tennis court; exercise room; watersports equipment rentals; children's programs; game room; concierge; activities desk; car-rental desk; salon; massage; babysitting; laundry service; coin-op washers and dryers. *In room:* A/C, coffeemaker, fridge, iron, safe.

Tambua Sands Beach Resort   This hotel sits in a narrow, 6.8-hectare (17-acre) grove of coconut palms beside a better white-sand beach than fronts the nearby Hideaway Resort. All virtually identical, the bungalows here have high peaked ceilings with tin roofs, and their front porches all face the lagoon (those closest to the beach cost slightly more than the "ocean view" units). Each has both a queen-size and single bed. A wooden footbridge crosses a stream flowing through the grounds and connects the bungalows with a swimming pool and plantation-style central building. The low-ceiling, open-air restaurant and bar are somewhat dark, but they do look out to the pool and the sea.

P.O. Box 177, Sigatoka (20km/12 miles east of Sigatoka). © **650 0399.** Fax 650 0265. www.tambuasandsfiji.com. 25 units. F$185–F$195 (US$120–US$127/£60–£64) double. AE, MC, V. **Amenities:** Restaurant; bar; activities desk; babysitting; game room; laundry service; massage; outdoor pool; grass tennis court; watersports equipment rentals. *In room:* Coffeemaker, fridge, no phone.

NEAR KOROLEVU

The Beachouse ★   Andrew Waldken-Brown, a European who was born in Fiji, and his Australian wife, Jessica, have turned his family's old vacation retreat—beside one of the finest beaches on the Coral Coast—into this excellent backpacker resort. The British TV show *Love Island* took over the premises in 2006 and built a charming South Seas stage set and swimming pool, which now serves as lounge, bar, and dining room providing inexpensive meals. Each dorm is screened and has its own ceiling fan, and all beds have reading lights. The upstairs is aimed at couples, with partitions separating roomettes, but the walls don't reach the ceiling; the accommodations also have ceiling fans and mosquito-netted double beds. More private for couples are the bungalow-like garden units, each of which has a double bed. All guests, including the campers who pitch their tents on the spacious lawn, share clean toilets and a modern communal kitchen. Although it lacks bures with bathrooms, the Beachouse is more intimate than the rocking Mango Bay Resort (see below).

P.O. Box 68, Korolevu (37km/23 miles east of Sigatoka). ℭ **0800/653 0530** toll-free in Fiji, or 653 0500. www.fijibeachouse.com. 12 units (none with bathroom), 48 dorm beds. F$93 (US$60/£30) double; F$30 (US$19/£10) dorm bed; F$23 (US$15/£7.70) per person camping. MC, V. **Amenities:** Restaurant; bar; activities desk; bike and watersports equipment rentals; game room; massage; outdoor pool; coin-op washers and dryers. *In room:* No phone.

Crusoe's Retreat   Only the foot-shaped swimming pool reminds me of when this low-key resort was known as Man Friday. It's still one of the Coral Coast's oldest hotels, but much has been done in recent years to improve it, including installation of new bathrooms with "his-and-her" shower heads and sinks in all units. It's a rough but scenic 4km (2½-mile) ride along a dirt road and a steep downhill descent to reach the resort. In fact, you'll have to climb uphill to guest units nos. 12 through 29. They have stunning views, but I prefer those down near the beach, especially the thatch-encased "seaside luxury" bungalows. They're not that luxurious by modern standards, but they are much more charming than the other, A-frame units here—and they may be air-conditioned and have outdoor showers by the time you arrive. In the meantime, all units have fans. The skimpy beach in front of the resort is augmented by sand held in place by a rock wall; it's much better in front of Namaqumaqua, the adjoining Fijian village. Crusoe's has what appears to be a grass tennis court, but don't bother bringing your racket.

P.O. Box 20, Korolevu (45km/28 miles east of Sigatoka). ℭ **650 0185.** Fax 650 0666. www.crusoesretreat.com. 29 units. F$258–F$310 (US$168–US$201/£84–£101) double. AE, MC, V. **Amenities:** Restaurant; 2 bars; activities desk; babysitting; laundry service; massage; outdoor pool; grass tennis court; watersports equipment rentals. *In room:* Coffeemaker, fridge, safe.

Mango Bay Resort   This beachside resort is the most popular on the Coral Coast among 25- to 35-year-olds, although its small bungalows and African safari–style tents appeal to travelers of any age who don't mind a lot of bustle or a poolside bar that can rock past midnight. Fortunately it's all spread out over several acres of lawn and palm trees, so the noise shouldn't seriously interfere with sleeping. Mango Bay is an eco-friendly place, so none of the natural thatched-roof units or dorms have air-conditioners. They do have ceiling fans, and both the bures and tents have their own bathrooms (the bures have outdoor showers). The tents have wood floors, front porches, and both double and single beds. The more expensive dorm has double beds separated by dividers, while the other has over-and-under bunk beds. Only the tents are screened, but every bed here has its own mosquito net.

P.O. Box 1720, Sigatoka (Sunset Strip, 40km/25 miles east of Sigatoka). ℭ **653 0069.** Fax 653 0138. www.mango bayresortfiji.com. 19 units (all with bathroom), 70 dorm beds. F$189–F$270 (US$123–US$175/£62–£88) double; F$36–F$45 (US$23–US$29/£12–£15) dorm bed. Rates include continental breakfast. AE, MC, V. No children 11 and under accepted. **Amenities:** Restaurant; 2 bars; laundry service; massage; outdoor pool. *In room:* Safe, no phone.

The Naviti Resort   A sister of the Warwick Fiji Resort & Spa (see below), this sprawling resort attracts mainly Australians and New Zealanders lured by its extensive activities and optional all-inclusive rates, which include all the beer and booze you can drink. The resort sits on 15 hectares (38 acres) of coconut palms waving in the trade wind beside a beach and dredged lagoon (you can wade to two islets). Or you can lounge beside two swimming pools, one with a shaded swim-up bar. Double-deck covered walkways lead from the central complex to two- and three-story concrete block buildings, two of them constructed in 2005. The older wings hold some of Fiji's largest hotel rooms (bathrooms have both tubs and walk-in showers). The two-room suites on the ends of the older buildings are especially spacious. The best units here, however, are 16 beachside bungalows, ranging from studios to two-bedrooms. Tall shingle roofs cover a coffee shop, a candlelit restaurant for fine dining, and a large lounge where a band plays most evenings. A fine Chinese restaurant looks out on an unchallenging 9-hole golf course.

P.O. Box 29, Korolevu (Queen's Road, 26km/16 miles east of Sigatoka). © 800/203-3232 or 653 0444. Fax 653 0099. www.navitiresort.com.fj. 224 units. F$268–F$296 (US$174–US$192/£87–£96) double; F$482–F$595 (US$313–US$386/£157–£193) suite or bungalow. Rates include breakfast. All-inclusive rates available. AE, DC, MC, V. **Amenities:** 3 restaurants; 3 bars; activities desk; babysitting; bike rentals; car-rental desk; children's programs; exercise room; game room; 9-hole golf course; Jacuzzi; laundry service; outdoor pool; room service; spa; salon; 5 tennis courts; watersports equipment rentals. *In room:* A/C, TV, coffeemaker, fridge, iron, safe.

Waidroka Bay Surf & Dive Resort   The easternmost of the Coral Coast resorts, this little lagoonside retreat has more in common with those at Pacific Harbour, which is much closer to here than is Korotogo. The lagoon here has no beach, so owners Boris and Karin Kaz—a German-Israeli couple who relocated here from New York City—specialize in diving, snorkeling, fishing, and surfing (Waidroka Bay is closer to Frigate Passage than either Pacific Harbour or Beqa Island). The guest bungalows flank their spacious, Mediterranean-style main building with a restaurant, bar, and large front porch opening to a swimming pool (with its own bar) set on a grassy lawn beside the palm-fringed lagoon. Guest quarters are either in bungalows (some have two bedrooms) or in a motel-like building. They are devoid of most island charms but all have sea views. Waidroka is 4km (2½ miles) south of the Queen's Road via a dirt track that literally climbs over a mountain before descending through a development of modest vacation homes.

P.O. Box 323, Pacific Harbour (50km/31 miles east of Sigatoka). © 330 4605. Fax 330 4383. www.waidroka.com. 11 units (all with bathroom), 70 dorm beds. F$165–F$250 (US$107–US$162/£54–£81) double. MC, V. **Amenities:** Restaurant; 2 bars; babysitting; laundry service; massage; outdoor pool. *In room:* No phone.

The Warwick Fiji Resort & Spa   Sitting on a palm-dotted beach with a bit more sand than you'll find at the Outrigger or the Hideaway, this complex reflects distinctive architecture from its origins as the Hyatt Regency Fiji. A sweeping roof supported by wood beams covers a wide reception and lobby area bordered on either end by huge carved murals depicting Captain James Cook's discovery of Fiji in 1779. A curving staircase descends from the center of the lobby into a large square well, giving access to the dining and recreation areas on the lagoon level. The medium-size guest rooms are in two- and three-story blocks that flank the central building. Each room has its own balcony or patio with a view of the sea or the tropical gardens surrounding the complex. The most expensive units are suites that directly face the lagoon from the ends of the buildings. The sand-floored Wicked Walu, under a thatched roof on a tiny island offshore, is the choice dining spot here. A free shuttle runs between the Warwick and its more family-oriented sister, the Naviti Resort.

P.O. Box 100, Korolevu (32km/20 miles east of Sigatoka). © 800/203-3232 or 653 0555. Fax 653 0010. www. warwickfiji.com. 250 units. F$412–F$647 (US$268–US$420/£134–£210) double; F$861 (US$559/£280) suite. AE, DC, MC, V. **Amenities:** 5 restaurants; 5 bars; activities desk; babysitting; business center; car-rental desk; children's programs; concierge-level rooms; exercise room; Jacuzzi; laundry service; massage; 2 outdoor pools; room service; salon; shopping arcade; spa; 4 tennis courts; coin-op washers and dryers; watersports equipment rentals. *In room:* A/C, TV, coffeemaker, iron, minibar, safe.

4 Where to Dine on the Coral Coast

In Sigatoka Town next to Jack's of Fiji, Roshni and Jean-Pierre Gerber's clean **Le Cafe Town** (© **652 0668**) offers inexpensive sandwiches, salads, curries, spaghetti, pizzas, fish and chips, and other snacks. Credit cards are not accepted. Le Cafe Town is open Monday to Saturday from 9am to 5pm. The Gerbers—she's from Fiji, he's Swiss, and both are chefs—also serve dinners at Le Cafe in Korotogo (see below). Although her original restaurant Le Cafe is better (see below), **Vilisite's Seafood Restaurant No. 2** (© **650 1030**) is on the Queen's Road in Sigatoka west of the river. It's open daily from 10am to 9:30pm.

Many Coral Coast hotels have special nights, such as meke feasts of Fijian foods cooked in a lovo, served buffet style and followed by traditional dancing.

As with the hotels above, I have organized the restaurants by location.

WEST OF SIGATOKA

Gecko's Restaurant REGIONAL   Occupying the veranda of one of the Western-style buildings at the Kalevu South Pacific Cultural Centre, this open-air restaurant offers a more affordable—but not nearly as good—alternative to the dining rooms at Shangri-La's Fijian Resort & Spa across the Queen's Road. You can have a breakfast of omelets and other egg dishes all day here. Lunch features a choice of sandwiches, burgers, fish and chips, curry, stir-fries, and other local favorites. Dinner sees a wide-ranging menu, which includes the house specialty, mud crabs with garlic sauce. There are Fijian meke shows here every night (call to see what's on).

Queen's Rd., in Kalevu South Pacific Museum opposite Shangri-La's Fijian Resort & Spa. © **652 0200**. Reservations accepted. Breakfast F$5–F$8 (US$3.20–US$5.20/£1.70–£2.70); lunch F$5–F$12 (US$3.20–US$7.80/£1.70–£4); main courses F$20–F$55 (US$13–US$36/£6.70–£18). MC, V. Daily 10am–10pm.

NEAR KOROTOGO

Beachside Cafe & Restaurant REGIONAL   An Indian family owns this open-air restaurant under a tin roof next to a convenience store, so curries are its most numerous offerings—although I picked a decent version of garlic prawns off the daily specials board. Fish and chips and stir-fried vegetables also appear. The Bula Bar has full service and billiards tables, although I prefer to imbibe at Le Cafe next door (see below).

Sunset Strip, Korotogo, west of the Outrigger on the Lagoon Fiji. © **652 0584**. Main courses F$8–F$17 (US$5.20–US$11/£2.70–£5.70). No credit cards. Daily 8am–10pm.

Le Cafe ★★ (Value) INTERNATIONAL   In addition to running Le Cafe Town in Sigatoka, Roshni and Jean-Pierre Gerber turn their attention to this little establishment, where they oversee the production of fish and chips, curries, pastas, and some reasonably good pizzas. The nightly specials board features the likes of fresh fish filet with lemon butter sauce, pepper or garlic steak, garlic prawns, and local lobster with Mornay sauce. A special lunch and dinner menu offers substantial servings of fish and chips, spaghetti, or burgers for F$7 (US$4.50/£2.50). Even if you don't dine here, the thatch-topped bar out front is a great place for a sunset cocktail during happy hour from 5 to 8pm daily.

Sunset Strip, Korotogo, west of the Outrigger on the Lagoon Fiji. © **652 0877**. Reservations accepted. Breakfast F$5.50–F$7.50 (US$3.60–US$4.90/£1.80–£2.50); lunch F$7 (US$4.50/£2.30); pizzas F$8.50–F$17 (US$5.50–US$11/£2.80–£5.70); main courses F$7–F$16 (US$4.50–US$10/£2.30–£5.30). No credit cards. Daily 8am–10pm.

Ocean Terrace Restaurant/EbbTide Cafe ✮ INTERNATIONAL   These two restaurants occupy the verandas overlooking the swimming pool at the Bedarra Beach Inn Fiji (see "Where to Stay on the Coral Coast," earlier in this chapter) and utilize the same kitchen. The downstairs Ebb Tide Cafe serves a daytime menu of salads, sandwiches, burgers, a few main courses, and 12-inch pizzas with a limited selection of toppings. At night the upstairs veranda turns into the romantic Ocean Terrace Restaurant, where the chef takes flight with his own versions of chicken and seafood curries, reef fish with a creamy lemon and coriander sauce, and beef with a vegetable and peanut stuffing. The evening menu is available in both restaurants.

Sunset Strip, Korotogo, in Bedarra Beach Inn Fiji. ✆ 650 0476. Reservations accepted. Ocean Terrace main courses F$17–F$27 (US$11–US$18/£5.70–£9). Ebb Tide sandwiches and burgers F$10 (US$6.50/£3.30), pizzas F$18 (US$12/£6), main courses F$9–F$20 (US$5.80–US$13/£3–£6.70). AE, MC, V. Ocean Terrace daily 6–9pm. Ebb Tide daily 10am–9pm.

NEAR KOROLEVU

Vilisite's Seafood Restaurant ✮✮ *Value* SEAFOOD/INDIAN/CHINESE   Vilisite (sounds like "Felicity"), a friendly Fijian who lived in Australia, operates one of the few non-hotel establishments in Fiji where you can dine right by the lagoon's edge. Come in time for a sunset drink and bring a camera, for the westward view from Vilisite's veranda belongs on a postcard. Her well-prepared cuisine is predominately fresh local seafood—fish, shrimp, lobster, octopus—in curry, garlic and butter, or coconut milk (the Fijian way). She offers five full seafood meals at dinner, or you can choose from chop suey, curry, shrimp, or fish and chips from a blackboard menu. Vilisite will arrange rides for dinner parties of four or more from as far away as the Outrigger on the Lagoon Fiji, but be sure to ask about the cost. You won't soon forget the view or this extraordinarily friendly Fijian, who certainly knows how to cook.

Queen's Rd., Korolevu, between the Warwick and the Naviti. ✆ 653 0054. Reservations recommended. Lunch F$2.50–F$15 (US$1.60–US$9.70/80p–£5); full dinners F$10–F$45 (US$6.50–US$29/£3.30–£15). MC, V. Daily 8am–10pm.

5 Island Nights on the Coral Coast

Coral Coast nightlife centers around the hotels and whatever Fijian meke shows they are sponsoring.

The **Fijian fire walkers** from Beqa, an island off the south coast (remember, it's pronounced M-*bengga,* not *Beck*-a), parade across the steaming stones to the incantations of "witch doctors" at least once a week at the **Hideaway Resort** (✆ 650 0177), **Outrigger on the Lagoon Fiji** (✆ 650 0044), and the **Warwick Fiji Resort & Spa** (✆ 653 0010). Call them or ask at your hotel for the schedule.

Gecko's Restaurant (✆ 652 0200) in the Kalevu South Pacific Cultural Centre has a 1-hour Fijian dance show Monday to Friday nights and a 3-hour version on Sunday evening. Call for reservations. The **Hideaway Resort** (✆ 650 0177) has a South Pacific show on Sunday and its excellent cabaret shows during the week.

6 A Resort on Vatulele Island

A flat, raised coral atoll 48km (30 miles) south of Viti Levu, **Vatulele Island** is known for its unusual red shrimp—that is, they're red while alive, not just after being cooked. The only way to see them, however, is to stay at Vatulele Island Resort, which is accessible only from Nadi Airport.

Vatulele Island Resort   Long a favorite haunt of Hollywood stars (it was built by Australian movie producer Henry Crawford), this super-luxe resort was recently bought by the Bangkok-based Six Senses Resorts & Spas (www.sixsenses.com), which plans to add a spa and to make other significant changes. Accordingly, I personally would opt for staying in another high-end resort until the dust settles here. Whatever happens, it still will reside beside one of Fiji's best beaches, a gorgeous, 1km-long (½-mile) beach of brilliantly white sand. In a blend of Santa Fean and Fijian native architectural styles, the bures and main building have thick adobe walls supporting Fijian thatched roofs. Most of the large, L-shaped bungalows have a lounge and raised sleeping areas under one roof; another roof covers an enormous bathroom that can be entered both from the bed/dressing area and from a private, hammock-swung patio. At the far end of the property, the private, exquisitely designed Vale Viqi (Pink House) delights honeymooners with its own private beach, plunge pool, and a unique two-person, face-to-face tub in the middle of its large bathroom. The Point, a two-story villa with its own pool, has a terrific view of the beach from its super-private perch atop a headland.

P.O. Box 9936, Nadi Airport (Vatulele Island, 50km/31 miles south of Viti Levu, a 30-min. flight from Nadi). ℰ **800/828-9146** or 672 0300. Fax 672 0062. www.vatulele.com. 19 units. US$924–US$2,079 (£462–£1040) bungalow. Rates include room, food, bar, all activities except sportfishing and scuba diving. 4-night minimum stay required. AE, DC, MC, V. Children 11 and under not accepted. **Amenities:** Restaurant; bar; laundry service; massage; room service; tennis court. *In room:* Coffeemaker, minibar, safe, no phone.

8

Pacific Harbour & Beqa Island

Pacific Harbour was begun in the early 1970s as a recreation-oriented, luxury residential community and resort (translated: a real-estate development). A number of expatriates have built homes here, and they have their own tourist information website at **www.pacificharbour-fiji.com**. Given the heat, humidity, and amount of rain it gets, Pacific Harbour is not the place to come for a typical beach vacation, although you can swim at all tides off 3km (2 miles) of deep, grayish sand. On the other hand, it does have an excellent golf course, fine deep-sea fishing, fabulous scuba diving both out in the **Beqa Lagoon** and along the coast (this is one place in Fiji where you can go on shark-feeding dives), and outstanding white-water rafting trips on the nearby **Navua River.** Local promoters aren't far wrong when they describe Pacific Harbour as "The Adventure Capital of Fiji."

It's also my favorite place to experience Fijian culture without visiting a village. Formerly known as the Pacific Harbour Cultural Centre & Market Place but now called the **Arts Village,** this shopping center on the Queen's Road serves both tourists and residents of the housing development. Although still troubled financially, it consists of colonial-style clapboard buildings joined by covered walkways leading to restaurants, a grocery store, boutiques, handicraft shops, a fancy swimming pool complex, and a fine cultural center (see below).

Offshore, rugged **Beqa Island** is nearly cut in two by Malumu Bay, making it one of Fiji's more scenic spots. Most of Fiji's famous fire walkers come from Dakuibeqa, Naceva, and Ruka villages on Beqa. The island is surrounded by the beautiful **Beqa Lagoon,** where more than a dozen dive sites feature both soft and hard corals. Among them is **Frigate Passage,** which has a 48m (158-ft.) wall for divers but is even better known for its powerful left-handed surf break over a relatively smooth coral reef.

1 Getting to & Getting Around Pacific Harbour

Pacific Harbour is on the Queen's Road, 30km (18 miles) west of Suva. The express buses between Nadi and Suva stop at the Pearl South Pacific Resort, where you'll also find taxis waiting in the parking lot. See "Getting Around Fiji" in chapter 3 for more information. **Thrifty Car Rental** (© **345 0655**) and **Hertz** (© **338 0981**) both have agencies in Pacific Harbour.

No regular ferry service runs between Pacific Harbour and Beqa Island; the resorts out there arrange transfers for their guests, either by boat from Pacific Harbour or by seaplane from Nadi.

Pacific Harbour

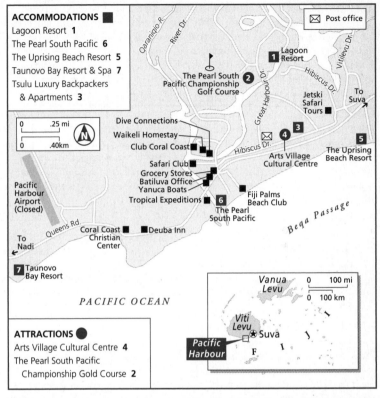

ACCOMMODATIONS ■
Lagoon Resort **1**
The Pearl South Pacific **6**
The Uprising Beach Resort **5**
Taunovo Bay Resort & Spa **7**
Tsulu Luxury Backpackers
  & Apartments **3**

✉ Post office

Qaraniqio R.
River Dr.
Lagoon Resort **1**
The Pearl South Pacific Championship Golf Course **2**
Great Harbour Dr.
Hibiscus Dr.
Jetski Safari Tours ■
Vitilevu Dr.
To Suva ↗

0   .25 mi
0   .40km

Dive Connections ─
Waikeli Homestay ─
Club Coral Coast ■
Hibiscus Dr.
4 ✉ **3**
Arts Village Cultural Centre
5 The Uprising Beach Resort

Safari Club ■
Grocery Stores
Batiluva Office
Yanuca Boats ─
Tropical Expeditions ■
6 The Pearl South Pacific
Fiji Palms Beach Club

Bega Passage

Pacific Harbour Airport (Closed)

Queens Rd.
To Nadi ←

Coral Coast Christian Center ■
■ Deuba Inn

7 Taunovo Bay Resort

PACIFIC OCEAN

ATTRACTIONS ●
Arts Village Cultural Centre **4**
The Pearl South Pacific
  Championship Gold Course **2**

Vanua Levu
0   100 mi
0   100 km

Viti Levu
Pacific Harbour
□ ★ Suva
F

---

2 Visiting the Arts Village ★

The centerpiece of the **Arts Village Cultural Centre** (© **345 0065**; www.arts village.com), on the Queen's Road, is a lakeside Fijian village, complete with thatched roofs over the grand chief's *bure* (bungalow) and the tallest traditional temple in Fiji. The shows and tours here tend to change. For example, the general manager outlined one set of tours for me, but when I got home, the website said something else. Accordingly, I hesitate to tell you the schedule and cost. Let's just say there are fire-walking shows, boat trips around the village, and tours into the village for visits with Fijians working at carving, weaving, boat building, and other crafts. All are worth doing, so call ahead to see what's going on when. Prices range from F$15 to F$75 (US$9.70–US$49/£5–£25). Children ages 6 to 16 are charged half price.

3 Scuba Diving, River Rafting & Other Outdoor Activities

FISHING

The waters off southern Viti Levu are renowned for their big game fish, especially when the tuna and mahimahi are running from January to May, and when big wahoos pass by in June and July. The women's world records for wahoo and trevally were set here. **Xtasea Charters** (© **345 0280;** www.xtaseacharters.com) can tailor excursions—from going for big ones offshore to trolling for smaller but exciting catch inshore. A full day of big game fishing costs about F$1,860 (US$1,208/£604). Reef fishing is less expensive, at F$1,050 (US$682/£341). Xtasea also has snorkeling trips to Beqa Lagoon for F$950 (US$617/£309). Up to six persons can be accommodated on each trip.

GOLF

Robert Trent Jones, Jr., designed the scenic 18-hole, par-72 **Pearl Championship Fiji Golf Course** (© **345 0905**), on the north side of the Queen's Road, at the Pearl South Pacific hotel (see p. 167). Some of its fairways cross lakes; others cut their way through narrow valleys surrounded by jungle-clad hills. Greens fees are F$40 (US$26/£13), and the pro shop has equipment for rent. The clubhouse restaurant is open daily from 7am to 7pm.

JET SKIING

An adventurous way to see Beqa lagoon is on a 60km (37-mile) excursion led by **Jetski Safari** (© **345 0933;** www.jetski-safari.com). Depending on weather conditions, you will speed across Beqa Passage and explore Beqa Island's picturesque Malumu Bay. The boats also stop for snorkeling on a tiny sand islet in the lagoon. Up to three persons can ride on each boat (realistically, two adults and one child) for F$285 (US$185/£93) per craft.

JUNGLE CANOPY RIDES

ZIP Fiji (© **930 0545;** www.zip-fiji.com) has strung wires in a rainforest between Pacific Harbour and Suva; you are strapped into a harness and ride from platform to platform high up in the jungle canopy, sometimes as fast as 50kph (30 mph). Some wires are 200m (650 ft.) long and 30m (98 ft.) up in the trees. The rides cost F$115 (US$75/£38) per adult; children ages 5 to 17 are charged half price. Reservations are required.

RIVER RAFTING & KAYAKING ✸✸✸

The South Pacific's best white-water rafting is with **Rivers Fiji** ✸✸✸ (© **800/ 446-2411** in the U.S., or 345 0147; fax 345 0148; www.riversfiji.com). This American-owned outfit uses inflatable rafts and kayaks for trips through the Upper Navua River Gorge, the "Grand Canyon of Fiji" and an official conservation area. I have met experienced rafters who say the Navua Gorge was one of their top experiences. The adventures cost about US$170 (£85) per person. It also has inflatable kayaking trips— "funyacking," it calls them—on the 'Luva River, another picturesque waterway up in the Namosi Highlands, for US$130 (£65) per person. Their 6-day multisport trips include kayaking down the 'Luva, sea kayaking in the Beqa Lagoon, and white-water rafting the Navua Gorge. Prices for the long trips start at US$2,375 (£1,188). Reservations are essential.

Videos and brochures often feature tourists lazily floating down a Fijian river on a raft made of bamboo poles lashed together. In the old days, mountain-dwelling Fijians really did use *bilibilis*—flimsy bamboo rafts—to float their crops downriver to market. They would discard the rafts and walk home. **Discover Fiji Tours** (© **345 0180;** www.discoverfijitours.com) takes you upriver by motorized canoe and usually brings you back on a bilibili (ask if the bilibili ride is included before you sign up). These 7-hour trips cost F$115 (US$75/£38) per person from Pacific Harbour, more from Nadi and the Coral Coast (see chapters 5 and 7). Reservations and a minimum of three passengers are required.

The Navua River is a scenic delight as it cuts its way through the foothills. Depending on how much it has rained recently, you'll have a few gentle rapids to negotiate, and you'll stop for dips in waterfalls that tumble right into the river. Wear swimsuits and sandals, but bring a sarong to wear in the Fijian village, where you'll be welcomed at a *yaqona* (kava) ceremony.

SCUBA DIVING 𝕽𝕽𝕽

Pacific Harbour is famous for its **shark-feeding dives,** especially over the nearby Shark Reef Marine Reserve. You're almost guaranteed to come close to large bull and tiger sharks as well as six reef species. You watch from behind a man-made coral wall while the dive master does the feeding. Only experienced divers need apply for these exciting excursions.

Beqa Adventure Divers (© 345 0911; www.fiji-sharks.com) pioneered the shark-feeding dives and charges F$110 (US$71/£36 for a one-tank excursion, and F$200 (US$130/£65) for two tanks. San Francisco–based **Aqua-Trek** (© 800/541-4334 or 345 0324; fax 345 0324; www.aquatrek.com) also has shark-feeding dives among its repertoire. Both companies also dive in Beqa Lagoon, and Aqua-Trek teaches resort diving and a full range of PADI courses.

4 Where to Stay in Pacific Harbour

Another option here is the **Lagoon Resort** (© 345 0100; www.lagoonresort.com), a 21-room hotel about 2km (1¼ miles) inland beside the Qaraniqio River and near the Pearl South Pacific Championship Golf Course. It attracts primarily divers and ardent golfers who don't care about a beachside location. The crew of the movie *Anaconda* stayed at the Lagoon and left behind the *Bloody Mary*, the rickety boat that played a leading role (it's now part of the bar). Rates range from about F$175 (US$114/£57) for a room to F$335 (US$218/£109) for a suite.

The Pearl South Pacific   This three-story resort is so cool, sexy, and stylish that it would be more at home in New York or Sydney—or even Suva—than here beside this long beach of deep, gray sand. Jazz music permeates the public areas, from the lobby bar before a waterfall wall to the oversize daybed loungers, where you can stretch out while enjoying a drink or reading a book. Most units are standard hotel rooms, but some have been transformed into luxurious, one-bedroom "Penthouse Suites," each with hardwood floors, its own decor, and butler service. Dining choices include an informal restaurant, a fine-dining outlet, and a bar out by the beach and swimming pool, where Sunday jazz brunches draw crowds of well-heeled locals.

P.O. Box 144, Deuba. © 345 0022. Fax 345 0262. www.thepearlsouthpacific.com. 78 units. F$310–F$370 (US$201–US$240/£102–£120) double; F$650–F$700 (US$422–US$455/£211–£228) suite. AE, DC, MC, V. **Amenities:** 4 restaurants; 4 bars; activities desk; fitness center; game room; golf course; laundry service; outdoor pool; room service; spa; 3 tennis courts; watersports equipment rentals. *In room:* A/C, TV, coffeemaker, fridge, high-speed Internet access, minibar.

Taunovo Bay Resort & Spa   This luxury resort—or more accurately, this luxury real estate development—opened after my most recent visit to Fiji, so I can only tell you what two travel agents told me after they stayed here. The developers are building and selling 450-sq.-m (4,700-sq.-ft.) four-bedroom villas equipped with most modern luxuries, including their own pools. The owners can then live in them or rent them out whole or as one-, two-, or three-bedroom suites, all with butler service. The travel agents, in fact, were quite impressed with the overall service here. A central complex serves both as clubhouse for the villa owners and restaurant and bar for resort guests, who perhaps will be enticed to invest in this rainy corner of paradise. Whether it succeeds on this side of Viti Levu is anyone's guess. I do know that they reduced the published room rates by half for the resort's first 6 months.

P.O. Box 351, Pacific Harbour. ℂ 877/696-3454 or 999 2227. Fax 345 0617. www.taunovobay.com. 44 units. US$350–US$2,500 (£175–1,250). Rates include full breakfast. AE, MC, V. **Amenities:** Restaurant; bar; concierge; fitness center; laundry service; outdoor pool; room service; spa; 2 tennis courts. *In room:* A/C, TV, coffeemaker, iron, kitchen, minibar, safe.

Tsulu Luxury Backpackers & Apartments

On the second floor of the Arts Village buildings, this is a virtual rabbit warren of apartments, hotel-style rooms, private dorm rooms, and multiple dormitories ranging from 4 to 24 bunks each. Although they are called apartments, some of the units actually share bathrooms, and all of their kitchens have hot plates instead of stoves. A coffee shop is on the premises, and guests can use the Arts Centre's large outdoor pool. Frankly, the Uprising Beach Resort is a better choice of dormitory accommodations than here (see below).

P.O. Box 397, Pacific Harbour. ℂ 345 0064. Fax 345 0866. www.tsulu.com. 24 units (8 with bathroom), 68 dorm beds. F$90 (US$58/£29) double; F$150–F$199 (US$97–US$129/£48–£65) apt; F$28–F$33 (US$18–US$21/£9–£11) dorm bed. Rates include continental breakfast. AE, MC, V. **Amenities:** Restaurant; bar; activities desk; fitness center; laundry service; outdoor pool. *In room:* A/C, TV (apts. only), kitchen (apts. only), no phone.

The Uprising Beach Resort *Value*

Opened in 2007, this "flashpacker" resort shares Pacific Harbour's long beach with the Pearl South Pacific. The 12 surprisingly spacious guest bungalows have both queen-size and single beds plus sitting areas, wet bars, and small front porches. You must go outside to reach their outdoor showers and cramped bathrooms, however, so a Fijian *sulu* (sarong) will come in handy. Consisting of one large, fan-cooled room with over-and-under bunk beds, the 24-bed dorm is quietly situated at the rear of the property. The central building with bar and inexpensive restaurant opens to an outdoor pool and the beach. Young guests and imbibing locals can keep the bar rocking until 1am, so I would avoid bure nos. 1, 2, 3, 7, 8, and 9, which are closest to the action. You can camp here and share the dorm's facilities, but bring your own tent. A full range of outdoor activities includes horseback riding and "horse-boarding" (you and your boogie board are pulled over the lagoon by a horse trotting along the beach).

P.O. Box 416, Pacific Harbour. ℂ 345 2200. Fax 345 2059. www.uprisingbeachresort.com. 12 units, 24 dorm beds, 20 tent sites. F$135–F$155 (US$88–US$101/£44–£51) double; F$30 (US$19/£10) dorm bed; F$10 (US$6.50/£3.30) per person camping. MC, V. **Amenities:** Restaurant; bar; laundry service; outdoor pool; watersports equipment rentals. *In room:* Coffeemaker, fridge.

5 Where to Stay on or Near Beqa Island

Cost-conscious travelers can stay at **Lawaki Beach House** (ℂ 992 1621 or 926 9229; www.lawakibeachhouse.com), on Beqa's southwestern coast. It has two simple bures with bathrooms and porches, a six-person dormitory, and space for campers. Rates

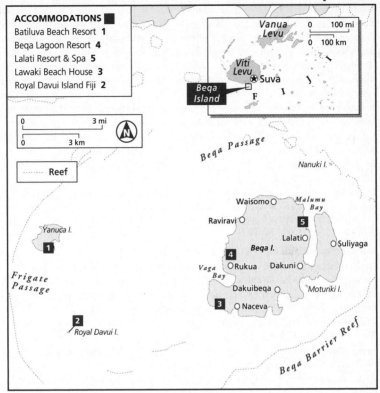

Beqa Island

ACCOMMODATIONS ■

Batiluva Beach Resort **1**
Beqa Lagoon Resort **4**
Lalati Resort & Spa **5**
Lawaki Beach House **3**
Royal Davui Island Fiji **2**

Reef

Vanua Levu

Viti Levu
★ Suva

Beqa Island
F

0   100 mi
0   100 km

0   3 mi
0   3 km

Beqa Passage

Nanuki I.

Waisomo ○   *Malumu Bay*

Raviravi ○

5

Lalati ○   ○ Suliyaga

Beqa I.

4

Vaga Bay   ○ Rukua   Dakuni ○

Dakuibeqa ○   *Moturiki I.*

3   ○ Naceva

Frigate Passage

Yanuca I.

1

2
Royal Davui I.

Beqa Barrier Reef

---

range from F$52 (US$34/£17) to F$95 (US$62/£31) per person, including meals. Lawaki Beach House does not accept credit cards.

You don't have to be a surfer dude to hang out at little **Batiluva Beach Resort** (✆ **345 0384** or 992 0019; www.batiluva.com), on hilly Yanuca Island near the western edge of Beqa Lagoon, but the big breaks on nearby Frigate Passage are its main attraction. Accommodations are in simple bungalows and dormitories. Rates are F$175 (US$114/£57) per person, including meals.

Beqa Lagoon Resort   On the island's north shore and once known as Marlin Bay Resort, this is the oldest hotel on Beqa. One advantage is that you can go scuba diving off the beach. Accommodations are in a variety of bungalows, from beachfront units with their own plunge pools to half a dozen beside a man-made pond with lily pads. Many feature Indian and Asian furniture. Least expensive are four rooms in a two-story building.

P.O. Box 112, Deuba. ✆ **800/592-3454** or 330 4042. Fax 330 4028. www.beqalagoonresort.com. 25 units. F$438–F$585 (US$284–US$380/£142–£190) bungalow. AE, MC, V. **Amenities:** Restaurant; bar; babysitting; laundry service; massage; outdoor pool; room service; watersports equipment rentals. *In room:* A/C, coffeemaker, fridge, safe, no phone.

Lalati Resort & Spa 🎭   This pleasant little resort sits near the mouth of narrow Malumu Bay, which nearly slices Beqa in two. As a result, it enjoys one of the most picturesque views of any Fiji resort. A jagged peak gives way to the azure Beqa Lagoon, while Viti Levu's southern coast lines the horizon (the lights of Suva can illuminate the sky at night). All buildings have tin roofs and ship-plank siding, lending a South Seas plantation ambience to the property. Bathrooms in the spacious guest bures open to both living rooms and bedrooms, and the larger honeymoon bure has a Jacuzzi and an outdoor shower. The bures lack air conditioning, but ceiling fans whip up a breeze. A swimming pool fronts the full-service spa, which has an air-conditioned lounge with TV and DVD player. The beach is almost nonexistent at high tide, but you can snorkel in deep water anytime from the resort's long pier, or kayak over to a lovely white-sand beach across the bay. Smoking is not allowed in any of the buildings here.

P.O. Box 166, Deuba. (📞 347 2033. Fax 347 2034. www.lalati-fiji.com. 7 units. US$310 (£155) per person. Rates include all meals and nonmotorized watersports. AE, MC, V. Children 13 and under not accepted. **Amenities:** Restaurant; bar; exercise room; Jacuzzi; laundry service; massage; outdoor pool; room service; spa; watersports equipment rentals. *In room:* Coffeemaker, minibar, no phone.

Royal Davui Island Fiji 🎭🎭   On a rocky, 3.2-hectare (8-acre) islet off Beqa's southwestern coast, Royal Davui provides competition for Fiji's other top-end, luxury resorts. The island has no flat land, however, so all but one of the bungalows sit up on the hillside. The trade-off for not being able to step from your bure onto the beach is that you will have a wonderful view. (Westward-facing units espy the sunset but can become uncomfortably warm in the afternoon sun, so I prefer one looking east toward Beqa.) Individually designed to fit among the rocks and old-growth forest, these spacious units have living rooms and bedrooms in separate buildings joined by a hallway. Each has a private plunge pool off the living room balcony, while their bedroom balconies hold two lounge chairs. Bathrooms have whirlpool tubs as well as showers. Part of each bathroom roof retracts to let in fresh air or sunshine. A walkway leads from the four-level reception building up to the open-air restaurant and bar. Guests can dine under the shade of a huge banyan tree (a remote, private space for honeymooners is facetiously dubbed the "fertilizer table").

P.O. Box 3171, Lami. (📞 330 7090. Fax 331 1500. www.royaldavui.com. 16 units. US$1,571–US$1,892 (£786–£946) double. AE, MC, V. Rates include meals, nonalcoholic beverages, all activities except scuba diving, game fishing, and spa treatments. **Amenities:** Restaurant; bar; laundry service; massage; outdoor pool; room service; spa; watersports equipment. *In room:* A/C, coffeemaker, iron, minibar, safe.

6 Where to Dine in Pacific Harbour

Oasis Restaurant REGIONAL   Owned by English expatriates Monica Vine and Colin Head, this airy dining room with widely spaced tables makes an excellent pit stop if you're driving between Nadi and Suva. The house specialty is vinegary London-style fish and chips. You can get tasty burgers, sandwiches, salads, curries, omelets, and English-style breakfasts all day. Evening sees the likes of pan-fried mahimahi, perhaps caught by one of the charter boat skippers having a cold one at the corner bar. Monica and Colin will let you use their computer with Internet access for F20¢ (US15¢/5p) per minute.

Queen's Rd., in Arts Village. (📞 345 0617. Reservations accepted. Breakfast F$6–F$13 (US$3.90–US$8.40/ £2–£4.30); snacks, sandwiches, and lunch F$5.50–F$16 (US$3.60–US$10/£1.80–£5.30); main courses F$15–F$35 (US$9.70–US$23/£5–£12). MC, V. Mon–Sat 9:30am–2:30pm and 6–9:30pm; Sun 10am–2:30pm and 6–9:30pm.

The Waters Edge Bar & Grill REGIONAL   Ex–New Yorker Renee Lange operates this open-air restaurant beside the big pond in the Arts Village. She provides a range of fare, from sandwiches and burgers to pizza and pasta, plus blackboard dinner specials on weekend nights, when she may have live jazz music.

Queen's Rd., in Arts Village. © **345 0146**. Reservations accepted. Sandwiches and burgers F$9–F$12 (US$5.80–US$7.80/£3–£4); pizza and pasta F$15–F$24 (US$9.70–US$16/£5–£8); main courses F$12–F$20 (US$7.80–US$13/£4–£6.70). MC, V. Mon–Thurs 8:30am–3pm; Fri–Sat 8:30am–9pm.

9

Kadavu

No other Fiji island is as rich in wildlife as is rugged **Kadavu,** about 100km (62 miles) south of Viti Levu. No cane toads, no iguanas, no mongooses, and no myna birds live on Kadavu to destroy the native flora and fauna in its hills and valleys. As a result, bird-watchers stand a good chance of seeing the endemic Kadavu musk (or shining) parrot, the Kadavu fantail, the Kadavu honeyeater, and the Kadavu whistling dove.

What you will not see on Fiji's least-developed large island is modern civilization. Kadavu has only two dirt roads, and they really don't go anywhere. Kadavu's 10,000 or so residents, all of them Fijians, live in 70 small villages scattered along the serrated coastline. With tourism in its infancy on Kadavu, villagers make their livings the old-fashioned way, by fishing and subsistence farming. Consequently, this is an excellent place to visit a village and experience relatively unchanged Fijian culture.

The country's fourth-largest island, skinny Kadavu is about 60km (37 miles) long by just 14km (8½ miles) wide—and that's at its widest point. Several bays, including **Galoa Harbour** and **Namalata Bay,** almost cut it into pieces. The Kadavu airstrip and **Vunisea,** the government administrative center, are on the narrow Namalata Isthmus between them. Vunisea has a post office, a school, an infirmary, and a few small shops, but it doesn't qualify as a town. The area around Vunisea saw its heyday in the 19th century, when whalers and other ships would anchor behind the protection afforded by **Galoa Island.**

When I first flew down to Kadavu, I was startled to see much of the north coast skirted by several kilometers of **Long Beach,** the longest uninterrupted strip of white sand in Fiji. Around a corner I could see **Matana Beach,** another jewel.

But Kadavu is best known for the **Great Astrolabe Reef,** which forms a barrier along its eastern and southern sides and encloses its neighbor, **Ono Island,** and several other small dry landmasses to the north. Named for French admiral Dumont d'Urville, who nearly lost his ship, the *Astrolabe,* on it in 1827, the reef is today one of Fiji's most famous scuba dive destinations. The lagoon and

---

⌒Tips Bring Local Currency

A post office and rudimentary hospital are in Vunisea, but Kadavu does not have a bank. Some but not all of the accommodations accept MasterCard and Visa credit cards, so bring sufficient Fijian currency if yours does not (see "Where to Stay & Dine on Kadavu" below for details).

---

mangrove forests along the coast also make Kadavu popular with sea kayakers.

Compared to Viti Levu, I found the weather to be cooler down here, thanks in large part to the southeast trade winds that blow strongly during much of the year.

1 Getting to & Getting Around Kadavu

Pacific Sun (© 800/294-4864 in the U.S., or 672 0888; www.pacificsun.com.fj) and **Air Fiji** (© 877/247-3454 in the U.S., 0800 347 3624 in Fiji or 672 2521; www.air fiji.com.fj) both fly to Kadavu daily from Nadi and Suva, respectively. Round-trip fare from Nadi on Pacific Sun is about F$182 (US$118/£59); from Suva on Air Fiji it is about F$222 (US$144/£72). The flights usually arrive and depart about midday, but they are notoriously late. The airstrip is at **Vunisea,** about midway along the island. See "Getting Around Fiji," in chapter 3.

Small ships haul supplies and passengers from Suva to Kadavu weekly, but the service is unreliable and anything but punctual. Fly instead.

The two dirt roads on the western end of Kadavu do not go anywhere near the accommodations, and a public transportation system is nonexistent. Consequently, there is no "Exploring Kadavu" section in this chapter because it cannot be done.

You will have to ride a boat to the resorts—10 minutes to Dive Kadavu/Matana Beach Resort, 30 minutes to Papageno Resort, 45 minutes or more to Matava—The Astrolabe Hideaway, and an hour or more to the eastern end (see "Where to Stay & Dine on Kadavu," below). Transfers usually are in small, open speedboats, so bring sun protection and light rain gear with you. No piers or wharfs have been built at the Vunisea airstrip or at the resorts, so you will get your feet wet wading ashore both coming and going.

Local boats land on both sides of the Namalata Isthmus, at the government wharf on the north, and at Galoa Harbour on the south. Really adventurous souls can hitch a ride or pay the owners for water taxi service, but it's an unreliable way to get around and most of the boats lack safety equipment.

2 Scuba Diving, Snorkeling, Kayaking & Other Outdoor Activities

The **Great Astrolabe Reef,** the world's fourth-longest barrier reef, skirts the eastern and southern sides of Kadavu and extends to the north around Ono and other islets. Much coral inside the Great Astrolabe is bleached (the northern reef is closed off even to live-aboard dive boats), but its outside slopes have plentiful hard corals and sea life, including a veritable herd of manta rays that gathers at the so-called Manta Pass on the south coast. In other words, the Great Astrolabe is best for hard corals and abundant sea life. It also is exposed to the usually strong southeast trade winds, which can make for rough boat rides and strong swells on the outer reef.

On the other hand, the **Namalata Reefs** and **King Kong Reef** off the usually protected north shore are known for colorful soft corals, and advanced divers can explore the 71m (235-ft.) *Pacific Voyager,* a tanker deliberately sunk in 1994 to form an artificial reef.

Diving here is handled by the resorts, which have their own operations (see "Where to Stay & Dine on Kadavu," below).

Kadavu is not Fiji's best **snorkeling** destination, since most of the lagoons are shallow close to shore, and the good coral is too far out for a safe swim. Exceptions are a colorful reef just off Dive Kadavu/Matana Beach Resort and around Waya Island off Matava—The Astrolabe Hideaway. You will need to pay your resort for a snorkeling excursion, or go along on a dive expedition to see the best coral and sea life.

Kadavu's many quiet bays, protected lagoons, and mangrove forests make it Fiji's top **kayaking** destination. The resorts have kayaks for their guests to use, and they will organize overnight paddling trips. Longer excursions are best arranged in advance. **Tamarillo Tropical Expeditions** (© **877/682-5433** in the U.S., 4/2399 855 in New Zealand; www.tamarillo.co.nz) offers guided 5- to 9-day Kadavu kayak expeditions. You paddle all day and stay in villages or resorts at night.

The resorts also organize **sport- and deep-sea fishing,** which is very good both in the lagoon and offshore. Marlin, sailfish, and wahoo are among the abundant fish in these waters.

The 11m (36-ft.) charter yacht *Safari* is based at Matava—The Astrolabe Hideaway (see below), from where it makes day sails, sunset cruises, and longer voyages. The boat has three staterooms, but usually only one couple at a time is allowed on overnight trips. Contact the resort for details.

3 Where to Stay & Dine on Kadavu

Given the difficulties getting around Kadavu, I have visited only the three resorts I recommend below. Next time I intend to see **Tiliva Resort** (© **333 7127;** www.tiliva resortfiji.com), on the far northeastern end of Kadavu facing Ono Island. It's the creation of Kim Yabaki, a native of Tiliva village who spent 20 years in the British army, and his Irish wife, Barbara. Their guests stay in large, chalet-style bungalows on a hillside overlooking their 7.2 hectares (18 acres), a beach, and the Ono Passage. Each unit has a kitchen, and the Yabakis have a restaurant and bar. Rates range from F$425 to F$530 (US$276–US$344/£138–£172) for a double, including all meals. Credit cards are accepted only if you book through Tiliva's website.

Nearby is the inexpensive **Waisalima Beach Resort & Dive Center** (©/fax **603 0486;** www.waisalimafiji.com), which has a restaurant, bar, simple Fijian-style bures, and a dormitory beside a sandy beach. Bures range from F$75 to F$150 (US$49–US$97/£25–£49) for a double, while dorm beds cost F$25 (US$16/£8.30) per person. Meals and transfers are extra, and credit cards are not accepted.

Nagigia Island Resort (© **603 0454;** www.fijisurf.com), on Nagigia Island off Kadavu's western end, was slated for major upgrades in 2008, though they had not taken place by press time. Given its proximity to the famous King Kong Breaks off Cape Washington, it remains one of Fiji's top surfing destinations.

Note: You must take a small boat to all Kadavu resorts, so be sure to ask if the transfers are included in the rates you are quoted.

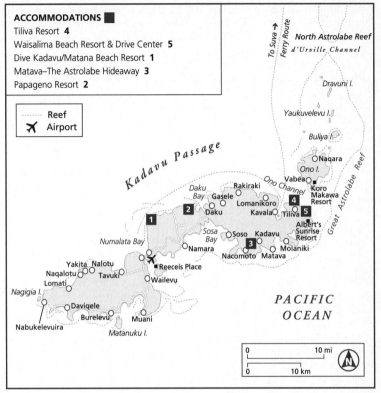

ACCOMMODATIONS ■

Tiliva Resort **4**

Waisalima Beach Resort & Drive Center **5**

Dive Kadavu/Matana Beach Resort **1**

Matava–The Astrolabe Hideaway **3**

Papageno Resort **2**

········· Reef

✈ Airport

Dive Kadavu/Matana Beach Resort 🍴 (Value)

Australians Rob and Rena Forster founded this resort in 1987 as Dive Kadavu but have added Matana Beach Resort to the name to take advantage of its setting beside one of Fiji's great beaches. Indeed, Matana Beach has soft white sand, the lagoon is deep enough for swimming and snorkeling over nearby coral heads at all tides, and the view westward along Kadavu's northern coast to Nabukelevu (Mount Washington), the extinct volcanic cone soaring above western Kadavu, is spectacular. The beachside "Jar Bar"—so called because drinks are served in Mason jars—takes full advantage of the view for sunset cocktails. Steps lead from there up to the hillside main building and its charming restaurant, bar, lounge, and library crammed with more than 1,000 of Rena's books. Two private honeymoon bures stand up on the hillside, while the others are beside the beach. Unit no. 3 is the largest, with living room, two bedrooms, one bathroom, and an expansive veranda. Units 5 and 6 share a building and can interconnect, making them popular with families and dive groups. Others are typical one-room bungalows. They fall short of today's standards of luxury, but they are spacious, comfortable, and have ceiling fans in case the trade winds aren't making their way in through the ample louvered windows. They also have outdoor rinse showers plus wash-off facilities and lock boxes for dive gear. In addition to diving and snorkeling, activities include fishing, waterfall hikes, village visits (Drue and Navautu villages share the beach), and kayak excursions. Bob keeps a boat on the south shore, so divers can easily go to both coasts from here. Only a 10-minute boat ride to Vunisea, this is the closest Kadavu resort to the airstrip.

P.O. Box 8, Vunisea, Kadavu. © **368 3502.** www.divekadavu.com or www.matanabeachresort.com. 10 units. US$150 (£75) per person. Rates include meals and nonmotorized watersports. 3-night minimum stay required. MC, V. **Amenities:** Restaurant; 2 bars; free kayaks and snorkeling gear; laundry service. *In room:* Safe, no phone.

Matava—The Astrolabe Hideaway ✦

On the edge of a lush, rainforested valley on Kadavu's southern side, this is the most environmentally friendly hotel in Fiji. All waste is either recycled, composted and used in the organic garden, or fed to the local pigs. Although the staff will crank up a small generator to charge your camera batteries, only 12-volt solar power passes through the wires here. Consequently, your electric razor and hair dryer will be useless. All guests are given kerosene lanterns at night, but my small flashlight was invaluable getting around after dark. The rather spartan but comfortable accommodations don't have fans, much less air-conditioners, but the prevailing trade winds usually make them unnecessary. Rooms do have mosquito nets over their beds and propane water heaters for their showers, but your hand basin shave will be with cold spring water. A natural look extends to all the units, which are predominately made of thatch and other local materials. The honeymoon and another unit are high up the hillside, giving them terrific views from their large decks. Others are down near the shoreline, which is not a beach except at low tide, when the lagoon turns into a massive sand flat. A small, picturesque beach is on Waya Island, a rocky outcrop a few hundred yards offshore. Given this setting, activities (other than doing absolutely nothing) are geared toward active travelers: diving, sea kayaking, hiking to nearby Kadavu Koro village, sailing, fishing, and snorkeling off Waya Island. The central restaurant-bar-lounge building was slated to be replaced in 2008 by a large sun deck with pizza oven and barbecue facilities. Matava was born in the 1990s as a surfing camp with dorms, very basic bungalows, and shared facilities, but present owners have greatly improved it in recent years. Although lacking luxuries, it's now one of the top places in Fiji to really get away from it all.

P.O. Box 63, Vunisea, Kadavu. © **333 6222.** www.matava.com. 12 units. F$120–F$215 (US$78–US$140/£39–£70) double. Rates include meals. MC, V. **Amenities:** Restaurant; bar; laundry service; watersports equipment rentals. *In room:* No phone.

Papageno Resort ✦

Beside one of the long, white beaches on Kadavu's northern shore, this resort is owned by Anneliese Schimmelpfennig, who's also proprietor of private elementary schools in Laguna Beach, California. She obviously is a collector of Pacific Islands tribal art, for the entire resort is a like a museum full of woodcarvings from Papua New Guinea, tapa cloth from Tonga, and other fabulous pieces. Formerly known as Papageno Eco Resort, this is still an environmentally friendly hotel, with organic gardens providing food, and both solar panels and a small hydroelectric dam supplying electricity. With a stream running through them, the 140 hectares (350 acres) are moist and lush, which means mosquitoes can be abundant. Consequently, the central building with restaurant and bar is fully screened, as are the accommodations. Ms. Schimmelpfennig's art-laden three bedroom, three-bathroom house leads the list as the Royal Bure. Next are the five Ocean View Bures, each with a queen-size bed and two twins, followed by five similar duplex Garden Bures. Least expensive are the four Garden Rooms in a motel-like building. All of the units are across the lawns and gardens from the beach. A single beachside building houses a bar and activities room, the latter frequented by yoga groups that like to visit here (ask if you can join in). As lovely as the beach is, the lagoon turns into a sand bank at low tide, so most activities—such as hikes to a nearby Fijian village and waterfall, snorkeling, and trips to visit manta rays swimming out by the reefs—take place away from the resort. The resort has its own PADI dive base.

P.O. Box 60, Vunisea, Kadavu. © **866/862-0754** or 600 3128. Fax 600 3127. www.papagenoecoresort.com. 15 units. US$255–US$385 (£128–£193) double. Rates include meals. AE, MC, V. **Amenities:** Restaurant; 2 bars; complimentary kayaks and snorkeling gear; laundry service; Wi-Fi. *In room:* Coffeemaker, fridge, no phone.

Suva

Neither the likelihood of frequent showers nor an occasional deluge should discourage you from visiting Suva, Fiji's vibrant, sophisticated capital city. Grab your umbrella and wander along its broad avenues lined with grand colonial buildings and orderly parks left over from the British Empire. Its streets will be crowded with Fijians, Indians, Chinese, Europeans, Polynesians, and people of various other ancestries.

Suva sprawls over a hilly, 26 sq. km (10 sq. mile) peninsula jutting like a thumb from southeastern Viti Levu. To the east lies windswept **Laucala Bay** and to the west, Suva's busy harbor and the suburbs of **Lami Town** and **Walu Bay.**

Jungle-draped mountains rise to heights of more than 1,200m (4,000 ft.) on the mainland to the north, high enough to condense moisture from the prevailing southeast trade winds and create the damp climate cloaking the city in lush green foliage year-round.

Suva was a typical Fijian village in 1870, when the Polynesia Company sent a group of Australians to settle land it acquired in exchange for paying Chief Cakobau's foreign debts. The Aussies established a camp on the flat, swampy,

mosquito-infested banks of **Nubukalou Creek,** on the western shore of the peninsula. When they failed to grow first cotton and then sugar, speculators convinced the new British colonial administration to move the capital from Levuka, which they did in 1882.

The commercial heart of the city still resides in the narrow, twisting streets near Nubukalou Creek, although you will find most of the sites, office buildings, interesting restaurants, and lively nightspots along broad **Victoria Parade,** the historic main drag where the British built their imposing colonial administrative center.

High-rise buildings are springing up all over downtown, a testament to Suva's position as the thriving commercial and diplomatic hub of the South Pacific islands and headquarters for several regional organizations.

As a result of the 2006 coup, the governments of Australia, New Zealand, and some other nations still caution against travel to Suva. Personally, the only sign of the coup I saw when I recently visited was the army's having turned the old Grand Pacific Hotel, on Victoria Parade, into a makeshift barracks. No soldiers were in

---

Impressions

The English, with a mania for wrong decisions in Fiji, built their capital at Suva, smack in the middle of the heaviest rainfall . . . Yet Suva is a superb tropical city.
—James A. Michener, *Return to Paradise,* 1951

evidence elsewhere, and even at the old hotel they were dressed in civvies.

Too many visitors spend only a day in Suva, which is hardly enough time to do justice to this fascinating city. You can easily spend 2 or 3 days walking its streets, seeing its sights, and poking your head into its multitude of shops.

1 Getting to & Getting Around Suva

GETTING TO SUVA

Suva is served by **Nausori Airport,** 19km (12 miles) northeast of downtown near the Rewa River town of Nausori. **Express buses** operated by **Nausori Taxi & Bus Service** (② 347 7583 in Nausori, or 330 4178 in Suva) are scheduled to depart the airport for downtown Monday to Friday at 8:30am, 9:30am, 11:30am, 2:30pm, 5pm, and 6:30pm. The fare is F$3 (US$1.90/£1) each way. That having been said, I always take one of several **taxis** waiting at the terminal, whose fares to downtown Suva officially are F$25 (US$16/£8.30). Allow at least 30 minutes for the taxi ride during midday, an hour during morning and evening rush hours.

Express buses leave **Nadi airport** daily for Suva, a ride of approximately 4 hours on the Queen's Road.

I never drive away from Nadi in my **rental car** (p. 52) without a good map of Suva, whose streets can seem like a confusing maze, especially at night.

See "Getting Around Fiji" in chapter 3 for more information.

GETTING AROUND SUVA

Hundreds of **taxis** prowl Suva's streets. Some have meters, but don't count on it. As a rule of thumb, F$2 to F$3.50 (US$1.30–US$2.30/70p–£1.20) will get you to the sites of interest, but plan on F$7 (US$4.50/£2.30) to the Raintree Lodge. If the taxi has a meter, make sure the driver drops the flag. The main **taxi stand** (② 331 2266) is on Central Street, behind the Air Pacific office in the CML Building on Victoria Parade, and on Victoria Parade at Sukuna Park (no phone). I have been very satisfied with **Black Arrow Taxis** (② 330 0541 or 330 0139 in Suva, or 347 7071 in Nausori) and **Nausori Taxi & Bus Service** (② 347 7583 in Nausori, or 330 4178 in Suva), which is based at the Holiday Inn Suva parking lot. Taxis also gather at the Suva Municipal Market.

Although usually crowded, local **buses** fan out from the municipal market from before daybreak to midnight Monday to Saturday (they have limited schedules on Sun). The fares vary but should be no more than F$2 (US$1.30/70p) to most destinations in and around Suva. *Word to the wise:* If you're going to ride the bus for the fun of it, do it in Nadi, where you won't get lost and aren't as likely to be robbed.

See "Getting Around Fiji" in chapter 3 for the phone numbers of the big **car-rental** firms.

Tickets are required to **park** on downtown streets Monday to Friday from 8am to 4:30pm, Saturday from 8am to 12:30pm. Buy the tickets at the silver machines in every block, and display them on your dashboard. On-street parking fees are F20¢ (US13¢/7p) per 15 minutes.

Suva

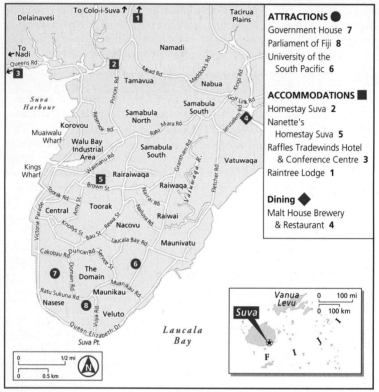

ATTRACTIONS ●
Government House **7**
Parliament of Fiji **8**
University of the
   South Pacific **6**

ACCOMMODATIONS ■
Homestay Suva **2**
Nanette's
   Homestay Suva **5**
Raffles Tradewinds Hotel
   & Conference Centre **3**
Raintree Lodge **1**

Dining ◆
Malt House Brewery
   & Restaurant **4**

FAST FACTS: Suva

The following facts apply to Suva. If you don't see an item here, see "Fast Facts: Fiji" in appendix A.

Bookstores The region's largest store is **University Book Centre** (📞 331 2500; www.uspbookcentre.com), on the University of the South Pacific campus on Laucala Bay Road (you can order online). **Dominion Book Centre,** in Dominion Arcade on Thomson Street behind the Fiji Visitors Bureau (📞 330 4334), has the latest newsmagazines and books on the South Pacific. Another good downtown choice is the book section of **Prouds** department store (📞 331 8686), in the Suva Central building on Renwick Road at Pratt Street.

Camera & Film **Caines Photofast,** corner of Victoria Parade and Pratt Street (📞 331 3211), sells a wide range of film, provides 1-hour processing of color-print film, and will download and print your digital photos.

Currency Exchange **ANZ Bank, Westpac Bank,** and **Colonial National Bank** have offices with ATMs on Victoria Parade, south of the Fiji Visitors Bureau. ANZ has a walk-up currency exchange window that is open Monday to Friday from 9am to 6pm, Saturday from 9am to 1pm. **GlobalEX,** on Victoria Parade at Gordon Street, cashes traveler's checks.

Drugstores **Suva City Pharmacy,** on Victoria Parade in the General Post Office building (© 331 7400), is the city's best drugstore. It's open Monday to Friday from 8:30am to 5:30pm, Saturday from 8:30am to 2pm.

Emergencies & Police The emergency phone number for **police** is © 917. For **fire** and **ambulance** dial © 911. Fiji Police's **central station** (© 331 1222) is on Joske Street, between Pratt and Gordon streets.

Eyeglasses Dr. Guy Hawley, an American eye specialist, practices at **Asgar & Co. Ltd.,** Queensland Insurance Centre, Victoria Parade (© 330 0433).

Healthcare Most expatriate residents go to the **Suva Private Hospital,** 120 Amy St. (© 331 3355). It's open 24 hours a day. **Colonial War Memorial Hospital,** at the end of Ratu Mara Road at Brown Street (© 331 3444), is the public hospital (but go to Suva Private Hospital if at all possible).

Internet Access Suva has dozens of Internet cafes, many of them on Victoria Parade, and wireless hotspots were being set up at press time. Operated by Fiji's major Internet service provider, **Connect Internet Cafe** (© 330 0777), in the General Post Office building, has high-speed broadband access for F$3 (US$1.90/£1) an hour. It's open Monday to Friday 8:30am to 8pm, Saturday 9am to 8pm, Sunday 10am to 6pm. You can print your e-mails, scan documents, and burn CDs here. The country's overseas phone company, **Fiji International Telecommunications Ltd. (FINTEL),** has broadband access at its headquarters (© 330 1655). It's open Monday to Saturday from 8am to 8pm and charges F$1.50 (US$1/50p) for 20 minutes. A wireless hotspot is at the **Esquires** branch on Renwick Road at Pratt Street (© 330 0082). It's open Monday to Friday 7am to 10pm, Saturday 8am to 10pm, Sunday 9am to 7pm.

Laundry & Dry Cleaning **Flagstaff Laundry & Drycleaners,** 62 Bau St. (© 330 1214), has full 1-day service.

Libraries **Suva City Library** on Victoria Parade (© 331 3433) has a small collection of books on the South Pacific. It's open Monday, Tuesday, Thursday, and Friday 9:30am to 6pm; Wednesday noon to 6pm; Saturday 9am to 1pm. The library at the **University of the South Pacific,** Laucala Bay Road (© 331 3900), has one of the largest collections in the South Pacific.

Mail Fiji Post's General Post Office is on Thomson Street, opposite the Fiji Visitors Bureau (Mon–Fri 8am–4:30pm, Sat 9am–noon).

Restrooms **Sukuna Park,** on Victoria Parade, has attended (and reasonably clean) public restrooms, on the side next to McDonald's. You must pay F70¢ (US45¢/25p) to use the toilets, or F$1.20 (US80¢/40p) for a shower. Restrooms are open Monday to Saturday 8am to 3:45pm.

Safety Street crime is a serious problem in Suva, so be alert at all times. Do not wander off Victoria Parade after dark; take a taxi. The busy blocks along Victoria Parade between the Fiji Visitors Bureau and the Holiday Inn Suva are relatively safe during the evenings (a local wag says the many prostitutes on the main drag keep the robbers away!), but always protect valuables from pickpockets. See "Safety" under "Fast Facts: Fiji" in appendix A.

Telephone & Fax You can make international calls, send faxes, and surf the 'net at **Fiji International Telecommunications Ltd.** (FINTEL; © **331 2933**), in its colonial-style building on Victoria Parade (Mon–Sat 8am–8pm).

Visitor Information & Maps The **Fiji Visitors Bureau** (© **330 2433**) has an information center in a restored colonial house at the corner of Thomson and Scott streets, in the heart of Suva. It's open Monday to Thursday 8am to 4:30pm, Friday 8am to 4pm, Saturday 8am to noon. The excellent *Suva and Lami Town* from the Department of Lands & Surveys is often available at Dominion Book Centre (see "Bookstores," above).

Water The tap water in Suva is safe to drink.

2 Exploring Suva

Although you could easily spend several days poking around the capital, most visitors come here for only a day, usually on one of the guided tours from Nadi or the Coral Coast. That's enough time to see the city's highlights, particularly if you make the walking tour described below.

Sitting on a ridge about 1km (½ mile) southeast of downtown, the **Parliament of Fiji,** Battery Road off Vuya Road (© **330 5811**), resides under a modern shingle-covered replica of a traditional Fijian roof. Parliament has not convened here since the 2006 coup, so call the main number or check with the Fiji Visitors Bureau before your visit.

THE TOP ATTRACTIONS

Fiji Museum ★★★   You'll see a marvelous collection of war clubs, cannibal forks, *tanoa* bowls, shell jewelry, and other relics in this excellent museum. Although some artifacts were damaged by Suva's humidity while they were hidden away during World War II, much remains. Later additions include the rudder and other relics of HMS *Bounty,* burned and sunk at Pitcairn Island by Fletcher Christian and the other mutineers in 1789 but recovered in the 1950s by the famed *National Geographic* photographer Luis Marden. Don't miss the *masi* (bark) cloth and Indian art exhibits in the air-conditioned upstairs galleries. The gift shop is worth a browse.

In Thurston Gardens, Ratu Cakobau Rd. off Victoria Parade. © 331 5944. www.fijimuseum.org.fj. Admission F$7 (US$4.50/£2.30) adults, F$5 (US$3.20/£1.70) students with IDs. Guided tours by donation. Mon–Thurs and Sat 9am–4:30pm; Fri 9:30am–4pm.

Suva Municipal Market ★★★   A vast array of tropical produce is offered for sale at Suva's main supplier of food, the largest and most lively market in Fiji. If they aren't too busy, the merchants will appreciate your interest and answer your questions about the names and uses of the various fruits and vegetables. The market teems on Saturday morning, when it seems the entire population of Suva shows up to shop and select television programs for the weekend's viewing: A telling sight about urban life in the modern South Pacific is that of a Fijian carrying home in one hand a bunch of taro roots tied together with *pandanus* (palm leaves), and, in the other, a collection of rented videocassettes stuffed into a plastic bag.

Usher St. at Rodwell Rd. The bus station is behind the market on Rodwell Rd. No phone. Free admission. Mon–Fri 5am–6pm; Sat 5am–1pm.

WALKING TOUR   SUVA

Start:	The Triangle
Finish:	Government House
Time:	2½ hours
Best Time:	Early morning or late afternoon
Worst Time:	Midday, or Saturday afternoon and Sunday, when the market and shops are closed and downtown is deserted

Begin at the four-way intersection of Victoria Parade, Renwick Road, and Thomson and Central streets. This little island in the middle of heavy traffic is called the Triangle.

❶ The Triangle

The modern center of Suva, in the late 1800s this spot was a lagoon fed by a stream that flowed along what is now Pratt Street. A marker in the park commemorates Suva's becoming the capital, the arrival of Fiji's first missionaries, the first public land sales, and Fiji becoming a colony.

From the Triangle, head north on Thomson Street, bearing right between the Fiji Visitors Bureau and the old Garrick Hotel (now the Sichuan Pavilion Restaurant), whose wrought-iron balconies recall a more genteel (but non-air-conditioned) era. Continue on Thomson Street to Nubukalou Creek.

❷ Nubukalou Creek

The Polynesia Company's settlers made camp beside this stream and presumably drank from it. A sign on the bridge warns against eating fish from it today—with good reason, as you will see and smell. Across the bridge, smiling Fijian women sit under a flame tree in a shady little park to offer grass skirts and other handicrafts for sale.

Pass to the left of the Fijian women across the bridge for now, and head down narrow Cumming Street.

❸ Cumming Street

This area, also on reclaimed land, was home of the Suva market until the 1940s. Cumming Street was lined with saloons, *yaqona* (kava) grog shops, and curry houses known as lodges. It became a tourist-oriented shopping mecca when World War II Allied servicemen created a market for curios. When import taxes were lifted from electronic equipment and cameras in the 1960s, Cumming Street merchants quickly added the plethora of duty-free items you'll find there today.

Return to Thomson Street, turn right, and then left on Usher Street. Follow Usher Street past the intersection at Rodwell Road and Scott Street to the Suva Municipal Market.

❹ Suva Municipal Market

This market is a beehive of activity, especially on Saturday mornings (see "The Top Attractions," above). Big ships from overseas and small boats from the other islands dock at Princes Wharf and Kings Wharf beyond the market on Usher Street.

Head south along wide Stinson Parade, back across Nubukalou Creek and along the edge of Suva's waterfront to Edward Street and the gray tin roofs of the Municipal Curio and Handicraft Centre.

❺ Municipal Curio and Handicraft Centre

In yet another bit of cultural diversity, you can haggle over the price of handicrafts at stalls run by Indians. (Don't try to haggle at those operated by Fijians, who sell by set prices and may be offended if you try to bargain.) It's best to wait until you have visited the Government Handicraft Centre before making a purchase (see "Shopping in Suva," below).

Continue on Stinson Parade past Central Street. The gray concrete building on the corner is the YWCA. When you get there, cut diagonally under the palms and flame trees across Sukuna Park.

❻ Sukuna Park

This park is named for Ratu Sir Lala Sukuna, founding father of independent Fiji. This shady waterfront park is a favorite brown-bag lunch spot for Suva's office workers. On the west side is the harbor and on the east, Victoria Parade. For many years only a row of flame trees separated this broad avenue from the harbor, but the shallows have been filled and the land has been extended into the harbor by the width of a city block. The large auditorium that stands south of the park is the Suva Civic Centre.

Head south on the seaward side of Victoria Parade and pass the cream-colored colonial-style headquarters of FINTEL, the country's electronic link to the world. You'll come to the Old Town Hall.

❼ Old Town Hall

A picturesque Victorian-era building, it features an intricate, ornamental wrought-iron portico. Built as an auditorium in the early 1900s and named Queen Victoria Memorial Hall, this lovely structure was later used as the Suva Town Hall (city offices are now in the modern Suva City Hall adjacent to the Civic Centre on the waterfront). The stage still stands at the rear of the Chinese restaurant.

Continue south on Victoria Parade until you come to the Suva City Library.

❽ Suva City Library

The U.S. industrialist and philanthropist Andrew Carnegie gave Fiji the money to build this structure. The central portion of the colonnaded building opened in 1909, with an initial collection of 4,200 books. The wings were added in 1929. Books on Fiji and the South Pacific are shelved to the left of the main entrance. (See "Fast Facts: Suva," above, for the library's hours.)

Keep going along Victoria Parade, past Loftus Street, to the corner of Gladstone Road, the locale for the Native Land Trust Board Building.

❾ Native Land Trust Board Building

This site is known locally as Naiqaqi ("The Crusher") because a sugar-crushing mill sat here during Suva's brief and unsuccessful career as a cane-growing region in the 1870s (see box, "My Word!," below). Ratu Sir Lala Sukuna, who prepared his people for independence (see "Looking Back at Fiji," in chapter 2), served as chairman of the Native Land Trust Board, which collects and distributes rents on the 80% of the country that is owned by the Fijians.

Across Gladstone Road you can't miss the imposing gray edifice and clock tower of the Government Buildings.

❿ Government Buildings

Erected between 1937 and 1939 (although they look older), these British-style gray stone buildings house the High Court, the prime minister's office, and several government ministries. Parliament met here until 1987, when Colonel Rabuka and his gang marched in and arrested its leaders. (If it ever meets again, Parliament will convene in its complex on Ratu Sukuna Road in the Muanikau suburb.) The clock tower is known as "Fiji's Big Ben." When it works, it chimes every 15 minutes from 6am to midnight.

Walk past the large open field on the south side of the building; this is Albert Park.

⓫ Albert Park

This park is named for Queen Victoria's consort, Prince Albert. The pavilion opposite the Government Buildings, however, is named for Charles Kingsford Smith, the Australian aviator and first person to fly across the Pacific. Smith was unaware that a row of palm trees stretched across the middle of Albert Park, his intended landing place. A local radio operator figured out Smith's predicament, and the colonial governor ordered the trees cut down immediately.

Walking Tour: Suva

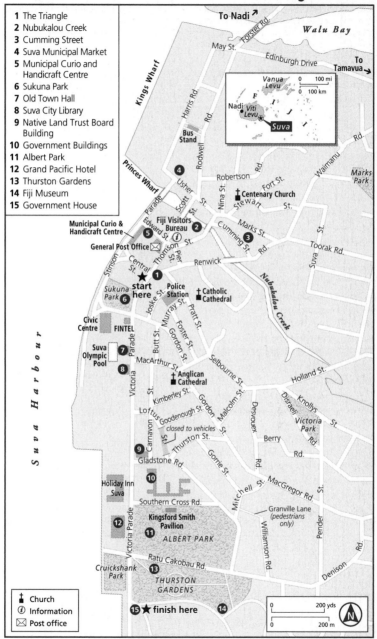

1 The Triangle
2 Nubukalou Creek
3 Cumming Street
4 Suva Municipal Market
5 Municipal Curio and Handicraft Centre
6 Sukuna Park
7 Old Town Hall
8 Suva City Library
9 Native Land Trust Board Building
10 Government Buildings
11 Albert Park
12 Grand Pacific Hotel
13 Thurston Gardens
14 Fiji Museum
15 Government House

To Nadi
Walu Bay
May St.
Edinburgh Drive
To Tamavua

Vanua Levu
Nadi • Viti Levu
Suva
F I J I
0 100 mi
0 100 km

Kings Wharf
Harris Rd.
Rodwell Rd.
Bus Stand
Princes Wharf
Usher St.
Scott St.
Nina St.
Fort St.
Robertson Rd.
Stewart St.
† Centenary Church
Waimanu Rd.
Marks Park
Marks St.
Toorak Rd.
Suva St.

Municipal Curio & Handicraft Centre
Fiji Visitors Bureau
5
2 (i)
Edward St.
Thomson St.
Pier St.
Cumming St.
3

General Post Office ⊠
Central St.
1
start here ★
Renwick Rd.

Stinson Parade
Parade

Police Station
Joske St.
Murray St.
Pratt St.
Foster St.
Gordon St.
† Catholic Cathedral

Sukuna Park 6

Nubukalou Creek

Civic Centre
FINTEL
Butt St.

Suva Olympic Pool
7
8
MacArthur St.
Selbourne St.
Holland St.

Victoria Parade
Victoria St.
† Anglican Cathedral
Kimberley St.
Gordon St.
Malcolm St.
Desvoeux Rd.
Knollys St.

Loftus St.
Goodenough St.
Carnavon St.
closed to vehicles
Thurston St.
Gorrie St.
Berry Rd.
Disraeli Rd.

Victoria Park

9
Gladstone Rd.
Holiday Inn Suva
10
Mitchell St.
MacGregor Rd.
Granville Lane (pedestrians only)

Southern Cross Rd.
12
Kingsford Smith Pavilion
11
ALBERT PARK
Williamson Rd.
Pender St.

Ratu Cakobau Rd.
Cruickshank Park
13
THURSTON GARDENS
Denison Rd.

15 ★ finish here
14

Suva Harbour

† Church
(i) Information
⊠ Post office

0 200 yds
0 200 m

185

The resulting "runway" across Albert Park was barely long enough, but Smith managed to stop his plane with a few feet to spare on June 6, 1928.

Opposite the park on Victoria Parade stands the Grand Pacific Hotel.

⑫ Grand Pacific Hotel

Vacant for years, this historic hotel was built in 1914 by the Union Steamship Company to house its transpacific passengers during their stopovers in Fiji. The idea was to make it look like they had never gone ashore: Rooms in the GPH were like first-class staterooms, complete with saltwater bathrooms and plumbing fixtures identical to those on an ocean liner. All rooms were on the second floor, and guests could step out onto a 4.5m-wide (15-ft.) veranda overlooking the harbor and walk completely around the building—as if walking on the ship's deck. When members of the British royal family visited Fiji, they stood atop the wrought-iron portico, the "bow" of the Grand Pacific, and addressed their subjects massed across Victoria Parade in Albert Park.

Continue south on Victoria Parade to the corner of Ratu Cakobau Road, and enter Thurston Gardens.

⑬ Thurston Gardens

Originally known as the Botanical Gardens, this cool, English-style park is named for its founder, the amateur botanist Sir John Bates Thurston, who started the gardens in 1881. Henry Marks, scion of a family who owned a local trading company, presented the drinking fountain in 1914. After G. J. Marks, a relative and lord mayor of Suva, was drowned that same year in the sinking of the SS *Empress* in the St. Lawrence River in Canada, the Marks family erected the bandstand in his memory.

Children can climb aboard the stationary *Thurston Express,* a narrow-gauge locomotive once used to pull harvested cane to the crushing mill.

Walk to the southeast corner of the gardens, where you will find the Fiji Museum.

⑭ Fiji Museum

At this fascinating museum, you can see relics and artifacts of Fiji's history (see "The Top Attractions," above). After touring the complex, take a break at the museum's cafe, under a lean-to roof on one side of the main building; it serves soft drinks, snacks, and curries.

Backtrack through the gardens to Victoria Parade and head south again until, just past the manicured greens of the Suva Bowling Club on the harbor, you arrive at the big iron gates of Government House.

⑮ Government House

This is the home of Fiji's president, guarded like Buckingham Palace by spit-and-polish Fijian soldiers clad in starched white *sulus* (sarongs). The original house, built in 1882 as the residence of the colonial governor, was struck by lightning and burned in 1921. The present rambling mansion was completed in 1928 and opened with great fanfare. It is closed to the public, but a colorful military ceremony marks the changing of the guard the first week of each month. Ask the Fiji Visitors Bureau whether a ceremony will take place while you're there.

From this point, Victoria Parade becomes Queen Elizabeth Drive, which skirts the peninsula to Laucala Bay. With homes and gardens on one side and the lagoon on the other, it's a lovely walk or drive. The manicured residential area in the rolling hills behind Government House is known as the Domain. An enclave of British civil servants in colonial times, it is now home to the Fiji parliament, government officials, diplomats, and affluent private citizens.

Fun Fact **My Word!**

Before the government buildings on Victoria Parade were erected between 1937 and 1939, the land under them was a swampy area called Naiqaqi, or "The Crusher," for the sugar mill that operated from 1873 to 1875 where the Native Lands Trust Board Building now stands. Naiqaqi was populated by shacks, some of them houses of ill-repute.

Local residents tell of a sailor who often visited the shacks while his ship was in port. He left Suva in 1931 for a long voyage, carrying with him fond memories of Naiqaqi—and, in particular, of one of its residents, a beautiful young woman named Annie.

The sailor's next visit to Suva was in 1940. Instead of a swamp, he found an imposing gray stone building standing where the old, familiar shacks had been.

"My word!" he exclaimed upon seeing the great new structures, "Annie has done well!"

COLO-I-SUVA FOREST PARK

At an altitude of 121 to 182m (400–600 ft.), **Colo-I-Suva Forest Park,** on the Prince's Road 11km (6½ miles) from downtown Suva (✆ **332 0211**), provides a cool, refreshing respite from the heat—if not the humidity—of the city below. You can hike the system of trails through the heavy indigenous forests and stands of mahogany to one of several lovely waterfalls that cascade into swimming holes. Bring walking shoes with good traction because the trails are covered with gravel or slippery soapstone. The park is open daily 8am to 4pm. Admission is F$5 (US$3.20/£1.70). Take a taxi or the Sawani bus, which leaves Suva Municipal Market every 30 minutes. Do not leave valuables unattended in your vehicle or anywhere else.

3 Shopping in Suva

Your walking tour of Suva will give you a good idea of where to shop for handicrafts, cameras, electronic gear, and clothing. Most of the city's top shops are along Victoria Parade and on Cumming Street. The largest and most reliable merchants are **Jack's of Fiji,** at Thomson and Pier streets, opposite the Fiji Visitors Bureau; **Prouds,** in the Suva Central building on Renwick Road at Pratt Street; and **Tappoo,** which has a large store at the corner of Thomson and Usher streets. Note that Jack's Suva store has a very small handicraft section; here, it's mostly a clothing and accessories outlet. The prices are fixed in these stores, but bargaining is the order of the day in Suva's so-called duty-free shops (see "'Duty-Free' Shopping," in chapter 5).

Suva has some fine tropical clothing outlets, several of them on Victoria Parade near the Regal Theatre. The upmarket resort- and beachwear specialist **Sogo Fiji** is on Victoria Parade, opposite the theater.

Stamp collectors will find colorful first-day covers from Fiji and other South Pacific island countries at the **Philatelic Bureau** (✆ **330 2022;** www.stampsfiji.com), on the first floor of the General Post Office. It's open Monday to Thursday from 8am to 4pm, Friday to 3:30pm. American Express, MasterCard, and Visa cards are accepted.

Tips Sword Seller Reprise

Although the government has chased most of them off the streets, you may still be approached by the **sword sellers** I warned you about under "Shopping in Nadi," in chapter 5. Avoid them!

HANDICRAFTS

Before buying handicrafts, be sure to visit the Fiji Museum and its excellent shop (see "The Top Attractions," above).

Government Handicraft Centre 𝒦 *Value*   Founded in 1974 to continue and promote Fiji's handicrafts, this shop has a limited selection of authentic merchandise (no war clubs carved in Asia are sold in this shop). Special attention is given to rural artisans who cannot easily market their works. You will see fine woodcarvings, woven goods, pottery, and masi cloth, and you will learn from the fixed prices just how much the really good items are worth. The Fijian staff is friendly and helpful.

Corner of Victoria Parade and MacArthur St., in rear of Ratu Sukuna House. 𝒞 **331 5869.** Mon–Thurs 8am–4:30pm; Fri 8am–4pm; Sat 8am–12:30pm.

Municipal Curio and Handicraft Centre   Having checked out the government center, you can visit these stalls and bargain with the Indian merchants (but not with the Fijians) from a position of knowledge, if not strength. Be careful, however, for some of the work here is mass produced and aimed at cruise-ship passengers who have only a few hours to do their shopping in Fiji.

Municipal Car Park, Stinson Parade, on the waterfront. 𝒞 **331 3433.** Mon–Thurs 8am–4:30pm; Fri 8am–4pm; Sat 8am–noon; Sun when cruise ships are in port.

4 Where to Stay in Suva

MODERATE

Holiday Inn Suva 𝒦   Formerly the Centra Suva and before that the Suva Travelodge, this hotel is the unofficial gathering place for the city's movers and shakers. The waterfront location couldn't be better, for Suva Harbour laps one side, the stately government buildings sit across Victoria Parade on the other, and the business district is a 3-block walk away. All units have been upgraded in recent years, which makes the mustiness caused by Suva's humid climate less apparent. Upstairs over the lobby, room nos. 263 to 281 face the harborside lawn and swimming pool, but they are less humid than rooms overlooking the water. The *Fiji Times* is delivered to your room daily on request. One room is equipped for guests with disabilities.

P.O. Box 1357, Suva (Victoria Parade, opposite government buildings). 𝒞 **800/465-4329** or 330 1600. Fax 330 0251. www.holiday-inn.com. 130 units. F$325–F$425 (US$211–US$276/£106–£138) double; F$585 (US$380/£190) suite. AE, DC, MC, V. **Amenities:** Restaurant; bar; activities desk; babysitting; business center; fitness center; access to nearby health club; laundry service; outdoor pool; room service; coin-op washers and dryers; Wi-Fi. *In room:* A/C, TV, coffeemaker, high-speed Internet access, iron, minibar, safe.

Homestay Suva 𝒦𝒦𝒦 *Value*   One of the top bed-and-breakfasts in the South Pacific islands, this gorgeous 1920s-vintage colonial home sits atop a ridge in the expensive Tamavua suburb. You will enjoy a stunning view while having breakfast or lounging on the covered veranda, which overlooks a ridge-top swimming pool and the

Where to Stay & Dine in Suva

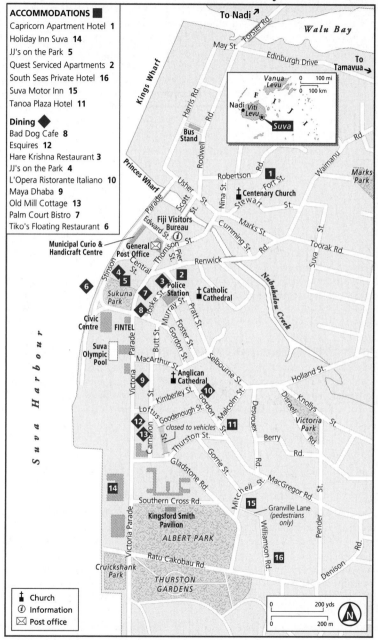

ACCOMMODATIONS ■
Capricorn Apartment Hotel **1**
Holiday Inn Suva **14**
JJ's on the Park **5**
Quest Serviced Apartments **2**
South Seas Private Hotel **16**
Suva Motor Inn **15**
Tanoa Plaza Hotel **11**

Dining ◆
Bad Dog Cafe **8**
Esquires **12**
Hare Krishna Restaurant **3**
JJ's on the Park **4**
L'Opera Ristorante Italiano **10**
Maya Dhaba **9**
Old Mill Cottage **13**
Palm Court Bistro **7**
Tiko's Floating Restaurant **6**

To Nadi ↗

Walu Bay

May St.

Edinburgh Drive

To Tamavua →

Kings Wharf

Harris Rd.

Rd.

Bus Stand

Rodwell

Foster Rd.

Waimanu

Rd.

Marks Park

Robertson

Nina St.

Fort St.

Stewart

St.

1

† Centenary Church

Marks St.

Suva St.

Toorak Rd.

Princes Wharf

Usher

Scott St.

Parade

Edward St.

Cumming St.

Rd.

Nubukalou Creek

Fiji Visitors Bureau ⓘ

Municipal Curio & Handicraft Centre

General Post Office ✉

Central St.

Thomson St.

Pier

Renwick

Stinson

6 ◆

Sukuna Park

4 ◆
5

3 ◆
Police Station

2

† Catholic Cathedral

7 ◆

Joske St.

Murray St.

Pratt St.

8 ◆

Foster St.

Gordon St.

Civic Centre

FINTEL

Butt St.

Suva Olympic Pool

MacArthur St.

Victoria Parade

9 ◆

† Anglican Cathedral ■

Selbourne St.

Holland St.

Knollys

Kimberley St.

10 ◆

Gordon

Malcolm St.

Desvoeux

Disraeli

Victoria Park

St.

Loftus

Goodenough St.

closed to vehicles

11

Berry

Rd.

Carnarvon St.

12 ◆
13 ◆

Thurston St.

Gorrie St.

Rd.

Gladstone Rd.

Mitchell

MacGregor Rd.

St.

Pender

14

Southern Cross Rd.

15

Granville Lane
(pedestrians only)

Victoria Parade

Kingsford Smith Pavilion

ALBERT PARK

Williamson Rd.

16

Denison

Rd.

Cruickshank Park

Ratu Cakobau Rd.

THURSTON GARDENS

† Church
ⓘ Information
✉ Post office

0   200 yds
0   200 m

N

Suva Harbour

Inset map:
Vanua Levu
0   100 mi
0   100 km
Nadi ● Viti Levu
F I J I
Suva

south coast of Viti Levu. The choice room is appropriately named Harbor View. Another upper room, the Nukulau, looks eastward across Laucala Bay to little Nukulau Island on the far-off reef. The three other rooms in the main house lack a view. Four more private and spacious "lodge" units in a building a few steps from the main house have kitchens and private balconies with sea views. Many guests here are business types, and this is a safe, friendly place for women traveling alone. Call for directions if you're driving, or take a taxi from downtown for F$3.50 (US$2.30/£1.20). Barking neighborhood dogs can disturb the peace at night, but that's common in residential areas throughout Fiji since their job is to protect against burglars.

265 Prince's Rd. (P.O. Box 16172, Suva). © 337 0395. Fax 337 0947. www.suvahomestay.com. 9 units, all with bathroom. F$168–F$200 (US$109–US$130/£55–£65) double. Rates include full breakfast. AE, MC, V. **Amenities:** Laundry service; outdoor pool. *In room:* A/C, TV, fridge, kitchen (in lodge units), no phone.

JJ's on the Park   Suva's only boutique hotel, JJ's on the Park isn't much to look at from the outside since it occupies the former YWCA Building, a stained concrete structure five stories high on the north side of Sukuna Park. But go inside and you'll find its comfortable rooms and suites are among Suva's best equipped. JJ's attracts business travelers seeking more luxuries and services than elsewhere. Accommodations range from smaller rooms without balconies to suites with two balconies and separate bedrooms. Balcony or not, every unit has a harbor view.

P.O. Box 12499, Suva (Stinson Parade, north side of Sukuna Park). © 330 5055. Fax 330 5002. www.jjsfiji.com.fj. 22 units. F$257 (US$167/£84) double; F$457–F$657 (US$297–US$427/£149–£214) suite. AE, DC, MC, V. No children accepted. **Amenities:** Restaurant; bar; activities desk; access to nearby health club; laundry service; room service; Wi-Fi. *In room:* A/C, TV, coffeemaker, fax machine (some units), fridge (stocked on request), high-speed Internet access, iron, safe.

Quest Serviced Apartments   Occupying two floors of the high-rise Suva Central building, these modern apartments are more secure than any accommodations in the city, since no one except guests are allowed past the reception desk. They range in size and price—from hotel room–like studios to three-bedroom apartments. They all have kitchenettes with fridges, toasters, and microwaves, but not cook stoves. The larger units have washers and dryers. A few have unfurnished balconies with city views. You can take the elevator down to Suva Central's food court. As the name implies, the apartments have daily cleaning service.

P.O. Box 686, Suva (Renwick Rd. at Pratt St., in Suva Central Building). © 331 9119. Fax 331 9118. www.questsuva. com. 32 units. F$139–F$330 (US$90–US$214/£45–£107) double. AE, MC, V. **Amenities:** Laundry service; Wi-Fi. *In room:* A/C, TV, coffeemaker, fridge, iron, kitchenettes (no stove).

Tanoa Plaza Hotel   Even sans balcony, you will have a commanding view over Suva, the harbor, and the south coast of Viti Levu from the top floors of this curving, nine-story building. Best of all are the executive suites on the top floor, which are larger and better appointed than the smallish regular rooms; they also feature small balconies, which the standard rooms do not. The neighborhood is quiet and residential, yet the hotel is only a 3-block walk from the shops on Victoria Parade (but you should take a taxi at night). Amenities include a pleasant first-floor restaurant serving breakfast, lunch, and dinner, and the swimming pool on the shady side of the building.

P.O. Box 112, Suva (corner Malcolm and Gordon sts.). © 331 2300. Fax 331 1300. www.tanoahotels.com. 60 units. F$210–F$235 (US$136–US$153/£68–£77) double; F$425 (US$276/£138) suite. AE, DC, MC, V. **Amenities:** Restaurant; bar; babysitting; laundry service; outdoor pool; room service; Wi-Fi (in lobby). *In room:* A/C, TV, coffeemaker, high-speed Internet access, iron, minibar, safe.

Tradewinds Hotel & Conference Centre   On the outskirts of town, the former Raffles Tradewinds Hotel & Conference Centre offers a location right on the picturesque Bay of Islands, Suva's yacht harbor. In fact, international cruising yachts tie up alongside the hotel's bulkhead. Comfortable rooms are in two waterfront wings on either side of the main building. Those on the Suva side are smaller and have angled balconies while those on the Nadi side are larger and have balconies facing directly to the bay. An attractively appointed lounge, bar, and restaurant open to the bay. Patrons also can dine on a covered barge moored to the dock. Facilities include a small bayside pool, tour desk, and large conference center across the Queen's Road. *Note:* Accor Hotels recently took over management of the property and announced plans to upgrade, after which it will be known as the Novotel Capital Suva Hotel & Convention Centre.

P.O. Box 3377, Lami Town (Queen's Rd. at Bay of Islands, a 10-min. drive west of Suva, 40-min. west of Nausori Airport). ⓒ **362 471.** Fax 361 464. 108 units. F$150 (US$97/£49) double. AE, MC, V. **Amenities:** 2 restaurants; 2 bars; activities desk; laundry service; outdoor pool; room service. *In room:* A/C, TV, coffeemaker, fridge.

INEXPENSIVE

Capricorn Apartment Hotel *(Value*   Although it's a steep, 2-block walk uphill from Cumming Street, Mulchand Patel's super-clean establishment is popular among Australians and New Zealanders who like to do their own cooking. The three-story, L-shaped building looks out on Suva Harbour and down the mountainous coast. Private balconies off each apartment share the view, as does a pear-shaped swimming pool on the Capricorn's grounds. Tropical furniture adorns all units, and the mattresses are new and among the firmest in Fiji. Mulchand and his friendly staff make sure these roomy efficiencies are kept spotless. Each unit has an air-conditioner, although (unscreened) windows on both sides of the building let the cooling trade winds blow through. The reception staff will sell you canned goods from its small on-premises store or have "Dial-A-Meal" deliver meals from local restaurants to your room.

P.O. Box 1261, Suva (top end of Saint Fort St.). ⓒ **330 3732.** Fax 330 3069. www.capricorn-hotels-fiji.com. 34 units. F$95–F$125 (US$62–US$81/£31–£41) double. AE, DC, MC, V. **Amenities:** Babysitting; laundry service; outdoor pool. *In room:* A/C, TV, coffeemaker, dataport, kitchen, safe.

Nanette's Homestay Suva *(Finds*   Almost hidden away on a side street behind Colonial War Memorial Hospital, Nanette MacAdam's two-story, white concrete house looks smaller from the road than it actually is. Upstairs she has a lounge, kitchen, and four breezy rooms, all with private bathrooms. One has its own balcony. Downstairs are three apartments, two of which have two bedrooms, and one of these has two bathrooms. All three have fully modern kitchens. The apartments are popular with overseas workers on assignment to the hospital. Guests are treated to continental breakfast, and they can barbecue on the big veranda off the guest lounge.

56 Extension St. (behind Colonial War Memorial Hospital). ⓒ **331 6316.** Fax 331 6902. nanettes@connect.com.fj. 7 units, all with bathroom. F$110 (US$71/£36) double; F$120–F$190 (US$78–US$123/£39–£62) apt. Rates include continental breakfast. MC, V. **Amenities:** Laundry service; Wi-Fi. *In room:* A/C, TV (apts only), kitchen (apts only), no phone.

Raintree Lodge   Backpackers flock to this rustic lodge beside a nearly round, quarry-turned-lake high in the hills near Colo-I-Suva Forest Park (see above). The climes are cool up here, and although "Raintree" refers to an acacia tree, it can rain a lot in this forest. Except for the vehicles passing on Prince's Road, you'll hear very little except the songs of tropical birds and insects. Built of pine and overlooking the lake, the bungalows are spacious, and their beds have mosquito nets (the windows are screened, too). All have ceiling fans and bathrooms with showers. Dormitories range in size from seven private rooms with double beds to a hall with 21 bunk beds. Their occupants share toilets, hot-water showers, and a kitchen. Locals love to drive up here for Sunday barbecue at the rustic and inexpensive **Raintree Restaurant,** where they vie for tables on the lakeside veranda. The lodge is F$7 (US$4.50/£2.30) by taxi or F95¢ (US60¢/30p) by public bus from downtown Suva.

P.O. Box 11245, LBE, Suva (Prince's Rd., Colo-I-Suva, opposite post office). © **332 0562.** Fax 332 0113. www.raintree lodge.com. 4 units, 45 dorm beds. F$165 (US$107/£54) bungalow; F$65 (US$42/£21) double dorm room; F$24 (US$16/£8) dorm bed. AE, MC, V. **Amenities:** Restaurant; bar; laundry service; outdoor pool; coin-operated washers and dryers. *In room:* TV, coffeemaker, fridge, no phone.

South Seas Private Hotel   Many backpackers stay at the Raintree Lodge (see above), but those who opt for the city usually end up at this large barracklike wooden structure with a long sunroom across the front (it can get hot in the afternoons). It's a friendly establishment with dormitories, basic rooms, a rudimentary communal kitchen, a TV lounge, and hand-wash laundry facilities. Bed linen is provided, but bring your own towel or pay a small deposit to use one of theirs. You will have to pay a refundable key deposit, too. Showers have both hot and cold water, and the rooms have fans that operate from 4pm to 7am.

P.O. Box 2086, Government Buildings, Suva (Williamson Rd. off Ratu Cakobau Rd., behind Albert Park). © **331 2296.** Fax 330 8646. www.fiji4less.com. 34 units (1 with bathroom), 42 dorm beds. F$58 (US$38/£19) double; F$18 (US$12/£6) dorm bed. AE, MC, V. *In room:* No phone.

Suva Motor Inn 🌟 *Value*   This three-story hotel is popular with business travelers who can't afford the rates elsewhere. It's also a good bet for budget-minded couples and families. Just uphill from Albert Park near the Government Buildings, the L-shaped structure bends around a tropical courtyard with a two-level swimming pool that has a Jacuzzi and a water slide. Opening to this vista is a small restaurant and a bar. Accommodations are in spacious studios and two-bedroom apartments, all with tropical cane-and-wicker furniture. The studios are fully air-conditioned, but only the master bedrooms of the apartments are cooled. Apartments have full kitchens; studios have refrigerators, toasters, coffeemakers, and microwaves. The staff will assist in arranging activities and excursions.

P.O. Box 2500, Government Buildings, Suva (corner of Mitchell and Gorrie sts.). © **331 3973.** Fax 330 0381. www. hexagonfiji.com. 47 units. F$150 (US$97/£49) double; F$195 (US$127/£64) apt. AE, DC, MC, V. **Amenities:** Restaurant; bar; laundry service; outdoor pool. *In room:* A/C, TV, coffeemaker, fridge, kitchen (apts only).

5 Where to Dine in Suva

MODERATE

JJ's on the Park   REGIONAL   On the harbor side of JJ's hotel, this lively bistro sports a Southwestern adobe theme, but that's as far it goes: The menu is strictly curries and other regional fare. Best bets are the substantial servings of fish and chips, burgers, salads, steaks, and rack of lamb. At dinner check the specials board for the fresh fish of the day. The bar here is a good place to slake a thirst during your walking tour of Suva (p. 183).

In JJ's on the Park, Stinson Parade, north side of Sukuna Park. © **330 5005.** Reservations recommended at dinner. Breakfast F$7.50–F$15 (US$4.90–US$9.70/£2.50–£5); burgers and salads F$12–F$18 (US$7.80–US$12/£4–£6); main courses F$18–F$39 (US$12–US$25/£6–£13). AE, DC, MC, V. Mon–Wed 7am–10pm; Thurs–Sat 7am–11pm (bar later).

L'Opera Ristorante Italiano ✪✪ ITALIAN   A long paneled corridor hung with historical photographs leads to this elegant restaurant and Suva's most refined dining. The menu offerings range up and down the Italian "boot" but always reflect a Tuscan origin. Dinners are served in true Italian fashion, beginning with an *apertivo* (pre-dinner drink), followed in order by antipasto, pasta, and a fish or meat *secondi* (main course). The weekday fixed-price business lunch is a good value at F$29 (US$19/£9.50). An extensive Sunday brunch is served.

59 Gordon St., at Kimberly St. ✆ **331 8602.** Reservations highly recommended. Pasta F$19–F$25 (US$12–US$16/£6.30–£8.30); main courses F$29–F$40 (US$19–US$26/£9.70–£13). AE, MC, V. Mon–Fri noon–2:30pm and 6–10pm; Sat 6–10pm.

Malt House Brewery & Restaurant ✪ INTERNATIONAL   Paul and Noeleene Roadley's microbrewery is a South Seas version of a German beer hall. Stop first at the bar, where the tender will offer small tastes to help you decide among the lager, ale, and dark beers. Romantic dining is out of the question here, but the noise from the bar and open dining area shouldn't distract from the seafood and steaks roasted in the wood-fired oven, which also produces pizzas large enough to feed two persons. The salads are dinner-size.

88 Jerusalem Rd., Vatuwaqa (4km/2½ miles from downtown; take a taxi). ✆ **337 1515.** Reservations accepted. Pizza F$15–F$19 (US$9.70–US$12/£5–£6.30); main courses F$18–F$30 (US$12–US$19/£6–£10). AE, MC, V. Daily 11am–10pm.

Tiko's Floating Restaurant SEAFOOD/STEAKS   Locals like to take out-of-town guests to this floating restaurant, which served years ago with Blue Lagoon Cruises. One hopes they don't lean to seasickness, for the old craft does tend to roll a bit when freighters kick up a wake going in and out of the harbor. Your best bets are the nightly seafood specials, such as *walu* (Spanish mackerel) and *pakapaka* (snapper). The fish is fresh, the service is attentive, and Jesse Mucunabitu, a terrific musician-singer, usually performs at dinner—all of which makes for a pleasant night out.

Stinson Parade at Sukuna Park. ✆ **331 3626.** Reservations recommended. Main courses F$17–F$40 (US$11–US$26/£5.70–£13). AE, MC, V. Mon–Fri noon–2pm; Mon–Sat 6–10pm.

INEXPENSIVE

Bad Dog Cafe PIZZA/STEAKS/SEAFOOD   Expatriate residents and professional Suvans—from their mid-20s on up—congregate in this sophisticated pub for after-work drinks and then hang around for good food, including some of Fiji's best pizzas. One pie will feed two adults of moderate appetite. Nor will you go wrong with char-grilled steaks or sushi-grade yellowfin tuna. An attractive, energetic, and good-natured waitstaff help make this Suva's top pub.

Victoria Parade, at MacArthur St. ✆ **331 2884.** Burgers, sandwiches, and salads F$8.50–F$12 (US$5.50–US$7.80/£2.80–£4); pizza F$13–F$16 (US$8.40–US$10/£4.30–£5.30); main courses F$11–F$30 (US$7–US$20/£3.50–£10). AE, MC, V. Mon–Wed 11am–11pm; Thurs–Sat 11am–1am; Sun 5–11pm.

Hare Krishna Restaurant ✪ *Value* VEGETARIAN INDIAN   This clean, casual restaurant specializes in a wide range of very good vegetarian curries—eggplant, cabbage, potatoes and peas, okra, and papaya to name a few—each seasoned delicately and differently from the others. Interesting pastries, breads, side dishes, and salads (such as cucumbers and carrots in yogurt) cool off the fire set by some of the curries. The items are displayed cafeteria-style near the entrance to the second-floor dining room, or get the all-you-can-eat *thali* sampler and try a little of everything. Downstairs has an excellent yogurt and ice-cream bar; climb the spiral stairs to reach the air-conditioned dining room. The Hare Krishna ownership allows no alcoholic beverages or smoking.

16 Pratt St., at Joske St. ℂ **331 4154.** Curries F$2–F$9 (US$1.30–US$5.80/70p–£3). No credit cards. Dining room Mon–Sat 11am–2:30pm. Downstairs snack bar Mon–Thurs 8am–7pm; Fri 8am–8pm; Sat 8am–3pm.

Maya Dhaba ★★ *(Finds* INDIAN   This chic, noisy Victoria Parade bistro is Suva's hottest and most urbane restaurant. Regardless of ethnicity, local couples and families all flock here for authentic Indian fare at extraordinarily reasonable prices. The menu runs the gamut of the Subcontinent, from Punjabi tandoori chicken *tikka* to huge vegetarian *masala dosa* (rice-flour pancakes wrapped crepelike around potato curry) from Madras. In fact, vegetarians will have many choices here. My old standby, butter chicken, has a wonderful smoked flavor here. Little guess work is required since the menu explains every dish.

281 Victoria Parade, between MacArthur and Loftus sts. ℂ **331 0045.** Reservations recommended. Main courses F$9–F$16 (US$5.80–US$10/£3–£5.30). MC, V. Daily 11am–3pm and 5:30–10pm.

Old Mill Cottage ★★★ *(Value* FIJIAN/INDIAN/EUROPEAN   One of the few remaining late-19th-century homes left in Suva's diplomatic-government section, these adjoining two-room clapboard cottages offer some of the most extraordinary home cooking in the South Pacific. Order at the cafeteria-like counters—one for breakfast, one for lunch—from among a choice of daily specials such as Fijian *palusami* (taro leaves in coconut milk), mild Indian curries, or European-style mustard-baked chicken with real mashed potatoes and peas. The vegetable plate is good value, since you can pick and choose from more than a dozen European, Fijian, and Indian selections. Diplomats (the U.S. Embassy is out the back door) and government executives pack the place at midday.

47–49 Carnavon St., near corner of Loftus St. ℂ **331 2134.** Breakfasts F$3–F$8 (US$1.90–US$5.20/£1–£2.70); meals F$2.50–F$9.50 (US$1.60–US$6.20/80p–£3.20). No credit cards. Mon–Fri 7am–6pm; Sat 7am–5pm.

Palm Court Bistro SNACK BAR   You can partake of excellent cooked or continental breakfasts (served all day) and a variety of other snacks and light meals at this walk-up carryout in the open-air center of the Palm Court Arcade. Order at the counter and then eat at plastic tables under cover, or go sit in the shade of the namesake palm in the middle of the arcade.

Victoria Parade, in the Palm Court Arcade, Queensland Insurance Centre. ℂ **304 662.** Reservations not accepted. Most items F$3.50–F$8.50 (US$2.30–US$5.50/£1.20–£2.80). No credit cards. Mon–Fri 7am–6pm; Sat 7am–3pm.

FOOD COURTS & COFFEE SHOPS

The city has two shopping mall–style food courts serving inexpensive European, Chinese, and Indian dishes. **Dolphins Food Court** is in the high-rise FNPF Place building on Victoria Parade at Loftus Street. The other is on the second floor of **Suva Central,** a modern building on Renwick Road at Pratt Street.

If you're hankering for a Big Mac, head for the **McDonald's** on Victoria Parade at the northern edge of Sukuna Park. A **Kentucky Fried Chicken** is on Victoria Parade next to the General Post Office.

Esquires COFFEE BAR   Formerly known as the Republic of Cappuccino, this coffee shop occupies the triangular corner of FNPF Place, on the Victoria Parade side of Dolphins Food Court. You can listen to recorded jazz while drinking your latte or cappuccino and eating your brownie, cake, or quiche at the tall tables by the big storefront windows. A second Suva location, on Renwick Road at Pratt Street (© **330 0082**), near the Fiji Visitors Bureau, has Wi-Fi for your laptop (see "Fast Facts: Suva" earlier).

Victoria Parade at Loftus St., in FNPF Place Building. © **330 0333**. Pastries and sandwiches F$2–F$6.50 (US$1.30–US$4.20/70p–£2.20). No credit cards. Mon–Fri 7am–11pm; Sat 8am–11pm; Sun 9am–7pm.

6 Island Nights in Suva

Nocturnal activities in Suva revolve around going to the movies and then hitting the bars—until the wee hours on Friday, the biggest night out.

Movies are a big deal, especially the first-run Hollywood and Indian "Bollywood" flicks at **Village 6 Cinemas** (© **330 6006**), on Scott Street at Nubukalou Creek, a modern, American-style emporium with six screens and a games arcade upstairs. Check the newspapers for what's playing and showtimes. Locals flock here on Sunday afternoon, when these plush, air-conditioned theaters offer a comfortable escape from Suva's sunshine and humidity.

Trap's Bar, 305 Victoria Parade, 2 blocks south of the Pizza Hut (© **331 2922**), is a popular watering hole where you're not likely to witness a fight. A band usually plays in the back room on weekends. **O'Reilly's,** on MacArthur Street off Victoria Parade (© **331 2968**), is an Irish-style pub that serves Guinness stout and sports on TVs (and it can get a bit rough, depending on who's winning the rugby matches).

Victoria Parade has a number of loud **discothèques** frequented by a young, noisy crowd.

Remember: Suva has a serious crime problem, so be careful when bar hopping. Guard your valuables, and always take a taxi to and from your hotel after dark, particularly if you've had a few drinks.

7 A Resort on Toberua Island

Reached by a 1-hour taxi-and-boat trip from Suva via the Rewa River delta, Toberua is a tiny, 1.6-hectare (4-acre) sand islet on the reefs off eastern Viti Levu. Palm-dotted and beach-encircled, it's too flat to draw moisture from the sky, thus isn't in the "rain belt" created by the mountains behind Suva. It is totally occupied by one resort.

Toberua Island Resort   This little resort is one of the oldest in Fiji but still going strong. Guests experience such an easygoing lifestyle that they are warned to take at least 4 days to slow down and grow accustomed to the pace. Actually, there's plenty to do: sunbathe, swim, snorkel, scuba dive, collect shells, sail, windsurf, visit nearby Fijian villages and uninhabited islands (including one with a protected booby colony), fish in the lagoon, or play a round of "reef golf" (which is exactly what it sounds like: holes and fairways are out on the reef at low tide). With 8m-high (27-ft.) roofs, the large, Fijian-style bures are cooled by ceiling fans. Each has its own modern bathroom with indoor and outdoor entrances. Deluxe bures face the ocean and have queen-size beds and at least two single beds, while premium bures have a king-size bed. The waterside dining room features excellent cuisine, with an emphasis on fresh seafood.

P.O. Box 3332, Nausori (Toberua Island, 19km/12 miles off Viti Levu). © **347 2777**. Fax 347 2888. www. toberua.com. 15 units. F$461–F$670 (US$299–US$435/£150–£218) double. AE, MC, V. **Amenities:** Restaurant; bar; activities desk; babysitting; laundry service; massage; saltwater outdoor pool; room service; free watersports equipment. *In room:* Coffeemaker, minibar, safe, no phone.

Rakiraki & Northern Viti Levu

Few travelers are disappointed by the scenic wonders on the northern side of Viti Levu. Cane fields climb valleys to green mountain ridges. Dramatic cliffs and spires bound a stunning bay. A narrow mountain road winds along the Wainibuka River, once called the "Banana Highway" because in preroad days Fijians used it to float their crops down to Suva on disposable *bilibili* rafts made of bamboo.

A relatively dry climate beckons anyone who wants to catch a few rays—so many rays that modern real estate developers call this the "Sun Coast." Local English-Fijian families appreciated the dryness long before the developers arrived, and some bought land and built vacation homes, especially on hilly **Nananu-I-Ra Island,** off the big island's northernmost point. They chose not to build along the main coast, which with a few exceptions is skirted by mangrove forests.

One family created the 6,800-hectare (17,000-acre) **Yaqara Estate,** Fiji's largest cattle ranch. Cowpokes still tend the steers, but the area is best known now for Fiji Water, which comes from artesian wells up in the hills above the ranch. A constant parade of trucks rumbles along the King's Road, either hauling bottles of Fiji Water to the port at Lautoka, and from there primarily to the United States,

or bringing back empty containers for more.

During World War II American soldiers built an airstrip near the Fijian village of **Rakiraki,** the chiefly headquarters from which Viti Levu's northern tip gets its name. The air base is long gone, but the charming hotel they frequented is still in business. Now the Tanoa Rakiraki Hotel, it's the last accommodations left from Fiji's colonial era.

Like the English-Fijians before them, today's sun-seeking visitors are attracted to a small peninsula near Rakiraki, to Nananu-I-Ra Island, and to great diving on the reefs offshore. Thanks to prevailing trade winds funneling between Viti Levu and Vanua Levu, this also is the windsurfing capital of Fiji—or surf kiting, the latest version of this arm-building sport. Despite the mangroves elsewhere, **Volivoli Point,** the island's northernmost extremity, has one of Fiji's great beaches.

There is only one drawback: It's a long way from Rakiraki to anywhere else in Fiji, and since there is no longer an airport up here, you must get to and from by car or bus via the King's Road. Consequently, most visitors are serious divers, windsurfers, and Australians and New Zealanders enjoying taking a break in the sun during the Austral winter from June through August.

1 Getting to & Getting Around Rakiraki

Some local hotels and backpackers' resorts either provide or arrange for their guests' transportation from Nadi, and it's always best to ask when you make your reservations. Since no airport serves this side of Viti Levu, all transportation is by rental

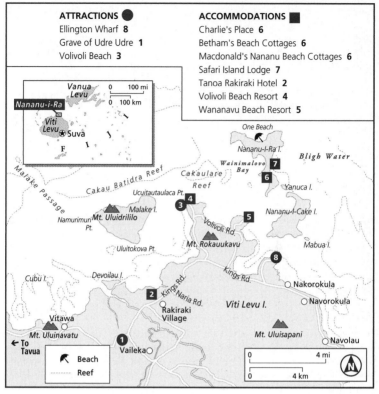

ATTRACTIONS ●
Ellington Wharf **8**
Grave of Udre Udre **1**
Volivoli Beach **3**

ACCOMMODATIONS ■
Charlie's Place **6**
Betham's Beach Cottages **6**
Macdonald's Nananu Beach Cottages **6**
Safari Island Lodge **7**
Tanoa Rakiraki Hotel **2**
Volivoli Beach Resort **4**
Wananavu Beach Resort **5**

car, taxi, or bus. Rakiraki is about a 2½-hour drive from Nadi International Airport.

The **King's Road** runs for 290km (180 miles) from Nadi Airport around the island's northern side to Suva—93km (58 miles) longer than the Queen's Road to the south. An unsealed portion through the central mountains between Rakiraki and Nausori can be treacherous, so I would not drive through that way during the rainy season from November through April, when bridges can wash out, and never at night.

Taxi fares from Nadi to Rakiraki are about F$90 (US$58/£29) each way.

Ellington Wharf, Volivoli Beach Resort, and the Tanoa Rakiraki Hotel are regular stops for **Feejee Experience** (© **672 5959;** www.feejeeexperience.com), the backpacker bus that circles Viti Levu counterclockwise daily.

The **Rakiraki Express** (© **670 0600**) operates a minivan between Nadi and Rakiraki daily. It leaves Nadi about 8:30am and costs F$27 (US$18/£9) per person each way. Call for reservations.

Sunbeam Transport Ltd. (© **666 2822**), **Reliance Transport Bus Service** (© **666 3059**), and **Akbar Buses Ltd.** (© **669 4760**) have express and local service via the King's Road between the Lautoka market and **Vaileka,** a predominately Indian town 1km (½ mile) off the King's Road near Rakiraki village. The one-way fare from Lautoka to Vaileka is about F$20 (US$13/£6.70).

Local taxis are available in Vaileka. The one-way fare from there to Elington Wharf or the northern tip of Viti Levu is about F$10 (US$6.50/£3.30).

Patterson Shipping Services (✆ **331 5644;** patterson@connect.com.fj) runs a ferry between Ellington Wharf and Nabouwalu on Vanua Levu, but the schedule is erratic. Bligh Water Shipping's ferry between Lautoka and Savusavu does not regularly stop at Ellington Wharf.

See "Getting Around Fiji," in chapter 3, for more information.

2 Exploring Rakiraki & Northern Viti Levu

The King's Road officially begins at Lautoka. To reach it by car from Nadi, follow the Queen's Road north and take the second exits off of both traffic circles in Lautoka.

From Lautoka, the King's Road first crosses a flat, fertile plain and then ascends into hills dotted with cattle ranches before dropping to the coast and entering Fiji's "Sugar Belt," its most productive sugar-growing area.

BA & TAVUA

The gorgeous steep hills of the **Ba Valley,** populated mostly by Fiji Indians, is second only to Suva in economic importance. The town of **Ba,** a prosperous farming and manufacturing community on the banks of the muddy Ba River, has one of Fiji's five sugar mills, and many of the country's most successful businesses are headquartered here. While most Fijian towns have the Western air of the British Raj or Australia, the commercial center of Ba is a mirror image of India. *Note:* The King's Road bypasses Ba, so watch for the exit leading into town.

Gravel roads twisting off from Ba into the valley offer some spectacular vistas. One of these roads follows a tributary into the central highlands and then along the Sigatoka River down to the Coral Coast. You can explore the Ba Valley roads in a rental car, but take the cross-island route only if you have a four-wheel-drive vehicle and a very good map.

From Ba, the King's Road continues to **Tavua,** another predominately Indian sugar town backed by its own much smaller valley reaching up to the mountains and the **Vatukoula Gold Mine,** whose workers lend a certain Wild West flair to Tavua. Although the mine has been troubled in recent years, it has produced more than 7 million ounces of gold since 1935. It's not open for tours, so don't bother driving up here.

Personally I wouldn't attempt this route, but the main road to Vatukoula, 8km (5 miles) inland, continues from the mine and crosses the central mountains to Suva. Along the way it passes the **Monasavu Hydroelectric Project,** which supplies most of Viti Levu's electrical power. The Monasavu Dam creates a lake directly in the center of Viti Levu, but it's so remote it has no facilities for visitors and is not worth the difficult trip to see.

⸢ *Fun Fact* **900 Men for Dinner**

Just before you reach the well-marked junction of the King's Road and the Vaileka cutoff, look on the right for the **Grave of Udre Udre.** Legend says the stones at the base of the tombstone represent every one of the 900 men this renowned cannibal chief had for dinner.

(*Tips* **Taking Care of Business**

To get any business done in Rakiraki, you'll have to go into Vaileka, which has the entire area's post office, police station, infirmary, major stores, and service stations.

Back on the King's Road, the enchanting peaks of the **Nakauvadra Range** keep getting closer to the sea as you proceed eastward. Legend says the mountains are home to Degei, the prolific spiritual leader who arrived with the first Fijians and later populated the country (see "The Dreaded Degei" box, in chapter 5). Where the flat land is squeezed between foothills and sea, cane fields give way to the grasslands and mesas of the Yaqara Estate cattle ranch. Offshore, conelike islands begin to dot the aquamarine lagoon.

RAKIRAKI

Although everyone refers to northernmost Viti Levu as Rakiraki, the commercial and administrative center is actually **Vaileka,** a predominately Indian town about 1km (½ mile) off the King's Road. Vaileka is home to the **Penang Mill,** the only one of Fiji's five sugar mills that produces solely for domestic consumption (the others export all their sugar). The 9-hole **Penang Golf Course** is near the mill; visitors who want to play it can make arrangements at their hotel (see "Where to Stay & Dine in Rakiraki," below).

With its fair share of the car-destroying road humps that populate every Fijian village, **Rakiraki** is on the King's Road, about 1km (½ mile) past the Vaileka junction. It's home of the *Tui Ra,* the high Fijian chief of Ra district, which encompasses all of northern Viti Levu. He likes to stroll over to the Tanoa Rakiraki Hotel (p. 200), on the village's eastern boundary.

Beyond the village, an unsealed gravel road makes a loop around the little peninsula at the top of Viti Levu. Kept in reasonably good condition for the Feejee Experience buses, this road is a marvelously scenic drive. At the northeastern corner you'll come to **Vilivoli Beach** ✰✰✰, now occupied by the inexpensive Volivoli Beach Resort. A snack bar is right at the beach, and the resort has public restrooms.

From Volivoli the gravel road runs along the shoreline to the peninsula's eastern side and Wananavu Beach Resort. Some of the freehold land up here is being sold as lots for vacation homes, which sit up on the hillsides.

East of the peninsula, a paved road leads off the King's Road to **Ellington Wharf,** the area's watersports center (see "Scuba Diving, Windsurfing & Other Watersports," below) and the jumping-off point for **Nananu-I-Ra,** a semiarid island that has inexpensive retreats (see "Nananu-I-Ra Island," below).

RAKIRAKI TO SUVA

From Ellington Wharf, the King's Road rounds the island's north point into **Viti Levu Bay,** whose surrounding mountains topped with basaltic cliffs, thumblike formations, and spires give it a tropical splendor. About 15km (9⅓ miles) from Rakiraki stands **St. Francis Xavier Church,** home of the unique *Naiserelagi,* or Black Christ mural painted by artist Jean Charlot in 1963.

From the head of the bay, the road begins to climb through rice paddies and more cattle country to the head of the winding **Wainibuka River.** This "Banana Highway" is a major tributary of the mighty Rewa River that eventually flows into the sea through a broad, flat delta northeast of Suva. The cool, often cloudy highlands of the Wainibuka Valley is old Fiji, with many traditional Fijian villages perched on the slopes along the river.

When driving through the valley, be careful on the many switch-back curves above the river. There are no shoulders to pull off on, and you will encounter several one-lane wooden bridges, which can be icy slick during the frequent rains. Also watch out for the huge buses that regularly ply this route, taking up the entire road as they rumble along at breakneck speeds.

Beyond the Wainibuka is the dairy farming region of eastern Fiji, source of the country's fresh milk and cheeses (be alert for cows on the road!). The small town of **Korovou,** 107km (66 miles) from Rakiraki, is the major junction in these parts. At the dead end, a left turn will take you to **Natovi Wharf,** where ferries depart for Savusavu and Taveuni. Turn right at the juncture to continue on to Nausori and Suva.

The King's Road goes directly south for 25km (16 miles) until it joins the Rewa River, now a meandering coastal stream. You soon come to bustling Nausori, the delta's main town. Follow the signs to a traffic circle and the four-lane bridge to Suva.

3 Scuba Diving, Windsurfing & Other Watersports

Although not as dramatic or scenic as in the Somosomo Strait between Vanua Levu and Taveuni (see chapter 14), the reefs off northern Viti Levu have colorful soft corals. They are relatively undiscovered, and the currents are not as strong as at other soft coral spots. Most require a boat ride, but the hulk of the cargo ship *Papuan Explorer* lies in 22m (72 ft.) of water only 150m (492 ft.) off Nananu-I-Ra Island. It was sunk in 1990 to create a reef, and experienced divers can swim inside the wreck.

The top dive operators in the area are **Kai Viti Divers** (© 669 3600; www.kaiviti divers.com), next to Wananavu Beach Resort, and **Ra Divers** (© 669 4622; www. ra-divers.com), at Volivoli Beach Resort (see below).

The strong trade winds, especially from June to August, put this area on the world's windsurfing maps, and **Ellington Wharf Water Sports Activity Center,** at Ellington Wharf (© 669 3333; www.safarilodge.com.fj), rents Windsurfers, sea kayaks, sail boats, snorkeling gear, and other toys. They also offer guided kayak trips, most in connection with Safari Island Lodge (see "Nananu-I-Ra Island," below). Owner Warren Francis conducts Fiji's only **kite-surfing school** here.

While the wind often whips from the southeast, Nananu-I-Ra and adjacent Nananu-I-Thake Island protect a usually quiet lagoon, creating a great spot for day sailing and kayaking. The islands are surrounded by fringing reefs, but the waters in between are deep enough to be dark blue.

4 Where to Stay & Dine in Rakiraki

Some of the new houses on the northern peninsula are available to rent as vacation homes, which appeal to Australians and New Zealanders on quick, get-away-from-it-all holidays. One is **Star Fish Blue** (© 828/277-7800 in the U.S.; www.starfish blue.com), a three-bedroom luxury villa adjacent to Wananavu Beach Resort, which manages a few others (see below). Star Fish Blue has its own swimming pool.

Tanoa Rakiraki Hotel ✪   Frequented primarily by business travelers, this establishment is one of the few remaining colonial-era hotels in Fiji. The two clapboard roadside buildings were built as guesthouses when U.S. soldiers were stationed at an airstrip nearby during World War II. One houses a tongue-and-groove-paneled bar and dining room (with a very limited menu). The other has an old-fashioned central hall with five rooms on either side. They have private bathrooms and air-conditioners but not phones. Two rooms are essentially dormitories and have four beds each. Out back, three modern two-story motel blocks have 36 rooms outfitted to international standards, with air-conditioned units, phones, and tiled shower-only bathrooms. The staff will arrange excursions to Vaileka and to Fijian villages, horseback riding, golfing, scuba diving, and treks into the highlands.

P.O. Box 31, Rakiraki (Rakiraki village, on King's Rd., 2.5km/1½ miles east of Vaileka, 132km/82 miles from Nadi Airport). © 800/448-8355 or 669 4101. Fax 669 4545. www.tanoahotels.com. 41 units. F$60–F$130 (US$39–US$84/£20–£42) double; F$30 (US$19/£10) dorm bed. AE, DC, MC, V. **Amenities:** Restaurant; bar; babysitting; laundry service; outdoor pool; tennis court. *In room:* A/C (in most units), TV, coffeemaker, fridge.

Volivoli Beach Resort   Opened in 2005, this is the top choice among backpackers in Rakiraki. Its sand-floor restaurant and bar face a mangrove swamp, but they are just around a bend from Volivoli Beach. This strip of white sand leads directly into deep water (no tidal flat here) and has a great view back across a bay to Viti Levu's mountains. At press time, the hotel consists of a lodge building containing four rooms (sharing two bathrooms) and 32 dorm beds, all on a hill with sea views—although bungalows are being added.

P.O. Box 417, Rakiraki. © 669 4511. Fax 669 4611. www.volivoli.com. 4 units, 32 dorm beds. F$100 (US$65/£33) double; F$25–F$27 (US$16–US$18/£8.30–£9) dorm bed. MC, V. **Amenities:** Restaurant; bar; laundry service; coin-op washers and dryers; watersports equipment rentals. *In room:* No phone.

Wananavu Beach Resort   The area's most luxurious accommodations are here near Viti Levu's northernmost point. "Beach Resort" is a bit of misnomer, for the resort's beach was created by removing a chunk of mangrove forest, leaving gray sand and a mud flat behind. Accordingly, Wananavu's prime appeal is to divers headed to the colorful reefs offshore, not to beach vacationers. The dining room, bar, and most of the duplex bungalows have fine ocean views. A few *bures* are down by the beach, but most occupy hillside perches.

P.O. Box 305, Rakiraki. © 669 4433. Fax 669 4499. www.wananavu.com. 31 units. F$220–F$450 (US$143–US$292/£72–£146) double. Rates include breakfast. AE, MC, V. **Amenities:** Restaurant; bar; babysitting; laundry service; outdoor pool; spa; tennis court. *In room:* A/C, coffeemaker, fridge, no phone.

5 Nananu-I-Ra Island

Hilly, anvil-shaped Nananu-I-Ra island, a 15-minute boat ride from Ellington Wharf, has long been popular as a sunny retreat for local Europeans who own beach cottages there (the island is all freehold land), and three local families still operate low-key resorts beside a long beach in the center of the island's western side. This is the narrowest part of the island, and you can walk over a hill to **Mile Long Beach** (yes, it actually is 1.5km/1 mile long) on the exposed eastern shore, Fiji's windsurfing headquarters. Although the lagoon is shallow at low tide, snorkeling is very good off the south coast.

Nananu-I-Ra's western third was a cattle ranch until 2005, and you might run into a stray head or two wandering around the island. Developers announced plans to turn the ranch into a luxury resort complex called the Talei (www.thetalei.com), but little had been done during my recent visit, except to close down Nananu Beach and Dive Resort, which was on the property.

Nananu-I-Ra once was on the backpackers circuit around Fiji, but today the young folk are more likely to stop at Volivoli Beach on the mainland. In addition to wind-surfing enthusiasts, most visitors are Australian and New Zealand couples, some of whom return year after year for inexpensive holidays in the sun. Indeed, this is one of the most cost-friendly places in Fiji to spend a quiet beachside vacation. Conse-quently, reserve well in advance from June through August.

WHERE TO STAY & DINE ON NANANU-I-RA ISLAND

The first three properties below sit side-by-side on the island's eastern shore. Fronted by a long beach, the land was once one parcel but the former owner divided it in sec-tions, one for each of three sisters of the Macdonal clan, one of Fiji's most prominent European families. Their children, and their spouses, operate them today.

All send open boats to pick up their guests at Ellington Wharf, 15 minutes away. Only Macdonald's Nananu Beach Cottages has a pier, elsewhere you will wade ashore.

The establishments usually turn off their electrical generators about 10pm so bring a flashlight.

Betham's Beach Cottages   On the beach next door to Charlie's Place, Betham's has five cottages, two rooms, and a four-bed dormitory. Built of concrete block or tim-ber, the one-bedroom cottages have kitchens and covered verandas, while the two rooms share a kitchen and a veranda. The dorm has its own bathroom and porch. A two-story house can be rented whole or as up- or downstairs. Every unit has an elec-tric fan, but their showers are cold-water. A pleasant restaurant-bar by the beach has picnic tables and Adirondack chairs for lounging while taking in the view of Viti Levu. A small store sells groceries and gift items.

P.O. Box 5, Rakiraki. ℂ/fax **669 4132** or 992 7132. www.bethams.com.fj. 7 units, 4 dorm beds. F$85 (US$55/£28) double; F$130 (US$84/£42) cottage; F$28 (US$18/£9) dorm bed. MC, V. **Amenities:** Restaurant; bar; free use of kayaks; laundry service. *In room:* Kitchen, no phone.

Charlie's Place   Louise Anthony has two cottages for rent on her end of the beach on Nananu-I-Ra's western side. Both are built of concrete blocks and stand up on a hill. They do not have fans, but from this perch they are more likely to catch the pre-vailing breezes than the units at Betham's Beach Cottages and Macdonald's Nananu Beach Cottages, which are down by the beach and thus shaded from the trade winds. Although simply furnished, the cottages are spacious. Each has a bedroom and a bath-room with cold-water shower. The higher unit has a sun porch with a fine view of the lagoon and Viti Levu, but mango and plumeria trees partially block the vista from the other bungalow's veranda. Louise doesn't have a restaurant, but you can walk to Betham's and Macdonald's, which do (be sure to reserve for dinner by 3pm at either of them).

P.O. Box 407, Rakiraki. ℂ **669 4676.** charlie's@connect.com.fj. 2 units. F$115 (US$75/£38) double. No credit cards. *In room:* Kitchen, no phone.

Macdonald's Nananu Beach Cottages   The Macdonald name lives on at this pleasant beachside property, whose sand-floor restaurant serves very good burgers and pizzas. Accommodations consist of two-bedroom cottages, a larger A-frame bungalow dressed up Fijian style, two rooms (each with two single beds), and a four-bunk dorm. Most do not have covered verandas like those at Betham's, but they are a bit more spa-cious and airy. The cottages have kitchens, and a small, well-stocked shop sells gro-ceries. All units have bathrooms whose showers dispense cold water. The lagoon here is shallow at low tide, but you can swim and snorkel off the end of the resort's long pier, which reaches deep water.

P.O. Box 140, Rakiraki. © **669 4633.** Fax 669 4302. www.macsnananu.com. 7 units, 4 dorm beds. F$85 (US$55/£28) double; F$120 (US$78/£39) cottage; F$25 (US$16/£8.30) dorm bed. MC, V. **Amenities:** Restaurant; bar; babysitting; free use of kayaks; laundry service. *In room:* No phone.

Safari Island Lodge   This eclectic property beside Mile Long Beach, on Nananu-I-Ra's windswept eastern side, is the creation of Warren Francis, an avid Australian wind-surfer who also owns Ellington Wharf Water Sports Activity Center (see "Scuba Diving, Windsurfing & Other Watersports," above). Consequently, about 60% of his guests come here to wind- or kite-surf. During my visit, he was building two lodges up on the hill above the resort to accommodate such groups. Each of these will have one private room with its own bathroom plus several dorm beds as well as a communal kitchen and a large veranda to take advantage of views across Bligh Water to Vanua Levu. Meantime, tin-roof beachside and oceanview bures suitable for couples have hardwood floors, front porches, and their own bathrooms. All the showers here have hot water. Bure windows are not screened, but mosquito nets hang over each double bed. Meals are served in the main house; it's across a lawn from the beach and has a large guest lounge with TV and DVD player. Narrow stairs lead up to a dorm that opens to a porch. Life is much live-lier here than at Charlie's, Betham's, and Macdonald's.

P.O. Box 939, Rakiraki. © **669 3333** or 669 3700. Fax 669 3366. www.safarilodge.com.fj. 6 units (4 with bathroom), 24 dorm beds. F$90 (US$58/£30) double; F$220–F$295 (US$143–US$192/£72–£96) cottage; F$30 (US$19/£10) dorm bed. MC, V. **Amenities:** Restaurant; bar; babysitting; free use of kayaks; kite-board and windsurf rentals; laundry serv-ice. *In room:* No phone.

12

Levuka & Ovalau Island

Fiji's Eastern Division consists of the Lomaviti Group of islands lying east of Viti Levu and south of Vanua Levu. On the largest of these, ruggedly beautiful **Ovalau,** some 32km (20 miles) off Viti Levu, **Levuka** was Fiji's first European-style town, and it still looks much as it did during its heyday before the government moved to Suva in 1882. In contrast to Suva, Levuka remains a charming example of what South Pacific towns were like in the 1870s.

Indeed, you may think you've slipped into the "Twilight Zone" as you stroll through Levuka, which has been nominated as Fiji's first World Heritage Site. Everything here seems to be from a century earlier: ramshackle dry-goods stores with false fronts, clapboard houses with tin roofs to keep them dry and shaded verandas to keep them cool, and round clocks in the baroque tower of Sacred Heart Catholic Church that seem to have stopped over a hundred years ago. Where the regular streets end, "step streets" climb to more houses up near the base of the jagged cliffs towering over the town.

Not that Levuka hasn't changed at all since its 19th-century days as one of the South Pacific's most notorious seaports. All but one of the 50 or more hotels and saloons that dispensed rum and other pleasures disappeared long ago. The sole survivor—the Royal Hotel—is now a

quiet, family-run establishment. The fist-fighting whalers and drifting beach bums went the way of the square-rigged ships that once crowded the blue-green harbor beyond the row of glistening ficus trees and park benches along Beach Street. Gone, too, are all signs of the pioneering merchants and *copra* (dried coconut meat) planters who established Levuka in the 1830s and who for years carried guns to protect themselves from its ruffians.

The 360m-tall (1,200-ft.) walls of basalt—which caused Levuka's ultimate demise by preventing its progress and expansion—create a soaring backdrop that ranks Ovalau in the big leagues of dramatic tropical beauty.

Despite its history, extraordinary scenery, and extremely hospitable residents, Levuka is relatively off the beaten tourist track. The volcano that created Ovalau has eroded into such rugged formations that it has left very little flat land and no decent beach; therefore, the island has not attracted resort or hotel development. But Levuka does have comfortable and charming accommodations in which to stay while meeting the friendly locals and learning about Fiji's history and culture.

Within sight of Levuka lies **Wakaya Island,** in the center of the Lomaviti Group. Another historic outpost, it's now home to the Wakaya Club, one of Fiji's finest little resorts.

1 Getting to & Getting Around Levuka & Ovalau

GETTING THERE
Air Fiji (② 877/247-3454 in the U.S., or 672 2251 in Nadi; www.airfiji.com.fj) has early-morning and late-afternoon flights to Ovalau's unpaved airstrip at Bureta, on the

Levuka & Ovalau Island

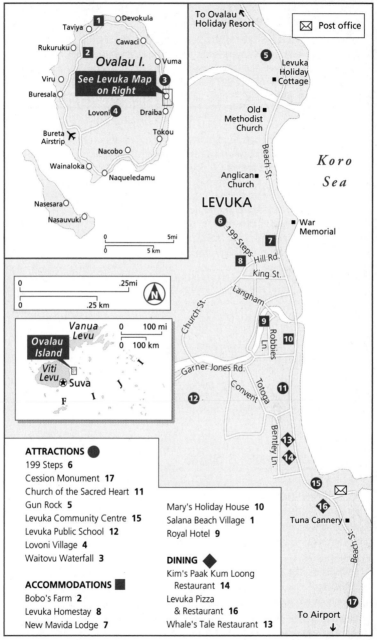

Post office

To Ovalau
Holiday Resort

Devokula
Taviya
Rukuruku
Cawaci
Ovalau I.
Vuma
Viru
Buresala
See Levuka Map on Right
Lovoni
Draiba
Bureta Airstrip
Tokou
Nacobo
Wainaloka
Naqueledamu
Nasesara
Nasauvuki

0   5mi
0   5 km

Levuka
Holiday
Cottage

Old
Methodist
Church

Beach St.

Koro
Sea

Anglican
Church

LEVUKA

War
Memorial

199 Steps
Hill Rd.
King St.
Langham

Church St.

Robbies Ln.

Garner Jones Rd.
Convent
Toroga
Bentley Ln.

0   .25mi
0   .25 km

Vanua
Levu
Ovalau
Island
Viti
Levu
Suva

0   100 mi
0   100 km

To Airport

Tuna Cannery

ATTRACTIONS
199 Steps **6**
Cession Monument **17**
Church of the Sacred Heart **11**
Gun Rock **5**
Levuka Community Centre **15**
Levuka Public School **12**
Lovoni Village **4**
Waitovu Waterfall **3**

Mary's Holiday House **10**
Salana Beach Village **1**
Royal Hotel **9**

ACCOMMODATIONS
Bobo's Farm **2**
Levuka Homestay **8**
New Mavida Lodge **7**

DINING
Kim's Paak Kum Loong
   Restaurant **14**
Levuka Pizza
   & Restaurant **16**
Whale's Tale Restaurant **13**

> ⌐ *Tips*   **Don't Leave Home Without It**
>
> You can see the prime sites in old Levuka in a day. The airstrip on Ovalau is not lighted, however, and rainy weather or delays can cause the one late afternoon flight to be canceled. If you do come over here on a day trip, bring your toothbrush and a change of clothes. If the flight doesn't come, Air Fiji will put you up at the Royal Hotel.

island's west coast. The round-trip fare from Suva is about F$128 (US$83/£43). Levuka is halfway around Ovalau on the east coast.

Patterson Shipping Services (© 331 5644; patterson@connect.com.fj) has bus-ferry connections from Suva to Buresala Landing, north of the airstrip.

The airstrip and ferry landing are at least 45-minute rides from Levuka via the very rough road that circles Ovalau; nevertheless, the ride to Levuka, on the other side of the island, is a sightseeing excursion in its own right. Bus fare from the airstrip or ferry landing into town is F$7 (US$4.50/£2.30); taxis cost about F$25 (US$16/£8.30).

For more information, see "Getting Around Fiji" in chapter 3.

GETTING AROUND

Levuka is a small town, and you can get to most places in 25 minutes by foot. Numerous taxis congregate on Beach Street; be sure you and the driver agree on a fare before departing.

Given the poor condition of Ovalau's roads, four-wheel-drive trucks with seats in the back—called "carriers" here—serve as the local bus service. They don't run after dark, so find out from the driver when—and whether—he returns to Levuka at the end of the day.

Ovalau Watersports (© 344 0166) and the **Royal Hotel** (© 344 0024) both rent bicycles for F$15 (US$9.70/£5) a day. The road around the southern part of the island is flat, but the north side is hilly.

FAST FACTS: Levuka & Ovalau

The following facts apply to Levuka town and Ovalau Island. If you don't see an item here, check "Fast Facts: Fiji" in appendix A.

Currency Exchange   **Westpac Bank** and **Colonial National Bank** have offices on Beach Street. Westpac Bank has an ATM. Most businesses here do not accept credit cards, so stock up on Fijian currency.

Emergencies   In an emergency, phone © **917** for police, © **911** for **fire** or **ambulance**. The **police station** (© 344 0222) is on Beach Street.

Healthcare   The **government hospital** (© 344 0088) is on Beach Street near the north end of town. No doctors are in private practice on Ovalau.

Internet Access   **Ovalau Watersports,** on Beach Street (© **344 0166;** www.owl fiji.com), has access for F$5 (US$3.25/£1.65) for 30 minutes.

Laundry   **Ovalau Watersports,** on Beach Street (© 344 0166), will wash, dry, and fold a load for F$10 (US$6.50/£3.30).

Mail The **post office** is on Beach Street at the main wharf. It's open Monday to Friday 8am to 5pm, Saturday 8am to noon.

Safety Levuka and Ovalau are safe to visit, but don't tempt the mortals: Keep an eye on your personal property.

Visitor Information The best bet for local information is **Ovalau Watersports,** on Beach Street (© **344 0166;** www.owlfiji.com). Its website has information about activities and accommodations, as does **www.levukafiji.com**.

Water The tap water in town is safe to drink.

2 Exploring Levuka & Ovalau

A WALKING TOUR OF TOWN

A walking tour of Levuka (pop. 3,745) should take about 2 hours. Begin at **Ovalau Watersports,** on the south end of Beach Street (© **344 0166;** www.owlfiji.com), the only scuba diving operation here; it also rents bicycles, does laundry, provides Internet access, books tours, and generally is the focal point for all visitors. German owners Andrea and Noby Dehm and their staff are fonts of information.

LEVUKA COMMUNITY CENTER ★★

Next door to Ovalau Watersports is the **Levuka Community Centre** (© **344 0356**), where you can explore the town's small but interesting history museum. In addition to displaying real Fijian war clubs and an excellent collection of shells (including ancient mother-of-pearl buttons), the museum chronicles Levuka's earliest European settlers, such as American David Whippy and Englishman Henry Simpson, who arrived on ships in the 1820s and stayed to found two of the country's most prominent families.

The center occupies the quaint old **Morris Hedstrom** store built in 1878 by two other early arrivals, Percy Morris and Maynard Hedstrom. The trading company they founded is now Fiji's largest department store chain ("MH" stores are all over the country). The company donated this dilapidated structure to the National Trust of Fiji. The Levuka Historical and Cultural Society raised money throughout the country to restore it and install a small branch of the Fiji Museum, a public library, a meeting hall, and a crafts and recreational center. The furniture is made of timbers salvaged from the rotting floor. The center is open Monday through Thursday from 8am to

---

Impressions

There appeared to be a rowdy devil-may-care sort of look about the whole of them; and the great part of the day, and the night too, seemed to be spent in tippling in public house bars. I dare say that of the row of houses that make Levuka, fully half are hotels or public houses. The amount of gin and water which is consumed must be amazing, for the bars are always crowded, and the representatives of white civilization always at it.

—Robert Philp (co-founder of Burns Philp trading company), 1872

1pm and from 2 to 4:30pm, Friday from 8am to 1pm and from 2 to 4pm, and Saturday from 8am to 1pm.

NASOVA & THE DEED OF CESSION 🌟🌟
South of the museum, the post office stands at the entrance to the **Queens Wharf.**
The drinking fountain in front marks the site of a carrier-pigeon service that linked
Suva and Levuka in the late 1800s. The Queens Wharf is one of Fiji's four ports of
entry (Suva, Lautoka, and Savusavu are the others), but along with domestic cargo, it
now primarily handles exports from the **tuna cannery,** established by the Pacific Fishing Company (Pafco) in 1964. Follow your nose to the cannery in the industrial
buildings south of the pier.

Keep going to **Nasova,** a village on the shore of the little bay about half a mile south
of the cannery. The **Cession Monument** 🌟🌟 now marks the site where Chief
Cakobau signed the deed ceding Fiji to Great Britain. Three stones in the center of
the grassy park at the water's edge commemorate the signing ceremony that took place
on October 10, 1874, as well as Fiji's independence exactly 96 years later and the 1974
centennial celebration of the Deed of Cession. Two meetinghouses—one traditional
Fijian-style, the other a modern building—stand across the road. The new one was
built in anticipation of a meeting of the Great Council of Chiefs in early 2007, but
the coup in December 2006 put an end to those plans.

South of Nasova, the **Old Levuka Cemetery** is tended to perfection by prison
inmates. Tombstones bear the names of many Europeans who settled here in the 19th
century—and some who met their demise instead.

BEACH STREET 🌟
Backtrack to the weathered storefronts of Levuka's 3-block-long business district along
Beach Street. Saloons no longer line this avenue; instead, the Indian- and Chinese-
owned stores now dispense a variety of dry goods and groceries. On the horizon
beyond the ficus trees and park benches lie the smoky-blue outlines of Wakaya, Makogai, and other Lomaiviti islands. The green cliffs still reach skyward behind the stores,
hemming in Levuka and its narrow valley. Walk along the waterfront, and don't hesitate to stick your head into the general stores for a look at their amazing variety of
goods: You could see an old fashion kerosene lantern displayed next to a modern
DVD player.

After the last store stands the **Church of the Sacred Heart,** a wooden building
fronted by a baroque stone tower. It was built by the Marist Brothers who came to
Levuka in 1858. The clock in the tower strikes once on the hour, and again—in case
you missed the number of chimes marking the time—1 minute later. Across Beach
Street stands a **World War I monument** to the Fijian members of the Fiji Labour
Corps who were killed assisting the British in Europe.

𝒇Moments   **Traveling Back in Time**

Having grown up in Edenton, a small town that still looks very much like it did
as North Carolina's colonial capital in the 1700s, I feel almost nostalgic in
Levuka, which hasn't changed much since it played the same role in Fiji.

Walk on across **Totoga Creek,** from whose bridge local youth like to dive off for a swim, to low **Niukaubi Hill,** on top of which is another World War I monument, this one to Levukans of English ancestry who died fighting as British soldiers in that conflict. Parliament House and the Supreme Court building sat on this little knoll before the capital was moved to Suva. They had a nice view across the town, the waterfront, and the reef and islands offshore. At the bottom of the hill is the **Levuka Club,** a colonial-era social club established by Indians, who weren't allowed in the European-dominated Ovalau Club.

Keep going north on Beach Street, which soon passes the 1904-vintage **Anglican Church** before arriving in the original Fijian village known as **Levuka.** The Tui Levuka who lived here befriended the early European settlers. Later, Chief Cakobau worshiped in the Methodist church that was built on the south side of the creek in 1869. John Brown Williams, the American consul, is buried in the village's Old Cemetery near the church. (Remember, good manners dictate that you request permission before entering a Fijian village.)

To the north, **Gun Rock** towers over Levuka village. In order to show the chiefs just how much firepower it packed, a British warship in 1849 used this steep headland for target practice. Beach Street now runs under the overhang of Gun Rock, where the Marist Brothers said their first Mass. The road didn't exist then, only a shingly beach where the sea had worn away the base of the cliff.

INLAND

Beyond Gun Rock lies the village of **Vagadaci,** where the Duke of York—later King George V—and his brother, the Duke of Clarence, once played cricket (the field is now covered by a housing project), but I usually turn around at Gun Rock and return to Hill Road, the first street inland south of the hospital. It leads to the **199 steps** that climb Mission Hill from the Methodist church to the collection of buildings comprising **Delana Methodist School.** For the energetic, the view from the 199th step is worth the climb.

From the church, cut down Chapel and Langham streets and take a look in the historic **Royal Hotel,** a sightseeing attraction in its own right (see "Where to Stay in Levuka," below). Even if you don't stay at Fiji's oldest operating hotel, have a look at its public rooms, for this ancient establishment is as much attraction as accommodations. It dates to about 1860 but was rebuilt in 1917 after a fire destroyed the original building. Except for installing ceiling fans and bathrooms, little seems to have been done to it since then. Not much imagination is required to picture W. Somerset Maugham or Robert Louis Stevenson relaxing in the comfortable rattan chairs in the charming lounge, slowly sipping gin-and-tonics at the polished bar, or playing a game of snooker at the antique billiard table. Note the large piece of tapa cloth, which was part of the bridal train of the late Queen Salote of Tonga.

After your visit to the hotel, keep going south along the banks of Togoga to the **Town Hall,** built in 1898 in honor of Queen Victoria's 50 years on the British throne; it still houses most of Levuka's city offices. Behind the Town Hall, **Nasau Park** provides the town's rugby and cricket field, bowling green, and tennis courts.

Now head uphill on Garner Jones Road along the creek until you get to the lovely white Victorian buildings with broad verandas of **Levuka Public School,** Fiji's first educational institution (opened in 1879) and still one of its best. A row of mango and sweet-smelling frangipani trees shade the sidewalk known as Bath Road between the school and the rushing creek. Walk up Bath Road, which soon turns into a "step street" as it climbs to a waterfall and concrete-lined swimming hole known as the **Bath.** Cool off at this refreshing spot before heading back down the steps to Beach Street.

ATTRACTIONS BEYOND LEVUKA

St. John's College, in the village of Cawaci north of Levuka, was founded by the Marist Brothers in 1884, primarily to educate the sons of ranking Fijian chiefs. The school sits on the grounds of **St. John's Church,** a Gothic Revival building typical of Catholic missions in the South Pacific. On a bluff overlooking the sea, the **Bishop's Tomb** holds the remains of Dr. Julian Vidal, the first Catholic bishop of Fiji.

Yavu, south of Levuka, is a hilltop overlooking the sea where, according to legend, a newly arrived chief lit a fire, which caught the attention of a chief who was already here. The two met at Yavu and agreed that one would be chief of the interior, while the other would rule the coastline. They placed two sacred stones at the spot to mark their agreement. The hilltop isn't marked, so go there with a guide (see "Organized Tours," below).

Waitovu, about a 50-minute walk north of town (look for its mosque), has the town's nearest waterfall. Ask permission, and the residents will show the way. You can dive into the top pool from the rocks above.

Rukuruku village on the northwest shore has a waterfall and Ovalau's sole swimming beach.

LOVONI VILLAGE ✿

A picturesque Fijian village in the crater of Ovalau's extinct volcano, **Lovoni** was the home of ferocious warriors who stormed down to the coast and attacked Levuka on several occasions in pre-colonial times. Chief Cakobau settled that problem in the 1840s by luring them into town to talk peace; instead, he captured them all and deported them to other parts of Fiji. Lovonians still bear a grudge against their coastal brethren. Some of them came down to Levuka during the 2000 insurrection and torched the Ovalau Club and the Polynesia Masonic Lodge, until then two of the town's landmarks. My friend Christine Moore Green and I took a bus up to Lovoni in 1977; it has changed little since then. The houses still are built of wood with corrugated iron roofs. Today's Lovonians have seen so many travelers wandering around their village that most are adept at pleasantly smiling while ignoring you. It rains a lot up in the crater, whose walls are carpeted with tropical rainforests.

ORGANIZED TOURS

The best way to see the town and environs on foot is in the company of Levuka native Noa "Nox" Vueti of **Nox Walking Tours** ✿. His 2-hour historical walking tour of town is well worth the F$10 (US$6.50/£3.30) per person. He also leads walks to Waitovu waterfall and climbs up to the top of the peak overlooking town; these trips cost F$15 (US$9.70/£5) per person. The climb to the peak takes 1½ hours each way and is not for anyone who is out of shape. Book either excursion through **Ovalau Watersports** (© 344 0166).

Epi's Inland Tour ✿ (© 362 4174 or 923 6011) departs at 11am and goes by truck to Lovoni village, up in the central crater. The visit includes a *sevusevu* (kava) welcoming ceremony and lunch of traditional Fijian food in the village, then a walk into a nearby rainforest. The trips cost F$50 (US$32/£16) per person if less than four go, or F$40 (US$26/£13) a head for four or more. You'll get back to town about 6pm. Reservations are required, so call Epi or book at the Royal Hotel (see "Where to Stay in Levuka," below).

Ovalau Watersports (© **344 0166**) organizes **Tea and** *Talanoa* visits with veteran Levuka residents "Bubu" Kara and Duncan Creighton, who serve tea and tell tales about the island's old days and explain Fijian culture and customs. *Talanoa* is Fijian for sitting down and having a long talk, and it's well worth F$14 (US$9.10/£4.70) to do just that with these knowledgeable locals.

3 Diving, Snorkeling & Hiking

Ovalau's lack of beaches means that watersports are limited here. One exception is the ubiquitous **Ovalau Watersports** (© **440 611;** www.owlfiji.com), which offers **scuba diving** and teaches PADI courses. Owner Noby Dehm has pioneered diving in the Lomaviti Islands and knows the area better than anyone. Nearby dive sites include several shipwrecks in and near Levuka harbor, and Levuka Pass, which is inhabited by a multitude of fish and sharks. Weather permitting, Noby also takes divers to Wakaya Passage, where manta rays congregate from June through August and hammerhead sharks are regularly seen. Noby charges F$140 (US$91/£46) for a two-tank dive and teaches PADI open-water courses for F$590 (US$383/£197). Snorkelers can go along on the nearby dive trips for F$40 (US$26/£13) each.

Ovalau is a fine place to go **hiking,** whether it's a long walk along the shoreline on either side of Levuka, or climbing into the mountains above the town. I don't, however, advise wandering into the mountains by yourself; instead, go with **Nox Walking Tours.** You'll be rewarded with some terrific views on his hike to the peak overlooking Levuka and the Lomaviti Islands. **Epi's Inland Tour** to Lovoni village includes rainforest hikes followed by a dip in the cool stream flowing through the village. See "Organized Tours," above.

4 Where to Stay in Levuka

Two local families welcome visitors on Ovalau's northern coast. **Silana Beach Village** is a seaside homestay with four *bures* (bungalows) and 10 dorm beds near Arovundi village, while **Bobo's Farm** has one Western-style cottage on a riverbank in the Rukuruku Valley. Both charge about F$56 (US$36/£18) per double including meals. Contact **Ovalau Watersports** (© **440 611;** www.owlfiji.com) for more information and reservations.

Levuka Homestay ⊛★★   After vacationing in Fiji several times, John and Marilyn Milesi gave up on the fast lane and relocated here from Perth, Australia. One of the top bed-and-breakfasts in Fiji, John and Marilyn's home overlooking Levuka is far and away the best place to stay here. You climb up stairs bordered by tropical foliage past three of their hotel-style rooms to the main house, where Marilyn serves breakfast on the veranda, whose view almost matches the quality of her cooking. The three units below the house are staggered down the hill and each has a porch, so they seem almost like small bungalows. They have old Levuka touches, such as tongue-and-groove plank walls, and windows that push out in the colonial style (they are not screened, but these units are air-conditioned). A fourth room is on the first floor of the Molesi's upstairs quarters. Although it is less private and not air-conditioned, it's carved out of the hill, which moderates the temperature. It also has twin beds, while the others have one queen-size bed each. Every unit has a ceiling fan and a small desk.

P.O. Box 50, Levuka, Ovalau. (✆ 344 0777. www.levukahomestay.com. 4 units, all with bathroom. F$144 (US$94/£47) double. Rates include full breakfast. MC, V. **Amenities:** Laundry service. *In room:* A/C (3 units), coffeemaker, fridge, no phone.

Mary's Holiday Lodge   This simple house on Beach Street offers very basic rooms, most of which have double beds. Others with cots serve as dormitories. A central hallway runs from the living room fronting Beach Street to a primordial communal kitchen in the rear. Frankly, I would opt for a room at the Royal Hotel rather than here.

P.O. Box 90, Levuka, Ovalau. (✆ 344 0013. 13 units (none with bathroom), 20 dorm beds. F$40 (US$26/£13) double; F$15 (US$9.70/£5) dorm bed. No credit cards. **Amenities:** Communal kitchen; washing machine. *In room:* No phone.

New Mavida Lodge   Levuka's only modern motel opened in 2006 on the site of the original Mavida Lodge, a terrific Fijian guesthouse where I spent Christmas of 1977, and which unfortunately burned down a few years ago. On Beach Street, this incarnation is entered via a two-story lobby with gleaming white tile floors. Hallways lead off to the rooms, each with a TV, telephone, and modern bathroom. The most expensive rooms have balconies, but I prefer to opt for one on the second floor with a lagoon and sea view. A large, fan-cooled room serves as a privacy-deprived dormitory with 10 cots; it has both male and female bathrooms en suite and two more across the backyard. Guests are served complimentary breakfast in the meeting room, but there is no restaurant on-site.

P.O. Box 4, Levuka, Ovalau. (✆ 344 0477. Fax 334 0533. newmavidalodge@connect.com.fj. 11 units, 10 dorm beds. F$80–F$120 (US$52–US$78/£26–£39) double; F$25 (US$16/£8.30) dorm bed. Rates include continental breakfast. No credit cards. **Amenities:** Internet access; laundry service; coin-op washers and dryers. *In room:* A/C, TV, coffeemaker.

Royal Hotel ⟨✿⟩   One of Levuka's fine old families, the Ashleys, has run the Royal for more than half a century with such attentive care that it seems more like a pension full of antiques than a hotel. Creaking stairs lead to the 15 rooms in the original building. Basic by today's standards, they are charming and all have ceiling fans, shower stalls, and toilets. Their unscreened windows push out, and some rooms have small sun porches with white wicker furniture (you can watch the local rugby matches from those on the backside of the building). A mosquito net hangs romantically over the queen-size bed in the honeymoon room, which has a fridge and sun porch. The largest room is the family unit on the north end of the building; it has a queen-size bed in a large room, two single beds in its sunroom, a sink, and a fridge.

Much more modern and spacious, six clapboard cottages between the old structure and Beach Street were built in 1998. Five of these are air-conditioned, although their louvered windows usually let in the sea breeze, and five have kitchens. Each has a front porch. Preferable to me are the Winifred, Ed, and Dot cottages, which face Beach Street and have kitchens. Next would be Kie and Kiku, beside the hotel's outdoor pool.

The dining room here serves breakfast all day but no other meals.

P.O. Box 47, Levuka, Ovalau. (✆ 344 0024. Fax 344 0174. www.royallevuka.com. 15 units, 6 cottages (all with bathroom). F$40–F$62 (US$26–US$40/£13–£20) double; F$83–F$119 (US$54–US$77/£27–£39) cottage. MC, V. **Amenities:**

Restaurant (breakfast only); bar; bicycle rentals; children's playground; exercise room; Internet access; laundry service; outdoor pool. *In room:* A/C (in 5 cottages); coffeemaker (in cottages); fridge (in 2 rooms and all cottages); kitchen (3 cottages); no phone.

5 Where to Dine in Levuka

None of Levuka's hotels serve lunch or dinner, so you will have to head to one of the following on Beach Street.

Kim's Paak Kum Loong Restaurant CHINESE/INDIAN/EUROPEAN   The best tables in this upstairs restaurant are out on the front porch overlooking Beach Street. The menu offers something for everyone in town: Fried fish and chips for Europeans, spicy curries for Indians, and *ika vakalolo* (fish steamed with coconut milk) for Fijians, plus several Chinese dishes including good won ton soup. Pan-fried fish in herbs and garlic and spicy Thai curries also are served. Only Chinese fare is served for breakfast and lunch.

Beach St., middle of town. (*C*) **344 0059**. Reservations not accepted. Main courses F$6.50–F$13 (US$4.20–US$8.40/£2.20–£4.30). No credit cards. Mon–Sat 7am–2pm and 6–9pm; Sun noon–2pm and 6–9pm.

Levuka Pizza & Restaurant PIZZA/REGIONAL   Crews from the tuna boats docking at the nearby cannery frequent this establishment for pizza, served in small and medium sizes with familiar toppings. They're not the best pies in the world, but they beat the basic local dishes such as fish, chicken, or beef stir-fries served with rice.

Beach St. (opposite main wharf). (*C*) **344 0429**. Reservations not accepted. Pizza F$8.50–F$19 (US$5.50–US$12/£2.80–£6.30); sandwiches F$2.50–F$5 (US$1.60–US$3.20/80p–£1.70). No credit cards. Mon–Sat 7am–2pm and 6–9pm; Sun 6–9pm.

Whale's Tale Restaurant REGIONAL   This cramped but pleasant restaurant in one of Beach Street's old storefronts is the best place to dine in Levuka. Australian Liza Ditrich and Fijian partner Sai Tuibua serve continental breakfasts as well as sandwiches, burgers, and pastas at lunch. At night they put cloths on the tables and offer omelets, burgers, pastas, stir-fries, and three-course dinners from a chalkboard menu, which usually includes a vegetarian selection.

Beach St., middle of town. (*C*) **344 0235**. Reservations not accepted. Lunch F$4–F$10 (US$2.50–US$6.50/£1.50–£3.50); main courses F$10 (US$6.50/£3.30); 3-course dinners F$17 (US$11/£5.70). No credit cards. Mon–Sat 11am–3pm and 6–9pm.

6 A Super-Luxury Resort on Wakaya Island

Within sight of Levuka, **Wakaya Island** is an uplifted, tilted coral atoll in the Koro Sea. Beaches fringe Wakaya's north and east coasts, and cliffs fall into the sea on its western side. Relics of a Fijian fort still stand on the cliffs. Legend says a chief and all his men leapt off the cliff to their deaths from there rather than be roasted by a rival tribe; the spot is now known as Chieftain's Leap. The only way to visit Wakaya, however, is to stay at:

The Wakaya Club ★★★   A 20-minute flight by private plane from Nausori Airport, 50 minutes from Nadi, this superdeluxe beachside facility is the brainchild of Canadian entrepreneur David Gilmour, who also introduced us to "Fiji" bottled water. Gilmour has sold off pieces of Wakaya for deluxe getaway homes. For a small fortune, you can rent one of these villas, including *Vale O,* Gilmore's own Japanese-influenced mansion high on a ridge overlooking the resort. Nicole Kidman (a regular guest) and other Hollywood types who don't own a private villa—or can't borrow a friend's—feel right at home in the club's large, super-luxurious bungalows. The gourmet food here is outstandingly presented. Guests dine in a huge thatched-roof beachside building or outside, either on a patio or under two gazebo-like shelters on a deck surrounding a pool with its own waterfall. The Fijian staff delivers excellent, unobtrusive service. Only the humongous Governor's and Ambassador's bures have TVs for DVD viewing. The latter, a 418-sq.-m (4,500-sq.-ft.) retreat, is the largest bure here.

P.O. Box 15424, Suva (Wakaya Island, Lomaviti Group). *©* **344 0128.** Fax 970/920-1225 or 344 0406. www.wakaya. com. 9 units. US$1,900–US$7,600 (£950–£3,800) bungalow. Rates include meals, bar, all activities except deep-sea fishing, scuba diving courses, and massages. Round-trip transfers US$960 (£480) per couple from Nadi, US$480 (£240) from Suva. AE, DC, MC, V. **Amenities:** Restaurant; bar; babysitting; 9-hole golf course; laundry service; massage; outdoor pool; room service; tennis courts. *In room:* Coffeemaker, high-speed Internet access, minibar.

7 Other Islands Near Ovalau

Before the Yasawa Islands became Fiji's backpacker heaven early this century, young folk would visit little islets near Ovalau for some serious sun and fun. Few young travelers come this way nowadays, though.

Leleuvia Island (*©* **343 4008**) is a tiny sand islet dotted with coconut trees and surrounded by a beach and good snorkeling in the lagoon. This was a hot backpacker destination in pre-Yasawa days, and expatriate management has been trying to stage a comeback. Basic accommodations range from about F$50 (US$32/£16) for a dorm bed to F$70 (US$45/£23) for a room or thatch hut, including meals. Credit cards are not accepted.

Caqalai Island Accommodation (*©* **343 0366**) is on a larger island of the same name (pronounced *Than*-ga-lai) owned by the Methodist Church, which means BYO since no alcohol is sold here. Simple bures cost about F$55 (US$36/£18) for a double, dorm beds are about F$45 (US$29/£15) per person, and you can camp for about F$35 (US$23/£12) per person, including all meals. No credit cards are accepted.

The **Royal Hotel** organizes day trips to Caqalai (see "Where to Stay in Levuka," above).

Fiji's first Indian indentured workers arrived in 1879 at **Yanuca Lailai Island,** off Ovalau's south coast, where they were quarantined for 2 months to make sure they weren't bringing cholera and other diseases into the islands. Today, it's home to **Lost Island Resort** (no phone), which has three Fijian bures and an eight-bed dorm. Rates are about F$45 (US$29/£15) per person in a bure, or F$40 (US$26/£13) in the dorm, including meals (no credit cards).

The easiest way to make reservations at Leleuvia, Caqalai, and Lost Island is through **Ovalau Watersports** (*©* **440 611;** www.owlfiji.com).

Hilly **Naigani Island,** about 11km (7 miles) northwest of Ovalau, is home to **Naigani Island Resort** (*©* **603 0613;** www.naiganiresort.com). Chinese interests reportedly have purchased the resort, and it's anyone's guess as to what they plan to do with it.

13

Savusavu

To me, the pristine islands of northern Fiji are what the old South Seas are all about. Compared to busy Viti Levu, "The North" takes us back to the old days of *copra* (dried coconut meat) planters, of Fijians living in small villages in the hills or beside crystal-clear lagoons. You will get a taste of the slow, peaceful pace of life up here as soon as you get off the plane.

The rolling plains of northern **Vanua Levu,** the country's second-largest island, are devoted to sugar-cane farming and are of little interest to anyone who has visited Nadi. **Labasa,** a predominately Indo-Fijian town and Vanua Levu's commercial center, reminds me of Dorothy Parker's famous quip, "There is no there there."

But Vanua Levu's southern side is quite another story. From Labasa, the paved Cross-Island Road traverses the rugged central mountains, where cheerful villagers go about life at the ageless pace of tropical islands everywhere. The Cross-Island then drops down to an old trading town with the singsong name **Savusavu.**

Vanua Levu's major sightseeing attraction, Savusavu is noted for its volcanic hot springs and magnificent scenic harbor—a bay so large and well protected by surrounding mountains that the U.S. Navy chose it as a possible "hurricane hole" for the Pacific Fleet during World War II. Today it is one of Fiji's major sailing centers and a popular stop for cruising yachties, who can clear Customs and Immigration here. The blue waters of the bay also are home to Fiji's first black-pearl farm.

The **Hibiscus Highway** starts at Savusavu and cuts south across a hilly peninsula to the airstrip before continuing along the south shore to Buca Bay. Although 19km (12 miles) of it is paved, this road is neither a highway nor lined with hibiscus (cows grazing beneath the palms ate them all), but it does run along a picturesque, island-strewn lagoon through the heart of Vanua Levu's copra region. This area has one of Fiji's largest concentrations of freehold land, which Americans have been buying in recent years. So many Yanks have bought here, in fact, that residents elsewhere in Fiji facetiously refer to Savusavu as "Little America." Although you'll drive past thousands of coconut palms, the number

Impressions

By now I was drowsy; the warm air blowing freely through the windowless bus brought smells of flowers, damp earth, and copra-drying fires, that seemed to blend and thicken as the day lengthened and colours became enriched.
—Ronald Wright, *On Fiji Islands,* 1986

of housing developments now rivals that of copra plantations along the Hibiscus Highway.

The coastal plain here is primarily a raised limestone shelf, meaning that the reef is shallow and the beaches cannot hold a candle to the sands on Taveuni (see chapter 14). Keep that in mind as you plan your vacation.

1 Getting to & Getting Around Savusavu

GETTING THERE

Air Fiji and **Pacific Sun** both fly from Nadi to Savusavu, and Air Fiji arrives here from Suva. Air Fiji's flights between Nadi and Taveuni usually stop here briefly, so don't let your travel agent send you all the way back to Nadi in order to get to Taveuni. The tiny Savusavu airstrip is on Vanua Levu's south coast. Hotel representatives meet guests who have reservations. A few taxi drivers usually meet the flights.

Bligh Water Shipping Ltd. and **Venu Shipping Ltd.** operate ferries to Savusavu from Suva. **Patterson Shipping Services** has bus-ferry connections from Natovi Wharf (north of Suva on eastern Viti Levu) to Nabouwalu on Vanua Levu. You connect by bus from Suva to Natovi and from Nabouwalu to Labasa. Local buses connect Labasa to Savusavu. In addition, Bligh Water Shipping Ltd. has service directly from Lautoka around Viti Levu's northern coast.

See "Getting Around Fiji" in chapter 3 for more information.

The small ferry *Amazing Grace* (© **927 1372** in Savusavu, 888 0320 on Taveuni) crosses the Somosomo Strait between Buca (*Boo*-tha) Bay and Taveuni 4 days a week. The one-way fare is F$25 (US$16/£8.30), including the bus ride between Savusavu and Buca Bay. Call for schedules and reservations.

GETTING AROUND SAVUSAVU

Budget Rent A Car (© **800/527-0700** or 885 0377 in Savusavu, 672 2735 in Nadi; www.budget.com) and **Carpenters Rentals** (© **885 0122** in Savusavu, 672 2772 in Nadi; rentals@carpenters.com.fj) both have offices in Savusavu. **Trip n Tour,** a travel agency in the Copra Shed (© **885 3154;** tripntours@connect.com.fj), rents bikes, scooters, cars, and SUVs. **Rock 'n Downunder Divers,** on the main street (© **885 3054;** rockndownunder@connect.com.fj), rents bicycles.

An incredible number of **taxis** gather by the market in Savusavu. The cars of **Paradise Cab** (© **885 0018** or 956026), **Michael's Taxi** (© **995 5727**), and **Blue Lagoon Cab** (© **997 1525**) are air-conditioned. Fares from Savusavu are F$4.50 (US$2.90/£1.50) to the airstrip, F$7 (US$4.50/£2.30) to Namale Resort, F$12 (US$7/£4) to Koro Sun Resort, and F$6 (US$3.90/£2) to the Jean-Michel Cousteau Fiji Islands Resort on Lesiaceva Point.

Local buses fan out from the Savusavu market to various points on the island. Most of them make three or four runs a day to outlying destinations, but ask the drivers when they will return to town. The longest runs should cost about F$6 (US$3.90/£2), with local routes in the F55¢ to F$1 (US35¢–US65¢/20p–35p) range.

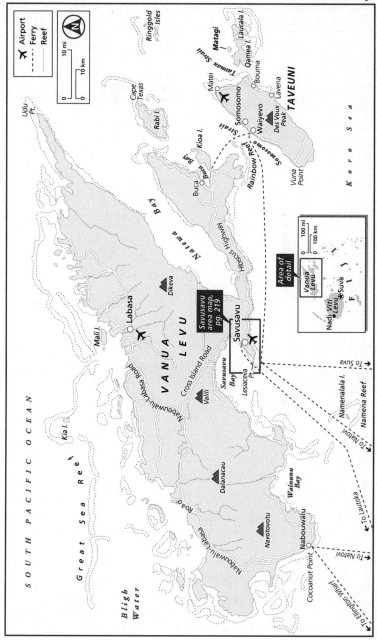

FAST FACTS: Savusavu

The following facts apply to Savusavu. If you don't see an item here, check "Fast Facts: Fiji" in appendix A.

Currency Exchange ANZ Bank, Westpac Bank, and Colonial National Bank have offices with ATMs on the main street.

Emergencies In case of an emergency, phone ☏ 917 for the police, and ☏ 911 for fire or ambulance. The police station (☏ 885 0222) is east of town.

Healthcare Dr. Joeli Taoi (☏ 885 0721) has an office and pharmacy in the Palm Court shops, on the main street. The government hospital (☏ 885 0800) is east of town, in the government compound.

Internet Access Xerographic Solutions, in the Copra Shed (☏ 885 3253), has broadband access in air-conditioned comfort for F10¢ (US5¢/5p) a minute.

Mail The post office is on the main street east of the downtown commercial district. It's open Monday to Friday 8am to 5pm, Saturday 8am to noon.

Safety Savusavu generally is a safe place to visit, but you should always keep an eye on your personal property.

Visitor Information Your best bet for local information is Trip n Tour, in the Copra Shed (☏ 885 3154); this travel agency arranges tours and also rents bikes, scooters, and cars. You can find information on the Web at the Savusavu Tourism Association's site (www.fiji-savusavu.com).

Water The tap water in town and at the resorts is safe to drink.

2 Exploring Savusavu

For practical purposes, Savusavu has only one street, and that runs along the shore for about 1.5km (1 mile). It has no official name, but everyone calls it Main Street. The **Copra Shed,** an old warehouse that has been turned into modern shops and a cafe, stands about midway along the shore. The airlines have their offices in the Copra Shed, along with the Savusavu Yacht Club and restaurants. A bit farther along is **Wai-tui Marina,** where cruising yachties come ashore.

Highlights of a stroll along the bay-hugging street are the gorgeous scenery and the volcanic **hot springs.** Steam from underground rises from the beach on the west end of town, and you can see more white clouds floating up from the ground between the sports field and the school, both behind the BP service station. A concrete pot has been built to make a natural stove in which local residents place meals to cook slowly

⟨Moments The Way It Used to Be

The old South Pacific of copra plantation and trading boat days still lives in Savusavu and southern Vanua Levu. It rains more up here in Fiji's north, but that makes the steep hills lushly green. The diving and snorkeling here are outstanding.

Savusavu

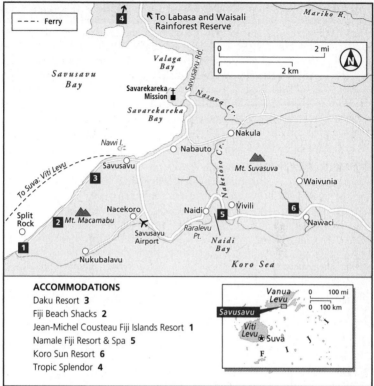

ACCOMMODATIONS

Daku Resort **3**

Fiji Beach Shacks **2**

Jean-Michel Cousteau Fiji Islands Resort **1**

Namale Fiji Resort & Spa **5**

Koro Sun Resort **6**

Tropic Splendor **4**

all day. Overlooking the springs and bay, the **Savusavu Hot Springs Hotel** has great views (see "Where to Stay in Savusavu," later in the chapter).

ORGANIZED TOURS

More than likely your hotel will have a choice of guided excursions in and around Savusavu. If not, **Trip n Tour,** in the Copra Shed (© **885 3154;** tripntours@ connect.com.fj), has a series of tours and excursions. One goes in search of the red prawns that grow in lakes on southeastern Vanua Levu (F$55/US$36/£18 per person). Another takes you to a copra and beef plantation, where you can see the modern-day version of the old South Seas coconut plantation. It costs F$35 (US$23/£12) per person. A full-day trip goes to **Waisali Rainforest Reserve** 🐾🐾, a 116-hectare (290-acre) national forest up in the central mountains; the outing, which includes a hike to a waterfall, costs F$125 (US$81/£41). The park has well-maintained gravel pathways. Reservations for the tour are essential.

Rock 'n Downunder Divers, on the main street (© **885 3054;** rockdown under@connect.com.fj), has half-day Fijian village visits for F$60 (US$39/£20). It also offers half- and full-day boat tours around Savusavu Bay for F$70 (US$45/£23) and F$120 (US$78/£39), respectively, and full-day cruises up a river on the bay's north shore for F$80 (US$52/£26).

3 Mountain Biking, Fishing, Scuba Diving & Sailing

The gray-sand beaches around Savusavu aren't the main reason to come here. The nearest beach to town is a shady stretch on Lesiaceva Point just outside the Jean-Michel Cousteau Fiji Islands Resort, about 5km (3 miles) west of town, which is the end of the line for westbound buses leaving Savusavu market. A half-moon beach is hidden away at **Naidi Bay,** an extinct volcanic crater, just west of Namale Resort on the Hibiscus Highway. The road skirts the bay, but the beach is not easy to see. Take a taxi or ask the bus driver to let you off at Naidi Bay—not Naidi village or nearby Namale Resort. The bar and restaurant at Namale Resort are not open to walk-in customers, so bring something to drink and eat.

ADVENTURE CRUISES 🏝🏝🏝

Ecotourism takes to sea with **Active Fiji** (© 885 3032; www.activefiji.com), which uses the luxurious, 42m (140-ft.) sailing schooner *Tui Tai* to make 7- and 10-day voyages from Savusavu. The boat goes to Taveuni, where you visit Bouma Falls; Kioa, where you spend time in that island's one village; and Rabi Island, which is inhabited by Micronesians who were relocated here after World War II when their home island of Banaba (Ocean Island) was made uninhabitable by phosphate mining. Some cruises go into the Lau Islands in eastern Fiji. The *Tui Tai* carries mountain bikes for land excursions as well as kayaks and diving and snorkeling gear for exploring the shoreline and reefs. The *Tui Tai* can accommodate 24 guests in air-conditioned cabins. Rates range from F$3,739 to F$8,722 (US$2,428–US$5,664/£1,214–£2,832) per person double occupancy, depending on the length of voyage and type of stateroom, and including all meals and activities.

FISHING

Ika Levu Fishing Charters (© 944 8506; www.fishinginfiji.com) uses 7.2 and 12m (24- and 41-ft.) boats for sportfishing excursions in the bays and offshore. Rates range from F$1,013 for half a day to F$1,688 for a full day (US$658–US$1,096/£328–£548). Each boat can take up to four fishers.

MOUNTAIN BIKING

The best way to explore Vanua Levu's mountains by bike is on a tour offered by **Naveria Heights Lodge** (© 885 0348; www.naveriaheightsfiji.com), whose three modern bungalows all have views of Savusavu Bay as well as private bathrooms. Daily rates are F$125 (US$81/£41) double, including breakfast, but they also offer "Adventure Weeks" for F$1,450 (US$942/£471) double, including meals and five biking and hiking excursions.

SAILING

Most sailboats vacate Savusavu during the hurricane season from November through March. Among those that stick around is *SeaHawk* **Yacht Charters** (© 885 0787; www.seahawkfiji.com). The *SeaHawk* is a cruising yawl built for famed yacht designer Ted Hood in 1969. It can carry eight passengers and is now used for half- and full-day sails, sunset cruises, and longer charters (3-day minimum) throughout Fiji. Rates range from US$150 to US$250 (£75–£125) per person per day plus food and beverages.

> **Tips When to Go Diving in Northern Fiji**
>
> Diving in northern Fiji is best from late May through October, when visibility reaches 36m (120 ft.) and more. Because of the strong currents, however, dives to such outer reef sites as the Great White Wall and Rainbow Reef can be strenuous any time of year.

SCUBA DIVING & SNORKELING ★★★

A very long boat ride is required to dive on the Rainbow Reef and Great White Wall, which are more easily reached from Taveuni than from Savusavu. But that's not to say that there aren't plenty of colorful reefs near here, especially outside the bay along the island's southern coast. The beautifully preserved Namena Barrier Reef, a wonderful formation nearly encircling Moody's Namena, is a 2½-hour ride away (see "A Resort on Namenalala Island," later in the chapter). Namena trips are not always possible, since it can be too rough to cross if the trade winds are blowing strongly out of the southeast. Most of the resorts have complete diving facilities (see "Where to Stay in Savusavu," below).

The best spot for snorkeling is over **Split Rock,** off the Jean-Michel Cousteau Fiji Islands Resort, but to access it you will have to stay at the resort or go on a snorkeling expedition with Savusavu town–based **Rock 'n Downunder Divers** (© 885 3054; rockndownunder@connect.com.fj), which also has scuba diving, teaches PADI diving courses, and rents snorkeling gear, kayaks, and bicycles.

Curly's Cruising/Bosun's Locker, on the main street opposite Waitui Marina (© 885 0122), has snorkeling trips to colorful reefs offshore for F$55 (US$36/£18) per person.

4 Shopping in Savusavu

Marine biologist Justin Hunter spent more than 10 years working in the U.S. before coming home to Savusavu and founding Fiji's first black-pearl farm out in the bay. You can shop for the results—including golden pearls grown only here—at **J. Hunter Pearls** ★★, on the western end of town (© 885 0821; www.pearlsfiji.com; Mon–Fri 8am–5pm, Sat 8am–1pm). Prices range from F$20 up to F$2,000 (US$13–US$1,299/£6.70–£650) for loose pearls. Justin has them set in jewelry, too, as well as some interesting items made from the mother-of-pearl shells (I prize my salad forks made from gleaming shells with tree-branch handles). For F$25 (US$16/£8.30), you can take a 30-minute boat tour of the farm at 9:30am and 1:30pm weekdays.

The mother-son team of Karen and Shane Bower display their paintings and sculpture, respectively, at the **Art Gallery,** in the Copra Shed (© 885 3054). They also carry black pearls and shell jewelry. Gallery hours are Monday to Friday from 9:30am to 1pm and 2 to 4:30pm, and Saturday from 9:30am to 12:30pm. Next door, **Taki Handicrafts** (© 885 3956) sells quality woodcarvings, tapa cloth, shell jewelry, and other items made in Fiji (Mon–Fri 8am–1pm and 2–4:30pm, Sat 9:30am–noon).

Another place to browse is the **Savusavu Municipal Market,** on main street (no phone), especially the handicraft stalls on the eastern side of the building. It's open Monday to Friday 7am to 5pm, and Saturday from 6:30am to 3pm.

5 Where to Stay in Savusavu

EXPENSIVE

Jean-Michel Cousteau Fiji Islands Resort ★★★ *Kids*   The finest family resort in the South Pacific bears the name of Jean-Michel Cousteau (son of the late Jacques Cousteau), who convinced the owners that a tropical resort could be both environmentally friendly and profitable. It is indeed environmentally friendly, from waste-water treatment ponds inhabited by frogs (nature's own mosquito control) to the lack of energy-guzzling air-conditioners in most buildings. Its outstanding Bula Camp teaches children about the tropical environment. My cousin Eve Silverman, who was 9 years old at the time, spent 5 days in the Bula Camp and sent in a Reader's Comment, as did her mother, Virginia Silverman (p. 224). Children 4 and under get their own full-time nannies at no extra cost. With the kids thoroughly occupied and mostly out of sight from 8:30am until 9pm, depending on their parents' wishes, this also is a fine couples resort. Guests of any age can take part in environmentally oriented activities such as visits to rain- and mangrove forests. An on-site marine biologist gives lectures and leads bird-watching expeditions and visits to Fijian villages. And divers are accompanied by guides skilled in marine biology.

The property looks like an old-time Fijian village set in a flat palm grove beside the bay near Lesiaceva Point. Reception and the resort's bar and dining areas (one for families, another for couples) are under large thatched roofs built like Fijian chiefs' and

---

Reader's Comment: A 9-Year-Old in Fantastic Fiji

I really didn't know what to expect when my Mom told me we were going to Fiji. Once we got there, I did so many things I had never done before, for example, snorkeling. Fiji is the best place to snorkel ever!

The Bula Club for kids [at Jean-Michel Cousteau Fiji Islands Resort] was awesome! There was always something new to do every day, like catching frogs and digging for hermit crabs. The Bula Club was fun because I had my own Fijian buddy, Mary, who played with me every day. She taught me how to whistle a hermit crab out of its shell. She also made me a farewell present, which was a lei made out of flowers.

It was fun meeting kids from other countries, like Australia, New Zealand, and Scotland. We actually saw a family from our hometown in California and she was on my soccer team 2 years ago! It is such a small world, isn't it?

I was a little worried about the food in Fiji, but discovered it is delicious. I ate the best pineapple in the world! On our way to the waterfall in the rainforest one day, our guide Sami bought it from Fijians who were walking along the road with pineapples on their backs. Sami cut it open with their machete. Sami served our pineapple on elephant ear leaves.

Another fun part about Cousteau resort was walking on the pier. You did not even have to try hard to see the bottom of the ocean. I saw beautiful exotic fish, like blue sea stars, yellow tang, zebra fish, sea cucumbers, needlefish, and giant clams. You could see even more when you got in the water.

The very best thing about Fiji is the people. So if you ever want to go to Fiji remember to bring your camera because Fiji is a FANTASTIC place!

—**Eve Silverman**, age 9, Laguna Niguel, California

Savusavu Town

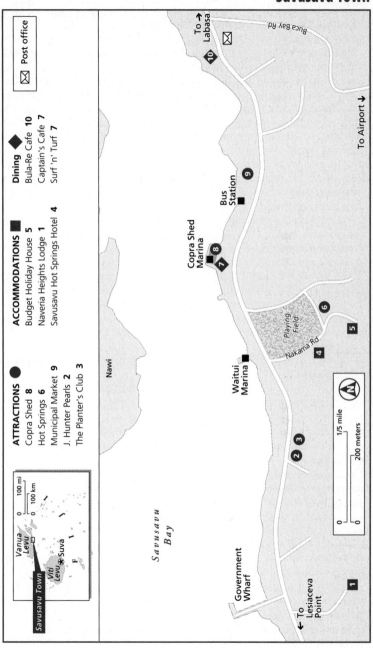

ATTRACTIONS ●
Copra Shed **8**
Hot Springs **6**
Municipal Market **9**
J. Hunter Pearls **2**
The Planter's Club **3**

ACCOMMODATIONS ■
Budget Holiday House **5**
Naveria Heights Lodge **1**
Savusavu Hot Springs Hotel **4**

Dining ◆
Bula-Re Cafe **10**
Captain's Cafe **7**
Surf 'n' Turf **7**

⊠ Post office

Reader's Comment: A Mother's View

When we stepped out of the van that brought us from the Savusavu airport to the Jean-Michel Cousteau Fiji Islands Resort, our luggage went one way, and my 9-year-old daughter, Eve, went another!

Eve was met by her Bula Club Buddy, Mary, who acted as her personal playmate/chaperone/concierge during our entire stay. While I was reading a book by the adult's pool or walking along the white sandy beach, the Bula Club offered her nonstop activities, exposure to the natural beauty and fun of the islands, and a nice, safe environment for her to experiment. She learned to snorkel, kayak, swim in the open ocean, the names of marine life and their habits, and games. She met new friends daily. Although she had the option of dining with me, she continuously chose to eat with her new friends. The bonds she made were quite strong with both the other children in the club as well as the Fijian caretakers.

Our Fiji experience changed both my daughter and me. From sharing kava with a Fijian chief in a rural village just outside Savusavu to watching her catch her breath as she jumped from a glass-bottom boat to snorkel for the first time, I watched her grow from a child into a young woman, open to new experiences, places, and people. She straddled the international date line on Taveuni, thrilled to stand in Wednesday and Thursday at the same time. She was amazed at the strange new culture we saw in villages, the beauty of the rainforests, the unusual tastes of the indigenous food and drink, and I was amazed at her ability to open up to it all. Fiji gave us both a safe place to grow as mother and daughter.

Both of us left part of our hearts and imagination in that beautiful place and we can't wait to go back to retrieve them.

—**Virginia Silverman,** Laguna Niguel, California

priests' houses. These impressive buildings sit next to an infinity pool just steps from one of the better beaches in the area. The central buildings have expensive wireless Internet access.

The thatched-roof guest *bures* (bungalows) have ceiling fans to augment the natural breezes flowing through the floor-to-ceiling wooden jalousie windows that comprise the front and rear walls. Most bures have porches strung with hammocks, and some of the smaller units have been enlarged to include a separate sleeping area, a plus for families. It's worth paying extra for more space and privacy in the split-level "villas" isolated at the end of the property. The award-winning honeymoon villa has its own swimming pool and a spa tub in its large bathroom. Only the honeymoon villa has a phone and is air-conditioned.

A full-service spa is planned; in the meantime, you can get massages and treatments in beachside bures, which become private dining venues after dark. Even the kids' cuisine is outstanding here.

Post Office, Savusavu (Lesiaceva Point, 5km/3 miles west of town). (℄ 800/246-3454 or 885 0188. Fax 885 0430. www.fijiresort.com. 25 units. US$575–US$2,200 (£288–£1,100) double. Rates include meals, soft drinks, airport transfers, and all activities except scuba diving. AE, MC, V. **Amenities:** Restaurant; bar; activities desk; babysitting; children's program; Wi-Fi (in main building); laundry service; massage; 3 outdoor pools; room service; scuba diving; tennis court; watersports. *In room:* A/C (in honeymoon villa), coffeemaker, iron, minibar, safe, no phone (except in honeymoon villa).

Koro Sun Resort   This property on Vanua Levu's southern coast has been considerably upgraded in recent years by its American owners, who will gladly sell you a piece of paradise and build a custom-designed home on it (the resort rents luxury villas already built by its landowners). The Hibiscus Highway runs along the shoreline, separating the property from the lagoon. The resort offers a bit of beach, and a swimming hole has been dredged into the shallow reef. A lagoonside restaurant and bar sit on a landfill by a marina, also blasted into the reef. Koro Sun sports two outdoor pools (the more attractive reserved for adults only), and a 9-hole, par-3 golf course. A dirt track leads around the course and through a rainforest to the resort's own refreshing cascades, where you can take a cold dip or be pampered in the spa's two screened bungalows. On the way are six "Raintree Villas" beside one of the fairways; each of these units has two bedrooms, a bathroom, its own pool, and a full kitchen. The land turns quickly from flat coastal shelf to hills, where most of the guest bungalows are perched, thus commanding views through the palms to the sea. All these hillside units have screened porches. One has a separate bedroom, another has two bedrooms. The octagonal honeymoon bure is the most deluxe and private. Down at sea level, the "garden" units lack views but have small front yards behind picket fences, plus four-poster beds with mosquito nets. All bungalows have outdoor showers behind high rock walls.

Private Bag, Savusavu (Hibiscus Hwy., 16km/10 miles east of town). © **877/567-6786** or 885 0262. Fax 885 0355. www.korosunresort.com. 24 units. US$320–US$550 (£160–£275) bungalow; US$800–US$1,200 (£400–£600) villa. Rates include meals and nonmotorized watersports. AE, MC, V. **Amenities:** 2 restaurants; 2 bars; babysitting; children's programs; 9-hole golf course; laundry service; massage; spa; free use of mountain bikes, snorkeling gear, and sea kayaks; 2 outdoor pools; scuba diving; 2 tennis courts. *In room:* A/C, TV (in villas), coffeemaker, fridge, high-speed Internet access (in villas), kitchen (in villas), no phone.

Namale – The Fiji Islands Resort & Spa ✹✹✹   Both luxurious and eclectic, this resort is owned by toothy American motivational author and speaker Anthony Robbins, who visits several times a year and conducts some of his get-a-grip seminars here (most participants sleep across the road, but those willing to pay a lot extra stay in the resort). Robbins obviously finds any dull moment distasteful, for he has built an air-conditioned gym with a wall-size TV for watching sports via satellite, an indoor basketball court, an electronic golf simulator, and a full-size bowling alley (I kid you not). These indoor toys will come in handy since the climate here is borderline rainforest, and the pebbly beaches are not reason alone to spend your entire vacation here. Nevertheless, Namale has excellent scuba diving and deep-sea fishing (the only two activities demanding an extra fee), plus windsurfing, horseback riding, and hiking. After all that, you can be pampered in the full-service spa, the most beautiful in Fiji. As my travel-writing friend John ("Johnny Jet") DiScala once wisecracked, this is "the kind of place Americans come when they really don't want to leave home."

This area has been geologically uplifted, so all buildings are on a shelf 3 to 6m (10–20 ft.) above sea level. The guest quarters are widely scattered in the blooming tropical gardens, thus affording honeymoon-like privacy if not a setting directly beside

---

Fun Fact **Do I Have a Deal for You**

Namale Fiji Island Resort & Spa has been a working copra plantation since the 1860s, when an Englishman bought it from the local chief for 10 rifles. Some of today's nationalistic Fijians would like to buy it back—at the same price.

the lagoon. The crown jewel is the "Dream House," a two-bedroom, two-bathroom minimansion with a kitchen, its own small pool, a whirlpool bathtub, and indoor and outdoor showers. Similarly equipped, the "Bula House" has only one bedroom, but its rental includes the two guest bungalows outside, and it has a Jacuzzi on its deck. Both the Dream and Bula houses have drop-down movie screens with wraparound sound systems. Two more "Grand Villas" have their own pools, separate buildings for sleeping and living, and a treehouselike platform for lounging with sea views. Your children can stay with you in these houses, but only if they're at least 12 years old (they are allowed in the other bungalows only if you rent one just for them).

Among the bungalows, the deluxe honeymoon bure also has its own swimming pool. Four more honeymoon bures have bathrooms with Jacuzzi tubs, separate showers with indoor and outdoor entrances, and their own ceiling fans. Six older bures are much less spectacular, but they are attractively appointed nonetheless. If you're traveling by yourself, you can stay in one of these, but not in the larger units. You'll have a walkie-talkie instead of a phone.

P.O. Box 244, Savusavu (Hibiscus Hwy., 11km/7 miles east of town). © 800/727-3454 or 885 0435. Fax 885 0400, or 619/535-6385 in the U.S. www.namalefiji.com. 15 bungalows, 3 houses. US$850–US$1,250 (£425–£625) double; US$1,950–US$2,100 (£975–£1,050) house. Rates include meals, drinks, all activities except spa services, scuba diving, and fishing. AE, MC, V. No children 11 and under accepted. **Amenities:** Restaurant; 2 bars; basketball court; free use of bikes; exercise room; game room; Jacuzzi; free laundry service; massage; 2 outdoor pools; spa; tennis court; watersports. *In room:* A/C (in houses and deluxe bungalows), coffeemaker, iron, kitchen (in houses), minibar, safe, no phone.

INEXPENSIVE

Although few backpackers visit Savusavu these days, the town has several properties offering inexpensive accommodations. The most comfortable dorm is at the Savusavu Hot Springs Hotel (see below).

Operated by an Indo-Fijian family of the Christian persuasion, **Budget Holiday House** (© 885 0149) offers very basic rooms in a simple wood frame house in a quiet setting on Nakama Road near the hot springs. It charges F$40 (US$26/£13) for a double, and credit cards are not accepted.

Daku Resort *(Value* This former church camp is now owned by Britons John ("J.J.") and Delia Rothnie-Jones, who renovated all of its accommodations. They also use it as a base for a variety of educational courses such as creative writing, quilting, bird-watching, sketching, and gospel singing (see their website for more activities). The tin-roof accommodations, main building with restaurant and bar, and outdoor pool sit in a lawn across Lesiaceva Point Road from a small beach. Ranging from hotel rooms to three-bedroom houses, the units are simple but clean and comfortable. Two "lodge" rooms share hot-water showers; all other units have their own bathrooms, some with outdoor showers. Savusavu town is a 25-minute walk from here.

P.O. Box 18, Savusavu (Lesiaceva Point Rd., 2km/1¼ miles west of town). © 885 0046. Fax 885 0334. www.daku resort.com. 19 units, 18 with bathroom. F$95–F$250 (US$62–US$162/£31–£81) double. AE, MC, V. **Amenities:** Restaurant; bar; babysitting; free use of kayaks, canoes, and snorkel gear; laundry service; outdoor pool; Wi-Fi. *In room:* A/C (2 units) , coffeemaker, fridge.

Savusavu Hot Springs Hotel *(Value* Once a Travelodge motel, this three-story structure sits on a hill in town, and its motel-style rooms afford the view through sliding glass doors opening to balconies. Units on the third and fourth floors have the best vantage. The less-expensive rooms on the lower levels are equipped with ceiling fans but lack air-conditioners. Ground-floor rooms are devoted to dormitory-style accommodations, which makes this my top backpacker's choice in the area. Most of these have double beds while two are equipped with four bunk beds each. The Decked Out restaurant serves all meals and opens to an outdoor pool surrounded by a wooden deck overlooking the bay. This isn't a fancy establishment, but it's clean, comfortable, friendly, and a very good value.

P.O. Box 208, Savusavu (in town). © **885 0195.** Fax 885 0430. www.hotspringsfiji.com. 48 units. F$95–F$125 (US$62–US$81/£31–£81) double; F$35 (US$23/£12) dorm bed. AE, MC, V (plus 4%). **Amenities:** Restaurant, bar; babysitting; laundry service; outdoor pool; coin-op washers and dryers. *In room:* A/C (most units), coffeemaker, fridge.

COTTAGE RENTALS

As on Taveuni (see "Where to Stay on Taveuni," in chapter 14), a number of expatriates have purchased land and built homes in or near Savusavu. Some live here permanently and have constructed rental cottages on their properties. Others rent out their homes when they're not here, either through rental programs such as at Koro Sun Resort (see above) or on the Internet. You don't want someone from the Fiji Hotel and Guest House Licensing Board (© **330 9866;** fax 330 2344; www.ag.gov.fj) knocking on your door in the middle of your siesta, so if you rent a cottage, ask if it is fully licensed and avoid any property whose owner avoids answering the question.

You won't have this problem at **Tropic Splendor** (© **851 0152** or 991 7931; www.tropic-splendor-fiji.com), on the north shore of Savusavu Bay, a 20-minute drive from town. Deserting the deserts of New Mexico, owners Susan Stone and Jeffery Mather relocated to this lush setting in 2001. They make sure you have all the comforts of home in their guest bungalow beside a beach of powdery, cocoa-colored sand. It has ceiling fans, a TV with DVD player, wireless Internet access, a king-size bed, a big wraparound porch with hammock, outdoor shower, and other amenities. They charge F$360 (US$234/£117) per day, with discounts for longer stays. MasterCard and Visa credit cards are accepted.

Another option is **Fiji Beach Shacks** (© **885 1002;** www.fijibeachshacks.com), whose "House of Bamboo" between town and Lesiaceva Point is anything but a shack. This two-level, two-bedroom, two-bathroom luxury home with outdoor pool is perched high on a hill overlooking Savusavu Bay. Rates are F$225 (US$146/£73) for a double per night, with a 3-night minimum stay required.

A RESORT ON NAMENALALA ISLAND

Back in the 1970s, Pennsylvanians Tom and Joan Moody (she pronounces her name "Joanne") opened a small, isolated resort in Panama's San Blas Islands, catering to serious scuba divers and others who just wanted a total escape. Terrorists attacked their peaceful outpost, however, shooting and nearly killing Tom and tying Joan up. Fortunately, Tom survived, but they soon left Panama. After searching the South Pacific, they settled on dragon-shaped Namenalala, a 44-hectare (110-acre) rocky ridge protruding from the Koro Sea about 32km (20 miles) south of Vanua Levu and covered with dense native forest and bush. The huge Namena barrier reef sweeps down from Vanua Levu and creates a gorgeous lagoon in which you can indulge your passion for diving. The Moodys have designated most of Namenalala as a nature preserve in order to protect a large colony of boobies that nest on the island, and **sea turtles** that climb onto the beaches to lay their eggs from November through February. The surrounding reef is now officially the **Namena Marine Protected Reserve.**

Moody's Namena ☆☆ ⓥ*alue*   Tom and Joan Moody opened this peaceful, remote resort in 1986. The Moodys have perched all but one of their comfortable bungalows up on the ridge so that they have commanding views of the ocean but not of one another. The walls of the hexagonal structures slide back to render both views and cooling breezes, so all beds have mosquito nets. Solar power runs the reading lights and fans, but you won't be able to plug in your hair dryer or shaver. Instead of treading sandy paths among palm trees, you climb crushed-rock pathways along the wooded ridge to the central building, where the Moodys provide excellent meals. They serve wine with dinner and sell beer, but they do not have a license, so bring some duty-free booze if you drink spirits. OCCUPIED/UNOCCUPIED signs warn guests that someone else is already cavorting on four of the island's five private beaches. Other activities include hiking, kayaking, swimming, snorkeling, deep-sea fishing, and scuba diving among the colorful reefs and sea turtles. Tom does not teach scuba diving, so you must be certified in advance. The Moodys will have you brought out from Savusavu on a fast sportfishing boat, a voyage of 1½ hours, or arrange to charter a seaplane for the 1-hour flight from Nadi.

Private Mail Bag, Savusavu. ⓒ **881 3764.** Fax 881 2366. www.moodysnamenafiji.com. 6 units. US$1,375 (£688) per person double occupancy for 5-night minimum stay (required). Rates include meals, boat transfers from Savusavu, and all activities except scuba diving. MC, V. Closed Mar–Apr. No children 15 and under accepted. **Amenities:** Restaurant; bar; game room; laundry service; massage. *In room:* Coffeemaker, no phone.

6 Where to Dine in Savusavu

Bula-Re Cafe ☆ INTERNATIONAL   For the money, this German-operated restaurant facing the harbor serves some of the best food in town. That's especially true of its awesome toasted-sesame-seed salad dressing. The house special is chicken schnitzel-style, but the menu ranges all over the world, from British fish and chips to Fijian *palusami*, a sweet combination of vegetables and meat or fish steamed with coconut milk in banana leaves. Spicy Indian-style curry prawns with almond rice will excite your taste buds. Vegetarians will have several choices here, including veggie pasta with a spicy cheese and curry sauce. Wednesday is *lovo* night, featuring a buffet of earth-oven Fijian foods for F$17 (US$11/£5.70) per person. You can get an espresso or latte to accompany breakfast or to recharge later in the day.

Main street, east end of town opposite the post office. ⓒ **885 0377.** Reservations recommended for dinner. Breakfast F$5–F$7 (US$3.20–US$4.50/£1.70–£2.30); main courses F$7.50–F$19 (US$4.90–US$12/£2.50–£6.30). No credit cards. Mon–Sat 9am–9:30pm; Sun 5–10pm.

Captain's Cafe INTERNATIONAL   With seating inside the Copra Shed or outside on a deck over the bay, this cafe is a pleasant place for a morning coffee, an outdoor lunch, and good steaks at dinner. Fresh fish is surprisingly tasty, too, especially the mahimahi in lemon butter. Other offerings are sandwiches, burgers, side salads, garlic bread, and reasonably good pastas and pizzas.

Main street, in the Copra Shed. ⓒ **885 0511.** Breakfast F$4–F$8 (US$2.60–US$5.20/£1.30–£2.70); burgers and sandwiches F$8–F$12 (US$5.20–US$7.80/£2.70–£4); pizza F$10–F$24 (US$6.50–US$16/£3.30–£8); main courses F$9–F$11 (US$5.80–US$7.10/£3–£3.70). No credit cards. Daily 7:30am–10:30pm.

Surf 'n' Turf ☆☆ INTERNATIONAL   Formerly a chef at Jean-Michel Cousteau Fiji Islands Resort, Vijendra Kumar now puts his skills to good use at this waterfront restaurant in the Copra Shed. As the name implies, a combination of steak and tropical lobster tail leads the list here, often accompanied by *ota miti,* the young shoots of the wood fern, my favorite Fijian vegetable. Vijendra also cooks very good Indian curries. His specialty is a six-course dinner cooked at your bayside table.

Main street, in Copra Shed. © **881 0966.** Reservations required for fixed-priced dinner. Main courses F$12–F$50 (US$7.80–US$32/£4–£16); fixed-course dinner F$50 (US$32/£16). No credit cards. Daily 10am–2pm and 6–10pm.

7 Island Nights in Savusavu

The resorts provide weekly Fijian *meke* nights and other entertainment for their guests. Otherwise, not much goes on in Savusavu after dark except at one local **nightclub,** which I have not had the courage to sample, and at three local **bars,** which I have.

For a step back in time, visit the **Planter's Club** ☆ (© **885 0233**), an ancient clapboard building near the western end of town. It's a friendly holdover from the colonial era, with a snooker table and a pleasant bar, where you can order a cold young coconut—add gin or rum, and you've got a genuine island cocktail. It's open Monday to Thursday from 10am to 10pm, Friday and Saturday 10am to 11pm, Sunday 10am to 8pm. You'll be asked to sign the club's register.

Yachties and the numerous expatriates who live here congregate at the wharf-side bars of the **Savusavu Yacht Club,** in the Copra Shed (© **885 0685**), and the nearby **Waitui Club** (© **885 0536**), upstairs at Waitui Marina. The yacht club is open Monday to Saturday 10am to 10pm and Sunday noon to 10pm. Waitui Club is open Monday to Thursday 10am to 8pm, Friday and Saturday 10am to 11pm.

14

Taveuni

One of my favorite places to hang out in Fiji is cigar-shaped Taveuni, just 6.5km (4 miles) from Vanua Levu's eastern peninsula across the Somosomo Strait. The country's third-largest island is one of the world's most famous scuba-diving spots. Although it is only 9.5km (6 miles) wide, a volcanic ridge down Taveuni's 40km (25-mile) length soars to more than 1,200m (4,000 ft.), blocking the southeast trade winds and pouring as much as 9m (30 ft.) of rain a year on the mountaintops and the island's rugged eastern side. Consequently, Taveuni's 9,000 residents (three-fourths of them Fijians) live in a string of villages along the gently sloping, lush western side. They own some of the country's most fertile and well-watered soil—hence Taveuni's nickname: the Garden Isle.

Thanks to limited land clearance and the absence of the mongoose, Taveuni is the best place in Fiji to explore the interior on foot in **Bouma National Heritage Park** and the gorgeous **Lavena Coastal Walk.** It still has all the plants and animals indigenous to Fiji, including the unique Fiji fruit bat, the Taveuni silk-tail bird, land crabs, and some species of palm that have only recently been identified. The **Ravilevu Nature Preserve** on the east coast and the **Taveuni Forest Preserve** in the middle of the island are designed to protect these rare creatures.

In a volcanic crater atop the mountains at an altitude of more than 810m (2,700 ft.) is **Lake Tagimaucia,** home of the rare *tagimaucia* flower that bears red blooms with white centers.

The surrounding waters are equally fascinating. With dozens of fabulous dive sites nearby, including the Rainbow Reef and its Great White Wall, Taveuni is the best place to explore Fiji's underwater paradise.

The little airstrip and most of Taveuni's accommodations are at **Matei,** on the northeastern corner of the island facing the small, rugged islands of **Qamea** and **Matagi,** homes of two of my favorite little offshore resorts (see "Resorts on Matagi & Qamea Islands," later in this chapter).

1 Getting to & Getting Around Taveuni

Both **Air Fiji** and **Pacific Sun** fly to Taveuni from Nadi, and Air Fiji has service from Suva and Savusavu. The hotels send buses or hire taxis to pick up their guests.

The large ferries from Suva stop at Savusavu before arriving at Waiyevo, and the small *Amazing Grace* crosses the Somosomo Strait between Waiyevo and Buca Bay daily.

See "Getting to & Getting Around Savusavu" in chapter 13, and "Getting Around Fiji" in chapter 3, for details.

Taxis don't patrol the roads here, but your hotel staff can summon one. I have been satisfied with **Taveuni Island Tours** (© 888 0221), **Nan's Taxi** (© 888 0705), and

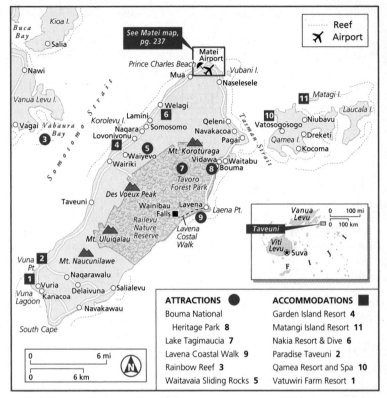

Map legend and labels:

- Reef
- ✈ Airport

ATTRACTIONS ●
Bouma National
 Heritage Park **8**
Lake Tagimaucia **7**
Lavena Coastal Walk **9**
Rainbow Reef **3**
Waitavaia Sliding Rocks **5**

ACCOMMODATIONS ■
Garden Island Resort **4**
Matangi Island Resort **11**
Nakia Resort & Dive **6**
Paradise Taveuni **2**
Qamea Resort and Spa **10**
Vatuwiri Farm Resort **1**

Ishwar's Taxi (© **888 0464**). None of the taxis have meters, so negotiate for a round-trip price if you're going out into the villages and having the driver wait for you. The official fare from the airstrip is F$2 (US$1.30/65p) to Maravu Plantation and Taveuni Island resorts, F$17 (US$11/£5.70) to Bouma Falls, and F$20 (US$13/£6.70) to Navakoca (Qamea) Landing, or Waiyevo.

Local **buses** fan out from Waiyevo to the outlying villages about three times a day from Monday to Saturday. For example, a bus leaves Waiyevo for Bouma at 8:30am, 12:15pm, and 4:30pm. The one-way fare to Bouma is no more than F$4 (US$2.60/

Tips Rough Road

Budget Rent A Car (© **800/527-0700** or 888 0291; www.budget.com) has an agency on Taveuni, but I always hire a taxi and driver instead (see "Getting to Taveuni & Getting Around"). Taveuni's main road, which runs along the west and north coasts, is paved between Waiyevo and Matei, but elsewhere it's rough gravel, winding, often narrow, and at places carved into sheer cliffs above the sea. A taxi and driver cost about F$150 (US$97/£50) for a full day, or about the same as a rental with insurance and gas.

£1.30). Contact **Pacific Transport** (*©* **888 0278**) opposite Kaba's Supermarket in Nagara.

Coconut Grove Beachfront Cottages in Matei (*©*/fax **888 0328**) rents bicycles for F$25 (US$16/£8.30) a day. See "Where to Stay on Taveuni," later in the chapter.

FAST FACTS: Taveuni

The following facts apply to Taveuni. If you don't see an item here, see "Fast Facts: Fiji" in appendix A.

Currency Exchange **Colonial National Bank** (*©* **888 0433**) has an office and an ATM at Nagara. It's open Monday to Friday from 9:30am to 4pm.

Electricity The resorts and hotels have their own generators since only Taveuni's villages have public electricity. Most generators are 220 volts but a few are 110 volts, so ask before plugging in your electric shaver.

Emergencies In an emergency, phone *©* **917** for the **police**, *©* **911** for **fire** or **ambulance**. The **police station** (*©* **888 0222**) is in the government compound. Taveuni is relatively safe, but exercise caution if you're out late at night.

Healthcare The **government hospital** (*©* **888 0222**) is in the government compound in the hills above Waiyevo. To get there, go uphill on the road opposite the Garden Island Resort, then take the right fork.

Internet Access **Lani's Digital Services**, in Nagara opposite Colonial National Bank (*©* **888 0259**), has Internet access for F$1.20 (US80¢/40p) per 10-minute interval. They also will burn your digital photos to CDs. Open Monday to Saturday from 7am to 7pm.

Mail The **post office** is in Waiyevo (Mon–Fri 8am–4pm, Sat 8am–noon).

Visitor Information There is no visitor information office on the island, but the **Taveuni Tourism Association** has a website at **www.puretaveuni.com**.

Water The tap water is safe to drink at the hotels on Taveuni but not elsewhere.

---

2 Exploring Taveuni

Taveuni is famous for shallow **Lake Tagimaucia** (*Tangi*-maw-thia), home of the rare *tagimaucia* flower bearing red blooms with white centers. Its sides ringed with mud flats and thick vegetation, the lake sits in the volcanic crater of **Des Voeux Peak** at more than 800m (2,700 ft.) altitude. It's a rare day when clouds don't shroud the peak.

The three-level **Bouma Falls** are among Fiji's finest and most accessible waterfalls, and the area around them is included in the **Bouma National Heritage Park** (see below). Past Bouma at the end of the road, a sensational coastal hiking track begins at **Lavena** village and runs through the Ravilevu Nature Reserve.

By tradition, Taveuni's **Somosomo** village is one of Fiji's most "chiefly" villages; that is, its chief is one of the highest ranking in all of Fiji, and the big meetinghouse here is a prime gathering place of Fiji's Great Council of Chiefs. Although Somosomo has a modern Morris Hedstrom supermarket, the predominately Indo-Fijian **Nagara** village next door is the island's commercial center.

> ### ⟨Moments⟩ Yesterday & Today
>
> The 180th meridian would have been the international date line were it not for its dividing the Aleutians and Fiji into 2 days, and for Tonga's wish to be on the same day as Australia. Even so, I love to stand here on Taveuni with one of my feet in today, the other in yesterday.

The administrative village of **Waiyevo** sits halfway down the west coast. A kilometer (½ mile) south, a brass plaque marks the **180th meridian** of longitude, exactly halfway around the world from the zero meridian in Greenwich, England. In addition to the aptly named Meridian Cinema, the village of **Wairiki** sports the lovely **Wairiki Catholic Mission,** built in the 19th century to reward a French missionary for helping the locals defeat a band of invading Tongans. A painting of the battle hangs in the presbytery.

The main road is rough, slow-going gravel from Wairiki to **Vuna Point** on Taveuni's southeastern extremity. On the way it passes **Taveuni Estates,** a real-estate development with a 9-hole golf course (you, too, can own a piece of paradise).

BOUMA NATIONAL HERITAGE PARK 𝒢𝒢𝒢

One attraction on everyone's list is **Bouma National Heritage Park** (© 888 0390) on Taveuni's northeastern end, 18km (11 miles) from the airstrip, 37km (23 miles) from Waiyevo. The government of New Zealand provided funds for the village of Bouma to build trails that lead to the three levels of **Bouma Falls.** It's a flat, 15-minute walk along an old road from the visitor center to the lower falls, which plunge some 180m (600 ft.) into a broad pool. From there, a trail climbs sharply to a lookout with a fine view of Qamea and as far offshore as the Kaibu and Naitoba islands east of Taveuni. The trail then enters a rainforest to a second set of falls, which are not as impressive as the lower cascade. Hikers ford slippery rocks across a swift-flowing creek while holding onto a rope. This 30-minute muddy climb can be made in shower sandals, but be careful of your footing. A more difficult track ascends to yet a third falls, but I've never followed it, and people who did have told me it isn't worth the effort.

Another trail, the **Vidawa Rainforest Walk,** leads to historic hill fortifications and more great views. Guides lead full-day treks through the rainforest, but you'll need to book at your hotel activities desk or call the park's **visitor center** (© **888 0390**) at least a day in advance. The trek ends at Bouma Falls. The hikes cost F$60 (US$39/£20) for adults, F$40 (US$26/£13) for children 12 to 17.

The park is open daily from 8am to 5pm. Admission is F$8 (US$5.20/£2.70) per person without a guide, F$15 (US$9.75/£5) with a guide. See "Getting to & Getting Around Taveuni," above, for information about how to get here.

HIKING 𝒢𝒢𝒢

In addition to the short walks in the Bouma National Heritage Park (see above), three other treks are worth making, depending on the weather. The relatively dry (and cooler) season from May to September is the best time to explore Taveuni on foot.

Best of all is the **Lavena Coastal Walk** 𝒢𝒢𝒢. It follows a well-worn, easy to follow trail from the end of the road past the park for 5km (3 miles), then climbs to **Wainibau Falls.** The last 20 minutes or so of this track are spent walking up a creek bed, and you'll have to swim through a rock-lined canyon to reach the falls (stay to the left,

---

(Fun Fact **Actors in Paradise**

On a clear day you can see **Naitaba Island**—once owned by the late Raymond Burr—from up the hills of Bouma National Heritage Park. Another actor, Mel Gibson, owns **Mago Island,** which lies beyond Naitaba.

---

out of the current). The creek water is safe to drink, but bring your own bottled water if you want to be on the safe side. You can do it on your own, but it's much more rewarding to go with a Bouma National Heritage Park guide for F$60 (US$39/£20) adults, F$40 (US$26/£13) children 12 to 17, including the F$12 (US$7.80/£4) per person admission you would otherwise have to pay to the village and walking track. Positioned on a peninsula, Lavena village has one of Taveuni's best beaches and a lodge where hikers can overnight for F$25 (US$16/£8.30) per person (𝄐 **923 9080;** ask for Maria).

An alternative to walking is to ride a boat along this spectacular coast with **Lavena Coastal Tour** (𝄐 **920 5834**). This half-day excursion costs F$50 (US$32/£16) per person and includes a picnic lunch at a waterfall. If the sea is calm, you may get to see **Savulevu Yavonu Falls,** which plunge precipitously into the sea.

High in the center of the island, a rough road leads to the top of **Des Voeux Peak** and **Lake Tagimaucia,** home of the famous flower that blooms from the end of September to the end of December. This crater lake is surrounded by mud flats and filled with floating vegetation. Beginning at Somosomo village, the hike to the lake takes about 8 hours round-trip. The trail is often muddy and slippery, and—given the usual cloud cover hanging over the mountains by midmorning—you're not likely to see much when you reach the top. Only hikers who are in shape should make this full-day trek. You must pay a F$25 (US$16/£8.30) per person "custom fee" to visit the lake, which includes a guide—an absolute necessity. Your hotel will make the arrangements. An alternative is to take a four-wheel-drive vehicle up Des Voeux Peak for a look down at the lake. The drive is best done early in the morning, when the mountain is least likely to be shrouded in clouds.

3 Scuba Diving, Snorkeling & Other Outdoor Activities

The hotels and resorts will arrange all of Taveuni's outdoor activities, although you should book at least a day in advance.

FISHING

Two charter boats will take you in search of big game fish offshore: American John Llanes's **Makaira Charters** (𝄐 **888 0686;** makaira@connect.com.fj) and New Zealander Geoffrey Amos's **Matei Game Fishing** (𝄐 **888 0371**). They charge about US$325 (£163) for half a day, US$525 (£263) for a full day for up to four fishers. Call for reservations, which are required.

GOLF

The real-estate development known as **Taveuni Estates,** about 7km (4⅓ miles) southeast of the 180th Meridian, has a scenic 9-hole golf course skirting the island's eastern shore. Reserve at the clubhouse (𝄐 **888 0044**), which serves lunch and has a bar. The greens fee is F$40 (US$26/£13), including clubs and a pizza.

HORSEBACK RIDING

Maravu Plantation Beach Resort & Spa (© **888 0555**) has horseback riding along a trail leading to the resort's wedding chapel on a ridge with views of both sides of Taveuni. **Vatuwiri Farm Resort** (© **888 0316;** www.vatuwirifiji.com) also has horses. See "Where to Stay on Taveuni," later in the chapter.

JET-SKIING

Paradise Taveuni (© **888 0125;** www.paradiseinfiji.com) has jet-skiing expeditions across the Somosomo Strait to Vanua Levu, a 45-minute ride each way. These cost F$400 (US$260/£130) per person, including lunch. Reserve at least 2 days in advance. See "Where to Stay on Taveuni," later in the chapter.

KAYAKING

It's great fun to kayak to the three little rocky islets off the north shore, near the airstrip. You can land on the islands for a bring-your-own picnic. **Coconut Grove Beachfront Cottages & Restaurant** (© **888 0328**), opposite the airstrip (see "Where to Stay on Taveuni," later in the chapter), rents two-person ocean kayaks for F$35 (US$23/£12) per half day, F$55 (US$36/£18) per full day. Owner Ronna Goldstein will prepare a picnic lunch with advance notice.

You can also rent kayaks and outrigger canoes from **Little Dolphin,** in Matei east of the airport (© **888 0130;** www.littledolphinontaveuni.com), for F$25 (US$16/£8.30) per day. It's across the main road from the lagoon.

SCUBA DIVING 𝒜𝒜𝒜

The swift currents of the Somosomo Strait feed the soft corals on the Rainbow Reef and its White Wall between Taveuni and Vanua Levu, making this one of the world's most colorful and famous scuba-diving sites. As a diver I met said, "It's like when you buy a pack of coloring pencils, except there aren't enough colors."

The Rainbow Reef and its Great White Wall are only 6.4km (4 miles) off Waiyevo, so the Garden Island Resort (see "Where to Stay on Taveuni," below) is the closest dive base, a 20-minute boat ride across the Somosomo Strait. The U.S. firm **Aqua-Trek** (© **800/541-4334** or 888 0286; www.aquatrek.com) manages the resort and has its dive base here. This five-star PADI operation has full equipment rental, NITROX, and teaches courses from beginner to dive master. Aqua-Trek's prices start at F$165 (US$107/£54) for a two-dive excursion.

With offices at Taveuni Estates and Wairiki, Carl Fox's **Taveuni Dive** (© **866/217-3438** or 888 0063; www.taveunidive.com) also is within reach of the Rainbow Reef. Carl charges US$95 (£48) for a two-tank dive.

At Matei on the northern end of Taveuni are Fijian-owned **Jewel Bubble Divers** (© **888 2080;** www.jeweldivers.com) and **Unibokoi Divers** (© **888 0560;** www. tovutovu.com).

Tips It All Depends on the Tides

Because of the strong currents in the Somosomo Strait, dives on Taveuni's most famous sites must be timed according to the tides. You can't count on making the dives you would like if the tides are wrong when you're here. A very good friend of mine spent 10 days on Matangi and Qamea islands and never did get out to the Rainbow Reef.

> ## *Tips* Beware of "Jaws"
>
> Ancient legend says that Taveuni's paramount chief is Fiji's highest ranking because sharks protect the island from enemies. True or not, shark attacks have occurred here. So be careful when you're swimming and snorkeling in the Somosomo Strait, and don't under any circumstances swim out to the edge of the reef. Swim and snorkel between 9am and 3pm to minimize the risk of a dangerous encounter.

Based at Paradise Taveuni on the island's southeastern end (see "Where to Stay on Taveuni," below), **Pro Dive Taveuni** (© **888 0125;** www.paradiseinfiji.com) specializes in diving the Vuna Lagoon, which has fewer soft corals but bigger fish.

All operators charge about F$120 (US$78/£39) for a one-tank dive.

SNORKELING & SWIMMING

If they aren't too busy with serious divers, most of the scuba operators will take snorkelers along. For example, **Aqua-Trek** at the Garden Island Resort has snorkeling trips to **Korolevu,** a rocky islet off Waiyevo (be careful out there because the currents can be very strong). The company will even take you snorkeling out to the Rainbow Reef, but book these trips well in advance.

You can also snorkel from a Fijian *bilibili* (bamboo raft) over the **Waitabu Marine Park** (© **888 0451**), a preserved reef that is part of Bouma National Heritage Park. These half-day bilibili ventures cost F$40 (US$26/£13) per scuba diver for four or more, F$20 (US$13/£6.70) per person for snorkeling only.

Some of the best do-it-yourself snorkeling is at the foot of the cliff off **Tramontu Bar & Grill** (see "Where to Dine on Taveuni," later in the chapter), and in the three little rocky islets off the north shore, near the airstrip (provided kelp from the nearby seaweed farms isn't drifting by). Also good for both snorkeling and swimming are **Prince Charles Beach, Valaca Beach,** and the lovely, tree-draped **Beverly Beach,** all south of the airstrip.

A fun outing is to **Waitavaia Sliding Rocks,** near Waiyevo (no phone), where you can literally slide over the rocks down a freshwater cascade. Be prepared to get a few bruises! The rocks are off the side road leading to Waitavala Estates, and admission is free.

4 Where to Stay on Taveuni

The majority of Taveuni's accommodations are near the airstrip at Matei, on the island's northeastern corner. A few small planes arrive and depart about 9:30am and again about 2:30pm, so it's not as if you're sleeping under the flight path of an international airport. I like to stay at Matei because I can walk to the airstrip-area hotels and restaurants in no more than 20 minutes. Other accommodations are in Waiyvo village, about halfway along Taveuni's northern coast, and near Vuda Point, on the southeastern end. Vuda Piont is at least an hour's drive from the airstrip.

AT MATEI

Bibi's Hideaway   Jim Bibi (prounced *Bim*-bee), who describes himself as "100% Fijian," retired as a teacher at the Fiji Institute of Technology in Suva in 1984 and bought this 32-hectare (80-acre) coconut plantation. He cleared away the brush by hand with a machete, and built five plywood-and-tin cottages, one for each of his

Matei

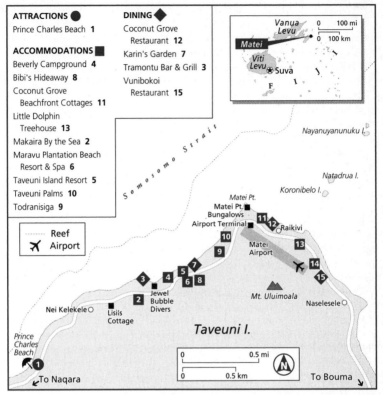

ATTRACTIONS ●
Prince Charles Beach **1**

ACCOMMODATIONS ■
Beverly Campground **4**
Bibi's Hideaway **8**
Coconut Grove
 Beachfront Cottages **11**
Little Dolphin
 Treehouse **13**
Makaira By the Sea **2**
Maravu Plantation Beach
 Resort & Spa **6**
Taveuni Island Resort **5**
Taveuni Palms **10**
Todranisiga **9**

DINING ◆
Coconut Grove
 Restaurant **12**
Karin's Garden **7**
Tramontu Bar & Grill **3**
Vunibokoi
 Restaurant **15**

children (they later added a sixth). Most of his offspring prefer the fast lane in Suva, however, so now he rents out their cottages. They are simple but clean and fairly spacious structures. Not all of their windows are screened, but mosquito nets hang over the beds, which range from two singles to a queen-size. One bungalow dedicated to backpackers has a kitchen and an outdoor shower. All showers here dispense cold water. Along with Vatuwiri Farm Resort (see below), this is a good place to get to know local residents.

P.O. Box 80, Waiyevo, Taveuni. ℰ **888 2014** or 888 0443. 6 units, all with bathroom. F$50–F$100 (US$32–US$65/£16–£33) double. No credit cards. **Amenities:** Laundry service. *In room:* Fridge (some units), no phone.

Coconut Grove Beachfront Cottages ★★★ ⟨*Value*⟩   Ronna Goldstein, who named this little gem not for the palm trees growing all around it but for her hometown in Florida, has three *bures* (bungalows) set beside a fine little beach next to her restaurant (see "Where to Dine on Taveuni," below). Ronna lives here, and the restaurant is on her big, breezy front porch with a terrific view of the sea and offshore islets. You can dine here or down by the beach. Next door, her Mango cottage has a great sea view from its large front porch. Down below, the Banana bure lacks the great view, but it's right by the beach and is more private. Almost on the beach, the Papaya bure is the smallest, but it's also the most private. All three have CD players and outdoor showers. Ronna's veteran staff will make you feel right at home, while Sophia, her friendly

Doberman, is in charge of guest relations. Ronna provides complimentary kayaks, snorkeling fins (bring your own mask), half-hour massages, and village visits. This is one of Fiji's great values. *Note:* Children 6 and under are not accepted here.

Postal Agency, Matei, Taveuni (opposite airstrip). ℂ/fax **888 0328**. www.coconutgrovefiji.com. 3 units. US$155–US$195 (£78–£98) double. Rates include tropical breakfast, afternoon tea, and 30-min. massage. MC, V. No children 6 and under accepted. **Amenities:** Restaurant; bar; bicycle rentals; laundry service; massage. *In room:* CD player, fridge, no phone.

Maravu Plantation Beach Resort & Spa 𝒢 (Value)

Although it has its own lovely beach across the road (a 5-min. downhill walk), this unusual retreat is set among 36 hectares (90 acres) of palms on a former *copra* (dried coconut meat) plantation. Most of the bures are laid out among grounds carefully planted with bananas, papayas, and a plethora of ginger plants and wild orchids. This plantation setting blocks the prevailing breezes, which means the property can get warm and humid during the day. Built in the style of South Seas planters' cottages, the guest bungalows have thatch-covered tin roofs and reed or mat accents that lend a tropical ambience. Situated about 5 minutes away from the main complex via wooden walkways spanning a small valley, six units have sea views and outdoor Jacuzzis. Nearby is the crown jewel, a tree-house bungalow. Four honeymoon bures have four-person-size whirlpool tubs under their outdoor showers, while four more honeymoon suites feature two rooms, outdoor showers, Jacuzzis, and sun decks surrounded by rock privacy walls. Only the older, "planters bures" don't have outdoor showers. With an emphasis on very good "nouvelle Fijian" cuisine, the dining room under the high thatched roof looks out to the lawns and a pool surrounded by an expansive deck. Wine lovers are in for a treat here, for owner Jochen Kiess, a former German lawyer, has accumulated a fine list. Since most of Maravu isn't directly on the beach, Jochen doesn't charge an arm and a leg, which makes it a good value. Horseback riding is included in the rates here, too.

Postal Agency, Matei, Taveuni. ℂ] **866/528-3864** or 888 0555. Fax 888 0600. www.maravu.net. 21 units. US$130–US$325 (£65–£163) per person double occupancy. Rates include full breakfast. AE, DC, MC, V. **Amenities:** Restaurant; bar; activities desk; babysitting; free use of bicycles; exercise room; laundry service; outdoor pool; room service; spa. *In room:* A/C, coffeemaker, minibar, no phone.

Nakia Resort & Dive

Jim and Robin Kelly were stuck in a traffic jam in Hawaii one morning when they decided to relocate to Taveuni and build this little resort, up in a coconut grove with a view of Somosomo Strait. Their central restaurant, with excellent home cooking utilizing produce from an organic garden, overlooks a swimming pool and is flanked by the plantation-style guest bungalows. Three of them have queen-size beds and are suited to couples, while their larger family unit has both king-size and double beds. All have porches with hammocks. A steep stairway leads down to a small beach (at low tide, at least), but like Taveuni Island Resort (see below), the hillside location means this is not the place for a typical beachside vacation. The Kellys have their own dive operation.

P.O. Box 204, Waiyevo, Taveuni. ℂ **888 1111**. Fax 888 1333. www.nakiafiji.com. 4 units. US$175–US$275 (£88–£138). AE, MC, V. **Amenities:** Restaurant; bar (beer and wine only); babysitting; laundry service; massage; outdoor pool; room service; free use of snorkel gear, kayaks, and mountain bikes. *In room:* Fridge, no phone.

Taveuni Island Resort

Once known as Dive Taveuni, this resort now relies on honeymooners for the bulk of its business (no kids 14 and under are allowed). If you are among these romantic souls, you're in for a very private, pampered stay with a fabulous view. You will be sorely disappointed if you expect to step out of your bungalow onto the beach, however, for this property sits high on a bluff overlooking

Somosomo Strait, and you will have to climb down it to reach the sand. STEEP DESCEND (SIC) PLEASE MIND YOUR STEP, a sign at the top of the walkway warns. To compensate, a hilltop pool commands a stunning view over the strait, as do the central building and the guest bungalows. Six of the units are hexagonal models built of pine with side wall windows that let in the view and the breeze. The most stunning view of all is from the spacious deck of the Veidomoni bure—or you can take in the vista from its open-to-the-sea outdoor shower. All other units also have outdoor showers as well as separate sleeping and living areas. One deluxe unit has a separate bedroom, and the luxurious Matalau villa has two master bedrooms and its own private pool.

Postal Agency, Matei, Taveuni. ℂ **866/828-3864** or 888 0441. Fax 888 0466. www.taveuniislandresort.com. 12 units. US$995 (£498) per person double; US$1,539 (£770) villa. Rates include all meals. AE, MC, V. Children 14 and under not accepted. **Amenities:** Restaurant; bar; free use of bicycles; laundry service; outdoor pool; room service; spa. *In room:* A/C, coffeemaker, minibar, safe.

Taveuni Palms 𝒜𝒜   This private little retreat in a coconut grove specializes in pampering guests in its two private bungalows, each of which has its own expansive deck, swimming pool, and small beach among the rocks and cliffs lining the coastline. Owners Tony and Kelly Acland have no need for a restaurant or bar. Instead, the staff prepares and serves your meals in your own dining room, on your deck, down by the beach, or just about any place you choose. The bungalows have sea views from their perches above the shoreline. Each also has two air-conditioned bedrooms with king-size beds, a big-screen TV to play DVDs, an outdoor shower, an intercom for ordering your meals, and its own kayaks and snorkeling gear. Taveuni Palms has its own dive master, and you can have your massage or spa treatment down by the beach.

P.O. Box 51, Matei, Taveuni. ℂ **888 0032.** Fax 888 2445. www.taveunipalmsfiji.com. 2 units. US$995 (£498) double. Minimum 5-night stay required. Rates include meals, nonalcoholic beverages, airport transfers, and most activities. AE, MC, V. **Amenities:** Babysitting; free use of kayaks; laundry service; massage; 2 outdoor pools; spa treatments; Wi-Fi. *In room:* A/C, TV (DVDs only), coffeemaker, fridge, kitchen.

Tovu Tovu Resort   Spread out over a lawn across the road from the lagoon, the Peterson family's simple bungalows have front porches, reed exterior walls, tile floors, ceiling fans, and bathrooms with hot-water showers. Three of them also have their own private cooking facilities. The Vunibokoi Restaurant is here, and it's a scenic walk to Coconut Grove Restaurant and others near the airport (see "Where to Dine on Taveuni," below).

Postal Agency, Matei, Taveuni. ℂ **888 0560.** Fax 888 0722. www.tovutovu.com. 5 bungalows. F$85–F$125 (US$55–US$81/£28–£41) bungalow. AE, MC, V. **Amenities:** Restaurant; bar; laundry service. *In room:* Kitchen (in 3 units), no phone.

AT WAIYEVO

Garden Island Resort 𝒜 *Value*   Built as a Travelodge in the 1960s, this waterside motel is now operated by the San Francisco–based dive company Aqua-Trek, which has its Taveuni base here. Most of the clientele are divers since this is the closest accommodations to the White Wall and its Rainbow Reef (a 20-min. boat ride away in normal conditions), but the friendly staff welcomes everyone. The Garden Island has no beach, but all rooms face a fine view over the Somosomo Strait to Vanua Levu. Each medium-size unit has a queen-size and a single bed, tropical-style chairs, a desk, and a tub/shower combo bathroom. All rooms except the dormitories are air-conditioned (the dorms have ceiling fans). Opening to a strait-side pool, the dining room serves meals, which always include vegetarian selections, at reasonable prices. Guests and nonguests can rent kayaks and go on snorkeling trips to Korolevu islet offshore and even to the Rainbow Reef with Aqua-Trek (p. 235). The hotel also arranges hiking trips and other excursions.

P.O. Box 1, Waiyevo, Taveuni. (©) **800/541-4334** or 888 0286. Fax 888 0288. www.aquatrek.com. 28 units, 8 dorm beds. F$240 (US$156/£78) double room; F$40 (US$26/£13) dorm bed. Room rate includes breakfast; dorm rate does not. AE, MC, V. **Amenities:** Restaurant; bar; babysitting; laundry service; massage; outdoor pool; room service; watersports. *In room:* A/C (except in dorms), coffeemaker, fridge, hair dryer, safe.

IN SOUTHEASTERN TAVEUNI

Paradise Taveuni 🐟🐟   An hour's drive south of the airport (or by jet ski, if you prefer), this pleasant property sits on the site of Susie's Plantation, which was a back-packer resort until present owners Allan and Terri Gorten took over and seriously upgraded it. This paradise doesn't have its own beach, but you can climb down the rocky shoreline directly into the lagoon. Or you can swim in the pool or walk 5 min-utes to a black-sand beach. The thatched-roof guest bures are reasonably spacious, with king-size beds and combination tub/shower bathrooms. The oceanfront models add Jacuzzis and outdoor showers. Allan is a chef, so the Pacific Rim cuisine served in the central building is very good. Pro Dive Taveuni (p. 236) is based here, and this also is the departure point for jet-ski tours to Vanua Levu.

P.O. Box 69, Waiyevo, Taveuni. (©)/fax **888 0125.** www.paradiseinfiji.com. 10 units. F$300 (US$195/£98) per person. Rates include meals. AE, MC, V. **Amenities:** Restaurant; bar; babysitting; free laundry service; massage; outdoor pool; room service; spa; Wi-Fi. *In room:* Coffeemaker, fridge, safe, no phone.

Vatuwiri Farm Resort   On a flat plateau at Vuna Point, this is not a resort but a farm stay, where you reside in one of two simple seaside bungalows while sharing a 720-hectare (1,800-acre) copra plantation, ranch, and farm with the Tarte family, whose ancestor, Englishman James Valentine Tarte, bought the land in 1871. He intended to raise cotton, but a precipitous drop in prices after the American Civil War halted that notion. Today the fifth generation of Tartes produces some 300 British tonnes (about 661,386 lb.) of copra a year and graze several hundred head of cattle beneath the coconut palms. You will share meals with the Tartes in their home over-looking the sea. Their bungalows sit on a rocky promontory, but the property has a long black-sand beach. You can go horseback riding on the beach and in the coconut groves here. Paradise Taveuni (above) and its dive base are about 5 minutes away.

C/o S. Tarte, Waiyevo, Taveuni. ((©) **888 0316.** www.vatuwirifiji.com. 2 units. US$300 (£150) double. Rates include all meals. MC, V. **Amenities:** Restaurant; bar. *In room:* No phone.

COTTAGE RENTALS

Several expatriate landowners on Taveuni rent out their own homes when they're away, or they have cottages on their properties to let.

One owner who did not move here from someplace else is Fiji-born May Gould-ing, who has two cottages at **Todranisiga,** her property south of the airstrip. The land slopes through coconut palms from the road down to the top of a seaside cliff, from where her planter-style bungalows look out over the Somosomo Strait. One of them has an alfresco shower—and I do mean alfresco, since nothing blocks you from the view, or the view from you! Or you can wash off in a claw-foot tub sitting on the lawn. You'll spend most of your time out on the porches enjoying the breeze, taking in the view, and perhaps cooking a light meal on the gas camp stove. May charges F$155 (US$101/£51) for a double. She does not accept credit cards. Contact her at Postal Agency, Matei, Taveuni (© **888 0680;** makaira@connect.com.fj).

Two others cottages with views are at American Roberta Davis's **Makaira By the Sea** (© **888 0686**; www.fijibeachfrontatmakaira.com), sitting above a cliff with a 180-degree view down over Prince Charles Beach and the sea (notwithstanding the website address, this is not a beachfront property). Built of pine, the cottages have queen-size beds, kitchens, porches, and both indoor and outdoor showers. Tramontu Bar & Grill is across the road (see "Where to Dine on Taveuni," below). Roberta charges F$125 to F$165 (US$81–US$107/£41–£54) per double, with discounts for longer stays. She does not accept credit cards.

Less charming but also with the same view as Makaira By the Sea is the one cottage at **Karin's Garden** (© **888 0511**; www.karinsgardenfiji.com), which Peter and Karin Uwe rent for US$185 (£93) per night. It's near the airstrip.

American Scott Suit has one cottage at his **Little Dolphin Treehouse** (© **888 0130**; www.littledolphinontaveuni.com). It's in the middle of his lawn across the road from the lagoon east of the airstrip. The shoreline consists of stones to prevent erosion from reaching the road, but someone has built stairs across this breakwater so you can go swimming. Scott's upstairs living quarters have a fine view of the lagoon, and you can see the offshore islands from the front porch; but you must go outside to reach the downstairs bathroom (with hot-water shower). Scott charges F$100 (US$65/£33) a night but does not accept credit cards.

CAMPING

Campers who like to sleep by the sea can find a beautiful (if not insect-free) site at Bill Madden's **Beverly Campground** (© **888 0326** or 888 0684), on Beverly Beach about 1.5km (1 mile) south of the airstrip. Maravu Resort's beach is next door to one side, and Jewel Bubbles dive base is on the other. Monstrous trees completely shade the sites and hang over portions of the lagoon-lapped shore. The campground has flushing toilets, cold-water showers, and a rudimentary beachside kitchen. Rates are F$10 (US$6.50/£3.30) per person if you bring your own tent, or F$20 (US$13/£6.70) if you rent one of theirs. A bed in the forgettable dorm costs F$20 (US$13/£6.70).

5 Where to Dine on Taveuni

Coconut Grove Restaurant 🕭🕭 INTERNATIONAL   American Ronna Goldstein consistently serves Taveuni's best fare at her little enclave, where she also rents cottages (see "Where to Stay on Taveuni," above). She offers breakfasts (her banana, coconut, and papaya breads are fabulous) and salads, soups, burgers, and sandwiches for lunch. Dinner offerings include a variety of local seafood dishes, spicy Thai and mild Fijian curries (I love the Thai fish), and homemade pastas. Saturday night features a buffet and Fijian musicians. Dining tables are on Ronna's veranda, which has a great view of the little islands off Taveuni, making it a fine place not just for lunch or dinner but to sip a great fruit shake or juice while waiting for your flight. She can also set you up for a romantic dinner under a cabana by her beach.

Matei, opposite airstrip. © **888 0328**. Reservations strongly advised by noon for dinner. Main courses F$14–F$25 (US$9.10–US$16/£4.70–£8.30). MC, V. Daily 8am–5pm and 6–9pm.

Karin's Garden INTERNATIONAL   Karin and Peter Roncaka prepare meals from their native Europe in the dining room of their home overlooking the beach and Somosomo Strait (see "Cottage Rentals" under "Where to Stay on Taveuni," above). Dining here is much like attending a dinner party with these longtime residents. Reservations are required by noon.

> **Tips Audrey's Sweet Somethings**
>
> East of the airstrip, **Audrey's Island Coffee and Pastries** (© 888 0039) really isn't a restaurant; it's the home of American Audrey Brown, Taveuni's top baker. She charges F$10 (US$6.50/£3.30) per serving for cakes with coffee, but doesn't accept credit cards. Audrey's is open daily from 10am to 6pm.

Matei, south of airstrip. © 888 0511. Reservations required by noon. Full meals F$30–F$35 (US$19–US$23/ £10–£12). No credit cards. Seatings daily 7pm.

Tramontu Bar & Grill REGIONAL   The best thing about this open-air, Fijian-owned cafe is its spectacular perch atop a cliff overlooking the Somosomo Strait, which makes it a fabulous spot to have a cold drink while watching the sun set into the sea. The local fare consists of the usual curries, grilled steaks, and chicken stir-fries, but I prefer the wood-fired pizzas. Tell them a day in advance if you'd like to eat seafood so they can acquire fresh lobster or fish; otherwise, stick to the other menu options.

Matei, south of airstrip. © 888 2224. Reservations recommended. Lunch F$15 (US$9.70/£5); pizza F$20–F$30 (US$13–US$19/£6.70–£10); main courses F$10–F$30 (US$6.50–US$19/£3.30–£10). No credit cards. Tues–Thurs 11am–2pm and 6–9:30pm; Fri–Sun 10am–10pm. Bar daily 11am–10pm.

Vunibokoi Restaurant REGIONAL   On the front porch of the main house at the Petersen family's Tovu Tovu Resort (see above), this plain but pleasant restaurant serves breakfast, lunch, and dinner, with a blackboard menu featuring home-cooked Fijian, Indian, and Western fare. I always make sure my trip coincides with the Vunibokoi's Friday night Fijian *lovo* food buffet, one of the most extensive and authentic such traditional feasts in the islands.

Matei, in Tovu Tovu Resort, 1km (½ mile) east of airstrip. © 888 0560. Reservations recommended. Main courses F$15–F$20 (US$9.70–US$13/£5–£6.70). AE, MC, V. Daily 8am–2pm and 6–9pm.

6 Resorts on Matagi & Qamea Islands ★★★

The northern end of Taveuni gives way to a chain of small, rugged islands that are as beautiful as any in Fiji; especially gorgeous are Matagi and Qamea. Their steep, jungle-clad hills drop to rocky shorelines in most places, but here and there little shelves of land and narrow valleys are bordered by beautiful beaches. The sheltered waters between the islands cover colorful reefs, making the area a hotbed for scuba diving and snorkeling. It's unfortunate that geography places them at the end of my coverage of Fiji, for they are home to two of my favorite resorts, both of which are beside two of Fiji's best beaches.

Another project (currently underway at press time) should be worth checking out after it opens in late 2008: **Aqua Club Beach Retreat** (www.aquaclubfiji.com), on the northern shore of Qamea. Plans call for luxury tented accommodations, like on safari in Africa.

ON MATAGI ISLAND

Matangi Island Resort ★★★ (Value   Matangi ranks high because of proprietors Noel and Flo Douglas and their daughter, Christine. Of English-Fijian descent, they own all of hilly, 104-hectare (260-acre) Matagi Island, a horseshoe-shape remnant of a volcanic cone, where in 1987 they built their resort in a beachside coconut grove on the western shore. A lounge building with a deck hanging out over the lagoon takes full advantage of gorgeous sunset views of Qamea and Taveuni. At first the Douglases catered to low-budget Australian divers, but, as their business grew, their clientele shifted to a mix of diving and nondiving American, Australian, and European adults (children 11 and under are no longer accepted here). Honeymooners can escape to three romantic bures 6m (20 ft.) up in the air, one of them actually in a shady Pacific almond tree. These units all have outdoor showers, as do some of the deluxe units down in the coconut grove beside the beach. You can also be taken to the spectacular half-moon-shape beach in aptly named Horseshoe Bay and be left alone for a secluded picnic on one of Fiji's outstanding beaches. Other nondiving activities include hiking, kayaking, bird-watching, sailing, windsurfing, and sportfishing. Except for the honeymoon bures, Matangi's bungalows are round, in the Polynesian-influenced style of eastern Fiji. Umbrella-like spokes radiating from hand-hewn central poles support reed-lined conical roofs. One bure is equipped for guests with disabilities. The tin-roofed central restaurant and bar building lacks the charm of Qamea's, but it overlooks a swimming pool.

P.O. Box 83, Waiyevo, Taveuni (Matagi Island, 20 min. by boat from Taveuni). (© 888/628-2644 or 888 0260. Fax 888 0274. www.matangiisland.com. 13 units. US$525–US$900 (£263–£450) double. Rates include meals and all excursions and activities except scuba diving, water-skiing, sportfishing, and island trips. AE, DC, MC, V. Children 11 and under not accepted. **Amenities:** Restaurant; bar; laundry service; massage; room service; spa; watersports; Wi-Fi (near office). *In room:* Coffeemaker, minibar, safe, no phone.

ON QAMEA ISLAND

Qamea Resort and Spa 🌴🌴🌴 *Value*   This luxury property has the most stunning main building and some of the most charming bures and of any resort in Fiji. In the proverbial lagoonside coconut grove beside a lovely beach, this entire property shows remarkable attention to Western comfort and Fijian detail. If I were to build a set for a South Seas movie, it would feature the original bungalows, all covered by 31-cen-timeter-thick (12-in.) Fijian thatch. Spacious and rectangular, each has an old-fash-ioned screen door that leads out to a porch that's complete with a hammock strung between two posts. Each unit is large enough to swallow the king-size bed, two over-size sitting chairs, a coffee table, and several other pieces of island-style furniture, some of it exquisitely handcrafted by the staff; and their bathrooms include outdoor show-ers. If you need more space, you can rent one of two private honeymoon villas at the end of the property, or even a split-level model that is twice the size of the regular units. Two large, luxuriously appointed "premium villas," which have swimming pools sunken into their front porches, are more spacious still. Qamea's centerpiece is the dining room and lounge under a soaring, 16m-high (52-ft.) priest's bure supported by two huge tree trunks. Orange light from kerosene lanterns hung high under the roof lends romantic charm for feasting on gourmet quality meals. You won't find a children's menu on hand because kids 15 and under are not accepted at the resort.

P.O. Matei, Taveuni (Qamea Island, 15 min. by boat from Taveuni). (© 866/867-2632 or 888 0220. Fax 888 0092. www.qamea.com. 16 units. US$690–US$995 (£345–£498) double. Rates include meals, airport transfers, and all activities except diving, sportfishing, and island tours. AE, MC, V. Children 15 and under not accepted. **Amenities:** Restaurant; bar; exercise room; laundry service; outdoor pool; spa. *In room:* A/C, coffeemaker, iron, minibar, safe, no phone (except in premium villas).

Appendix A: Fast Facts, Toll-Free Numbers & Websites

1 Fast Facts: Fiji

The following facts apply to Fiji in general. For more destination-specific information, see the "Fast Facts" sections in chapters 5, 7, 10, 12, 13, and 14.

AMERICAN EXPRESS Fiji does not have a full-service American Express representative.

AREA CODES Fiji does not have domestic area codes. The country code for calling into Fiji is **679.**

ATM NETWORKS & CASHPOINTS See "Money & Costs," p. 56.

BUSINESS HOURS Stores are generally open Monday to Saturday from 8am to 5pm, but many suburban stores stay open until 6pm and even 8pm. Sunday hours are from 8:30am to noon, although some tourist-oriented stores are open later. Shops in most hotels stay open until 9pm every day. Government office hours are Monday to Thursday from 8am to 4:30pm. Banking hours are Monday to Thursday 9:30am to 3pm, Friday 9:30am to 4pm.

CAMERA & FILM **Caines Photofast,** the largest processor of Kodak films, has shops in the main towns where you can also download and print digital photos.

CURRENCY See "Money & Costs," p. 56.

CLIMATE See "When to Go," p. 40.

CUSTOMS Fiji's **Customs allowances** are 200 cigarettes; 2 liters of liquor, beer, or wine; and F$400 (US$260/£132) worth of other goods in addition to personal belongings. Pornography is prohibited. Firearms and nonprescription narcotic drugs are strictly prohibited and subject to heavy fines and jail terms. Any fresh fruits and vegetables must be declared and are subject to inspection and fumigation. Customs will X-ray all of your luggage upon arrival. See "Customs" in chapter 3 for information about what you can bring home from Fiji. You will need advance permission to bring any animal into Fiji; if not, your pet will be quarantined.

DRIVING RULES See "Getting Around Fiji," p. 50.

DRUG LAWS Marijuana is grown illegally up in the hills, but one drive past the Suva Gaol will convince you not to get caught buying it—or smuggling narcotics or dangerous drugs into Fiji.

DRUGSTORES The main towns have reasonably well-stocked pharmacies, or "chemists." Their medicines are likely to be from Australia or New Zealand. Many pharmacists will dispense medications without a prescription if you have your original bottle from home. The Morris Hedstrom department stores throughout Fiji carry a wide range of toiletries, including Coppertone, Colgate, and many other familiar brands.

ELECTRICITY Electric current in Fiji is 240 volts, 50 cycles. Many hotels have converters for 110-volt shavers, but these are not suitable for hair dryers. The plugs are the angled two-prong types used in Australia and New Zealand. Outlets have on/off switches mounted next to them.

EMBASSIES & CONSULATES The **U.S. Embassy** is at 31 Loftus St., Suva (℡ **331 4466;** www.amembassy-fiji.gov). Other major diplomatic missions in Suva are **Australia,** 37 Princes Rd., Tamavua (℡ **338 2211**); **New Zealand,** 10th Floor, Reserve Bank of Fiji Building, Pratt Street (℡ **331 1422**); **United Kingdom,** Victoria House, 47 Gladstone Rd. (℡ **331 1033**); **Japan,** Second Floor, Dominion House, Thomson Street (℡ **330 2122**); **France,** Seventh Floor, Dominion House, Thomson Street (℡ **331 2233**); **People's Republic of China,** 147 Queen Elizabeth Dr. (℡ **330 0215**); and **South Korea,** Eighth Floor, Vanua House, Victoria Parade (℡ **330 0977**).

EMERGENCIES The **police** emergency number is **917** throughout Fiji. The emergency telephone number for **fire** and **ambulance** is ℡ **911.**

ETIQUETTE & CUSTOMS See "Fijian Village Etiquette" and "'Grog' Etiquette" under "The Islanders," in chapter 2. Modest dress is the order of the day, particularly in the villages. As a rule, don't leave the hotel swimming pool or the beach in bathing suits or other skimpy attire. That includes low-slung pants and shorts that show everything from your navel down to your you-know-what. If you want to run around half naked, go to Tahiti, where the French think it's cool. The Fijians do not.

FIREARMS Guns are illegal in Fiji, and persons found with them could be fined severely and sentenced to jail.

GAMBLING Fiji has no casinos, but you can play the local lottery.

HEALTHCARE Medical and dental care in Fiji are not up to the standards common in the industrialized world. Most hotels have private physicians on call or can refer one. Doctors are listed at the beginning of the White Pages section of the Fiji telephone directory, under the heading "Medical Practitioners." See the

"Fast Facts" section in destination chapters for specific doctors and clinics.

HITCHHIKING Local residents seldom hitchhike, so the custom is not widespread, nor do I recommend it. Women traveling alone should never hitchhike in Fiji.

HOLIDAYS For more information on holidays, see "When to Go," in chapter 3.

INSECTS Fiji has no dangerous insects, and its plentiful mosquitoes do not carry malaria. The only dangerous animal is the bolo, a venomous snake that is docile and rarely seen.

INSURANCE Medical Insurance Most U.S. health plans (including Medicare and Medicaid) do not provide coverage in Fiji, and the ones that do often require you to pay for services upfront and reimburse you only after you return home.

As a safety net, you may want to buy travel medical insurance, particularly if you're traveling to a remote or high-risk area where emergency evacuation might be necessary. If you require additional medical insurance, try **MEDEX Assistance** (℡ **410/453-6300;** www.medex assist.com) or **Travel Assistance International** (℡ **800/821-2828;** www.travel assistance.com; for general information on services, call the company's **Worldwide Assistance Services, Inc.,** at ℡ **800/ 777-8710**).

Canadians should check with their provincial health plan offices or call **Health Canada** (℡ **866/225-0709;** www. hc-sc.gc.ca) to find out the extent of their coverage and what documentation and receipts they must take home in case they are treated overseas.

Travelers from the U.K. should carry their European Health Insurance Card (EHIC), which replaced the E111 form as proof of entitlement to free/reduced cost medical treatment abroad (℡ **0845 606 2030;** www.ehic.org.uk). Note, however, that the EHIC only covers "necessary medical treatment," and for repatriation costs, lost money, baggage, or cancellation, travel insurance from a reputable company should always be sought (www.travelinsuranceweb.com).

Travel Insurance   The cost of travel insurance varies widely, depending on the destination, the cost and length of your trip, your age and health, and the type of trip you're taking, but expect to pay between 5% and 8% of the vacation itself. You can get estimates from various providers through **InsureMyTrip.com**. Enter your trip cost and dates, your age, and other information, for prices from more than a dozen companies.

U.K. citizens and their families who make more than one trip abroad per year may find an annual travel insurance policy works out cheaper. Check **www.money supermarket.com**, which compares prices across a wide range of providers for single- and multi-trip policies.

Most big travel agents offer their own insurance and will probably try to sell you their package when you book a holiday. Think before you sign. **Britain's Consumers' Association** recommends that you insist on seeing the policy and reading the fine print before buying travel insurance. **The Association of British Insurers** (© 020/7600-3333; www.abi.org.uk) gives advice by phone and publishes Holiday Insurance, a free guide to policy provisions and prices. You might also shop around for better deals: Try **Columbus Direct** (© 0870/033-9988; www.columbusdirect.net).

Trip Cancellation Insurance   Trip-cancellation insurance will help retrieve your money if you have to back out of a trip or depart early, or if your travel supplier goes bankrupt. Trip cancellation traditionally covers such events as sickness, natural disasters, and State Department advisories. The latest news in trip-cancellation insurance is the availability of expanded hurricane coverage and the **"any-reason"** cancellation coverage—which costs more but covers cancellations made for any reason. You won't get back 100% of your prepaid trip cost, but you'll be refunded a substantial portion. **Travel-Safe** (© **888/885-7233;** www.travelsafe.com) offers both types of coverage. Expedia also offers any-reason cancellation coverage for its air-hotel packages. For details, contact one of the following recommended insurers: **Access America** (© 866/807-3982; www.accessamerica.com); **Travel Guard International** (© 800/826-4919; www.travelguard.com); **Travel Insured International** (© 800/243-3174; www.travelinsured.com); and **Travelex Insurance Services** (© 888/457-4602; www.travelex-insurance.com).

INTERNET ACCESS   See "Staying Connected," in chapter 3.

LANGUAGE   English is an official language of Fiji and most residents can speak it to some degree. See appendix B for useful Fijian and Hindi phrases.

LIQUOR LAWS   The legal drinking age is 21. Most grocery stores sell beer, spirits, and wines from Australia and New Zealand. Both beer and spirits are produced locally and are considerably less expensive than imported brands, which are taxed heavily. While local Bounty rum is okay, the other stuff is rotgut. I bring quality brands of liquor with me. The locally brewed Fiji beer is served in a short bottle and known as a Stubbie. Fiji Gold is a lighter lager than Fiji Bitter. Most bars also sell Australian and New Zealand beers.

LOST & FOUND   Be sure to tell all of your credit card companies the minute you discover your wallet has been lost or stolen and file a report at the nearest police precinct. Your credit card company or insurer may require a police report number or record of the loss. Most credit card companies have an emergency toll-free number to call if your card is lost or stolen; they may be able to wire you a cash advance immediately or deliver an emergency credit card in a day or two.

MAIL All the main towns have post offices operated by **Fiji Post** (www.post-fiji.com.fj), and there is a branch at Nadi International Airport, across the entry road from the terminal. Allow at least a week for delivery of airmail letters from Fiji. Surface mail to North American and Europe can take 2 months or more. Mail moves faster if you use "Fiji Islands" on envelopes and packages sent here. Post offices usually are open Monday to Friday from 8am to 4pm. **FedEx, UPS,** and **DHL Express** all have express service into and out of Fiji.

MEASUREMENTS Fiji is on the metric system. See the chart on the inside front cover of this book for details on converting metric measurements to nonmetric equivalents.

NEWSPAPERS & MAGAZINES Two national newspapers are published in English: the *Fiji Times* (www.fijitimes.com) and the *Fiji Sun* (www.sun.com.fj). Both appear daily and carry a few major stories from overseas. The international editions of *Time* and the leading Australian and New Zealand daily newspapers are available at some bookstores and hotel shops. Published monthly in Suva, the excellent *Island Business Magazine* (www.islandsbusiness.com) covers South Pacific regional news.

PASSPORTS Allow plenty of time before your trip to apply for a passport; processing normally takes 3 weeks but can take longer during busy periods (especially spring). And keep in mind that if you need a passport in a hurry, you'll pay a higher processing fee.

For Residents of Australia: You can pick up an application from your local post office or any branch of Passports Australia, but you must schedule an interview at the passport office to present your application materials. Call the **Australian Passport Information Service** at ✆ **131-232,** or visit the government website at www.passports.gov.au.

For Residents of Canada: Passport applications are available at travel agencies throughout Canada or from the central **Passport Office,** Department of Foreign Affairs and International Trade, Ottawa, ON K1A 0G3 (✆ **800/567-6868;** www.ppt.gc.ca).

For Residents of Ireland: You can apply for a 10-year passport at the **Passport Office,** Setanta Centre, Molesworth Street, Dublin 2 (✆ **01/671-1633;** www.irlgov.ie/iveagh). Those 17 and under and 66 and over must apply for a 3-year passport. You can also apply at 1A South Mall, Cork (✆ **021/272-525**) or at most main post offices.

For Residents of New Zealand: You can pick up a passport application at any New Zealand Passports Office or download it from their website. Contact the **Passports Office** at ✆ **0800/225-050** in New Zealand or 04/474-8100, or log on to www.passports.govt.nz.

For Residents of the United Kingdom: To pick up an application for a standard 10-year passport (5-year passport for children 15 and under), visit your nearest passport office, major post office, or travel agency or contact the **United Kingdom Passport Service** at ✆ **0870/521-0410** or search its website at www.ukpa.gov.uk.

For Residents of the United States: Whether you're applying in person or by mail, you can download passport applications from the U.S. State Department website at **http://travel.state.gov.** To find your regional passport office, either check the U.S. State Department website or call the **National Passport Information Center** toll-free number (© 877/ 487-2778) for automated information.

POLICE   The nationwide emergency police number is © **917** throughout Fiji. The non-emergency numbers are © **670 0222** in Nadi, 334 3777 in Suva.

RADIO & TV   The Fijian government operates two nationwide AM radio networks with programming in Fijian and Hindi. Several private stations operate on the FM band in Suva and Nadi. The best is Radio Fiji Gold, which carries news bulletins on the hour and world, regional, and local news reports and weather bulletins daily at 7am and 6pm. The interim government has approved licenses for at least two more TV channels to join Fiji One, heretofore the country's sole over-the-air station. Fiji One has local news and weather at 6pm daily. The schedules are carried in the local newspapers. Many hotels have Sky TV, a pay system with the BBC, sports, and a few other channels.

SAFETY   Property theft, armed robberies, burglaries, and home invasions are common. Caution is advised at all times, especially in Suva. Stick to the main streets everywhere after dark, and take a taxi back to your hotel if you're out late at night. Do not leave valuables in your hotel room or unattended elsewhere, including in rental cars and tour buses. Women should not wander alone on deserted beaches and should be extremely cautious about accepting a late-night lift back to their hotel or hostel.

SMOKING   Smoking is legally prohibited in many public buildings in Fiji, but not at hotels, businesses, and restaurants. Ask for a nonsmoking room at your hotel and an outside table at restaurants.

TAXES   Fiji imposes a 12.5% value added tax (VAT) on most goods and services. These "VAT-inclusive prices," or VIP, are included in most prices. In addition, you will pay a 5% hotel tax. Hotels are not required to include the VAT and hotel tax in the rates they quote outside Fiji, so be sure to ask whether a quoted room rate includes all taxes and fees. You will not be entitled to a VAT refund when you leave the country.

TELEGRAPH, TELEX & FAX   Telegraph, telex, and fax services are provided at **Fiji Post** offices nationwide. Fiji Post also is an agent for **Western Union** (© **800/325-6000;** www.westernunion. com), as is **Forex** in Nadi Town (© **670 1666**). You can telegraph (wire) money, or have it telegraphed to you, very quickly over the Western Union system, but this service can cost as much as 15% to 20% of the amount sent. Most hotels have **fax machines** available for guest use (be sure to ask about the charge to use it).

TELEPHONE   See "Staying Connected," in chapter 3.

TIME   Local time in Fiji is 12 hours ahead of Greenwich Mean Time. Although the 180° meridian passes through Taveuni, all of Fiji is west of the international date line, so it's 1 day ahead of the United States and shares the same day with Australia and New Zealand. Translated: When it's 5am on Tuesday in Fiji, it's noon on Monday in New York and 9am on Monday in Los Angeles. Fiji does not observe daylight saving time.

TIPPING   Tipping is discouraged throughout Fiji unless truly exceptional service has been rendered. That's not to say that the porter won't give you that where's-my-money look once he figures out you're an American.

USEFUL PHONE NUMBERS

Air Pacific/Pacific Sun airlines © 672 0888

Air Fiji © 0800 347 3624 toll-free or 672 2521

Fiji Visitors Bureau © 672 2433 in Nadi, 330 2433 in Suva

Nadi Airport flight arrival and departure information ℂ 672 7777

U.S. Dept. of State Travel Advisory ℂ 202/647-5225 (manned 24 hr.)

U.S. Passport Agency ℂ 202/647-0518

U.S. Centers for Disease Control International Traveler's Hotline: ℂ 404/332-4559

WATER Except during periods of continuous heavy rain, the tap water in the main towns and at the resorts is safe to drink. Elsewhere I opt for the famous Fiji or other bottled water, which is widely available at shops and hotels.

2 Toll-Free Numbers & Websites

MAJOR U.S. AIRLINES

(*flies internationally as well)

Alaska Airlines/ Horizon Air
ℂ 800/252/7522
www.alaskaair.com

American Airlines*
ℂ 800/433-7300 (in U.S. or Canada)
ℂ 020/7365-0777 (in U.K.)
www.aa.com

Continental Airlines*
ℂ 800/523-3273 (in U.S. or Canada)
ℂ 084/5607-6760 (in U.K.)
www.continental.com

Delta Air Lines*
ℂ 800/221-1212 (in U.S. or Canada)
ℂ 084/5600-0950 (in U.K.)
www.delta.com

Hawaiian Airlines*
ℂ 800/367-5320 (in U.S. and Canada)
www.hawaiianair.com

Northwest Airlines
ℂ 800/225-2525 (in U.S.)
ℂ 870/0507-4074 (in U.K.)
www.flynaa.com

United Airlines*
ℂ 800/864-8331 (in U.S. and Canada)
ℂ 084/5844-4777 in U.K.
www.united.com

US Airways*
ℂ 800/428-4322 (in U.S. and Canada)
ℂ 084/5600-3300 (in U.K.)
www.usairways.com

Virgin America*
ℂ 877/359-8474
www.virginamerica.com

MAJOR INTERNATIONAL AIRLINES

Air New Zealand
ℂ 800/262-1234 (in U.S.)
ℂ 800/663-5494 (in Canada)
ℂ 0800/028-4149 (in U.K.)
www.airnewzealand.com

Air Pacific
ℂ 800/227-4446 (U.S. and Canada)
www.airpacific.com

American Airlines
ℂ 800/433-7300 (in U.S. and Canada)
ℂ 020/7365-0777 (in U.K.)
www.aa.com

Continental Airlines
ℂ 800/523-3273 (in U.S. or Canada)
ℂ 084/5607-6760 (in U.K.)
www.continental.com

Delta Air Lines
ℂ 800/221-1212 (in U.S. or Canada)
ℂ 084/5600-0950 (in U.K.)
www.delta.com

Emirates Airlines
ℂ 800/777-3999 (in U.S.)
ℂ 087/0243-2222 (in U.K.)
www.emirates.com

Hawaiian Airlines
ℂ 800/367-5320 (in U.S. and Canada)
www.hawaiianair.com

Korean Air
ℂ 800/438-5000 (in U.S. and Canada)
ℂ 0800/413-000 (in U.K.)
www.koreanair.com

Pacific Blue
℃ 13 16 45 (in Australia)
℃ 0800 67 0000 (in New Zealand)
www.flypacificblue.com)

Polynesian Airlines
℃ 21 261 (in Samoa)
www.polynesianairlines.com

Qantas Airways
℃ 800/227-4500 (in U.S.)
℃ 084/5774-7767 (in U.K. or Canada)
℃ 13 13 13 (in Australia)
www.quantas.com

United Airlines*
℃ 800/864-8331 (in U.S. and Canada)
℃ 084/5844-4777 (in U.K.)
www.united.com

Virgin Atlantic Airways
℃ 800/821-5438 (in U.S. and Canada)
℃ 087/0574-7747 (in U.K.)
www.virgin-atlantic.com

BUDGET AIRLINES

AirTran Airways
℃ 800/247-8726
www.airtran.com

Frontier Airlines
℃ 800/432-1359
www.frontierairlines.com

JetBlue Airways
℃ 800/538-2583 (in U.S.)
℃ 801/365-2525 (in U.K. or Canada)
www.jetblue.com

Jetstar (Australia)
℃ 866/397-8170
www.jetstar.com

Ryanair
℃ 1 353 1 249 7700 (in U.S.)
℃ 081/830-3030 (in Ireland)
℃ 087/1246-0000 (in U.K.)
www.ryanair.com

Southwest Airlines
℃ 800/435-9792 (in U.S., U.K., and Canada)
www.southwest.com

Spirit Airlines
℃ 800/772-7117
www.spiritair.com

Ted (part of United Airlines)
℃ 800/225-5561
www.flyted.com

WestJet
℃ 800/538-5696 (in U.S. and Canada)
www.westjet.com

CAR-RENTAL AGENCIES

Avis
℃ 800/331-1212 (in U.S. and Canada)
℃ 084/4581-8181 (in U.K.)
www.avis.com

Budget
℃ 800/527-0700 (in U.S.)
℃ 087/0156-5656 (in U.K.)
℃ 800/268-8900 (in Canada)
www.budget.com

Europcar
℃ 877/940-6900 (U.S. and Canada)
℃ 870 607 5000 (in U.K.)
www.europcar.com

Hertz
℃ 800/645-3131
℃ 800/654-3001 (for international reservations)
www.hertz.com

MAJOR HOTEL CHAINS

Hilton Hotels
℃ 800/HILTONS (445-8667) (in U.S. and Canada)
℃ 087/0590-9090 (in U.K.)
www.hilton.com

Holiday Inn
℃ 800/315-2621 (in U.S. and Canada)
℃ 0800/405-060 (in U.K.)
www.holidayinn.com

Mercure Hotels
℃ 800-515-5679 (US and Canada)
℃ 0870 609 0961 (UK)
www.mercure.com

Novotel Hotels
℡ 800/NOVOTEL (668-6835)
(U.S. and Canada)
℡ 0870 609 0962 (U.K.)
www.novotel.com

Radisson Hotels & Resorts
℡ 888/201-1718 (in U.S. and Canada)
℡ 0800/374-411 (in U.K.)
www.radisson.com

Sheraton Hotels & Resorts
℡ 800/325-3535 (in U.S.)
℡ 800/543-4300 (in Canada)
℡ 0800/3253-5353 (in U.K.)
www.starwoodhotels.com/sheraton

Sofitel Hotels
℡ 800/763-4835 (in U.S. and Canada)
℡ 0870 609 0961 (in U.K.)
www.sofitel.com

Westin Hotels & Resorts
℡ 800-937-8461 (in U.S. and Canada)
℡ 0800/3259-5959 (in U.K.)
www.starwoodhotels.com/westin

Wyndham Hotels & Resorts
℡ 877/999-3223 (in U.S. and Canada)
℡ 050/6638-4899 (in U.K.)
www.wyndham.com

Appendix B: Languages

Fiji has three official languages. To greatly oversimplify, the Fijians speak Fijian, the Indians speak Hindi, and they all speak English to each other. Schoolchildren are taught in their native language until they are proficient (but not necessarily fluent) in English, which thereafter is the medium of instruction.

Although you may not get into serious conversations in English with everyone here—and you may have trouble understanding English spoken with heavy Fijian or Hindi accents—you should have little trouble getting around and enjoying the country.

1 Fijian

Some knowledge of Fijian will come in handy, if for no other reason than the bewildering pronunciation of Fijian place names.

FIJIAN PRONUNCIATION

Fijian uses vowel sounds similar to those in Latin, French, Italian, and Spanish:

a as in b*a*d
e as in s*ay*
i as in b*ee*
o as in g*o*
u as in kangar*oo*.

Some Fijian consonants, however, sound very different from their counterparts in English, Latin, or any other language. In devising a written form of Fijian, the 19th-century Wesleyan missionaries decided to use some familiar Roman consonants in unfamiliar ways.

It would be easier for English speakers to read Fijian had the missionaries used a combination of consonants—*th,* for example—for the Fijian sounds. Their main purpose, however, was to teach Fijians to read and write their own language. Because the Fijians separate all consonant sounds with vowels, writing two consonants together confused them.

The missionaries came up with the following usage:

b sounds like *mb* (as in reme*mb*er)
c sounds like *th* (as in *th*at)
d sounds like *nd* (as in Su*nd*ay)
g sounds like *ng* (as in si*ng*er)
q sounds like *ng + g* (as in fi*ng*er)

In addition, most Fijians roll the letter *r* in an exaggerated fashion, like the Spanish *r* taken to extreme.

FIJIAN NAMES

The unusual pronunciation is most evident in Fijian place names such as Nadi, which is pronounced *Nahn-di*. There are many other names of people and places that are equally or even more confusing.

Here are some Fijian names with their pronunciations:

Ba	mBah
Bau	mBau
Beqa	*mBeng*-ga
Buca	*mBu*-tha
Cakobau	Thack-*om*-bau
Kadavu	Kan-*dah*-voo
Korotogo	Ko-ro-*ton*-go
Labasa	Lam-*ba*-sa
Mamanuca	Ma-ma-*noo*-tha
Nadi	Nahn-di
Tabua	*Tam*-bua
Tobura	Toom-boo-roo-ah
Tubakula	Toom-ba-*koo*-lah

FIJIAN WORDS, PHRASES & NUMBERS

You are likely to hear these Fijian words and phrases during your stay, and you can impress your hosts by counting to 10 in Fijian:

English	Fijian	Pronunciation
PHRASES		
best regards	**lololma**	low-*low*-mah
European person	**kaivalagi**	kai-vah-*lahng*-ee
good morning	**ni sa yadra**	nee sah *yand*-rah
good night	**ni sa moce**	nee sah *mo*-thay
hello	**bula**	*boo*-lah
hello (formal)	**ni sa bula**	nee sahm *boo*-lah
house/bungalow	**bure**	*boo*-ray
kava	**yaqona**	yon-*gon*-na
man	**turaga**	too-rang-ah
no, negative	**sega**	*san*-gah
sarong	**sulu**	*sue*-loo
tapa cloth	**masi**	*mah*-see
thank you	**vinaka**	vee-*nah*-kah
thank you very much	**vinaka vaka levu**	vee-*nah*-kah *vah*-ka *lay*-voo
toilet/restroom	**valelailai**	vah-*lay* lie lie
yes	**io**	*ee*-oh
you're welcome	**siga na lega**	sing-a nah *leng*-ah
NUMBERS		
1	**dua**	*doo*-ah
2	**rua**	roo-ah
3	**tolu**	*toh*-loo
4	**vaa**	*vah*-ah
5	**lima**	*lee*-mah
6	**ono**	*oh*-no
7	**vitu**	*vee*-too
8	**walu**	*wah*-loo
9	**ciwa**	*thee*-wah
10	**tini**	*tee*-nee

2 Fiji Hindi

The common everyday language spoken among the Fiji Indians is a tongue peculiar to Fiji. Although it is based on Hindustani (Fiji Indians have little trouble understanding most dialogue in Bollywood movies), it is somewhat different from that language as spoken in India.

Originally known as "Fiji Bat," it grew out of the need for a common language among the immigrants who came from various parts of the subcontinent and spoke some of the many languages and dialects found in India and Pakistan. Thus it includes words from Hindi, Urdu, Tamil Nadu, a variety of Indian dialects, and even English and Fijian. You'll see what I mean by tuning into a Hindi radio station.

If you want to impress the Fiji Indians, try these phrases in Fiji Hindi:

English	Fiji Hindi	Pronunciation
hello and goodbye	**namaste**	na-*mas*-tay
how are you?	**kaise?**	ka-*ee*-say
good	**accha**	*ach*-cha
I'm okay	**Thik hai**	teak high
right or okay	**rait**	right

Index

See also Accommodations & Resorts and Restaurant indexes, below.

RESTAURANTS

The new way to
get AROUND town.

Make the most of your stay. Go Day by Day!

Fun destinations for all ages!

FROMMER'S® COMPLETE TRAVEL GUIDES

Alaska
Amalfi Coast
American Southwest
Amsterdam
Argentina
Arizona
Atlanta
Australia
Austria
Bahamas
Barcelona
Beijing
Belgium, Holland & Luxembourg
Belize
Bermuda
Boston
Brazil
British Columbia & the Canadian
  Rockies
Brussels & Bruges
Budapest & the Best of Hungary
Buenos Aires
Calgary
California
Canada
Cancún, Cozumel & the Yucatán
Cape Cod, Nantucket & Martha's
  Vineyard
Caribbean
Caribbean Ports of Call
Carolinas & Georgia
Chicago
Chile & Easter Island
China
Colorado
Costa Rica
Croatia
Cuba
Denmark
Denver, Boulder & Colorado Springs
Eastern Europe
Ecuador & the Galapagos Islands
Edinburgh & Glasgow
England
Europe
Europe by Rail

Florence, Tuscany & Umbria
Florida
France
Germany
Greece
Greek Islands
Guatemala
Hawaii
Hong Kong
Honolulu, Waikiki & Oahu
India
Ireland
Israel
Italy
Jamaica
Japan
Kauai
Las Vegas
London
Los Angeles
Los Cabos & Baja
Madrid
Maine Coast
Maryland & Delaware
Maui
Mexico
Montana & Wyoming
Montréal & Québec City
Morocco
Moscow & St. Petersburg
Munich & the Bavarian Alps
Nashville & Memphis
New England
Newfoundland & Labrador
New Mexico
New Orleans
New York City
New York State
New Zealand
Northern Italy
Norway
Nova Scotia, New Brunswick &
  Prince Edward Island
Oregon
Paris
Peru

Philadelphia & the Amish Country
Portugal
Prague & the Best of the Czech
  Republic
Provence & the Riviera
Puerto Rico
Rome
San Antonio & Austin
San Diego
San Francisco
Santa Fe, Taos & Albuquerque
Scandinavia
Scotland
Seattle
Seville, Granada & the Best of
  Andalusia
Shanghai
Sicily
Singapore & Malaysia
South Africa
South America
South Florida
South Korea
South Pacific
Southeast Asia
Spain
Sweden
Switzerland
Tahiti & French Polynesia
Texas
Thailand
Tokyo
Toronto
Turkey
USA
Utah
Vancouver & Victoria
Vermont, New Hampshire & Maine
Vienna & the Danube Valley
Vietnam
Virgin Islands
Virginia
Walt Disney World® & Orlando
Washington, D.C.
Washington State

FROMMER'S® DAY BY DAY GUIDES

Amsterdam
Barcelona
Beijing
Boston
Cancun & the Yucatan
Chicago
Florence & Tuscany

Hong Kong
Honolulu & Oahu
London
Maui
Montréal
Napa & Sonoma
New York City

Paris
Provence & the Riviera
Rome
San Francisco
Venice
Washington D.C.

PAULINE FROMMER'S GUIDES: SEE MORE. SPEND LESS.

Alaska
Hawaii
Italy

Las Vegas
London
New York City

Paris
Walt Disney World®
Washington D.C.

FROMMER'S® PORTABLE GUIDES

Acapulco, Ixtapa & Zihuatanejo
Amsterdam
Aruba, Bonaire & Curacao
Australia's Great Barrier Reef
Bahamas
Big Island of Hawaii
Boston
California Wine Country
Cancún
Cayman Islands
Charleston
Chicago
Dominican Republic

Florence
Las Vegas
Las Vegas for Non-Gamblers
London
Maui
Nantucket & Martha's Vineyard
New Orleans
New York City
Paris
Portland
Puerto Rico
Puerto Vallarta, Manzanillo &
    Guadalajara

Rio de Janeiro
San Diego
San Francisco
Savannah
St. Martin, Sint Maarten
    St. Bart's
Turks & Caicos
Vancouver
Venice
Virgin Islands
Washington, D.C.
Whistler

FROMMER'S® CRUISE GUIDES

Alaska Cruises & Ports of Call

Cruises & Ports of Call

European Cruises & Port

FROMMER'S® NATIONAL PARK GUIDES

Algonquin Provincial Park
Banff & Jasper
Grand Canyon

National Parks of the American West
Rocky Mountain
Yellowstone & Grand Teton

Yosemite and Sequoia &
    Canyon
Zion & Bryce Canyon

FROMMER'S® WITH KIDS GUIDES

Chicago
Hawaii
Las Vegas
London

National Parks
New York City
San Francisco

Toronto
Walt Disney World® & (
Washington, D.C.

FROMMER'S® PHRASEFINDER DICTIONARY GUIDES

Chinese
French

German
Italian

Japanese
Spanish

SUZY GERSHMAN'S BORN TO SHOP GUIDES

France
Hong Kong, Shanghai & Beijing
Italy

London
New York
Paris

San Francisco
Where to Buy the Best o

FROMMER'S® BEST-LOVED DRIVING TOURS

Britain
California
France
Germany

Ireland
Italy
New England
Northern Italy

Scotland
Spain
Tuscany & Umbria

THE UNOFFICIAL GUIDES®

Adventure Travel in Alaska
Beyond Disney
California with Kids
Central Italy
Chicago
Cruises
Disneyland®
England
Hawaii

Ireland
Las Vegas
London
Maui
Mexico's Best Beach Resorts
Mini Mickey
New Orleans
New York City
Paris

San Francisco
South Florida including
    the Keys
Walt Disney World®
Walt Disney World® for
    Grown-ups
Walt Disney World® witl
Washington, D.C.

SPECIAL-INTEREST TITLES

Athens Past & Present
Best Places to Raise Your Family
Cities Ranked & Rated
500 Places to Take Your Kids Before They Grow Up
Frommer's Best Day Trips from London
Frommer's Best RV & Tent Campgrounds in the U.S.A.

Frommer's Exploring America by RV
Frommer's NYC Free & Dirt Cheap
Frommer's Road Atlas Europe
Frommer's Road Atlas Ireland
Retirement Places Rated